PRAISE FOR *OPERATIONAL RISK MANAGEMENT IN FINANCIAL SERVICES*

'An insightful book and a highly engaging, practical and useful guide to operational risk management.'
Veronica Lazenby, Chief Risk Officer, Jupiter Asset Management

'Understanding, mitigating and transferring operational risks is a critical part of building resilience. This book lays out best practice in a straightforward and practical way that should improve the ability of a critical sector to weather incidents and disruptions.'
Michael Berkowitz, Founding Principal, Resilient Cities Catalyst, former acting Global Head of Operational Risk at Deutsche Bank

'Elena Pykhova teaches and writes in simple, clear and engaging language. As well as her lectures and classes, her book is a must-read for anyone willing to learn about practical and value-added operational risk management.'
Daniela Biagi, Head of Group Academy, London Stock Exchange Group

'A very practical, refreshingly enjoyable and lively read, covering all aspects of operational risk management. An essential guide for all individuals responsible for implementing risk management practices in their organizations or those interested to stay current and improve their operational risk solutions.'
Qing Yang, Executive Vice Dean, Global Finance Academy, Bank of China University

'This outstanding book gives an excellent insight into the practical application of operational risk management in financial services, an important topic in the current unprecedented environment. It offers sensible advice to practitioners.'
Miguel Borg, Chief Risk Officer, Bank of Valetta

'In a world that is growing ever more complex and uncertain, effective operational risk management in financial organizations is needed more than ever. This book offers many practical insights that can help operational risk professionals to overcome the unexpected and create value for their organizations.'
Simon Ashby, Professor of Financial Services, Vlerick Business School

'A must-read from one of the industry's leading figures that provides essential guidance for anyone involved in operational risk. By anchoring the chapters against a holistic operational risk management framework, the author enables readers to relate the contents to their own frameworks.'
Andrew Sheen, Director, AJ Sheen Consulting and Fellow of the Institute of Operational Risk

'Such an outstanding journey through the main topics of operational risk. This book develops critical thinking about predefined concepts of risk, provides remarkable new insights into the changing landscape and explores methods, approaches and practices that are very relevant nowadays.'
William Varela, Group Chief Risk Officer, Mercantil Santa Cruz Financial Group

'This book really brings operational risk to life, written by someone who has clearly spent time at the coal-face and fronted many of the challenges that operational risk professionals experience. While offering a comprehensive description of a classic framework, the author appraises the practical challenges of implementation rather than offering an academic or textbook solution, while also considering current themes such as FinTech, Covid and operational resilience. This is a thought-provoking read, whether you are starting your operational risk journey or are a seasoned operational risk professional.'
Paul Neale, Head of Operational Risk Management, Mizuho International Plc

'If you are in the business of managing operational risk or need to know how to deal with it, then read this book! It is well written, setting out how to work on and improve a firm's operational risk framework with easily understandable tools, methods of working and industry examples. Elena Pykhova has always been passionate about operational risk as a discipline and that passion really comes out in this book.'
John Dick, Head of Risk, Bank of Communications, China, London Branch

'A well-written book that in a simple way explains the key concepts of managing operational risk. It offers practical solutions for adding value through operational risk management, by providing management with actionable insight into their universe of risks.'
Siv Rosseland, Head of Group Operational Risk, DNB

'An informative guide to managing operational risk in the ever-more complex business world. This book brings together the latest thinking, drawn from the author's experience in applying sound risk management practice in the field.'
Adam Seager, Chief Risk Officer for a global specialty insurance firm

'Having worked together on a number of committees, panels and forums, I have seen Elena Pykhova's inspirational and practical approach in action, which shines through in this book. It is highly recommended as both a detailed repository of current thinking and as a practitioner's guide to the role that operational risk should play in every firm, promoting the achievement of its business opportunities while managing its operational risks effectively.'
Sean Titley, Director of Enterprise and Operational Risk, Metro Bank and member of the Institute of Risk Management Advisory Committee on Operational Risk

'I am sure readers of this book will value the author's ability to draw out and articulate how to implement best practices within their organizations, particularly benchmarking against relevant peers.'
Barry Murphy, Managing Director, Risk and Compliance, British Business Bank

Operational Risk Management in Financial Services

A practical guide to establishing effective solutions

Elena Pykhova

KoganPage

First published in Great Britain and the United States in 2021 by Kogan Page Limited

2nd Floor, 45 Gee Street
London
EC1V 3RS
United Kingdom
www.koganpage.com

122 W 27th St, 10th Floor
New York, NY 10001
USA

4737/23 Ansari Road
Daryaganj
New Delhi 110002
India

Kogan Page books are printed on paper from sustainable forests.

ISBNs

Hardback   978 1 78966 709 7
Paperback   978 1 78966 708 0
Ebook   978 1 78966 711 0

British Library Cataloguing-in-Publication Data

A CIP record for this book is available from the British Library.

Library of Congress Cataloging-in-Publication Data

Names: Pykhova, Elena, author.
Title: Operational risk management in financial services : a practical guide to establishing effective solutions / Elena Pykhova.
Description: 1 Edition. | New York : Kogan Page, 2021. | Includes bibliographical references and index.
Identifiers: LCCN 2021010405 (print) | LCCN 2021010406 (ebook) | ISBN 9781789667080 (paperback) | ISBN 9781789667097 (hardback) | ISBN 9781789667110 (ebook)
Subjects: LCSH: Financial services industry–Management. | Operational risk. | Risk management.
Classification: LCC HG173 .P95 2021 (print) | LCC HG173 (ebook) | DDC 332.068/1–dc23
LC record available at https://lccn.loc.gov/2021010405
LC ebook record available at https://lccn.loc.gov/2021010406

Typeset by Integra Software Services, Pondicherry
Print production managed by Jellyfish
Printed and bound by CPI Group (UK) Ltd, Croydon, CR0 4YY

CONTENTS

LIST OF FIGURES AND TABLES

ABOUT THE AUTHOR

 **Elena Pykhova** is an operational risk executive specializing in the strategy, design and implementation of firm-wide operational risk frameworks. Based in London, she is a renowned operational risk trainer who for many years has run public and in-house training courses in the UK and internationally for world-leading organizations including the London Stock Exchange Group Academy, the Moller Institute, University of Cambridge, and Risk.net. Elena is also a thought leader, influencer, and founder of a prominent industry think tank, the Best Practice Operational Risk Forum. She is chair of the Operational Risk Expert Panel at the Association of Foreign Banks in London, and a former Director for Education at the Institute of Operational Risk. Passionate about the operational risk discipline, Elena founded her training and consulting practice, The Op Risk Company Ltd, after 20 years of experience in senior roles at Fortune 500 companies. She is a frequent speaker at conferences and writes articles for Thompson Reuters, Advantage Talent, Inc, *Operational Risk & Regulation* and other publications.

PREFACE

Operational Risk Management in Financial Services: A practical guide to establishing effective solutions reflects my passion for the operational risk discipline and the value it delivers to the enterprise. No other domain in financial services is so extensive and all-encompassing, yet at the same time relatively young and still evolving as a discipline. These factors together mean that operational risk is perhaps the most exciting and interesting field to explore in the whole financial services sector. I am delighted to be sharing my passion for this fascinating and important topic, and invite the reader to embark on a journey distinguished by three main features: a practical approach, simplicity and engaging insights.

A practical approach

I came into operational risk from executive leadership roles in operations: running round-the-clock global foreign exchange and money market settlements, processing billions of dollars a day, at American Express; managing busy retail branches with customers queuing at tellers' tills in Citibank Tunisia; and starting up an internal control unit at Citibank Russia, where a dozen initial recruits helped to shape the bank from its inception. My personal experience in these roles taught me to apply a pragmatic approach to operational risk management. When designing and implementing frameworks and tools, I always question whether these tools would have enabled me to *do my job better*. Operational risk management is about the *value proposition* of risk: finding practical ways of embedding risk management into the organization to add value. This has been my personal mantra in group head roles across American Express, Standard Chartered, VTB Capital and Deutsche Bank as well as many executive assignments with a broad range of clients in my consultancy practice.

Simplicity

Simplicity is another essential element. As Albert Einstein is alleged to have said, 'If you can't explain it simply, you don't understand it well enough.' From an early age I was accustomed to dealing with complexity and translating it into simplicity: my parents are nuclear physicists, my brother studied and worked in the field of laser physics, and for my own degree I chose applied mathematics, admiring the beauty of logic and order. When teaching operational risk classes, I always aim to find ways of relaying complex information in a simple manner, and to communicate in language that is engaging and easily understood. Many of my courses, for example in mainland China, are run with a consequential translator. This construct demands an extra degree of clarity and simplicity when formulating and expressing thoughts. Research demonstrates that our brains can process three chunks of information comfortably. So, throughout the book you will find uncomplicated three-step approaches that help explain the different concepts being outlined: three steps for implementing operational risk practices, three questions for risk identification, the 'Scope–Methodology–Integration' trilogy… and many more besides.

Engaging insights

Another feature of the operational risk journey that is apparent to me is the vital importance of open debate and the sharing of experiences among operational risk practitioners – especially at times when the discipline is actively evolving. To this end, I have been leading industry work in operational risk for over a decade, first as chair of the operational risk expert panel at the Association of Foreign Banks in London, managing round table discussions and overseeing working groups and papers on good practices. This is a role that I am proud to still be carrying out today. Subsequently I spearheaded the creation of the Best Practice Operational Risk Forum, comprising senior risk practitioners from over 50 diverse and geographically spread financial services firms. One positive development that has emerged from the Covid-19 pandemic is that the Best Practice Forum has expanded even further, as our meetings have moved online. I have been delighted to welcome many new international participants who are now joining the Forum's monthly calls from locations all over the globe. On these calls we share valuable insights – under Chatham House rules to preserve confidentiality – and conduct frequent live polls which enable rapid snapshots of current practices in every single area of operational risk. The Forum's work is reflected in the book, where every chapter contains industry benchmark sections, providing a reader with a perspective of where the industry stands on each particular topic. I also make a point of posting regular insights, reports and briefings on LinkedIn. If these are of interest, you can continue reading them by following my consultancy practice, The Op Risk Company Ltd.

Many friendships emanated from these years of industry work, and I am grateful to every one of my colleagues who has shared my passion for operational risk management over the years. A group of us even formed an Operational Risk Dinner Club, which we are looking forward to reinstating after we are all safely through the Covid-19 pandemic.

ACKNOWLEDGEMENTS

I am grateful to Amy Minshull from Kogan Page, whose phone call initiated this project. Amy somehow managed to convince me, quickly and effortlessly, that I was well capable of writing a book and absolutely should do it: little did I know at that stage the effort involved. I would also like to thank the Kogan Page editors, Adam Cox and Heather Wood, who have been working with me, inspiring and encouraging me throughout the whole journey. I am immensely grateful to Howard Walwyn from Prism-Clarity, who provided clarity when it was needed. Thank you also to many of my good friends – risk experts around the world who read the draft chapters, taking time to comment on and improve the content.

I am also hugely grateful to my clients: I am fortunate to be working with so many inspiring people who continue to place their trust in me as we work to continuously enhance their operational risk management practices. I thank the many industry partners who believe in me, hosting and promoting my training courses, including the London Stock Exchange Academy, Risk.net and the Moller Institute, University of Cambridge. The book assimilates all the knowledge and experience I have gained over the years. It is thanks to all of you that this book has become possible.

My family deserves a special mention. Most of the writing of this book happened during the Covid-19 pandemic, while I had a full-time consulting contract and multiple teaching assignments. The chapters were created in the evenings, at weekends, on planes and in hotels during occasional spells of permitted travel. We went through lockdowns, my son's cancelled GCSE exams, and my daughter's university year abroad being cut short as a result of the pandemic. In the midst of the turmoil, my family not only supported my writing but also kept themselves (and me) positive during difficult times. My husband taught the kids to take on responsibilities such as cooking challenging North African dishes, not to mention taking care of household duties. I thank them wholeheartedly for their patience and support.

I hope that readers will appreciate the practical solutions, tips and hints that appear throughout this book, and will relate to the challenges highlighted in the chapters. I also trust that the book will help to distil the common myth that operational risk is a boring discipline; and that instead it will inspire more and more practitioners from across different disciplines to apply for roles in the Operational Risk department.

01

Operational risk

Definition and taxonomy

What this chapter covers: This introductory chapter starts with reflections on what risk is, and how to encourage employees to think about risk without viewing it as an alien subject. The chapter provides a definition of Operational Risk and examines its evolution. It then presents the Risk Taxonomy as the essential glue that binds the framework together, laying the foundation for effective operational risk management. It proceeds to emphasize the importance of an appropriate classification system. Finally, the chapter contains an industry study and the results of live polls with industry practitioners.

FURTHER READING

- Operational Riskdata eXchange Association (2019) *ORX Reference Taxonomy*
  Why recommended: The ORX reference taxonomy is the latest positive industry development, presenting a coherent and up-to-date classification system.

- Daniel Kahneman (2012) *Thinking, Fast and Slow,* Penguin Books
  Why recommended: After all, risk management is about decision making. This international bestseller by Nobel Laureate Daniel Kahneman explores how our minds work and provides practical techniques to help us make better decisions.

Introduction: value-added risk management

Organizations – some more than others, admittedly – take a natural interest in managing their people, systems and processes, and the threats posed by the external environment. Business units and support functions were handling these things well before operational risk was defined in the Basel Accord; and they would continue to do so, even if operational risk practitioners were not part of the equation.

The key question, therefore, is about the value proposition of the risk function. Are operational risk professionals providing end-users with the tools that enable them to do their job *better*? Or do risk frameworks merely add an administrative burden, and hinder employees' experience, rather than enhancing it?

This book is about the *value proposition* of risk: simple, practical ways of embedding operational risk management into your organization to add value.

Helping employees to think about risk

What is *risk* and how do we think about it? Without oversimplifying, risk is an intuitive concept: perhaps without always realizing it, we are managing risk and taking risk-based decisions every day. As individuals, we have an internal compass that guides our risk perception. The tuning of the compass is highly personalized; something perceived as alarming by some may be normal for others, and so our reactions vary. Risk takers may welcome thrilling situations, while other more conservative individuals may prefer to stay as far away as possible from anything remotely threatening.

For over two decades I have been running training courses on operational risk, and I usually start these sessions with a simple exercise: asking participants to exchange stories about something *risky* they have done and getting each group to decide who is the *riskiest* person in their team. This always sets the room in motion: no formal definitions or lengthy explanations are required about what *risk* is. Invariably fascinating stories are told by attendees representing different cultures, nationalities and geographic locations. I consider myself very fortunate to have heard so many of them.

This exercise is particularly helpful because it enables attendees to consider some important concepts as well as draw parallels with the world of operational risk management.

Risk taking for reward

The anecdotes that feature most frequently in these stories are related to extreme sports such as bungee jumping, mountain biking and skydiving. It never fails to fascinate me how many financial services professionals engage fearlessly in activities which are essentially quite dangerous. They illustrate *risk taking* – actively seeking *risk for reward* – doing exciting things while at the same time recognizing that they contain threats.

Risk assessment

It is worth exploring how participants *assessed the risk* and what precautions they took before deciding to (for instance) jump out of a plane with a parachute. These might include:

- researching the service provider to ensure it was a reputable establishment;
- asking to be accompanied by a master instructor on the dive;
- taking out insurance.

These kinds of precautions immediately highlight some important concepts. First, the notion of *inherent risk* – risk without any associated controls. Second, the idea of *risk reduction* via the application of *controls*. Third, the related notion of *residual risk* – the level of risk remaining after the application of controls – which the individual has accepted before choosing to proceed. This example also introduces the concept of a *risk assessment*, which will be outlined in Chapter 5.

Risk mitigation

Many of the courses I run are in countries with different cultures and languages, sometimes alongside a translator. In some languages the word *risk* has a negative connotation and is associated with *danger* or individual participants may attribute this meaning. For them hearing the word *risk* conjures up threats and hazards in their minds. Consequently, their stories sometimes involve snowstorms, floods or explosions. These examples in turn illustrate that risk is not always intentionally sought; there is no reward to be gained and therefore the level must be *mitigated downwards*, by any means possible. This summarizes the key dilemma around the nature of operational risk, discussed in Chapter 9, which invites readers to form a view on whether operational risk is taken for return or, akin to a snowstorm, imposed from the outside and not intentionally sought – with reduction or mitigation being left as the only option.

Impact and likelihood

Sometimes, the accounts contain examples of *materialized* risk; perhaps a skiing accident which (thankfully) resulted in only a minor injury. When risk materializes it turns into a *risk event*, as presented in Chapter 4. This illustrates that *risk* is something that has not happened yet and may (or may not) happen in the future; introducing the uncertainty of outcome and the twin dimensions of *likelihood* and *impact*. In the skiing accident example the impact was described as minor; but before the trip took place its outcome was unknown.

Risk appetite

I asked a group of international participants at a course I delivered at Cambridge University to identify the *riskiest* person in their group. They all pointed immediately to the head of the delegation. This was because, on arrival, they had rented a bicycle and gone out exploring the picturesque town on their own. The group perceived this decision as 'very adventurous' due to a lack of familiarity with the layout of the town, not to mention the language barrier, which it was felt would diminish their opportunity to ask for help if needed. The head of the delegation, by contrast, argued that they were well-travelled and used to exploring unknown places, and would continue to do so throughout the stay.

This discussion articulates the fact that people have different individual *risk appetites*, ranging from conservative to expansionary. Similarly, financial services firms have distinct *risk appetites* to suit their size, nature and business model. The example also highlights the importance of *risk conversations*, encouraging people to talk openly about risk, and to compare notes on the magnitude of risk being taken and the quality of controls in place.

Every key concept in operational risk management can be explained via real-life stories of this kind; the list of examples and respective parallels that can be drawn is endless. The main objective of the introductory exercise to the training course is to encourage participants to embrace *risk* and actively converse on the topic. Bringing in examples from personal experience demonstrates that we are already continually reflecting on risk-related matters; and it should be no different when it comes to running a financial services business.

Within a corporate environment, it is essential to find ways of inspiring employees to think and talk about risk, in as many ways as possible.

Defining operational risk

Definition and its evolution

The well-known definition of operational risk presented by the Basel Framework is 'the risk of loss resulting from inadequate or failed internal processes, people and systems or from external events'.[1] Put simply, the regulators concluded that financial services firms could sustain major damage due to risks *other than* credit and market risks. Consequently, a broad range of threats was grouped under the umbrella of operational risk, as depicted in Figure 1.1; and firms were requested, for the first time, to put capital aside to guard against such losses.

Needless to say, the spectrum of the operational risk discipline based on this definition is very wide-ranging, covering deliberate or accidental actions of employees, malfunctions of technological systems and broken processes. The categories of risk covered by this definition are distinct, not homogeneous and require specialist knowledge. This is an interesting phenomenon which has always prompted questions about the identity of operational risk practitioners and the expectation that they need to be masters of all trades.

FIGURE 1.1 Operational risk in a picture

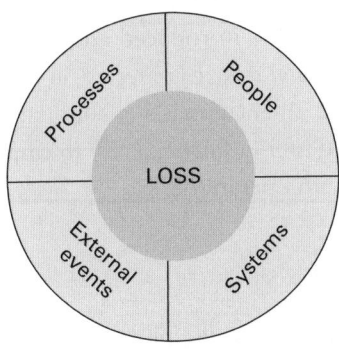

That very breadth of the scope should, however, be viewed as the greatest advantage of the operational risk discipline: no other domain in financial services is so extensive or all-encompassing in scope. Coupled with the fact that it is still a relatively young and evolving discipline, operational risk is perhaps the most exciting and interesting financial services field in which to explore and build a career.

Operational risk, not operations risk

Arguably, the name *operational risk* does not do the discipline justice; whether in English or other languages, it is often mistakenly associated with the *Operations Department* and the potential errors and failures that emanate from operational processing. When my training slides are translated into various languages, I always double-check the definition and frequently have to correct the fact that the word has been translated as *operations*. What was confusing a decade ago is still so nowadays. So it is important to emphasize:

Operational Risk ≠ Operations Risk

The educational journey is far from complete, within both financial services firms and the regulatory authorities themselves. In 2017, the European Securities and Markets Authority (ESMA) issued a pioneering document on the application of distributed ledger technology to the securities market.[2] Under the 'Key Risk' section, however, operational risk still called out only errors and glitches; while other sub-components such as cyber, fraud and money laundering – which should have been mentioned under the same heading – appeared under separate and distinct titles.

In recent years, potential fragmentation was somewhat exacerbated by *conduct risk* being unhelpfully introduced and treated by many firms as a risk distinct from operational risk. To reiterate, in this book operational risk is viewed in its broadest, all-encompassing context. In some organizations, it has even been renamed to *non-financial risk* to emphasize the breadth and remove the confusion with operations.

Just loss no longer works

The roots of the operational risk discipline lay in the Basel *Capital* Accord; the word *capital* relaying the primary focus of prudential regulatory directives on *risk measurement* and the adequacy of internal financial resources. The Basel Committee disclosed, in a study of 30 major banks, that the value of losses crystallizing from operational risk failures between 1998 and 2000 amounted to €2.6 billion;[3] as a result, it became a significant enough concern to warrant an introduction of a capital charge.

In reality there are other important impacts of operational risk failure, in addition to financial losses incurred by the firm itself. These include customer detriment, reputational damage and market instability. Following high-profile mis-selling scandals and significant technology failures, both firms and regulators nowadays are paying close attention to conduct and operational resilience. While the Basel Framework itself is primarily *inwardly focussed* on the firm's financial resources, supervisors around the world would argue that organizations also need to have an *outward* view: considering the harm that their wrongdoing may be causing to clients and markets. This friction creates an interesting divergence: a growing number of organizations are coming to the view that the definition which cites only *loss* is no longer fully reflective of today's environment. The universe of operational risk is thus expanded, by amending the first part of the standard Basel definition to:

- the risk of **direct or indirect** loss resulting from...;
- the risk of **actual or potential financial** loss or **client harm** resulting from...; or even more broadly...
- the risk of **not achieving strategic objectives** due to inadequate or failed internal processes, people and systems or from external events.

Link to strategy and value proposition

As a business value proposition, operational risk management has a clear purpose. Its primary goal is to provide tools to business units on the ground to enable them to make well-informed and risk-aware decisions. Even though the Basel description specifically excludes strategic risk from its scope, expanding the definition of operational risk to be more of an enterprise-wide discipline – and specifically linking it to business objectives – makes a lot of sense and immediately bears fruit. Having a conversation with a chief executive and senior managers on what keeps them awake at night inevitably brings more strategic aspects into the discussion. A narrowly defined scope, on the other hand, creates barriers to a free-flowing conversation. It means business-related concerns are expressly carved out and demonstrates clearly that the focus of operational risk should be limited to 'operational' concerns, such as fraud and the like.

The traditional definition of risk cited by the International Organization for Standardization (ISO) is 'the effect of uncertainty on objectives'.[4] This definition purposely focusses on *objectives*; not the whole realm of uncertainties, but rather their specific impact on what needs to be achieved. Similarly, the Committee of Sponsoring Organizations of the Treadway Commission (COSO) stresses the position of risk in relation to mission and strategy.[5]

This may be the missing link in how operational risk is distinguished from other disciplines. At times there is a tendency within the operational risk domain to go its own way, creating lists of all the things that can possibly go wrong due to processes, people or systems, but not always seeing the vital connection to what matters most: the firm's business goals. Expanding the definition to include an explicit link to business objectives elevates the brand and straightaway brings risk practitioners to the strategy table.

In 2018, I conducted a study to understand industry practices around these definition questions, the results of which are presented in Table 1.1. They demonstrate that, while the majority of practitioners are still using the original Basel definition, we are also seeing a positive shift in the industry, re-positioning operational risk where it can help derive the maximum possible business benefit.

As part of the same study, operational risk professionals voted on their presence at the strategy table. The outcome in Table 1.2 reflects a common complaint among practitioners that the operational risk function is not routinely called upon when major discussions and decisions are taking place. This result provides yet more impetus to expand the definition and promote the standing of the discipline.

TABLE 1.1 Industry study: definition of operational risk

Operational risk definition	% Firms
Using Basel definition	56
Expanded to broader than *loss*	13
Expanded to include strategy or link to objectives	23
Other expanded	8

TABLE 1.2 Industry study: operational risk function at the strategy table

Operational risk function at the strategy table	% Firms
Yes	25
Occasionally involved in some strategic decisions	49
Not involved in making strategic decisions	26

Operational risk taxonomy and its evolution

At the heart of operational risk management is the Risk Taxonomy, which provides further explanation and definition of the scope of what is included in the discipline.

OPERATIONAL RISK TAXONOMY

The taxonomy is a risk classification system which defines and distinguishes different categories of operational risk, enabling it to capture the complete risk universe.

What is the main purpose of this taxonomy? In practice it serves several different uses, as highlighted below.

Common language and areas of focus

Classification introduces a common language of risk, enabling the organization to use consistent terminology. It also allows firms to bring certain themes into the spotlight, by specifically calling them out in separate categories, which helps to focus attention on them during risk identification exercises. There is an additional benefit from the regulatory requirement to map internal taxonomy to standard Basel Committee categories which are described further in the chapter. It means that not only do firms have a common language but there is also an *industry* common language that can be used for benchmarking purposes.

Risk measurement

In the early days, the primary use of the taxonomy tended to be for *risk measurement*. It enables firms to allocate losses – which we can think of as crystallized operational risks, as discussed in Chapter 4 – to a specific named category. This helps firms analyse their loss profile, understand the distribution of loss amounts across the spectrum of possibilities, and evaluate the adequacy of their capital.

Risk identification

As the operational risk discipline has matured, the use of categorization for *risk management* purposes has gradually been increasing. For example, during the risk assessment process outlined in Chapters 5 and 6, risk categories provide a helpful reminder that a whole range of themes need to be addressed, from fraud to system failures, ensuring that no material risks are omitted from the review.

Back-testing

The taxonomy is the essential glue that links the framework elements together. If the tools introduced in subsequent chapters all apply the same classification, it is possible to compare and contrast their outputs against each other, which helps to tell a coherent story.

Aggregation and reporting

Following on from this, categorization allows a structure to be imposed on large quantities of operational risk data, allowing the aggregation, analysis and reporting of themes in a meaningful way, and enabling areas of concern to be highlighted.

INTRODUCTION OF OPERATIONAL RISK TAXONOMY

The Basel taxonomy consists of seven *categories*, or types, described in Figure 1.2. (Note: the terms 'category' and 'type' will be used interchangeably throughout the rest of this chapter.)

Basel classification has been used by many organizations since the very early days of the operational risk discipline, and is now deeply embedded in the core tools of the framework which capture, process and analyse relevant data.

A further nomenclature exists for each of the main (or *level 1*) categories. We can think of these as *level 2* sub-categories (or sub-types) of risk. The Basel Framework, for instance, splits *internal fraud* into more detailed sub-categories, such as *unauthorized activity* and *theft and fraud* (see Table 1.3).

FIGURE 1.2 Seven operational risk categories, Basel Committee

1	**Internal fraud**
2	**External fraud**
3	**Employment practices and workplace safety**
4	**Clients, products and business practices**
5	**Damage to physical assets**
6	**Business disruption and system failures**
7	**Execution, delivery and process management**

TABLE 1.3 Taxonomy sub-categories

Level 1 category	Level 2 sub-category
1. Internal fraud	1.1 Unauthorized activity
	1.2 Theft and fraud

Typically, firms define a hierarchy with two to three levels, though some organizations go up to five levels, creating a comprehensive catalogue of detailed individual risks. A taxonomy with more than three levels may, however, become too granular and burdensome to use.

Evolution of operational risk taxonomy

While many firms continue to apply the original Basel classification, it is recognized across the industry that it is becoming dated. Increasingly, organizations are taking the opportunity to design a bespoke, fit-for-purpose listing tailored to their own needs. The publication of an updated reference taxonomy by the ORX, summarized in Figure 1.3, has enabled some firms to accelerate progress in adopting a more current categorization system.[6]

FIGURE 1.3 Sixteen operational risk categories, ORX

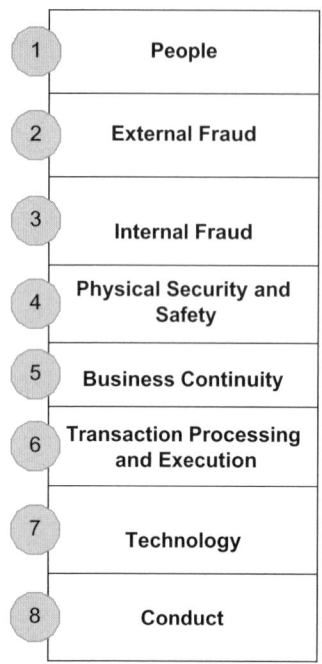

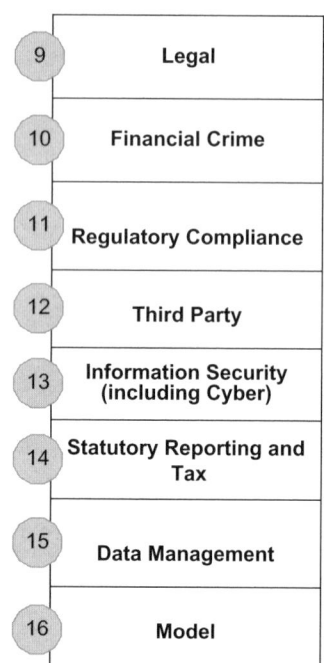

To create a fit-for-purpose taxonomy, organizations should aim to:

- use simple language which is understood at all levels of the organization;

- shape the categories to reflect the most significant risks in their business;

- create the best possible value for risk identification and management purposes.

Simplifying the language

The Basel Committee naming conventions are not entirely obvious or intuitive to employees on the ground who may be less familiar with operational risk as a discipline. While the term *execution, delivery and process management* is easily recognized by most risk practitioners, it is less meaningful to other departments. To help improve embeddedness, a better value proposition is to deliver the risk framework in the language that people in the business actually use. For example, as seen in Figure 1.3, *employment practices and workplace safety* has been effectively renamed by ORX as merely *people* – a more sensible and intuitive expression of that risk type.

Reflecting the current landscape

Over the years the operational risk landscape has evolved markedly, providing yet another reason for a refresh of the Basel taxonomy. For example:

- *Outsourcing* – given firms' increasing reliance on third parties and in view of new requirements such as the European Banking Authority's guidelines,[7] this needs to be *promoted* into its own level 1 category rather than displayed as part of *execution, delivery and process management*.

- *Cyber* – for which the Financial Stability Board has developed a whole lexicon of its own – needs to be reflected with adequate language.[8]

- *Clients, products and business practices* is too wide-ranging and includes several distinct topics, including *legal* and *financial crime*. If a firm is assessing its exposure to and appetite for, say, *legal risk* – which is specifically called out by the Basel Framework as part of operational risk – it would be beneficial to have that risk as a distinct category.

- On the other hand, examples such as cheque kiting – a form of unauthorized chequing account activity which Basel lists as level 3 under *execution, delivery and process management* – are becoming less pertinent in the digital age.

Considering best value for risk management purposes

As discussed earlier in the chapter, taxonomy allows firms and practitioners to consciously focus attention on specific themes; it is therefore a powerful risk management tool. For example, where the firm is reliant on a significant number of complex spreadsheets and end-user computing applications (EUCs), it may introduce *models* as a level 1 category. This will emphasize the importance of the topic and encourage end-users to identify and assess *model risk*, defined as the risk of incorrect model design or poor implementation. Areas such as trading, finance and market risk commonly use elaborate models, sometimes in the form of spreadsheets, which take assumptions, perform computations and produce critical outputs that are used for decision-making. There are plenty of industry examples of model errors that have caused significant losses and reputational damage to the enterprise, signifying the importance of *model risk* management.

TABLE 1.4   Taxonomy example: *product* category

Level 1 category	Subject Matter Expert	Definition	Level 2 sub-categories
1. Product	Head of Product Development	The risk of product flaws or defects, failure to adhere to specification.	1.1 Product defects 1.2 Failure to adhere to product specification 1.3 Inadequate new/change product approval process

Similarly, if the organization is actively launching new products and value propositions, it may feel appropriate to distinguish a level 1 *product* category, as described in Table 1.4.

Product does not appear as a level 1 category in either the Basel or ORX taxonomies; while *model* is present in the ORX but not the Basel level 1 categorization. This discrepancy illustrates that it is useful to refer to industry sources as a guide rather than a rule, and to develop a customized classification scheme. The challenge, of course, is that businesses evolve over time and the scheme has to be meaningful at the moment of creation and yet have the flexibility to evolve in line with business needs.

Cause, event and impact: use of the bow-tie

Generally, the purpose of the operational risk taxonomy is to classify *events*. It is worth discussing this in more detail, highlighting a perpetual operational risk management challenge around *cause*, *event* and *impact*.

- *cause* leads to an event;
- *event* is a specific occurrence, or something that goes wrong;
- *impact* is the consequence of an event.

Staff fatigue may be a *cause* of, for instance, a transactional error or failure to process a payment (an *event*), leading to financial loss, client detriment and other consequences (*impacts*), as outlined in Figure 1.4.

FIGURE 1.4 Cause–Event–Impact bow-tie

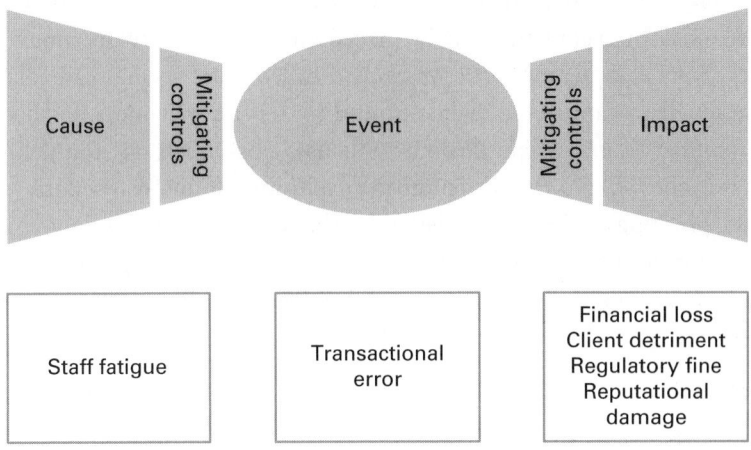

This well-known model, named after its resemblance to a bow-tie, is helpful in differentiating between causes, events and impacts, leading to a neater taxonomy containing *events* (and excluding causes and impacts). The bow-tie model will be further referred to in subsequent chapters of the book. In the earlier example, the event falls under the category *transaction processing and execution*; while staff fatigue, being a *cause*, does not belong in the *event* taxonomy.

That said, it has to be acknowledged that there are endless cause–event–impact chains in operational risk management due to the sheer breadth of the discipline and interconnectedness of various elements. One event can become the cause of another; for instance, miscommunication (cause) can result in an erroneous transaction (event); in turn an erroneous transaction (cause) may corrupt a system, leading to system failure (event).

PRACTICAL TIP: 'PIN THE BOW-TIE'

To untangle the cause–event–impact chain, practitioners may adopt an approach of 'pinning the bow-tie', whereby the *cause* is ascertained first to distinguish the *event*. Alternatively, employees may choose to 'pin' the *impact* (for example, on the end-customer), working backwards to the *event*. The latter approach is easier and more readily understood by the business units and support functions.

A note on exclusivity, which is a useful design concept when setting the taxonomy. It is important to provide clear guidance to avoid the overlap where a risk or event can easily be placed into two or more taxonomy categories. For example, the *third party* (also called outsourcing) category may be designed to capture all events caused by service providers. In this case, *information security* type dealing with data loss, theft or non-deliberate data breaches should clearly denote the exclusion of third-party data-related events, pointing to their coverage under the respective category.

To summarize, when designing the taxonomy, adopt a pragmatic approach, and configure to the extent possible 'clean' event-type categories which are:

- exhaustive;

- mutually exclusive;

- resonant with end-users; and

- aiding the most in risk management.

Importantly, be prepared to invest in the analysis of captured data – and recategorization of it where necessary – accepting that perfection is not feasible in this space. Additionally, maintain mappings to the original Basel categories for industry benchmarking purposes.

Most debated taxonomy categories

There are areas of taxonomy that are actively debated and deserve attention, outlined below.

PEOPLE

The first one is *people* category, where both the Basel and ORX taxonomies only count occurrences such as employment lawsuits (*events*). The firms, however, frequently wish to encourage the identification and monitoring of risks related to employees being overstretched, or not having the right skillset. If business functions are urged to record threats to capacity or capability, that might enable the firm to receive signals and proactively act before the problem becomes serious. In this case, the overall employee life cycle from on-boarding to off-boarding – including *well-being*, which became a particular focal point during the Covid-19 pandemic – is included in the *event-type* taxonomy to capture the entire range of people-related matters.

CHANGE

Another topic which justifies review, as it often leads to arguments, is the topic of *change*. Inadequate change management is usually a *cause* of events such as errors or failed regulatory reporting obligations. Therefore, it has no place in the original Basel or ORX *event-type* taxonomies. However, due to the increasing change agenda within all organizations, change is often now built into the classification system in its own right; to prompt staff to reflect on the magnitude of corporate transformation and address the pressures of too much change before things go wrong.

CONDUCT

While *conduct* is sometimes presented it its own right (including by ORX), it is best to treat it as an overarching term to identify the multitude of risks that may result in poor customer outcomes (also see Chapter 12 for further definitions). Arguably, many risks residing in the categories such as *people, financial crime, information security* may have conduct implications. They may however also apply to the *technology* category, where for example, underinvestment in systems leading to technology failure is a behavioural matter, as it reflects a lack of customer care: the customer not being at the heart of strategic decisions, prioritization and allocation of budget. Consequently, a conduct *lens* can be applied to almost any risk or event to reflect the fact that it has specific (customer or market) consequences, leading to reporting on conduct risk via consolidation of one or more taxonomy categories.

OPERATIONAL RESILIENCE

Similarly, *operational resilience* according to the Basel Committee is an 'outcome that benefits from the effective management of operational risk'.[9] Similarly to *conduct*, it is best not to shoehorn it into a separate category due to the potential for duplication with other risk types (see Chapter 14 for more details).

In 2020, I led a comparative analysis of operational risk taxonomies across the financial services sector. Presented below in Table 1.5 are examples from six firms, anonymized and slightly modified to preserve confidentiality.

The study demonstrates the expected degree of divergence, and proves that there is no 'right' solution to the taxonomy question. Companies are actively tailoring the nomenclature to suit their needs, splitting or collapsing categories and introducing their own terminology. And while there are some common groupings such as *fraud* and *information technology*, unique types – for example *transparency* or *customer and employee communication* – also appear.

TABLE 1.5 Industry study: operational risk taxonomies

Firm 1	Firm 2	Firm 3	Firm 4	Firm 5	Firm 6
Internal Fraud	Economic Crime	Financial Crime	Fraud	Third-party Liability	Fraud
External Fraud	Rogue Trading and	People	Financial Crime	Health and Safety	Health, Safety and
Unauthorized Activity	Market	Health and Safety	Staff	Buildings and Premises	Security
Employment Practices	Abuse	Model	Health and Safety	Transparency Risk	Model Governance
Personal and Physical	Employment Practices	Conduct	Valuation	Communications	Technology
Security	Health, Safety and	Technology & Cyber	Compliance	Information Technology	Business Resilience
Compliance Risk	Environment	Security	Legal	Cyber	Business Process
Information Technology	Facilities Management	Operational Resilience	Tax	Business Continuity	Change Management
Risk	Product Flaws	Data Security	Systems	Data Quality and	Supplier Management
Continuity Risk	Regulatory Compliance	Execution, Delivery &	Data	integrity	
Processing Risk	Legal Compliance	Process Management	Booking & Processing	Estate Management	
Control Risk	Customer and Employee	Change Management	Accounting	Reporting	
	Communication	Supplier	Collateral	Third-party Risk	
	Information Technology		Insurance		
	Management		Project		
	Payments Transactions		Outsourcing		
	Member Service				
	Financial, Regulatory and				
	Critical Monitoring and				
	Reporting				

Role of taxonomy in risk management by risk category

A well-defined taxonomy sets the foundation for effective *management* of operational risk not only at the overall level, but also by *risk category*; that is where the naming conventions and appropriateness of the categorization scheme become even more apparent. It is likely that all the risk types decided on are already being managed by the enterprise, and that experts are in place to provide specialist advice. The critical role of the operational risk function, therefore, is to *orchestrate* and *coordinate* the various activities, bringing together a wealth of existing expertise while avoiding unnecessary duplication.

> A subject matter expert (SME) for a given taxonomy category can be defined as a knowledgeable senior individual who is able to provide expertise and advice on that category, including:
>
> - contributing to its definition and level 2 composition;
> - providing expert opinion on operational risk data recorded under the category;
> - defining operating policies and standards; and
> - contributing to operational risk appetite statement and measures (discussed in Chapter 9).

Organizational structures often naturally lend themselves to the SME concept, with the head of Human Resources, for example, being the natural SME for the *people* category, the Chief Technology Officer for *technology*, the head of the Legal department for *legal* – and so on. Partnership with SMEs enables operational risk teams to agree each taxonomy category and set the foundation for continuous collaboration in risk management. Operational risk teams must not apply an overly rigid approach, instead consulting with SMEs and incorporating their views. It is better to find the right middle ground to arrive at a sensible and meaningful classification, rather than aiming for a perfect categorization that does not achieve organizational buy-in.

Where a partnership with SMEs is not achieved, operational risk practitioners face a challenge of a high degree of fragmentation – and lack of coordination – of their activities. They will be managing operational risk at

FIGURE 1.5 Governance forums aligned to risk categories

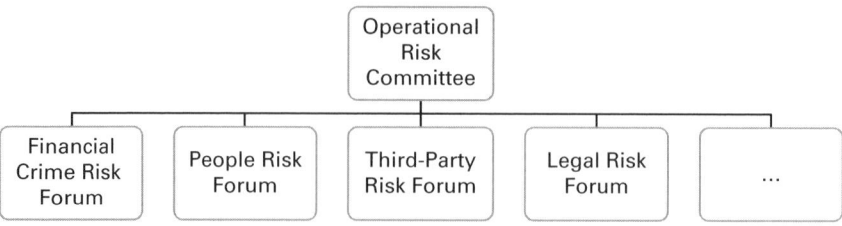

an aggregate level, whereas their respective SMEs are dealing with each category individually on the ground. Bringing the framework together and integrating the activities helps greatly in ensuring effective and value-added risk management. That is where governance forums aligned to the risk categories, as described in Figure 1.5, are most effective.

These kinds of lower-level forums allow firms to dedicate sufficient attention and perform a deep dive into risk categories. They also bring together the operational risk function, SMEs, and business units and support functions, enabling much needed coordination. Not all categories are equal; some will require a forum with more frequent meetings, while other less material ones could benefit from either an annual review or coverage as an agenda item at the overall operational risk committee. The benefit of establishing dedicated forums has to be weighed against the cost of running additional meetings.

While roles may vary from firm to firm, an example of responsibilities is presented in the box below.

The operational risk function is responsible for:

- leading the design and development of the operational risk taxonomy in consultation with SMEs;

- working closely with each respective SME to define each level 1 category and its level 2 components;

- establishing and coordinating governance forums aligned to the taxonomy categories, to provide appropriate depth and quality of risk management discussions for each risk type (Note: the forums may be chaired by the SME or the operational risk function, depending on the firm's approach and governance arrangements);

- analysing operational risk data, validating and reclassifying it as needed;

- leading the definition of the appetite, overall and by risk category;

- reporting on the aggregate level of operational risk and by risk category;

- providing oversight and challenge to first line areas.

First line business units and support functions will in turn:

- apply taxonomy to identify material risks that may prevent achievement of their objectives;

- involve SMEs as needed in risk and control identification and management;

- participate in governance forums; and

- correctly report and categorize operational risk data.

Common challenges and good practices

Common challenges and good practices when developing an operational risk taxonomy are described below.

Common challenges

NO ELEGANCE IN THE SOLUTION

I had a discussion with a senior practitioner searching for an elegant operational risk taxonomy, with no cross-overs between causes, events and impacts, and with data falling neatly into allocated places. It is hardly feasible to strive for perfection. But nor it is advisable to have 'dirty data', a term that often applies when events, causes and control failures all end up in the categorization system, creating an entangled and unreconcilable array of data. It is best to apply a practical solution, such as a bow-tie structure, to arrive at a sensible classification that is meaningful to the firm; while accepting that this will inevitably mean some detailed data analysis is required.

DATA CLEAN-UP AND RECATEGORIZATION

Continuing from the first challenge, the importance of continuous clean-up and recategorization of operational risk data is sometimes underestimated. For example, when logging events, employees may erroneously classify payment errors under *people*, reasoning that it is a human error. These

OREs need to be moved to the correct category, such as *transaction processing and execution*. This kind of clean-up is an ongoing activity which has to be factored into the day-to-day responsibilities of risk practitioners (whether first or second line), because invariably they are the firm's main experts in taxonomy. This kind of challenge can be also mitigated, however, by more training of the end-users.

LABORIOUS PROCESS OF INTRODUCING CHANGES

Once classification is embedded into the operational risk software, it takes a substantial effort to introduce any changes. This is because previous data – related to past operational risk events, risks and controls – will need to be re-mapped to the new classification. In large international organizations it may take years to move to a new classification scheme. It is best, therefore, to invest effort up-front into developing a system and classification that is well thought through from the start.

OPERATIONAL RISK DISINTEGRATION

At times, the Operational Risk department is operating as a standalone function, dedicating insufficient attention to building synergies with the SMEs who, in practice, manage risk categories on the ground. Lack of alignment with SMEs, ambiguity in roles and responsibilities and absence of joint forums for robust management by risk category may lead to either duplication of activities or even disintegration. It is crucial to focus on developing relationships and establishing clarity in roles and responsibilities for effective risk management.

Good practices

DEVELOPING EXPERTISE

There will be instances where an unusual event may arise which raises questions on how it should be incorporated into the existing scheme. It is crucial to develop expertise on these cases within the Operational Risk department – perhaps even to appoint a taxonomy 'guru' who can interpret arbitrary cases and provide effective guidance.

CREATING SUPPLEMENTARY CLASSIFICATION SYSTEMS

Some firms use the term 'taxonomy' more widely and create other data categorization structures in addition to *event-type* classification. Most common are classifications for causes and impacts (being the left- and right-hand bows of the bow-tie). For example, a rudimentary causal taxonomy can be based on the definition of operational risk, and include:

- people;
- systems;
- processes; and
- external events.

More developed causal types are expansive, incorporating considerations around staff unavailability; failure of governance; climate change – although the jury is still out on how this topic, which is gaining significant attention from both firms and regulators – should be treated from a taxonomy perspective; approaching it as a *cause* enables examination of how it influences a variety of materializing risks. Reference taxonomies for cause and impact issued by ORX provide a good starting point for organizations.[10]

There may also be a separate classification scheme for control types; for example, by using *Preventative–Detective–Directive–Corrective* categories, as explored in Chapter 5.

CONSISTENT USE OF TAXONOMY BY OTHER FUNCTIONS

It is good practice to strive for consistent use of taxonomy by other functions; for example compliance and internal audit, as well as specialist areas such as IT and facilities management, who may have separate systems for recording technology incidents or health and safety breaches. Failure to align may result in duplication of effort, varying criteria, confusion for end-users and fragmentation of valuable risk data. In contrast, a unified categorization system utilized by all functions enables data to be compared and contrasted effectively, increasing the quality and depth of analysis.

Industry benchmark, 2020

The operational risk taxonomy is the essential glue that ties together all the elements of the framework. The Best Practice Operational Risk Forum examined the state of maturity of the tool, and variances in its application, recognizing the vital importance of taxonomy and its place in the framework.

Only 20 per cent of respondents felt they had got their taxonomy right, while the remaining 80 per cent were either already redesigning it or planning to implement improvements, as described in Figure 1.6.

FIGURE 1.6 Industry poll: satisfaction with taxonomy

Satisfied with Operational Risk Taxonomy

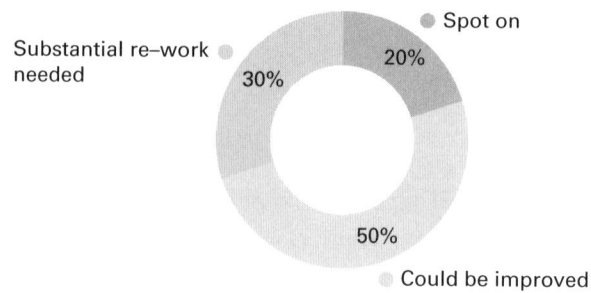

Best Practice Operational Risk Forum, 2020

FIGURE 1.7 Industry poll: use of Basel taxonomy

Using Basel Op Risk categories

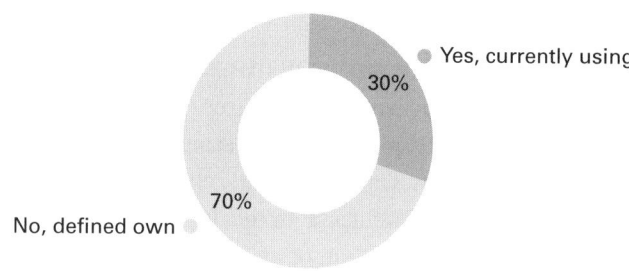

Best Practice Operational Risk Forum, 2020

As presented in Figure 1.7, a minority (30 per cent) continue to use Basel risk event types while still aiming to move to a more up-to-date and intuitive classification. Categories such as *people, outsourcing* and *data* read better than *execution, delivery* and *process management*. Participants agreed that the reference taxonomy published by ORX is a very useful guide for those firms considering making changes.[11]

Implementing a change to the taxonomy is a large undertaking which requires re-mapping of large quantities of old data to the new categories. However, as Nelson Mandela said, 'It always seems impossible until it's done.' Defining and adopting the right taxonomy, which fully reflects the business model of the organization, results in significantly more meaningful risk identification, management and reporting, based on risk categories that are well understood across the firm.

Practical workplace exercise

Reflecting on the content of this chapter, review the definition of operational risk and the existing classification system used in your firm, considering:

1 Is the definition fit for purpose? Does it position the discipline relative to the firm's business objectives?

2 Is the taxonomy easy to understand, up to date and effective?

3 Are the taxonomy categories exhaustive and mutually exclusive to the extent possible?

4 What works well and should be retained?

5 What can be improved? Note down potential improvements.

MAKE A DIFFERENCE (MAD) ACTION

Note down one action you will take after reading this chapter that will make a positive difference to how the operational risk taxonomy is defined and treated in your firm.

In summary, this chapter introduced operational risk and discussed the importance of the risk taxonomy, as well as challenges related to its development and implementation.

Moving on, the next chapter outlines the framework, and the key tools used to identify, manage and mitigate operational risk.

Notes

1   Basel Committee on Banking Supervision, Basel Framework, www.bis.org/
    basel_framework/ (archived at https://perma.cc/96FE-VF9B)

2   European Securities and Markets Authority (2017) *The Distributed Ledger
    Technology Applied to Securities Markets*, www.esma.europa.eu/system/files_
    force/library/dlt_report_-_esma50-1121423017-285.pdf?download=1
    (archived at https://perma.cc/88XL-E6FK)

3   Basel Committee on Banking Supervision (2002) *The Quantitative Impact
    Study for Operational Risk: Overview of individual loss data and lessons
    learned*, www.bis.org/bcbs/qis/qisopriskresponse.pdf (archived at https://perma.
    cc/CZ7Z-7TV6)

4   International Organization for Standardization (2009) ISO 31000:2009, www.
    iso.org/standard/43170.html (archived at https://perma.cc/QC2G-Z8WR)

5   Committee of Sponsoring Organizations of the Treadway Commission (COSO)
    (2017) *2017 Enterprise Risk Management: Integrated framework*, www.coso.
    org/Pages/erm.aspx (archived at https://perma.cc/RKP9-BZ4Z)

6   Operational Riskdata eXchange Association (ORX) (2019) *ORX Reference
    Taxonomy*, managingrisktogether.orx.org/operational-risk-taxonomy (archived
    at https://perma.cc/Z9QC-WC6L)

7   European Banking Authority (2019) *EBA Guidelines on Outsourcing
    Arrangements*, www.eba.europa.eu/regulation-and-policy/internal-governance/
    guidelines-on-outsourcing-arrangements (archived at https://perma.cc/4X3C-
    LZ6Z)

8   Financial Stability Board (2018) *Cyber Lexicon*, www.fsb.org/2018/11/
    cyber-lexicon/ (archived at https://perma.cc/CWD6-EGUD)

9   Basel Committee on Banking Supervision (2020) Consultative Document,
    Principles for Operational Resilience, www.bis.org/bcbs/publ/d509.pdf
    (archived at https://perma.cc/5857-EJ8V)

10 Operational Riskdata eXchange Association (ORX) (2020) *ORX Cause and
    Impact Operational Risk Reference Taxonomy*, managingrisktogether.orx.org/
    operational-risk-reference-taxonomy/orx-cause-impact-reference-taxonomy
    (archived at https://perma.cc/DN4Q-CZN2)

11 Operational Riskdata eXchange Association (ORX) (2019) *ORX Reference
    Taxonomy*, managingrisktogether.orx.org/operational-risk-taxonomy
    (archived at https://perma.cc/88N6-8PYP)

02

Operational risk framework and its implementation

What this chapter covers: This chapter builds a foundation which is then used throughout the book, introducing the Operational Risk Framework and explaining its key components. Each subsequent chapter will commence with a visual diagram of the framework, clearly denoting the element it addresses, and providing a coherent link between all the chapters. The chapter also outlines a structured three-step approach for implementing and embedding operational risk management, presenting a range of practical tools which can help in the deployment process.

FURTHER READING

- Basel Committee on Banking Supervision (2020) Consultative document, *Revisions to the Principles for the Sound Management of Operational Risk*
  Why recommended: Since the early days, the Basel Principles have been the key document to study for operational risk practitioners, and the latest 2020 update forms a solid base for a benchmarking exercise.

- Gerd Gigerenzer (2015) *Risk Savvy: How to make good decisions*, Penguin Books
  Why recommended: An operational risk framework needs to be built out with a simple and pragmatic approach in mind, one that will resonate with the end-users. This mode of thinking aligns with this excellent suggested book, whose author believes that the best decisions are arrived at using common sense and listening to your gut.

Introducing the framework and its components

Every firm embarking on an operational risk journey requires a framework that provides a structure for implementing operational risk management throughout the entire organization. It needs to present a simple yet coherent picture of the essential pieces of the puzzle, and to outline how they join together. The framework should be easy to understand, as it will be communicated to senior management as well as employees at the coal face, serving as an anchor and a key reference point for a whole range of discussions related to operational risk management.

While there is no one-size-fits-all approach, an example of the framework is described in Figure 2.1, and serves as a base for the rest of the chapters in the book. Let's examine these framework components in more detail.

To begin with, each practitioner needs to answer a single question: what tools do I need in my operational risk toolbox? Four core elements are positioned in the middle section of the diagram. They work together in an integrated fashion to ensure the company identifies, assesses and manages the operational risks that it faces. The life cycle of each core element is described in subsequent chapters of the book.

Core tools

OPERATIONAL RISK EVENTS

Operational risk events (OREs) are the oldest and the most common of the four core elements. They enable an organization to act promptly following an incident, to minimize the impact from the incident escalating, and to derive valuable lessons learned. Even more, they allow the firm to achieve a clear understanding of its loss profile and evaluate the adequacy of its capital resources.

RISK ASSESSMENTS

Risk assessments are a key forward-looking framework component. They supplement the backward-looking OREs while still taking them into consideration, permitting management to identify and mitigate risks before they crystallize into events. They enable the organization to bring focus to gaps and weaknesses, providing management with a powerful tool for strengthening the control environment.

FIGURE 2.1 Holistic operational risk management framework

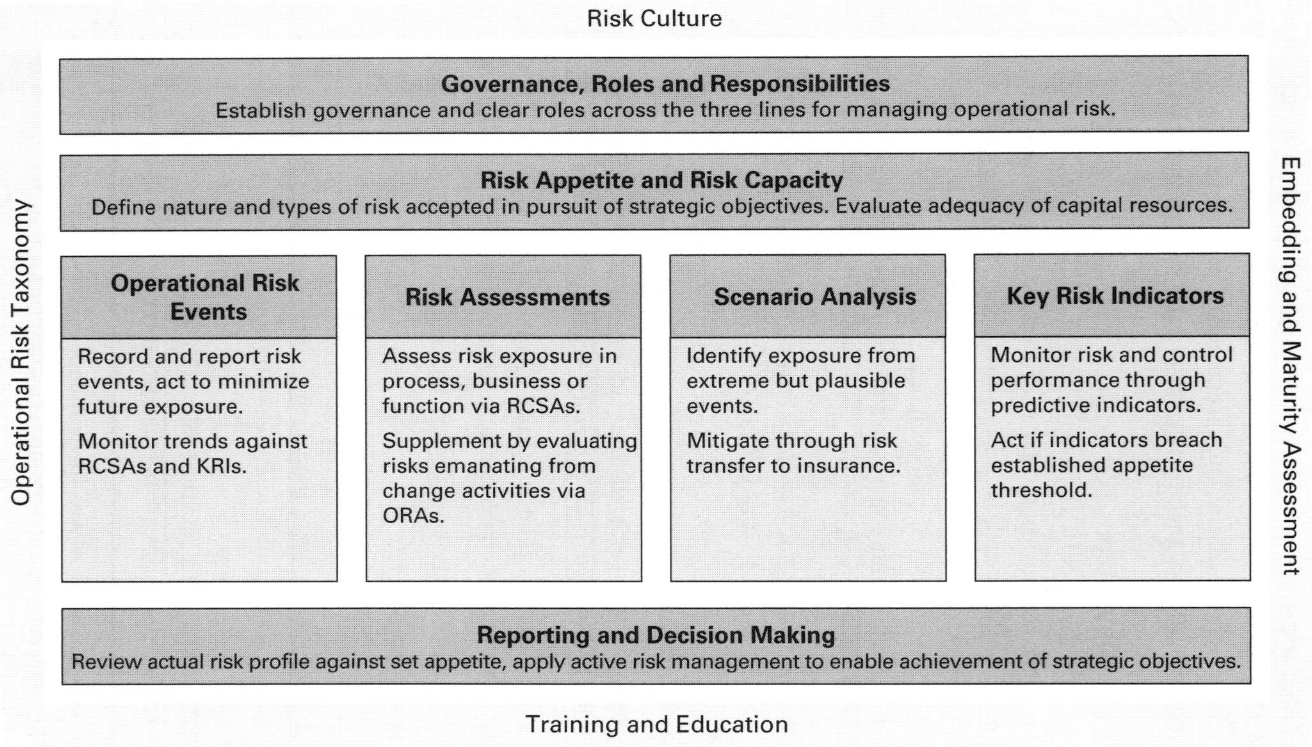

Embedding and Maturity Assessment

Risk Culture

Governance, Roles and Responsibilities

Establish governance and clear roles across the three lines for managing operational risk.

Risk Appetite and Risk Capacity

Define nature and types of risk accepted in pursuit of strategic objectives. Evaluate adequacy of capital resources.

Operational Risk Events	**Risk Assessments**	**Scenario Analysis**	**Key Risk Indicators**
Record and report risk events, act to minimize future exposure.	Assess risk exposure in process, business or function via RCSAs.	Identify exposure from extreme but plausible events.	Monitor risk and control performance through predictive indicators.
Monitor trends against RCSAs and KRIs.	Supplement by evaluating risks emanating from change activities via ORAs.	Mitigate through risk transfer to insurance.	Act if indicators breach established appetite threshold.

Reporting and Decision Making

Review actual risk profile against set appetite, apply active risk management to enable achievement of strategic objectives.

Training and Education

Operational Risk Taxonomy

SCENARIO ANALYSIS

Scenario analysis is an instrument that utilizes proactive risk assessment thinking and applies it to extreme but plausible circumstances. It augments the ORE dataset by adding considered scenarios which – even if they are synthetic – build on the knowledge derived from the other core tools. It is just as valuable for risk management as for measurement purposes.

KEY RISK INDICATORS

Key risk indicators (KRIs) are used to monitor the risk and control environment of the organization. KRI information, assimilated and presented in the form of a dashboard, is indispensable for observing the behaviour of the most significant risks identified during forward-looking exercises.

Practitioners can of course change the composition of this toolbox, filling it with the right components to suit the needs of their own organization. For example, they may decide to:

- segregate *external loss data* into a distinct framework element (in this book, it forms part of OREs); or

- add control assurance or process mapping as separate components (here, both are addressed as part of risk assessments); or

- remove KRIs – not all firms adopt this element, although in this book KRIs are viewed as an extremely useful mechanism.

It is up to the second line operational risk team to find the best fit, and the tools most suitable to the nature, size and business model of the firm.

Linking components

Once the core tools have been agreed upon, it is time to link them via *governance arrangements*, *risk appetite* and *risk reporting*, as displayed in Figure 2.1, stretching above and below the main toolset.

GOVERNANCE, ROLES AND RESPONSIBILITIES

Clear responsibilities are particularly important to operational risk management, where similar roles may be being performed by first line operational risk coordinators as well as by independent second line risk teams. Equally important are the roles of subject matter experts, risk and control owners, and members of the board, senior management and governance committees, all working collaboratively to multiply the power of risk management.

RISK APPETITE AND RISK CAPACITY

Operational risk appetite is the most nascent of the framework components. Once it is well developed, however, it converges the core elements and becomes an irreplaceable mechanism for decision making.

REPORTING AND DECISION MAKING

Reporting is the window through which operational risk teams communicate with management across the organization, the board and senior committees. This is where the results from all the toolbox instruments are consolidated in a meaningful way, answering the vitally important *so what?* question, and supporting a wide range of tactical and strategic decisions.

Supporting elements

Finally, the framework relies on other supporting elements, highlighted in Figure 2.1 on the perimeter around the main components. They include:

- *Risk culture*, given that operational risk is closely linked to and largely dependent on the culture of the organization.
- *Training and education*, without which it would be impossible to embed solid practices firm-wide.
- *Maturity assessment*, which a firm may want to carry out once it has embarked on its risk management implementation journey, to evaluate where it has got to relative to the desired state, and set improvement strategies.
- *Taxonomy*, used for setting the foundation for operational risk management by risk category (covered in Chapter 1).

Three essential steps for implementing operational risk management practices

Where do we start with implementing operational risk management practices in our organization? This question, which was topical at the inception of the operational risk discipline, remains relevant now. There are still plenty of firms starting from scratch for a whole range of valid reasons, perhaps opening a new branch or applying for a new banking licence. But even for a well-established firm, it is equally important to benchmark the framework

FIGURE 2.2   Three steps for implementing an operational risk framework

that is already in place, to set your direction of travel and define sensible next steps. Whether your firm is in the first category or the second, there are a number of crucial steps to follow, some of which are more challenging while others are easier to accomplish (Figure 2.2).

Step 1: External and internal requirements

UNDERSTANDING RULES AND REGULATIONS

The first step always consists of identifying the minimum requirements set by relevant regulators, assembling the list of applicable documents and understanding both the *letter* and the *spirit* of the rules. It is worth installing yourself in a comfortable chair and putting on your reading glasses. This stage is key. It builds a solid foundation by forcing firms to actively interpret their fundamental obligations, as well as more nuanced elements, for example:

- Subtle differences in the position of the second line operational risk function, which is expected to provide assertive *challenge* in some jurisdictions but to exhibit helpful *support* in others. These kinds of expectations influence the second line approaches, for instance, scenario analysis and KRIs; whether it oversees the process or assists first line units in completing the tasks.

- Requirements related to control *testing* if, for example, the firm is subject to Sarbanes–Oxley regulation;[1] these rules have a meaningful impact on the risk and control self-assessment (RCSA) methodology, and require a defined approach to testing rather than a purely judgemental assessment of controls.

- The obligation under certain jurisdictions to have a mandatory internal control function, which influences the entire set-up and operation of the Risk Department.

KEEPING UP TO DATE WITH REGULATORY REQUIREMENTS

Understanding regulatory requirements for operational risk management is not a one-off exercise. It is critical to achieve clarity as to who is responsible for horizon scanning and picking up changes as they come along. This helps to avoid gaps and grey areas which often exist between compliance and operational risk teams. Sometimes it is assumed that Compliance is performing holistic horizon scanning, and full reliance is placed on their process. In practice, though, the compliance function may be excluding certain topics from its scanning process; for instance, some aspects of prudential regulation, 'best practice' industry guidance, or even selected geographies. Operational risk teams need to ensure agreement on the scope of such processes, and maybe even perform their own reviews of what is a continuously changing regulatory agenda.

For international firms, the most rigorous expectations will usually prevail and be applied across the entire organization. Branches and subsidiaries of international institutions, especially those situated in locations subject to stricter rules, are frequently driving the operational risk value proposition for the whole firm – often including the head office. This can create friction between the head office and the affiliate, whose voice is not always taken into due consideration. In these cases, the local entity needs to take a firm lead in creating any necessary addendums to the group's policies and practices, and in ensuring that it continues to maintain those higher standards locally, withstanding the rigours of regulatory scrutiny.

DEVELOPING AN INTERNAL VALUE PROPOSITION

Particularly important at the outset, and at the same time as understanding the external rules, internal requirements also need to be assimilated. Essentially, this process involves analysing the firm's strengths and weaknesses, to determine the key selling points of operational risk management. While undeniably there are many generic advantages of prudent risk management, what *specific benefits* will resonate *the most*? Those particular benefits should be the ones most emphasized during discussions with the chief executive and the business units; they represent cards that will be put squarely on the table in subsequent conversations. Examples of the benefits that operational risk management brings – and the corresponding framework tools that enable their realization – are presented in Table 2.1.

TABLE 2.1   Benefits and corresponding framework tools

Benefits of operational risk management	Corresponding framework tools to help realize the benefits
Well-developed strategy, risks to strategic objectives are well understood and weighed up	Top-down strategic risk assessment with chief executive and senior management team Scenario analysis to explore the impact of extreme events
Enhancement of internal control environment, revenue protection	Bottom-up risk identification process, prioritizing the controls that need to be strengthened and potentially tested Lessons learned from OREs, leading to error reduction
Improved decision making	Risks and opportunities assessment, as described in Chapter 6, enabling the firm to take balanced decisions by weighing up its risks and opportunities Applying risk appetite and key risk indicators to guide mitigation and, at the same time, enable agreement on when to accept the risk and do nothing
Process optimization, efficiency and increased operational resilience	Bottom-up process risk assessment; identifying risks and controls while creating end-to-end process maps, which allow the firm to streamline the entire set of activities and achieve a view based on business processes or services
Strong risk culture	All framework tools; with emphasis on increased transparency, no blame, accountability, risk-awareness and risk reward
Regulatory compliance	All framework tools; regulatory conformance is a hugely important yet – rightly – the last element on the list. The organization needs to find the benefits of risk management which lead to compliance, but not the other way around

A word of caution: operational risk loss reduction is frequently seen as a tempting reason for establishing a framework. But this may be a hard sell for a small to medium-sized firm that does not have much history of losses (see Chapter 13 for further details).

Step 2: Conducting benchmarking

Regulatory directives are commonly principle-based and do not prescribe rigidly how to implement the framework or operate the tools. That is where, historically, the Basel Committee Principles for the sound management of operational risk have provided exceptionally useful directional guidance.[2] The Basel Principles, revised several times over the years, with the latest consultation paper issued in 2020, succinctly articulate fundamental requirements and remain the primary source for comparative analysis against existing practices. Despite being targeted at banks, they can be applied broadly to insurance, asset management or any other financial services activity, especially in sectors where fewer sources of literature are available compared to banking.

Second line operational risk teams, in conjunction with relevant subject matter experts, must conduct benchmarking analysis against these requirements – at a minimum performing a line-by-line comparison of the Basel Committee's 12 principles and 60+ detailed supporting statements vs the firm's current practices.

The Basel Principles can be supplemented by industry best practice; derived, for instance, from prior experience, from interactions with fellow practitioners, and from specialist industry guidance, such as papers issued by the Institute of Operational Risk.[3] Throughout the book, additional recommended reading of this kind is included at the start of each chapter.

KEEPING UP TO DATE WITH INDUSTRY BEST PRACTICE

Best practices evolve. One of the most important things to do when embarking on an operational risk implementation journey is to create strong links with other practitioners in the industry. There are plenty of forums, discussion groups and professional organizations across the financial services industry, examples of which are outlined in Chapter 11. These kinds of interactions are instrumental for keeping up with peers and closely following good industry practices as they develop.

Part of the purpose of the benchmarking analysis is to judgementally evaluate to what extent the Basel Principles (at a minimum) are already being applied, and to identify gaps and improvement areas. Conclusions can either be presented for each principle individually; or, with a bit more work, structured into themes which correspond to the individual components of the operational risk framework, as depicted in Figure 2.1. Results can be documented with the help of round ideograms, often used in qualitative comparative analysis for presenting the degree to which an item meets a

FIGURE 2.3   Example extract from benchmarking study

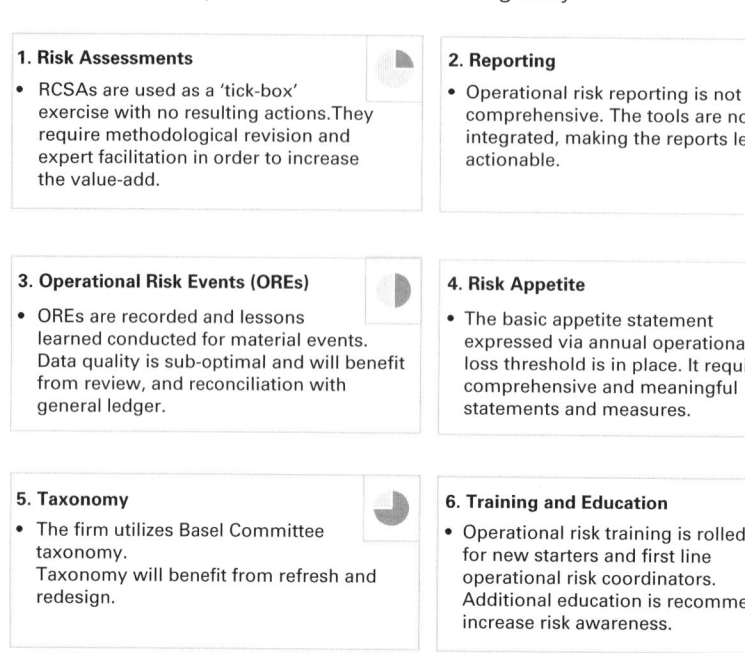

1. Risk Assessments

- RCSAs are used as a 'tick-box' exercise with no resulting actions. They require methodological revision and expert facilitation in order to increase the value-add.

2. Reporting

- Operational risk reporting is not comprehensive. The tools are not integrated, making the reports less actionable.

3. Operational Risk Events (OREs)

- OREs are recorded and lessons learned conducted for material events. Data quality is sub-optimal and will benefit from review, and reconciliation with general ledger.

4. Risk Appetite

- The basic appetite statement expressed via annual operational risk loss threshold is in place. It requires more comprehensive and meaningful statements and measures.

5. Taxonomy

- The firm utilizes Basel Committee taxonomy.
  Taxonomy will benefit from refresh and redesign.

6. Training and Education

- Operational risk training is rolled out for new starters and first line operational risk coordinators. Additional education is recommended to increase risk awareness.

Priority 1: least embedded, in need of enhancement

Priority 2: partially embedded, will benefit from improvement

Priority 3: embedded, consider enhancing

particular criterion. An example extract of this kind of analysis is provided in Figure 2.3.

The benchmarking study extract in Figure 2.3 demonstrates that the organization perceives that – relative to other framework elements – it is *risk assessments* and *reporting* that are least embedded and most in need of enhancement. Training and education, on the other hand, has been evaluated as well *embedded* and requires less focus.

Step 3: Planning implementation

The benchmarking exercise outlines the 'as-is' state of operational risk management, effectively defining the point of departure. It constitutes a starting point, enabling the firm to plan its next steps.

Subsequently, the benchmark can be translated into a practical implementation plan, with specific milestones and their timelines agreed and endorsed by senior management. This plan needs to consider the resource

FIGURE 2.4 Swimlane plan: operational risk implementation

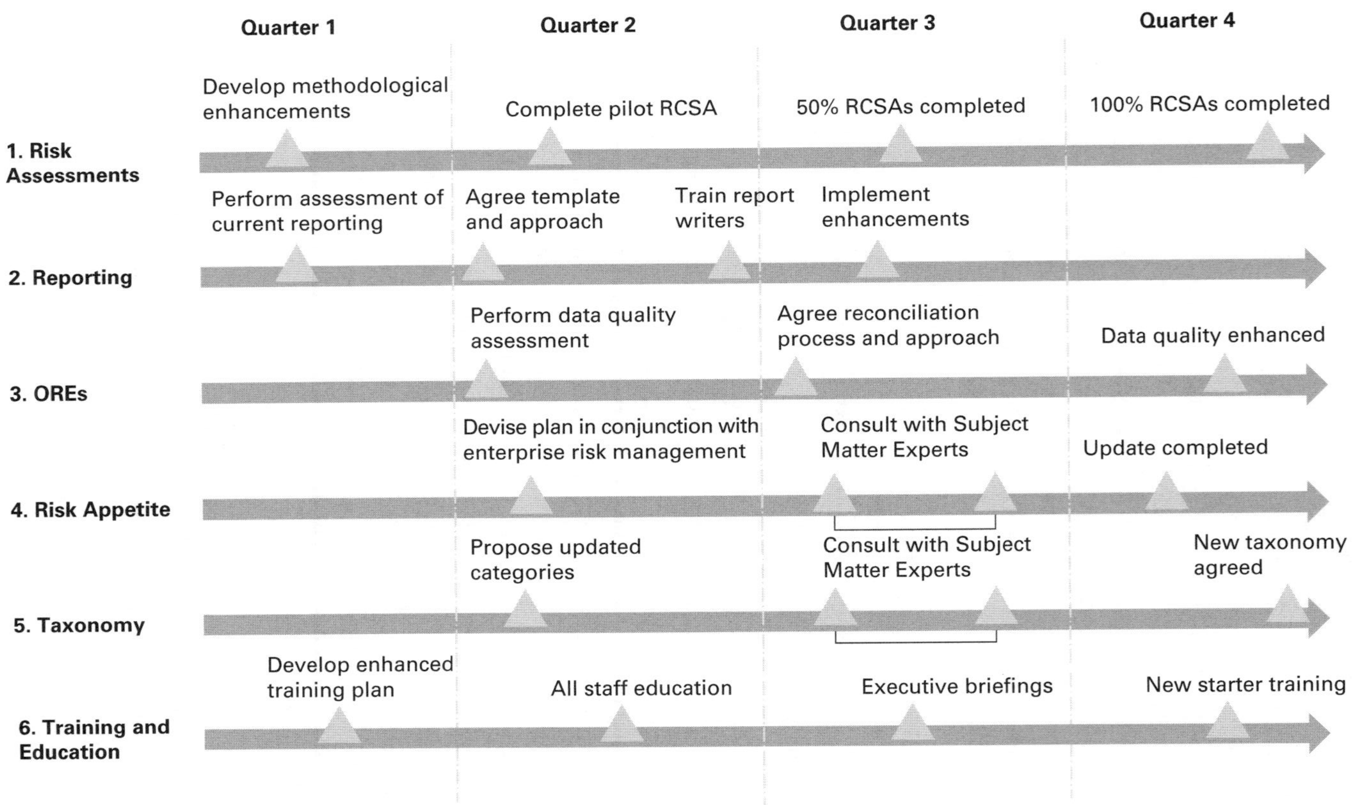

	Quarter 1	Quarter 2	Quarter 3	Quarter 4
1. Risk Assessments	Develop methodological enhancements	Complete pilot RCSA	50% RCSAs completed	100% RCSAs completed
2. Reporting	Perform assessment of current reporting	Agree template and approach	Train report writers	Implement enhancements
3. OREs		Perform data quality assessment	Agree reconciliation process and approach	Data quality enhanced
4. Risk Appetite		Devise plan in conjunction with enterprise risk management	Consult with Subject Matter Experts	Update completed
5. Taxonomy		Propose updated categories	Consult with Subject Matter Experts	New taxonomy agreed
6. Training and Education	Develop enhanced training plan	All staff education	Executive briefings	New starter training

requirements to complete each task, and to set a realistic time frame within which it can be accomplished.

An example of a resulting 'swimlane' plan, with the key themes highlighted in Figure 2.3 now split into implementation milestones, is presented in Figure 2.4.

In conclusion, it may be a daunting prospect to start up a new function – and to spearhead the development of operational risk practices within the organization – completely from scratch. If you have landed in such a situation, bear in mind that it will be a very exciting and enriching journey. All operational risk professionals had to start somewhere, and most, myself included, have since grown very fond of what is an outstandingly interesting discipline.

Common challenges and good practices

Common challenges

INSUFFICIENT THOUGHT GIVEN TO VALUE PROPOSITION

Operational risk implementation can sometimes be triggered by an unsatisfactory audit report or regulatory criticism; regulatory compliance then becomes the primary impetus for developmental activities. A lack of consideration of the internal value proposition – and an absence of explicit articulation or marketing of it – results in operational risk management being perceived as an administrative burden, with unclear value emanating from the function. This leads to first line business units pushing back, and refusing to use the tools or embed the practices. Even when pressed for time, it is crucial for the operational risk practitioner to invest strong effort in developing and articulating their value proposition: with a view to attracting interest and agreement across the board and achieving true engagement from first line units.

THREE-STEP PROCESS NOT FOLLOWED

In my consulting practice, I occasionally receive questions from practitioners which reflect the fact that Step 1 – namely understanding external and internal requirements – has not been completed properly. For example, a request to determine whether an organization really needs to conduct control testing or can instead adopt a judgemental evaluation of control effectiveness? The short answer to these questions is: it depends. As articulated in the three-step approach, there may (or may not) be a regulatory requirement for control testing, depending on the jurisdictions the firm operates in. Or the firm may actively aspire to perform testing if that will enhance the internal value proposition. Applying a structured three-step approach enables the firm to conduct thorough research and find answers to these kinds of questions before starting its implementation.

ABSENT OR OVERLY COMPLICATED FRAMEWORK DIAGRAM

Some organizations have developed their operational risk policies and procedures yet have failed to create a single pictorial diagram describing the framework and its key elements. This is challenging for visual learners, who absorb information through pictures. It may also mean that operational risk teams themselves are somewhat unclear how in reality the different pieces join together. At the other extreme, I have seen diagrams that require larger (eg A3-size) paper because they are so complicated that they do not fit onto an ordinary (eg A4-size) page. An easy-to-understand visual framework is a necessity. As per the classic quote attributed to Albert Einstein, 'If you can't explain it simply, you don't understand it well enough.'

Good practices

CREATING A PLAN

It is good practice in all cases to have an annual plan; whether the framework needs to be designed from scratch or is only undergoing minor enhancements (in more mature practices). Operational risk is still very much a developing discipline. New guidelines keep emerging. Testament to that are the Basel Committee Principles, which have been updated yet again in 2020. Discussing the response to the Basel consultative document with industry practitioners, it was clear that the most successful risk teams completed a prompt gap analysis, evaluated the differences, considered their value proposition, and incorporated additional tasks into their annual plan.

PRIORITIZING TASKS FOR IMPLEMENTATION

While prioritization sounds like an obvious concept, at times firms' implementation plans contain unachievable targets, with multiple milestones all falling due at the same time, rather than being spread throughout the year in a more manageable fashion. It is good practice to involve the operational risk team – or even broader business teams – in a ranking exercise, asking them to vote on their top three priority enhancements. Team members can be supplied with pretend tokens and requested to 'put their money' on the three tasks that they believe will generate most value. The votes are then summed and the improvements receiving most support can be scheduled for speedier delivery.

ACHIEVING A BALANCED PLAN FOCUSSED ON VALUE-ADD

More and more unregulated firms are aspiring to implement solid operational risk management practices. Kudos to these organizations. They approach the implementation straight from an internal value proposition perspective, coupled with industry best practice. This can only make the value-add stronger. However, even with regulatory-driven priorities, the overall plan must be balanced. It should combine key regulatory deliverables with targets that the firm aspires to achieve for itself. From this point of view, it is important to have a constructive dialogue with the supervisors, pushing back on the deadlines and milestones to achieve the right plan, one that first and foremost makes sense to the firm as well as to the supervisor.

Industry benchmark, 2020

Drastic changes to the operational risk landscape, such as the rapid growth and adoption of financial technology (FinTech) – not to mention the Covid-19 pandemic – prompted the Best Practice Operational Risk Forum to contemplate whether the current framework and its tools remain fit-for-purpose.

Operational risk and FinTech

With the continued evolution of FinTech, it is prudent to question whether the current toolset enables firms to effectively identify, assess, manage and report on FinTech-driven operational risks. This exact question has been deliberated by the Basel Committee,[4] which explored a number of issues including:

- the capture and control of new FinTech-driven risks;
- prompt reporting and mitigation;
- change risk assessment prior to the launch of new FinTech-driven processes;
- appropriate risk appetite and risk culture; and
- adequate staff capacity and capability.

FIGURE 2.5   Industry poll: operational risk and FinTech

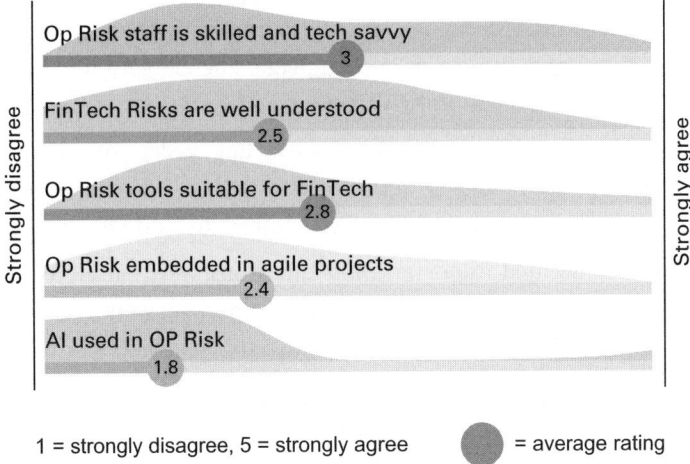

Op Risk and FinTech space

1 = strongly disagree, 5 = strongly agree   = average rating

Best Practice Operational Risk Forum, 2020

Industry practitioners voted on the progress they have made encompassing FinTech into various aspects of their operational risk framework. The results are presented in Figure 2.5.

It is apparent from Figure 2.5 that, overall, organizations are either at the early stages or in the midst, rather than towards the end, of their FinTech journeys. Firms appeared to have satisfactory staff skills and capabilities, which were markedly present in cases where technology specialists were consciously recruited into the second line of defence to oversee and challenge the Information Technology (IT) department. The use of innovative technologies such as artificial intelligence (AI) for operational risk purposes was still at its inception, however, and received the lowest score.

Framework elements were perceived as adequate overall and well suited to supporting FinTech. Particularly effective were:

- scenario analysis, enabling firms to examine extreme but plausible events; and

- operational risk assessments (ORAs) of new products and change initiatives, as they allow firms to get 'under the skin' of new technological developments, on a timely and proactive basis, prior to the product being launched and change implemented.

Other tools were deemed equally valuable, at times supplemented by IT-specific granular controls and activities:

- RCSAs: an excellent tool which encourages conversations between risk practitioners and technology specialists, requiring the formulation of key overarching concerns in a simple language. These are usually accompanied by more detailed technology-driven assessments.

- KRIs: monitoring the behaviours of key risks and controls, and highlighting the results of IT monitoring and surveillance, which are more immediate tools used for scanning threats and vulnerabilities.

- OREs: still deemed important, but questions were raised as to whether FinTech-related events are captured comprehensively by external loss data consortia.

Consequently, practitioners should be aiming to facilitate more FinTech-related scenarios (see Chapter 8) and finding ways to join agile projects and change initiatives, enabling them to initiate more risk conversations (as discussed in Chapter 6). This is in addition to consistently applying all the other framework elements, to derive value across the firm.

Operational risk and Covid-19 pandemic

The Covid-19 pandemic and the widespread move to a new working from home (WFH) environment also raised questions around the fitness of the operational risk framework. The majority of practitioners (58 per cent, as presented in Figure 2.6) were confident that the core components of their framework remained relevant and effective. Specifically, top-down and bottom-up RCSAs were seen as a valuable tool to derive timely knowledge on increasing risk and weakening controls. Exactly *how* the framework elements were implemented, however, needed further adaptation to the new working environment. Successful operational risk teams were those that proactively reached out to first line business units and support functions to jointly assess the changing risk and control profile and enable management to take timely decisions.

In conclusion, it is the role of operational risk professionals to remain on guard given the changing environment, and to challenge the status quo. This will ensure that the most appropriate framework is built out, whether that consists of adapting traditional tools, or a redesign of the way the tools are

FIGURE 2.6   Industry poll: operational risk and Covid-19 pandemic

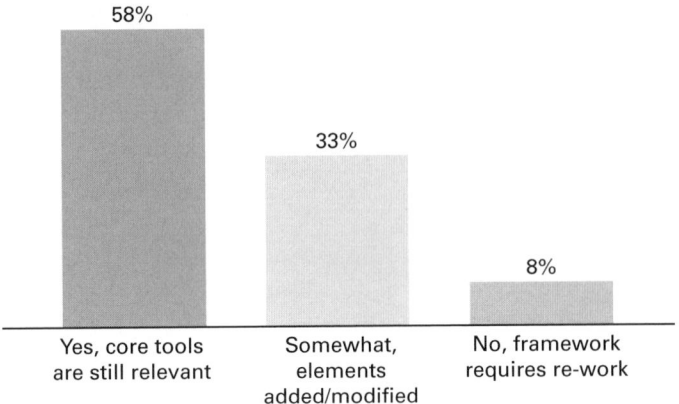

Operational Risk framework remains fit for purpose in Covid-19 / WFH

- 58% — Yes, core tools are still relevant
- 33% — Somewhat, elements added/modified
- 8% — No, framework requires re-work

Best Practice Operational Risk Forum, 2020

applied and operated. Most important, it is vital not to over-complicate. If the framework is intuitive and has been designed with simplicity in mind, it will guide employees to take risk-based decisions by applying common sense – and even their gut feel – defined by Gerd Gigerenzer as judgement that 'appears quickly in consciousness, whose underlying reasons we are not fully aware of, yet is strong enough to act upon'.[5]

Practical workplace exercise

Consider key points and ideas presented in this chapter. Obtain and review the operational risk framework used in your firm, questioning:

1 Is there a clear picture of how the framework elements operate together, in an integrated fashion?

2 Has the firm conducted a benchmark against the Basel Committee Principles and other industry documents?

3 Is there a clear implementation plan outlining priorities for the current year?

4 What works well and should be retained?

5 What can be improved? Note down potential improvements.

MAKE **A D**IFFERENCE (MAD) **A**CTION

Note down one action you will take after reading this chapter that will make a positive difference to how the firm's operational risk framework is defined and implemented.

In summary, this chapter introduced the operational risk framework and discussed some possible approaches to its implementation.

Moving on, the next chapter starts a deep dive into each of the framework components, commencing with the role of the three lines of defence in operational risk management.

Notes

1 The Sarbanes–Oxley Act of 2002, www.sec.gov/about/laws/soa2002.pdf (archived at https://perma.cc/9H8R-WXX3)

2 Basel Committee on Banking Supervision (2020) Consultative document, *Revisions to the Principles for the Sound Management of Operational Risk*, www.bis.org/bcbs/publ/d508.pdf (archived at https://perma.cc/264K-FXGJ)

3 Institute of Operational Risk (2021) Sound Practice Guidance, www.ior-institute.org/sound-practice-guidance (archived at https://perma.cc/L7VE-FNFD)

4 Basel Committee on Banking Supervision (2018) *Implications of FinTech Developments for Banks and Bank Supervisors*, www.bis.org/bcbs/publ/d431.pdf (archived at https://perma.cc/5VQA-88RN)

5 Gerd Gigerenzer (2015) *Risk Savvy: How to make good decisions*, Penguin Books

03

The three lines of defence model

Its application to operational risk management

What this chapter covers: The chapter examines how the concept of the Three Lines of Defence is applied to operational risk management and implemented in practice by individuals that embody the different lines (Figure 3.1). It analyses the role of the first line operational risk coordinators and introduces Problem Solvers, Postmen and Champions. The chapter then concentrates on the second line operational risk function and presents Drifters, Diminishers and Multipliers. The role of internal audit is briefly discussed, recognizing that there is commonly less confusion around the tasks carried out by the third line. The chapter highlights common challenges and good practices and includes an industry benchmark.

FURTHER READING

- Institute of Internal Auditors (2013) IIA Position paper, *The Three Lines of Defence in Effective Risk Management and Control*

- Institute of Internal Auditors (2020) *The IIA's Three Lines Model*
  Why recommended: The first paper is an essential read on the fundamental nature of the three lines of defence from the Institute of Internal Auditors, for those willing to learn from the source. It is supplemented by the second document issued in 2020, which provides an updated position of the Institute towards the three lines model.

- Dr Simon Ashby, Dr Cormac Bryce and Dr Patrick Ring (2019) *Risk and Performance: Embedding risk management*, ACCA
  Why recommended: A must-read research paper from three acclaimed professors, providing an insight on some of the practical aspects of embedding risk management.

FIGURE 3.1 Focus of Chapter 3: responsibilities across the three lines

Embedding and Maturity Assessment

Risk Culture

Governance, Roles and Responsibilities
Establish governance and clear roles across the three lines for managing operational risk.

Risk Appetite and Risk Capacity
Define nature and types of risk accepted in pursuit of strategic objectives. Evaluate adequacy of capital resources.

Operational Risk Events
Record and report risk events, act to minimize future exposure.

Monitor trends against RCSAs and KRIs.

Risk Assessments
Assess risk exposure in process, business or function via RCSAs.

Supplement by evaluating risks emanating from change activities via ORAs.

Scenario Analysis
Identify exposure from extreme but plausible events.

Mitigate through risk transfer to insurance.

Key Risk Indicators
Monitor risk and control performance through predictive indicators.

Act if indicators breach established appetite threshold.

Reporting and Decision Making
Review actual risk profile against set appetite, apply active risk management to enable achievement of strategic objectives.

Training and Education

Operational Risk Taxonomy

Overview: 3LOD model, its benefits and challenges

The somewhat controversial Three Lines of Defence (3LOD) model, which had its origins in military planning and sports management, is now firmly engrained into the DNA of financial services firms. It is widely viewed as an important factor in the successful embedding of enterprise risk management, while at the same time attracting a fair share of criticism due to its inefficiencies and challenges. In simple terms, the success or failure of a 3LOD model depends on how the concept is implemented in practice. And this is particularly relevant to operational risk management, where, as articulated in Chapter 2, fairly similar roles may be performed by the first line of defence operational risk coordinators as well as by independent second line risk teams. An opportunity to work collaboratively? Or to generate conflicts, trip over each other and duplicate tasks?

Let's start by discussing the 3LOD concept, which is described in the position paper written by the Institute of Internal Auditors (IIA). Essentially, IIA distinguishes between the three groups (or lines) involved in effective risk management:[1]

- functions that own and manage risks;
- functions that oversee risks;
- functions that provide independent assurance.

IIA argues that 'risk management normally is strongest when there are three separate and clearly defined lines of defence'.[2]

A typical application of the 3LOD model in financial services is presented in Figure 3.2.

As outlined in the schematic:

- First line business units and support functions are *risk owners* – a term also used by the International Organization for Standardization (ISO) – who have the authority to manage risk and are accountable for doing so.[3] They have primary responsibility for establishing a robust control environment, complying with policies and executing day-to-day risk and control management.

- The second line oversees the activities of the first line and provides objective review and constructive challenge, flagging to the board and senior committees if the level of risk is not commensurate with the risk appetite set by the board. Generally, functions such as risk management and compliance are within the second line of defence, although interpretation varies across firms.

FIGURE 3.2   Three lines of defence in financial services

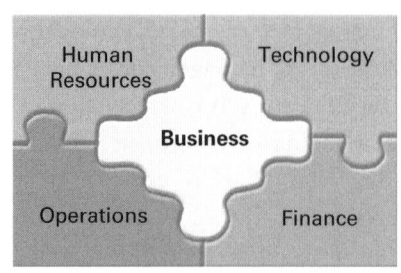

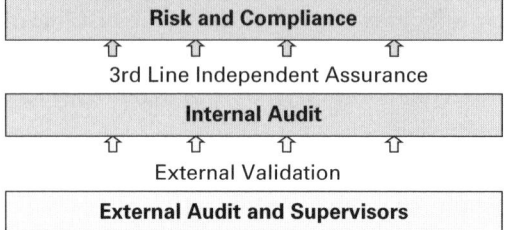

2nd Line Risk Oversight and Challenge	Design framework
Risk and Compliance	Provide training
⇧ ⇧ ⇧ ⇧	Oversee and challenge
3rd Line Independent Assurance	
Internal Audit	Develop and execute on risk-based plan
⇧ ⇧ ⇧ ⇧	
External Validation	Provide external validation
External Audit and Supervisors	

Identify, Assess, Manage and Report on risk

Maintain adequate internal control environment

- The third line, internal audit, is independent of both business units and supports functions and second line departments. It is responsible for providing assurance about the design and operation of the internal risk and control framework via a programme of risk-based reviews.

The concept of the three lines of defence can be illustrated with a picture. France, 1895, the Montparnasse train station in Paris: an iconic photograph of a Granville–Paris train, trying to make up for lost time, entering the station at too high a speed, crushing through the wall of the station and tumbling onto the street. Miraculously, none of the passengers died.[4]

You can imagine a control room engineer sending warning signals to the driver: 'Attention, attention, you are running too fast, please slow down.' The driver increases his speed, ignoring the message from the control room.

The first line of defence, train drivers, own the risks and make choices over whether to control them effectively or not. Front-office staff who sell products to clients, employees processing payments and information technology personnel maintaining systems all belong to the first line.

The second line, control room operators, communicate warning signals, pointing out when the level of risk is too high. Not being in the front line, however, they cannot stop the train from crashing.

The third line inspect both the train tracks and the set-up of the control room, ensuring that the whole enterprise, comprised of first and second lines, is positioned effectively for delivering on its objectives.

Some of the benefits and challenges of the 3LOD are outlined in Table 3.1 below.

The 3LOD concept has particular significance to operational risk. To embed good practices, processes and behaviours, first line business units and support functions commonly appoint operational risk coordinators. This practice helps immensely with spreading operational risk knowledge; however, it can also confuse the 3LOD structure.

In theory, placing operational risk experts in the first line should double the benefits. It is the same discipline, after all, so operational risk practitioners in both the first and second lines must work together, completely in sync, towards a common goal of augmenting the value of risk management within the organization. In practice, however, models are implemented by people; consequently, a great deal depends on the personalities of the individuals and the way they embody the different lines of defence. The relationship and dynamics between coordinators and the Risk Department may result in productive outcomes, but they can also lead to unpleasant and avoidable experiences.

TABLE 3.1 Benefits and challenges of the 3LOD model

Benefits	Challenges
The structure of defined lines provides a level of confidence to the firm's board of directors and senior management.	3LOD can result in duplication of activities. Who, for example, is performing control testing?
It allocates clear roles – risk management, risk oversight and risk assurance.	It is debatable what functions form the second line of defence; application across the industry varies.
The model aims to embed enterprise risk management at all levels across the firm and enhance risk communication.	The concept can cause confusion within the organization; do employees know what line they represent?
It serves as a protection mechanism. Functions work effectively together within their line to prevent and/or mitigate significant failures.	One of the key challenges of the 3LOD model is trust. If lines are fully segregated, trust between them may be low.
Regulators and many professional bodies, including the Institute of Internal Auditors and Institute of Directors, endorse the concept.	The use of the 3LOD model alone should not be regarded as a guarantee of success.

FIGURE 3.3 Operational risk personnel in first and second lines of defence

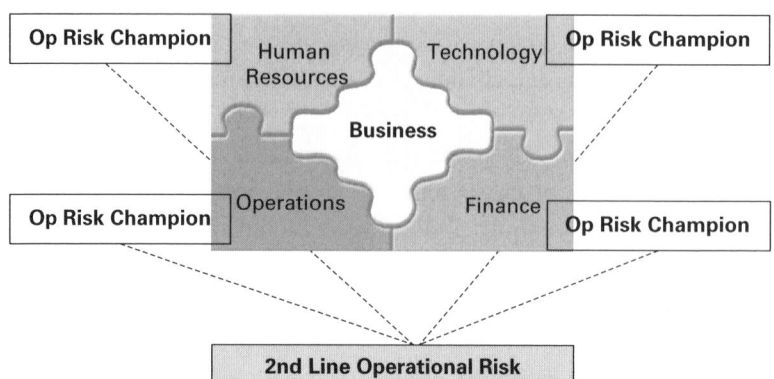

It is therefore important to examine operational risk manager roles in more detail, focussing on finding practical solutions to making the spiders' web of operational risk professionals across the two lines, depicted in Figure 3.3, work effectively and efficiently. Note that the role of the third line, internal audit, is usually clearly defined and well established, so rarely generates many questions or challenges.

First line operational risk: problem solvers, postmen and champions

An organization's policy will often require all heads of business units and support functions to nominate an operational risk lead: a named individual who serves as both a subject matter expert (SME) on operational risk matters and a key liaison point between the business and the second line Risk department.

The theory is well known and understood. Where it becomes interesting is when it comes down to practical implementation. In reality, who are the operational risk coordinators and what is it that they do? Let's review three types of coordinator roles, depicted in Figure 3.4.

The problem solver

Problem solvers, sometimes also called 'risk hunters', are tasked with identifying risks and 'fixing' them, by coming up with action plans, enhancing controls

FIGURE 3.4 First line operational risk role types

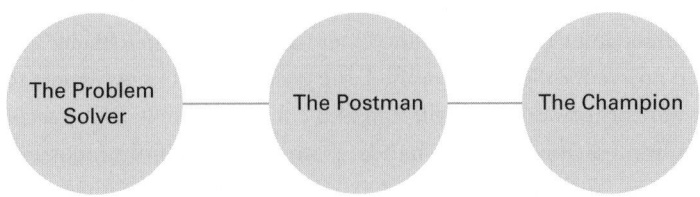

or delivering process improvements. In this model the duty of providing operational risk management for the whole business unit falls on one individual, while the rest of the staff contentedly abdicate their responsibilities. 'How do we manage operational risk? We are very good at it. Please see our colleague around the corner: it is their role and they will tell you all about it.'

Problem solvers also carry the burden of remediation and mitigation activities for the risks that they themselves have identified. They are expected to add value by repairing broken processes and plastering over the cracks of poor controls. The more risks they discover, the more issues they have to solve.

Organizations with less mature risk cultures use problem solvers as a way of ticking the operational risk box, and demonstrating externally that someone is in place performing all the required activities. The problem solvers' approach indicates that the respective heads of business units or support functions are not accepting the accountability they have been allocated for the management of operational risk.

The postman

Postmen see their role as receiving a message from the centre and delivering it to the business unit or function. In many organizations, the first line operational risk coordinator is a part-time role. Coordinators are busy people; throughout the day they are occupied with important tasks within their direct area of responsibility. On top of their regular duties, they will engage with the Operational Risk department as and when the second line calls a meeting, receive the transmitted information, and pass it on to their colleagues and department head. For example:

- 'Operational Risk is implementing a new policy: please find this attached.'
- 'Operational Risk is initiating a firm-wide RCSA refresh: please complete per the stipulated deadline.'
- 'The template for loss reporting has changed: please familiarize yourselves with the new form.'

The second line usually trains coordinators on key tools and processes. Occasionally, therefore, messages will also be relayed in the other direction, from business unit to the second line Operational Risk department. For example, when an event or loss is identified, the postmen will know where to locate the relevant form, and how to fill it in and communicate with the second line.

Given limited time on their hands, postmen are mainly focussed on the administrative side of operational risk processes, rather than the actual quality of risk management, which requires more time and thought. They frequently complain that the additional duties of being a coordinator, on top of their daily tasks, are burdensome. I have had many interactions with coordinators via public and in-house training courses that I deliver specifically for first line personnel. Having surveyed over 200 coordinators over the last 15 years, a fair share of them operate as postmen. Generally they spend around 2 per cent to 15 per cent of their time on operational risk.

The champion

Champions are engaged and passionate operational risk specialists in the first line of defence. They focus on the essence of risk management, ensuring that material risks are identified and mitigated. They take the initiative and spearhead enhancements, with business unit employees giving them proper support while also understanding that risk management is everyone's responsibility.

For example, champions will not only contribute to the Risk and Control Self-Assessment (RCSA) process, but will also consider:

- how to meaningfully engage all employees in risk identification, to ensure their voice is heard – perhaps suggesting a discussion or live poll that can be conducted at the next departmental meeting;
- how to best share the results, so that all employees can consistently articulate the top operational risks of the unit;
- the status and behaviour of material risks, whether actions are being taken to remediate them, and how business units can work collectively with other functions;
- whether RCSA results are used in other initiatives, for example, when developing new products or engaging in regulatory programmes;
- what learnings, whether successes or failures, can be shared with other business units or support functions (also see RCSAs, Chapter 5).

(Note: subsequent chapters of the book contain a checklist with proposed champion responsibilities for each of the core operational risk tools – events, RCSAs, ORAs, KRIs and scenario analysis.)

How do organizations step up from using problem solvers and postmen and instead develop an effective and engaged group of operational risk champions? The answer is a combination of contributory factors, which range from very complex (for example, getting the culture right) to very simple (such as having a clear profile of the coordinator role):

- Tone from the top: both across the firm overall and within respective business units or support functions, recognizing the value of operational risk management.

- Understanding the *why* of risk management, integrating risk into decision-making, aligning the effort to better customer experiences and shareholder outcomes.

- Full ownership: it is the role of the first line to manage risks and maintain a sound control environment, and it is a team effort where everyone is accountable for sound risk management.

- Acknowledgement of additional responsibilities allocated to the champion, allowing sufficient time for them to be undertaken effectively.

- Incentives: these can be financial, via increased pay or a reward for significant achievements. They can also be developmental: for example, studying or obtaining a professional qualification in operational risk management; participating in cross-functional initiatives to increase exposure to other departments and disciplines; or joining relevant external forums and committees as a member. This latter incentive is not sufficiently used. Having chaired various operational risk industry forums over the last 20 years, my observation is that typically less than 10 per cent of attendees are from the first line.

- Praise and recognition of good work: this sounds obvious but does not always happen.

- A clear job description: again this sounds basic, but many champions are operating 'blind', without a clear role profile.

- An appropriate framework and set of tools developed by the second line, which enable and do not hinder the risk management process.

- And another key factor: ample direction, guidance, training and engagement from multipliers in the second line of defence (see below).

Second line operational risk: drifters, diminishers and multipliers

Second line operational risk plays a crucial role in determining the success or failure of risk management. Not only via the design of an appropriate framework and tools, but via the attitude and value proposition represented by the second line, which ultimately matter just as much and have a significant influence on risk outcomes. Different role types are presented in Figure 3.5.

The drifter

Despite working in the second line operational risk function, drifters seem unsure of their role and the definitive risk product that they are expected to be producing. The Operations department is processing payments. Information Technology is maintaining systems. Human Resources is administering payroll. Their output is clear and well understood. Aside from periodic reports to the governance committees, however, drifters are often found deliberating about potential outputs. They understand the objective of providing independent oversight and challenge, but they cannot quite see how to implement this in practice. Their CV may contain tasks with unclear value, for example:

- attended business unit's meetings;
- requested regular updates;
- collated information from business unit and repackaged for risk reporting;
- communicated RCSA deadlines and monitored completion within schedule.

They drift from meeting to meeting, but rarely contribute, present or provide insights. They are more focussed on the administrative side of risk management ('RCSAs completed within the timeline?', 'Operational risk events reported via the right template?') than on the actual management of risks

FIGURE 3.5 Second line operational risk role types

that are important to the business. Over the years, I have conducted job interviews for over 50 second line candidates; and while some came across brilliantly, others struggled to articulate the ways in which they added value to the organization. Which risks have diminished as a result of their role? Which controls have improved? What was their contribution to the firm's ability to achieve its strategy and business objectives?

The diminisher

In her inspirational book about leadership, *Multipliers: How the best leaders make everyone smarter*, Liz Wiseman introduces the concept of diminishers and multipliers. Diminishers, according to Wiseman, 'stifled others and diluted the organization's crucial intelligence and capability', while multipliers 'brought out the intelligence in others and created collective, viral intelligence'.[5] That concept, applied to leadership, can be extrapolated to describe two more types of second line operational risk functions.

Diminishers tend to place emphasis on the role of *independent challenge* entrusted to them by the board and senior committees. They see themselves as advisors to the firm's executives, accentuating the need for the separation between business units and the Operational Risk department. This may include physical segregation, with diminishers located on a different floor or isolated area, which has the effect of widening the gap between first and second lines. They are formal, unapproachable and do not tend to socialize. Diminishers believe that they:

- are *entitled* to attend first line business unit or support function meetings;
- are not here to be liked;
- are independent and therefore cannot discuss, advise or facilitate workshops;
- should be provided with information (for example, RCSAs, KRIs, scenarios) which they will then autonomously challenge.

Under this model the first line, lacking sufficient explanation, education and advice about the context lying behind these processes, ends up producing sub-optimal results and then facing criticism and adverse commentary. This not only strains the relationship but also results in reduced motivation on the part of the first line to manage its own operational risks. Diminishers diminish the work of first line business units and support functions, ultimately creating a negative risk management brand.

The multiplier

In contrast, multipliers work in collaboration with the first line, actively positioning them for success. They are informal, approachable, likeable and do not hesitate to work closely with business units and support functions. They also have a clear value proposition and focus on risk management, not risk administration.

> In research published by ACCA, the authors emphasized the importance of informal risk management mechanisms, in addition to formal policies and governance structures, and stressed that the people skills of the risk team are key.[6] They argued that a less formal, integrated accountability approach recognizes distinct roles within the three lines of defence, yet still 'allows greater levels of collaboration and cooperation between the individuals responsible for conducting these roles'.

This softer and more integrated approach is also adopted in the revised three lines model (note: the word *defence* has been dropped), where the IIA states that first and second line roles may be 'blended or separated' and emphasizes that the second line provides '*assistance* with managing risk'.[7]

A good way of thinking about second line operational risk responsibilities is by outlining a spectrum of roles and assigning them a RAG (red, amber, green) rating:

- core second line operational risk roles (green zone);
- legitimate second line roles with safeguards (amber zone);
- roles that second line should not undertake (red zone).

Outlining the zones will guide the multipliers to find the right balance, being *supportive* and at the same time *firm*, providing ample assistance yet not doing the job on behalf of the first line.

GREEN ZONE

Core second line operational risk multiplier roles:

- Mastermind the framework and design the tools that suit the size, nature and culture of the organization; continuously evolve them based on feedback.

- Analyse information, having the privilege of seeing the overall picture and risk profile of the firm; report to management committees but also circle back to the business units and support functions.

- As a trusted advisor, contribute to the firm's strategy and business plan, scrutinize and influence risk decisions, and provide early warnings.

- Educate, educate, educate. Create engaging, fun and light-hearted training programmes (see Operational Risk Training, Chapter 11).

- Collaborate with business units and support functions to achieve quality outcomes. Workshop facilitation deserves a special mention in this context. Expert facilitation adds great value and does not contradict the 3LOD model. Necessary challenge can be performed during the workshop and subsequently minuted for evidence. Note that it is just as acceptable for first line champions to lead the workshops, as long as they have been fully trained and possess the right skills and expertise to perform this role. On the other hand it is detrimental to ask the first line to undertake this kind of facilitation if they are not ready or do not have the necessary skills; or to require two separate operational risk discussions with the business, one with the first line and a subsequent additional meeting for second line to challenge.

- Invest in developing an engaged network of champions, helping to multiply their capabilities and potential; hold periodic meetings to share successes and challenges.

- Act as a centre of excellence on operational risk; participate in external industry forums and professional bodies, actively seeking to develop more professional knowledge and benchmark one's own practices.

- Be accessible and available for informal advice when needed.

AMBER ZONE

Legitimate operational risk responsibilities, to be performed *as long as* they do not replace the accountability of the first line for risk management (to be adopted with caution):

- Conduct thematic reviews, based on identified trends and themes.

- Perform assurance, carry out periodic or ad hoc spot checks and control tests.

- Provide one-off help to business units or support functions when, for example, assisting with the roll-out of RCSAs; an operational risk expert can be temporarily seconded to the first line in exceptional circumstances.

- Champion the establishment of a risk culture, in close collaboration with senior management.

RED ZONE

What second line teams should not do:

- Manage operational risks on behalf of the first line; this debate was topical a decade ago, and the industry has moved on since to recognizing the right roles and responsibilities.

- Complete RCSAs (or manage other tools) on behalf of business units or support functions.

- Assume accountability for implementing control improvements and deal with actions instead of first line responsible functions.

- Take decisions on behalf of the business whether to accept or remediate risk.

- Serve as administrative assistants or note takers rather than risk managers.

- Always agree. It is valuable to have an honest second line opinion, regardless of its position; whether it agrees with the first line view or not.

A note about the third line of defence: the Chartered Institute of Internal Auditors has developed a similar spectrum of audit responsibilities with assigned RAG ratings to clearly distinguish and delineate the role of the audit function; a very useful and practical document well worth a read.[8] As it relates to operational risk management, there is rarely confusion around the tasks of internal audit colleagues who execute independent reviews. One area of frequent disputes though relates to the *ownership* of audit findings. At times, all findings related to operational risk management are erroneously attributed to the second line operational risk function, even when the weaknesses arise from the first line business units. It is important to acknowledge the accountability of the first line in the risk management process, and allocate the findings accordingly.

Recipe for success: when multipliers work with champions

The power of risk management is increased when *multipliers* in the second line work with *champions* in the first line.

To begin with, it is essential for the second line Operational Risk department to deliberate, decide and agree on the *what* and the *how* of second line risk management. Often this will be done most effectively using a vehicle such as a strategy day or awayday (or, during the Covid-19 pandemic, a virtual awayday), to enable a full debate free of distractions.

SECOND LINE OPERATIONAL RISK ESSENTIAL QUESTIONS

- *What* are the products that the second line is producing, apart from policies and periodic reports to the governance committees? Will business units and support functions benefit from these products?

- *How* will the second line work with first line businesses and embedded champions, via what formal and informal interactions? Per ACCA, is the balance of formal and informal mechanisms appropriate?[9] If not, what needs to be done differently and how will second line achieve it?

A similar process, again perhaps via a strategy day, then needs to take place between the second and first line operational risk personnel, who must come to an agreement on the joint plan for success. Some questions to consider in this process may include the following.

JOINT FIRST AND SECOND LINE OPERATIONAL RISK ESSENTIAL QUESTIONS

- Are roles clearly *articulated* and is there a good understanding of each other's responsibilities, to avoid *gaps* and *duplication*? For example, how will the first line operational risk coordinator engage with business units on new products and change initiatives, and what exactly will the second line do?

- Are second line interactions with business units *effective*? For example, if both groups need to review certain outputs – be it a strategy, business plan or RCSA – is it feasible for all concerned to do that at the same meeting rather than conducting separate sessions?

- How is the *output* of the second line *different* to what the first line produces? For example, if the first line creates reports to governance committees, the second line may be able to append their clearly articulated opinion to the report. In this case, governance committees will have the benefit of both views. And finally:

- What does success mean? How will it be measured and what needs to be done to achieve it?

It is also good practice to have periodic catch-ups with other second line functions, for example Compliance, as well as with Internal Audit, to increase collaboration and eliminate inefficiencies to the extent possible.

To summarize, when multipliers work with champions, the collaboration creates great chemistry, leading not only to thoughtful and productive risk management, but also to enjoyable days at the workplace.

Common challenges and good practices

Challenges

Challenges that firms may encounter when implementing operational risk roles and responsibilities across the three lines of defence include the following.

INFORMATION NOT SHARED

The concept of the lines of defence is also used in sport. In football, players pass the ball to each other to help the team to score a goal. In financial services, employees operating within different lines do not always pass the ball. Information is not always willingly shared by internal audit or risk departments, and business units may be reluctant to provide full disclosure to the second and third lines. Developing the culture of openness and investing in relationship building is essential for the groups to work effectively together.

OPERATIONAL RISK SUPERHERO CHARACTER

In the early years of the millennium another archetypal second line operational risk practitioner – Superman/Superwoman – was responsible for actually managing operational risk on behalf of the organization, stepping way out of their mandate to oversee and challenge the first line. This archetype is now rarely seen, as operational risk practices have matured and roles and responsibilities have matured with them.

LACK OF SUPPORT FOR CHAMPIONS

Insufficient support is provided to the first line coordinators, who end up doing extra work on top of their daily tasks, without incentivization or recognition. This is a cultural issue and, unfortunately, it sometimes takes a major loss, unsatisfactory audit or regulatory censure to prompt the organization to focus on how they perform risk management.

DUPLICATION OF ACTIVITIES

Unnecessary duplication of activities may arise if groups act in an uncoordinated manner. For example, business units developing a new product will often have a risk identification session with the first line coordinator. Subsequently, the second line Operational Risk department will request a separate meeting to provide independent challenge. This kind of duplication only causes confusion ('Another meeting with Operational Risk?'). Joint strategy days, and obtaining agreement on how the lines actually work together, help to minimize this kind of inefficiency.

VALUE-ADD OF SECOND LINE QUESTIONED

If the second line is characterized by drifters who do not generate outputs, it may become difficult for the first line to articulate what it is that the risk function does, which results in their questioning its value.

BUSINESS UNITS NOT ENGAGED

Business units and support functions may blame operational risk tools and use them as an excuse for not being willing to engage in risk management. While it is important to have a sensible framework, an organizational culture of doing the right thing always needs to come first, even if the tools to achieve that are still in development and have not yet reached perfection.

CONFUSION OVER LEGAL DEPARTMENT

Questions frequently arise whether the Legal department belongs to the first or second line. The jury is out on this across the industry, and opinion is split. Around half of the firms I have interacted with over the years consider Legal to be within the first line; the other half disagrees and has Legal in the second line.

CRITICISM OF THE 3LOD

There are many critics of the 3LOD model across the industry, including a group on LinkedIn using the hashtag #kill3lod, which advocates for complete elimination of the structure. Arguments used by this group include slower decision-making, due to the need for sign-offs from first and second lines, which is particularly challenging in an age of technological advancement and revolution. The model is also criticized for promoting wrong behaviours, including encouraging employees to rely on someone else to oversee their work ('Two more lines of defence behind me will surely check what I am doing'), rather than accepting accountability themselves.

Good practices

WORK IN COLLABORATION

There is great power in the model of multipliers working closely and cooperatively with champions. Two lines acting in collaboration go a long way towards shaping good practices and behaviours. Invest in creating a solid champion network and cherish the relationship. It will pay back.

SHARE EXPERIENCE

Other peer risk disciplines – namely credit, market and liquidity risk – do not have the same issues with the 3LOD model, as there is no need for a credit risk coordinator within, for example, a Human Resources department. Consequently, it is good practice for Operational Risk to regularly confer and share experiences with other functions that use a distributed model, such as business continuity and information security.

EVALUATION

First line champions usually have a direct reporting line to the business or function they support. When managers are conducting performance appraisals of first line champions, it is good practice to also solicit feedback from members of the second line Operational Risk department, who can opine on how well the champion performed relative to the first line group.

DISCUSSIONS WITH RISK TAKERS

Even with first line coordinators in place, it is essential for the second line to have a dialogue with risk takers and decision makers in business units and support functions. First line coordinators, especially in full-time roles, can sometimes block the second line's access to the business unit. Avoiding blockages like this ensures that communication does not become partial – with risk practitioners talking amongst themselves – and prevents the decline in the effectiveness of conversations.

MAKE OWNERSHIP TANGIBLE

A reader of one of my LinkedIn articles commented on the term *ownership*, noting that in their view it is a *care factor*. Aligning risk management efforts to tangible things that employees care about, for example, enhanced customer experiences or more resilient processes, helps to present the case and explain why risk management is so important.

SECOND LINE IN ADVISORY CAPACITY

Once the framework is embedded and the first line becomes more mature, the second line can take a step back and act in more of an advisory capacity. A measure of success is the number of times the second line is approached for advice; if business units and support functions regularly call on Operational Risk, that demonstrates trust and recognition of value.

Industry benchmark, 2019

Results from a live poll at the industry Best Practice Operational Risk Forum revealed that where the operational risk champion is a part-time role, the champions do not allocate sufficient time to operational risk management, as seen in Figure 3.6.

Having an effective and engaged group of operational risk champions in the first line of defence is essential for embedding risk management practices throughout the organization; and is a common model implemented by many firms.

Overall, while the scores from the live poll painted a positive picture, they also demonstrated that further improvements could be made (see Figure 3.6):

FIGURE 3.6 Industry poll: first line operational risk role

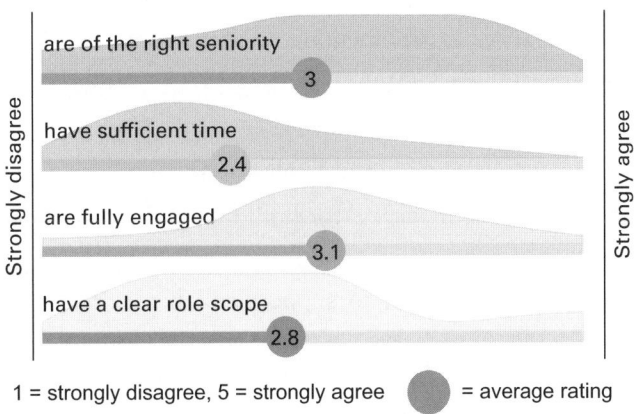

Best Practice Operational Risk Forum, 2019

- Engagement: this element rated relatively high and can be further increased using both financial incentives and non-financial benefits, including: training, making the role more exciting via information sharing, participation in themed reviews and other activities.

- Seniority: this was an interesting one. What indeed is the right level of seniority for a champion? If too senior – sometimes the department head takes on the role – it sets the right tone from the top but may not be practical due to the extensive workload. If too junior – the champion has insufficient experience and understanding – it may decrease the value-add.

- A clear role scope: it is important to have a description of responsibilities. This is easy to create and goes a long way towards reaching agreement and understanding the expectations of the role – so represents a useful quick win.

- And the main challenge – not enough time to spare – reflects the nature of the part-time champion position, where 'add-on' operational risk tasks are viewed as a second priority.

That said, to quote the ancient Chinese philosopher and writer Lao Tzu: 'Time is a created thing. To say "I don't have time" is to say "I don't want to."'

Operational risk is an exciting discipline, and practitioners need to continue to invest in enhancing its brand and reputation, making the first line champion a highly desirable and sought-after position; helping to make progress towards the goal of 'time flies when you are having fun'.

Practical workplace exercise

Reflect on the ideas discussed in this chapter. Obtain role profiles of the second line operational risk function and, if available, first line champions. Review the descriptions, considering:

1 Are the roles sufficiently clear? Do they articulate how the functions will collaborate and avoid gaps and duplication?

2 Are there measures of success for both first and second line operational risk personnel?

3 What good practices exist to support collaboration between first and second line operational risk practitioners; for example, joint strategy days, relationship building measures, education or similar activities?

4 What can be improved? Note down potential improvements.

A suggested role description for a risk champion is provided in Appendix 1.

MAKE **A D**IFFERENCE (MAD) **A**CTION

Please outline the key learnings and note down one specific action you will take after reading this chapter, to enhance your existing practices relating to the 3LOD and its application to operational risk management.

In summary, this chapter discussed the concept of the 3LOD and proposed ways of increasing the power of risk management via effective collaboration of the first and second line functions.

Moving on, the next chapter starts with a deep dive into the first core tool of the framework, operational risk events.

Notes

1 Institute of Internal Auditors (2013) Position paper, *The Three Lines of Defence in Effective Risk Management and Control*, na.theiia.org/standards-guidance/Public%20Documents/PP%20The%20Three%20Lines%20of%20Defense%20in%20Effective%20Risk%20Management%20and%20Control.pdf (archived at https://perma.cc/4AM3-2SEM)

2 Institute of Internal Auditors (2013) Position paper, *The Three Lines of Defence in Effective Risk Management and Control*, na.theiia.org/standards-guidance/Public%20Documents/PP%20The%20Three%20Lines%20of%20Defense%20in%20Effective%20Risk%20Management%20and%20Control.pdf (archived at https://perma.cc/D5HG-PT4G)

3 International Organization for Standardization (ISO) (2018) *ISO 31000:2018, Risk Management – Guidelines*, www.iso.org/standard/65694.html (archived at https://perma.cc/K98D-KUHW)

4 History Daily (2019) Montparnasse Derailment: When a train went through a station walls, historydaily.org/montparnasse-derailment-when-a-train-went-through-a-stations-walls (archived at https://perma.cc/JD72-65B5)

5 Liz Wiseman (2015) *Multipliers: How the best leaders make everyone smarter*, HarperBusiness

6 Ashby, A, Bryce, C and Ring, P (2019) *Risk and Performance: Embedding risk management*, www.accaglobal.com/gb/en/professional-insights/risk/risk-and-performance.html (archived at https://perma.cc/U5QE-V3AU)

7 Institute of Internal Auditors (2020) *The IIA's Three Lines Model*, na.theiia.org/about-ia/PublicDocuments/Three-Lines-Model-Updated.pdf (archived at https://perma.cc/879L-ZZA7)

8 Chartered Institute of Internal Auditors (2017) Position paper, *Risk Management and Internal Audit*, www.iia.org.uk/resources/risk-management/position-paper-risk-management-and-internal-audit (archived at https://perma.cc/U8HK-3KQA)

9 Ashby, A, Bryce, C and Ring, P (2019) *Risk and Performance: Embedding risk management*, www.accaglobal.com/gb/en/professional-insights/risk/risk-and-performance.html (archived at https://perma.cc/VT5A-SEAA)

04

Operational risk events

What this chapter covers: The chapter incorporates multiple industry benchmarks and includes a sample template for operational risk event reporting (Figure 4.1). Operational Risk Events (including losses) are the oldest and the most common operational risk component, and are now implemented by firms in many countries worldwide. The chapter commences with revisiting the basics, including definitions and examples, and then delves into practical matters: examining how to establish an effective collection process, considering the human element of reporting, and ensuring data completeness and accuracy. It addresses the evolution of the tool in the rise of technology incidents, regulatory non-compliance and data breaches; and advocates for broadening the scope of the tool from losses only to operational risk events, moving away from focussing on solely *risk measurement* and capital calculation to active *risk management*.

FURTHER READING

- European Banking Authority (2008) Compendium of Supplementary Guidelines on Implementation Issues of Operational Risk (CP21)
  Why recommended: Although this document is slightly dated, it is one of the best explanatory guides for those looking for practical examples of losses, boundary events and other concepts.

FIGURE 4.1   Focus of Chapter 4: operational risk events

Embedding and Maturity Assessment

Risk Culture

Governance, Roles and Responsibilities
Establish governance and clear roles across the three lines for managing operational risk.

Risk Appetite and Risk Capacity
Define nature and types of risk accepted in pursuit of strategic objectives. Evaluate adequacy of capital resources.

Operational Risk Events	Risk Assessments	Scenario Analysis	Key Risk Indicators
Record and report risk events, act to minimize future exposure. Monitor trends against RCSAs and KRIs.	Assess risk exposure in process, business or function via RCSAs. Supplement by evaluating risks emanating from change activities via ORAs.	Identify exposure from extreme but plausible events. Mitigate through risk transfer to insurance.	Monitor risk and control performance through predictive indicators. Act if indicators breach established appetite threshold.

Operational Risk Taxonomy

Reporting and Decision Making
Review actual risk profile against set appetite, apply active risk management to enable achievement of strategic objectives.

Training and Education

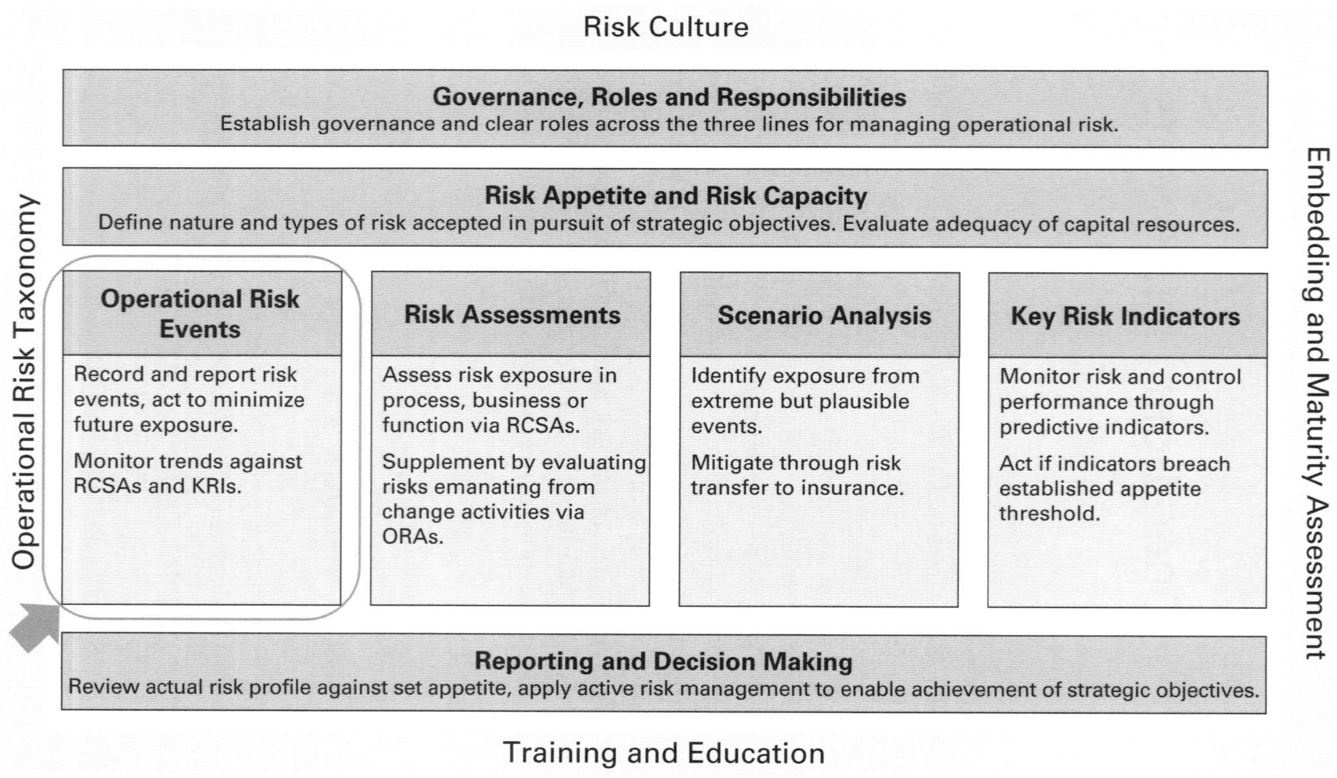

Overview: importance of operational risk events

Emanating from its original definition, operational risk is the risk of *loss* resulting from inadequate or failed internal processes, people and systems or from external events. If the firm does not have a clear understanding of its loss profile and has no preview into the common cases of failures, it will be significantly less equipped for managing forward-looking risks effectively.

Historically, losses were the first operational risk component deployed by organizations, while *appetite*, for example, was introduced at a much later stage. For banks, loss data collection was the earliest Basel Committee requirement, primarily as a prerequisite to the development of a credible risk *measurement* system, enabling evaluation of how much capital is needed for operational risk. Early on, banks set up collection processes, striving to accumulate several years' worth of accurate and comprehensive event data. Hence the relative embeddedness of the tool which, according to the Basel Committee, is now reasonably well established and more fully implemented than other operational risk framework components.[1]

The journey, however, is far from complete. The results of multiple industry polls presented in this chapter demonstrate that financial services firms need to persevere in enhancing this seemingly basic instrument. They need to step away from mere regulatory compliance, working in collaboration with other departments to avoid multiple parallel reporting processes. And they need to continue contributing positively to the development of a *no blame* culture that is conducive to staff speaking up and raising incident reports.

Defining scope and thresholds

Operational risk losses occur when operational risk materializes. Examples of operational risk losses include:

- a cashier steals $1,000 from the till;
- a payment of $200,000 is sent to the wrong customer and not returned;
- a bank's ATM is vandalized, and has to be repaired at a cost of $7,000;
- an employee files a lawsuit against the firm, resulting in a court settlement of $70,000;
- late filing of regulatory reports leads to a fine of $10,000.

Further examples illustrate various types of potential *outcomes*:

- a foreign exchange deal is booked with an erroneous amount; correcting the error leads to a *gain* of $37,000 due to a favourable market move (ie a fortuitous *gain* instead of a loss);

- technology disruption occurs just outside of trading hours (a *near miss*);

- a duplicate payment of $50,000 is sent by error, and returned within five days (also a near miss, sometimes also termed a *rapidly recovered* loss);

- a payments system outage results in multiple delayed payments to customers (an event which has an *impact on clients* as well as potential future monetary loss to the firm).

These cases demonstrate the complexity of operational risk, which can crystallize into a variety of *financial* as well as *non-financial* (client, reputational, regulatory) outcomes.

The scope of loss data collection depends on the business model of the organization as well as local regulatory guidance and priorities. Some firms concentrate on negative and quantifiable impacts on the profit and loss of the organization – actual operational risk losses. There is however a marked drive in the industry towards more active *management* of operational risk, which places increasing emphasis on non-financial outcomes. Adopting this kind of more inclusive approach is beneficial; therefore, the more encompassing term *risk event* (or incident) is adopted – a broader term than *loss*.

> Operational Risk Events (OREs) are transactions/events that arise due to failed processes, people or systems or from the external environment, resulting in actual or potential financial exposure and/or client harm, reputational damage or regulatory censure.

For explanation purposes, it can be stated that an ORE is an event which leads the *actual outcome* of a business process to differ from its *expected outcome*; this emphasizes the erroneous or undesirable nature of the incident.

Recognizing the need for clarity, various regulatory publications have considered different elements as constituting an operational risk loss. They directed institutions towards focussing on the *actual losses*;[2] while acknowledging that recording the other types of incident represents good practice, whether or not their impact is quantifiable.

DEFINING THE SCOPE OF OPERATIONAL RISK LOSS

1   Actual losses (including direct charges to P&L, external costs, provisions and pending losses).

2   Near misses.

3   Operational risk profits/gains.

4   Opportunity costs/lost revenues.

5   Timing impacts (financial mis-statements, ie negative economic impacts booked in a given fiscal period due to operational risk events, but impacting the cash flows of previous periods).

In 2012, in my role as Chair of the Operational Risk Expert Panel of the Association of Foreign Banks in the UK, I led a group study with branches and subsidiaries of foreign banks to understand what elements were in fact collected by different institutions. The results, presented in Table 4.1, demonstrate the divergence in firms' approaches.

Direct charges and *external costs* are easily recognizable and are captured by most firms, while *gains* and *near misses* are in scope of only some organizations. A minority account for *opportunity costs*, due to the difficulty of estimating the amount; however, there is an increasing desire to capture lost opportunities, especially those incurred by technology downtime. The Basel Committee also acknowledges this variance, concluding that 'only a few

TABLE 4.1 Industry study: scope of loss data collection

Element	% of firms collecting
Direct charges	100
External costs incurred as a consequence of the event	80
Provisions	40
Pending losses	40
Near misses	60
Profits/gains	70
Opportunity costs/lost revenue	20
Timing impacts	20

banks collect and analyse information relating to *all* internal operational risk events, including losses, near misses and profitable events.'[3]

Further definitions of frequently encountered event types are presented below.

> A near miss, or a *nil loss*, is an operational risk event that has occurred but did not ultimately result in a loss. Effectively, in this instance, the firm was lucky. However, as its controls have failed, the next time this event happened it could just as easily lead to a monetary loss or other significant non-financial consequences.

Note the following two alternative definitions used in the industry:

1 An event that could have happened but did not, due to a *secondary* or *supplementary* control preventing it from taking place – for example, a transaction input error was corrected by an authorizer. This interpretation can be administratively burdensome and is not recommended (and, in the end, this is the reason that firms have such controls in place anyway).

2 A possible nuance, to replace *supplementary* with *non-routine* or *out of the firm's control* – for example, a transaction input error was also missed by the authorizer, but was discovered by chance due to a batch failure and the subsequent need to manually re-input all transactions. It is best not to over-complicate. Applied in practice, the definition highlighted in the box is better and easier for end-users to comprehend.

Boundary events touch on our neighbouring disciplines of credit and market risk, with examples below:

• A loan is made to a client based on a fraudulent application via electronic identity fraud (phishing), leading to a loss of $15,000. This is a *boundary* event relating to both operational and credit risks, where both risks have materialized. Another way to describe it is as a lending loss that would not have otherwise occurred, resulting from an internal failure of people, processes and systems.

• A trader position taken in excess of prescribed limits, supplemented by an unfavourable market move, causes a loss of $200,000. This is also a *boundary* event, covering operational and market risk respectively.

Threshold setting

Thresholds for loss data gathering contribute to the deliberations on what should be in scope. Based on the Basel Committee study of 119 banks, 10 respondents applied a *zero* threshold, another 10 set €10,000 while most chose an amount somewhere in between.[4]

In 2012 I led a similar survey of smaller-sized banks in the UK. This study concluded that all participants applied a limit below or equal to £5,000, with 50 per cent setting a *zero* threshold, effectively capturing all OREs regardless of the amount. This result seems to support the view that a low limit is beneficial for smaller-sized organizations.

TABLE 4.2   Industry study: loss data collection threshold

Threshold	% of firms applying
0	50
£500	10
£1,000	20
£1,250	10
£5,000	10

To develop a fit-for-purpose threshold, consider the following factors:

✓ Size of the organization: a lower amount is suitable for smaller-sized firms which generally have fewer OREs, and typically lower impact values.

✓ History of past events: a lower limit is beneficial for start-ups or organizations that do not have a sufficient history of past data. This allows the firm to gather more events, thus learning from its own experiences of failure and enhancing the internal control environment as it does so.

✓ Capital calculation: losses below the threshold should be immaterial for capital calculation purposes; this may be supported by statistical evidence.

✓ Cost of collection: the ORE collection process is costly, and for larger companies this has to be balanced against the benefits. In these cases usually a higher limit is appropriate. Considerations need to include employees' time, and whether any system or software will be used, as opposed to a manual spreadsheet-based method.

✓ Risk management: active risk management provides impetus for including in scope any material events that have a non-financial impact.

✓ Tone from the top: the set threshold gives an indication of management's expectations of the quality of the ORE process.

Unified impact rating grid

Essentially, regulatory compliance aside, the firm needs to capture incidents that it deems important, without establishing a cottage industry of collecting every minor error and issue. This requires understanding of what, in fact, is meant by *important*. Without written and agreed guidelines this interpretation will inevitably vary from person to person.

To this end, the operational risk function should take the lead in coordinating an aligned Organizational Impact Rating Grid, applicable for assessing OREs as well as evaluating the impact of the risks discussed in Chapters 5 and 6. This kind of grid can be also adopted by compliance and internal audit for rating their issues and findings, and by information technology colleagues for assessing technology incidents. An example of a harmonized grid is presented in Figure 4.2. It guides the end-user to consider a range of consequences, being financial, client, reputational and regulatory. The category with the highest impact determines the overall rating.

A harmonized grid has substantial benefits, including:

- the introduction of a common language and universal meaning of *Low* vs *Very High* across the organization, enabling comparability of events, issues or findings of the same rating;
- help for end-users in prioritizing their focus and actions;
- aid in determining escalation depending on materiality;
- management of risks, events and issues within a set *appetite*.

Each impact category needs to be correctly calibrated, with input from compliance, finance, internal audit and other relevant subject matter experts, and approved by the governance committee. To establish what constitutes a material financial consequence, it is helpful to conduct an analysis of internal and external loss data.

In this way, using a unified grid, operational risk can define the scope and threshold for ORE collection of, for example *Moderate* and above.

FIGURE 4.2   Unified impact rating grid

Impact	Description
Very High	**Financial:** Actual/potential loss greater than $xxx **Client:** Serious client detriment/large proportion impacted **Reputation:** Deep damage to the brand and market value, sustained media coverage **Regulatory:** Formal investigation up to suspension of licence
High	**Financial:** Actual/potential loss between $xx and $xxx **Client:** High level of detriment **Reputation:** Market commentary, serious damage to the reputation, brand and value **Regulatory:** May prompt investigation or regulatory action
Moderate	**Financial:** Actual/potential loss between $x and $xx **Client:** Moderate impact/small proportion or segment **Reputation:** One-off media coverage, minor damage to reputation, brand and value **Regulatory:** Potential enquiry or one-off fine
Low	**Financial:** Actual/potential loss below $x **Client:** Minor impact or complaints **Reputation:** Inconsequential **Regulatory:** Unlikely to result in any regulatory action

The advantage of this approach is that other impacts, in addition to financial, are accounted for; while minor issues can still be carved out to avoid cluttering the dataset and overwhelming employees with unnecessary administration.

In conclusion, the first rudimentary step of agreeing the scope of ORE in practice requires active thought and strategizing. As will be seen from the industry benchmark later in the chapter, fewer than half of the organizations participating in the live poll admitted to having a scope that is fit for purpose.

ORE life cycle: from identification to root cause analysis

The life cycle of an operational risk event is described below:

- **Identify and notify:** employee identifies and raises potential event.
- **Escalate:** material events are escalated to senior management.

- **Report:** operational risk event report is completed within set time frame.
- **Resolve and close:** action plan is created; actions tracked until resolution; root cause analysis is performed for more significant events.
- **Analyse:** analysis, trend examination, aggregation and reporting are carried out.
- **Validate:** reconciliation is performed against books and records and other sources to ensure completeness and accuracy.

Identify and notify

Due to the breadth of the operational risk discipline, and the endless possibilities of an event occurring, OREs cannot easily be located in (and extracted from) the organization's books and records. Against this background, other discovery channels can be helpful, including: a) results of day-to-day control and reconciliation checks; b) source documents for passing accounting entries related to fines, penalties, compensations and write-offs; c) customer complaints; d) technology incident reports; and e) the results of quality assurance and inventory reviews.

However, the primary mechanism for capturing OREs when things go wrong is to rely on employees. Business units and support functions operating at the coal face need to be able to:

- understand what an ORE is, visualize examples and recognize an event when it occurs;
- know how to report it once discovered and have the means to do so;
- know who to ask in case of doubt.

The completeness of event reporting remains a challenge for many firms, for multiple reasons:

- employees not wanting to draw attention to their own failure;
- arguments as to who owns the ORE;
- the consequence of having to manage the follow-up root cause analysis and remediation efforts; and
- a lack of understanding, with an unclear ORE definition possibly leaving too much to judgement.

To address the latter point, it is useful to compile a list of possible ORE examples, to provide clarity and assist employees in recognizing an incident.

Potential events for a Human Resources department may include:

- payroll calculated incorrectly; employee underpaid;
- delivery of payslips to the wrong address by an outsourced provider;
- spreadsheet containing employee personal data placed on a public drive and accessed by unauthorized personnel;
- disgruntled member of staff threatens a lawsuit, resulting in an out-of-court settlement (Note: it is important to remember that out-of-court settlements count as operational risk events);
- failure of payroll system results in delayed salary disbursement.

The list of possible incidents for a trading business may comprise:

- wrong trade amount (fat-finger error);
- an error in model design, leading to incorrect valuation of the deal;
- erroneous valuation of a position due to a failure in updating prices;
- trading system upgrade, causing errors in transaction reports made to the regulatory authorities;
- client order taken on an unrecorded mobile phone; client subsequently claims not to recognize the order; trade reversed at a loss.

Similar lists can be prepared and discussed with each business unit and support function. Continuous, tailor-made employee training and education is essential to keep up a solid level of understanding. The 2012 industry study mentioned above included a survey on the level of confidence that events are indeed being reported by staff as required. Only 60 per cent of respondents had high confidence that a majority (over 90 per cent) of OREs were being captured, as illustrated in Table 4.3.

TABLE 4.3 Industry study: confidence in completeness of ORE reporting

Confidence level	% Firms
High: 90% and above	60
Medium high: 70%	30
Medium low: 50%	10

Escalate

Material events need to be escalated promptly. Escalation is becoming more important over time, involving rapid alert to senior management at the very early stages of an incident, to enable customer and stakeholder communication and speedy resolution. Especially with technology downtime, impacted clients may turn to social media to flag service unavailability; the very last resort in finding out about your own event should be from the customer themselves. Major incidents may necessitate swift assembly of the crisis management team, who will take the lead in coordinating follow-up action.

Some OREs also have to be notified to the regulators, depending on local supervisory guidelines, which vary by jurisdiction. Supervisors frequently set an amount above which they have to be informed of a loss within a given period of time; or outline types of impacts, for example, involving customer harm, which require to be promptly escalated.

The definition of what is *material* is also changing. A decade ago, materiality was mostly expressed in financial terms.

DEFINITIONS OF MATERIAL

Example 1

Material OREs are events where actual or potential loss ≥ $500,000. These events need to be immediately notified to the head of Finance, head of Risk, chief operations officer and the head of respective business or function.

When you add in client harm, reputational damage and regulatory censure, significance can be expressed via a combination of financial and non-financial impacts.

Example 2

Material OREs are events with *High* or *Very High* impacts in any of the categories (financial, client, reputational or regulatory) defined in the unified rating grid. They need to be immediately notified to the Operational Risk department, which will in turn inform relevant stakeholders and escalate to the Chief Operating Officer, Chief Risk Officer, Head of Compliance and the Head of respective business or function. The chief operating officer may initiate a crisis management process and will ascertain the need for client and regulatory communication.

Depending on the nature of the event, there may be other participants in the chain. Cases of fraud or financial crime will be routed to Human Resources, Fraud Prevention, Legal or some combination of the above. There are advantages in directing all events via the operational risk function, which can serve as a central point to determine subsequent escalation.

Report

The Operational Risk department usually develops a reporting template. A standard form is useful to stipulate minimum requirements, including important dates – the dates of occurrence, discovery and accounting – and an example template has been provided in Appendix 2. Reporting needs to be completed within a set timeline, which can vary significantly from firm to firm, from 24 hours up to 90 days. Rapid recording is encouraged, to relay the essence of the issue, rather than waiting for all facts to come to light. It is best to just get the record in, and if necessary add to it as new details emerge.

In many instances, the area that discovers the event is not the one that caused it; for example, the Finance department identifies an incorrect booking made by Operations. Who is responsible for filing the ORE? To avoid a heated debate, it is good practice for the *identifying business unit or support function* to report the incident, regardless of whether or not they are at fault. This helps speed up the process and prompts departments to work in collaboration. The operational risk function can assist in moderating complex cross-functional events where multiple areas are involved.

A reporting process can be established in one of two ways:

- Reporting is made available to all employees, for example, via a chat line, a link to a form on the firm's intranet site, or a paper template. Any member of staff can then complete a report and submit it directly to required recipients, ensuring swift notification. Investing in automation and streamlining the process via built-in menus and predefined distribution lists enhances the end-user experience and makes the tool straightforward and easy to use. All-staff reporting of this kind requires a higher level of maturity of the organization, where employees have reasonable knowledge and understanding of OREs. The approach works best in firms where the culture is conducive to accepting bad news and reacting constructively, focusing on resolution rather than pointing fingers.

- Reporting is accessible only to a smaller group of nominated first line operational risk champions within each business unit and support function.

These risk champions are usually trained on various aspects of OREs and other operational risk tools, which enables a significant increase in the quality of the reports, and a weeding down of false alerts. This approach may however slow down the reporting process because the risk champion becomes a key dependency.

It is possible to combine both options in a two-step process, allowing all employees to flag an event which is then routed to the champion for subsequent review.

An industry study conducted in 2020 revealed a definitive move towards simplifying the reporting process. As many as 50 per cent of respondents had a short and simple online incident reporting form available to all staff, either via the firm's intranet portal or as part of the operational risk system. Another 25 per cent used paper templates and the remaining 25 per cent limited access to first line champions, in order to increase the quality of submissions (see Table 4.4).

TABLE 4.4   Industry study: operational risk event reporting process

ORE Reporting	% Firms
Paper template available to all employees	25
System or online intranet module available to all employees	50
Reporting by champions only	25

Resolve and close

Until now, we have been discussing the event identification and reporting process. One of the fundamental challenges faced by operational risk professionals is ensuring that OREs are not merely seen as a *reporting exercise*. Even the name given in the Basel Accord, *internal loss data*, invites the use of the word *collection* next to it. A lot of focus is placed on the gathering aspect – scope, template, timeline – to the extent that sometimes the most important element, *active risk management*, is underemphasized.

Essential learnings can be derived from OREs when thought, time and effort are invested in understanding what controls have failed and why. *Material* OREs necessitate an exhaustive root cause analysis, sometimes called a *deep dive* or *lessons learned*. The operational risk function can facilitate this process, lend guidance and expertise, and provide a standard template to ensure consistency in the approach. Analysis can be completed via a workshop with subject matter experts (SMEs), and with the right stakeholders in the room a discussion will usually suffice. The firm may also apply techniques such as 5 Whys or fishbone (Ishikawa) diagrams, which are widely employed in the Six Sigma process improvement methodology:[5]

- 5 Whys prompt continual asking of the *why* question, to drill down into the problem and get to its true origin;
- a fishbone diagram is useful in exploring distinct groups of causes; for example, what are the people-, system- or process-related causes of the incident.

> Where a deeper analysis of root causes and failed controls is not completed, the firm will end up merely *counting* the loss occurrences, their volume and value; without understanding *why* they happened and *how* to prevent the next event from materializing.

Following the in-depth study, action plans must be created, with owners and target dates, to prevent future reoccurrence. The second line Operational Risk department usually monitors the progress of these plans and escalates to the relevant governance committees any OREs which have not closed by the target resolution date. Operational Risk can also take a more active role and sign off on the actions, to confirm that the intended control enhancements actually address the risk.

Lastly, OREs can serve as a trigger to consider revision of other tools, such as RCSAs, KRIs and scenarios.

Analyse

Analysis, trend examination, aggregation and reporting are crucial activities which bring value to the organization. Correct event classification using the risk taxonomy category, and tagging it against the primary responsible business unit and legal entity, help build a solid foundation for the analysis.

The second line Operational Risk department has a view of the entirety of the firm's ORE data and is best placed to conduct the analysis. The questions to consider include:

- What is the overall story – has there been an increase/decrease in the number or value of OREs? It is helpful to analyse incidents relative to transaction volume: if a business unit doubles its transaction processing but OREs go up by only 10 per cent, that could be interpreted as positive news.

- What can be said about the firm's risk profile? Are there certain risks that are continuously materializing?

- Are OREs occurring in different areas but with the same root cause? Another useful tool borrowed from Six Sigma, Pareto analysis, can be applied to the ORE data, with a view to finding a few key drivers which contribute to the majority of failures.[6]

- Is there a particular day of the month when events take place (eg month-end)?

- What are the weak spots, where controls appear to fail repeatedly? This is particularly a concern if prevention measures have already been implemented.

- What is the rate of near misses to actual monetary losses? This reflects the strength of preventative controls.

- What is the length of time between the date of event occurrence and the date of discovery? This provides insight on the performance of detective controls.

- Is there a cluster of events that occurred during a short period of time, which may be connected?

- Are OREs being reported within the timeline set by the policy? This provides a good reflection of the firm's culture.

- Integration with other tools – are the reported OREs consistent with the outputs of other tools, such as RCSAs (see Chapter 5) and KRIs (Chapter 7)?

In short, a meaningful story around the OREs needs to be relayed to senior management and appropriate governance committees (see Chapter 10, Operational Risk Reporting).

Another powerful technique is to present trends and findings back to first line business units and support functions, who can sometimes feel that their reported OREs seem to disappear into a black hole without any follow-up feedback. This kind of reporting back can be done, for example, in a quarterly review session with each business unit, where the department's own events are discussed and additional firm-wide analysis is shared by the second line operational risk team.

Validate

The validation stage focusses on data accuracy and completeness. Sound data collection, and the quality and integrity of the collected data, are crucial – for risk management purposes as well as measurement – to generate capital outcomes that are aligned with the firm's operational loss exposure. The Basel Framework requires banks to 'have processes to independently review the comprehensiveness and accuracy of loss data'.[7]

Validation steps may include regular reconciliation of OREs recorded in the operational risk system or spreadsheet to the firm's accounting records. This ensures that losses are correctly reflected in the general ledger; and in the opposite direction, checks that the respective general ledger entries correspond to what is captured in the system.

An additional *certification* mechanism can be used, where business units are asked to attest to the completeness and accuracy of OREs in the reporting period. To facilitate this process, it is good practice to provide departments with the OREs they have submitted, and to seek written confirmation from the department head that no other incidents have taken place.

Firms may find it useful to open a separate general ledger account for recording OREs, ensuring transparency and ease of reconciliation. As an example, in a trading business all gains and losses commonly end up in the same profit and loss account. This makes it very difficult to extract entries related to operational risk events from the normal day's P&L; a dedicated account helps in this process.

EXTERNAL LOSS DATA

External events provide excellent case studies and enable a firm to proactively consider the question *could this happen to us*? Data can be obtained from various sources, including newspaper articles or a paid subscription to external loss data consortia. It is the role of the operational risk function, both second line personnel and first line champions, to institute a disciplined approach for examining external events, selecting those cases that are most relevant, and following up by facilitating workshops on the events with subject matter experts.

Addressing the human element

Another key ORE challenge is linked to the culture of the organization: ensuring that employees feel comfortable and empowered to speak up when things go wrong. Fostering a *no blame* environment and emphasizing the value of lessons learned will encourage staff to raise issues. The operational risk function is often a catalyst of positive change in this direction; providing training to employees on the value of OREs, as well as requesting senior management to avoid reacting to events with negative comments or an immediate demand for the responsible employee's name. The operational risk function can also be a mediator, especially when transmitting bad news up the chain of the organization, focussing constructively on addressing the cause rather than naming and shaming members of staff. Needless to say, the second line operational risk should not have a role in any post-event disciplinary proceedings.

Operational risk helps transition from a *who did this?* style comeback from management to a *how do we solve this?* type reaction. Alas, this is a broader cultural challenge that cannot be solved by operational risk alone, even if mammoth efforts are made. In some organizations, the fear of reprisal significantly impedes the firm's ability to make effective reports and hence to derive true value from the lessons learned.

Unfortunately, OREs are always 'bad news'; with the rare exception when an incidental gain is incurred instead of a loss. Over time, this can create a negative brand to the process, and if not managed, can spread to affect the reputation of the whole operational risk discipline. Positive energy needs to be consciously injected by:

- focussing on lessons learned;
- presenting the results of deep dives which demonstrate process enhancements implemented as a result of the incident;
- sharing details of events between departments, to promote common learning and help avoid similar problems in other areas;
- celebrating success, highlighting any positive employee or customer feedback that relates to improved processes.

Treatment of system failures, data breaches and conduct-related events

As discussed in the first chapter, the operational risk discipline is moving away from solely focussing on regulatory capital calculations, and the definition of operational risk as the risk of just *loss* is no longer truly reflective of today's environment. Following recent technology incidents, firms' operational resilience is being brought into the spotlight, including a prominent UK parliamentary inquiry into IT failures and their impact on consumers.[8] Supervisors are constantly asking organizations to assess how their failures are impacting *their clients* and the *markets* they operate in. This conflict between the letter of the earliest Basel Committee requirement and the evolution of the financial services environment has created a divergence; either firms need to expand their treatment of operational risk losses to incorporate other non-financial impacts, or they need to create alternative parallel processes which capture events with client, reputational and regulatory outcomes.

Specifically, there are three areas of challenge: system failures, data breaches and conduct-related events.

System failures

These are subject to continual debate between operational risk and information technology colleagues, due to the lack of integration between the ORE process and IT helpdesk incident management. Major (not all) technology incidents usually turn into operational risk events, and a mechanism needs to be in place to guide decision-making: at what point does system failure become an ORE? As one example, the criteria can be agreed by instituting a unified rating grid as discussed earlier in the chapter. But end-users also need to be educated as to what notification route they should follow, be it via the IT helpdesk or an operational risk *material* event escalation channel.

System failures may not immediately translate into a clear financial loss to the firm. However, with increased reliance on technological solutions they are becoming more and more impactful to clients. The speed of escalation, customer and regulatory communication and event resolution is vital. Will operational risk practitioners acknowledge this, step up to the challenge, and incorporate technology failures into the ORE process? Or, with the evolution of operational resilience, will a new breed of operational resilience specialists emerge? Assuming the role of incident coordinators, these new specialists will hold a central position and orchestrate all the processes around significant technology incidents, including any necessary liaison with required stakeholders from various disciplines. The need for integration between risk and resilience is also discussed in Chapter 14.

Data breaches

The EU Global Data Protection Regulation (GDPR) introduced a dramatic increase in penalties for poor data management. Prompt identification and reporting of actual and potential violations is now part of every firm's priorities. Good practice is to use an existing operational risk event reporting channel for data-related issues. This requires an update to the ORE policy to clarify the scope. But it also relies on an increase in the speed of ORE submission, to comply with GDPR timelines, as well as good coordination between operational risk and data protection officers, to ensure prompt circulation and actioning of the report. In a similar way to a technology failure, a data breach may not generate an immediate and obvious loss, but does have an impact on the customer (or employee if it is an employee-related event). Equally, data breaches may emanate from a failure on the part of a third-party provider of outsourced services. Those kinds of failures should be logged as OREs, and the firm must both oversee resolution of the incident and ensure that the supplier introduces measures to prevent reoccurrence.

The alternative is to create a separate data breach reporting process, with a different (yet another) template for the end-user, a separate policy, training and education. Unfortunately, many organizations choose this route; but it is confusing for the employees at the coal face, who already have multiple templates to complete for different purposes.

Conduct-related events

This is another field where the ORE process can be a conduit for capturing and escalating material breaches, rather than creating an equivalent compliance reporting mechanism. For example, an incident where a new product is traded with a client prior to formal sign-off from the new product approval committee. Although it has zero financial impact, this represents a severe misconduct and internal policy breach. Similarly, an account opened for a client prior to customer due diligence (CDD) verification, where the CDD is completed 10 days later with no exceptions, epitomizes a lucky escape. There could have been significant consequences for the firm if the new client was subject to sanctions, or was operating outside the firm's target market and ended up not being approved. Even if a financial penalty was avoided, from a risk management perspective it is beneficial to examine the causes of this event and derive lessons learned.

The operational risk function needs to work closely with compliance to agree on a joined-up approach. End-users will always favour having a single channel for raising all types of exceptions, which are then routed to respective SMEs, whether compliance, operational risk, IT or data protection.

In terms of reflecting events that have conduct implications, an ORE template can include a flag or a field which addresses behavioural elements. This enables any conduct-related events to be easily extracted from the over-all database and subjected to subsequent analysis.

Covid-19: operational risk event – or not?

The Covid-19 pandemic has posed a big challenge for the ORE process. The industry reacted in different ways when it came to logging risk events. In May 2020, I conducted a live poll with members of the Best Practice Operational Risk Forum, with a view to understanding whether Covid-19, a seemingly classic operational risk event by definition, was actually treated as such by financial services firms. Were organizations capturing conse-quences such as additional costs incurred while establishing home working arrangements for employees? Did they treat as OREs one-off deep cleaning of the office, expenses related to maintaining building and security, trading losses as a result of the disruption, external consultancy fees and other exceptional costs?

Almost half of respondents (47 per cent) were undecided and still consid-ering the right treatment, while 41 per cent were not attributing extra costs to Covid-19 pandemic, instead considering them as necessary enhancements which may simply have been accelerated by the circumstances. Just 12 per cent captured losses, following guidance issued by the Operational Riskdata eXchange Association (ORX) on loss data reporting.[9]

This clear divergence in approaches emanates from the blurring of lines between the event and the 'new normal' way of working and living. For example, the price of additional screens and computer equipment installed in employees' houses can be perceived as a long-term investment in enhanced business continuity capabilities – or it can be counted as a loss. Deep clean-ing of the office, while a one-off event in the beginning, clearly linked to the pandemic, is becoming a normal practice and cannot continue to be attributed to the virus indefinitely.

Consistency in the treatment of events is important for comparative analysis, especially for firms that use external loss data consortia. Divergence will result in distorted loss profiles, which will be exaggerated for firms who are counting in Covid-19 impacts, and lowered for others who choose to reflect the consequences in their routine expenses rather than as OREs.

Roles and responsibilities

It is the responsibility of first line business units and support functions to identify, escalate and report OREs in compliance with the requirements stipulated by the policy. Business units agree on and fund control improvements to prevent incidents reoccurring, and track the enhancements until they have been fully implemented. They also need to use OREs as a trigger to consider any necessary updates to other operational risk tools – risk and control self-assessments and key risk indicators.

First line operational risk champions, embedded in the business, play a crucial role as risk coordinators, ensuring that OREs are used effectively to improve risk management.

An ORE checklist for first line risk coordinators is presented below.

FIRST LINE RISK COORDINATOR CHECKLIST: ORES

✓ All staff in the department are trained on operational risk events.

✓ Employees understand the importance of learning from incidents and are encouraged to raise them.

✓ Root cause and trend analysis are performed, actions are taken to improve control environment.

✓ Completeness of events is ensured through validation or attestation.

✓ Risk coordinators share lessons learned from OREs.

✓ Relevant external events are examined: can they happen to us?

The second line Operational Risk department is responsible for establishing policy requirements, providing training and education to end-users, conducting overall trend analysis, and providing insights to help derive the maximum value out of past events. The second line back-tests OREs against other tools in the framework, to ensure consistency, and derives key views on risk measurement and capital adequacy.

Operational risk specialists are often catalysts of cultural change, especially in firms where speaking up and raising incidents may be challenging. The function works in close partnership with first line business units, promoting and facilitating cross-functional learning.

Common challenges and good practices

Common challenges

Potential challenges related to operational risk events can include the following.

RELUCTANCE TO RAISE ORES

This is a very real hurdle especially in organizations characterized by a blame culture, where the first question is usually *who did it?* The operational risk function plays a key role in positively influencing the culture and encouraging transparency and no blame; but there are limits to what a single department can accomplish. Using data analytics and artificial intelligence can help to surface incidents automatically, placing less reliance on personnel and removing the emotion from the process. This is an embryonic area but one definitely worth exploring further.

LACK OF ACTION FOLLOWING THE EVENT

The necessary improvements are identified but are not completed on time due to other priorities, insufficient budget, apathy or for other reasons. In these cases, actions turn overdue and target dates are extended multiple times. To avoid this scenario a pragmatic approach needs to be adopted, differentiating between minor and material matters. For insignificant events, improvements may be too costly and risk acceptance is the optimum solution. If the event and corresponding actions are material, however, they need to be treated with the same rigour as internal audit action plans.

LACK OF OWNERSHIP OF CROSS-FUNCTIONAL INCIDENTS

Where multiple areas are involved in an event, none of the business areas are willing to step up and lead remediation, passing the accountability around: *this is not my event.* In such instances the Operational Risk department can moderate the resolution, facilitating conversations and agreeing the right steps forward.

OVER-ENGINEERED ORE FRAMEWORK AND TEMPLATE

Simply put, business units hesitate to use the ORE mechanism. If the form is too complicated and appears to provide no value then the reporting hurdle may not even be attempted. Simplifying the process ensures that, from an end-user perspective, it adds value compared to the time and effort invested.

ADMINISTRATION INSTEAD OF RISK MANAGEMENT

There is some risk that the whole ORE exercise can become solely about form completion; especially if thresholds are inappropriately low, combined with over-zealous employees in the Operational Risk department who duly chase each event, action and target date regardless of materiality. While it is important to have a disciplined approach to logging and analysing events, it is equally essential to apply a risk-based perspective and common sense when it comes to minor issues.

UNBALANCED OPERATIONAL RISK ENGAGEMENT

Criticism is sometimes directed towards the Operational Risk department to the effect that it is only visible when there has been an operational risk event. And while the business unit is determinedly focussing on investigating and resolving the incident, operational risk is unhelpfully following up every hour demanding submission of the ORE report. It is true that the second line needs to be actively involved at all stages of the event management process; but this should not be the only time it ever engages with end-users. Relationship building, understanding each other's roles and working in partnership throughout the whole risk management life cycle are key to effective risk management.

Good practices

TRAINING AND EDUCATION

Engaging and interactive training sessions, which are tailored to reflect examples relevant to business units and support functions, increase understanding about OREs and make the process more accessible. Educational programmes need to be continuous, to account for new joiners.

TREND ANALYSIS

It is good practice to invest time in conducting trend analysis at firm-wide level, to really understand the story that OREs present. To some extent, the loss profile reveals a firm's strengths and weaknesses, and this valuable knowledge should guide the organization when taking key decisions – for example when it is considering major business changes, expansion or investment in new product lines.

EXAMINATION OF DECLINE IN OREs

While any increase in the value and number of events is concerning and should be investigated, a sharp drop is equally worrying. This can occur due to process improvements that the firm has implemented; but it can also occur as a result of a new leader stepping in and propagating *no errors/no losses* type objectives, instilling fear in any employees who deliver unpopular messages. Consequently, the absence of OREs may not necessarily be good news, and the operational risk function needs to keep its ears to the ground, evaluating the situation and understanding what has caused it.

SHARING LEARNING

The second line Operational Risk department can lead a forum with first line champions to share relevant events, learnings and success stories. This process encourages debate and prompts champions to develop their own network, enhancing their ability to reach out to each other and compare notes. Is it worth mentioning that event sharing is particularly valuable in large organizations with the same activity being undertaken in various geographical locations. Fraudsters may identify a weakness in a firm's system and undertake the same fraud in different jurisdictions and locations. Sharing of incidents can prevent this from happening.

DATA CONFIDENTIALITY

Organizations need to ensure that customer or employee names and personal details are removed from the text of all event reports. Litigation, fraud and financial crime events contain sensitive details, so it is important that only a respective loss amount is recorded in the ORE report, supplemented by a reference number for the respective file which contains full details and is retained in the Human Resources or Legal department. This is particularly important when capturing sensitive data like pay-offs to staff.

In jurisdictions where firms are subject to bank secrecy or data privacy laws, client and transaction information should be relayed outside the jurisdiction only to the degree permitted by local privacy laws.

CELEBRATING SUCCESS

This is particularly important given that OREs intrinsically have a negative connotation embedded in their name (*incidents*, *losses*). Operational risk needs to emphasize improvements, focussing on lessons learned, and to encourage first line business units and support functions to adopt the same attitude. Recognition of timely and disciplined reporting, reward for process enhancements and, especially if available, client feedback related to perfected processes turn the focus from *what went wrong* to *what works well and has been improved*. This tool is not used nearly enough in most firms.

KNOWLEDGE OF THE SECOND LINE OPERATIONAL RISK FUNCTION

Due to their direct use in *risk measurement*, OREs require in-depth knowledge and proficiency with definitions and attributes. To name a few, these attributes include gross and net amounts, reference dates, and timing impacts (which, for example, should be captured when they span more than one financial accounting period and give rise to legal risk).[10] As described in Chapter 11 which covers training and education, operational risk policy setters must be able to not only articulate how the ORE process works but also explain: *why* a particular approach and scope was selected; what considerations went into the decision; which home and host supervisory guidelines have been examined; what cost/benefit analysis has been conducted; and whether cultural aspects have been considered.

Industry benchmark, 2020

The Best Practice Operational Risk Forum composed of practitioners from a range of financial services firms examined the topic of operational risk losses.

Addressing cultural aspects: good progress or still work to be done?

As described in Figure 4.3, when it comes to culture, just 8 per cent of live poll participants believed that their firms took a consistent, constructive approach to accepting that mistakes occur, focussing on solutions and lessons learned across the whole organization. This is a tribute to leadership setting the right tone. To quote US author Arnold Glasow, 'A good leader takes a little more than his share of the blame, a little less than his share of the credit'.

The majority of respondents perceived that their firms contained different pockets of culture, largely due to different managers encouraging right – or wrong – behaviours in their respective areas. Some 17 per cent were

FIGURE 4.3 Industry poll: first line attitude to reporting OREs

1LoD attitude to Op Risk loss reporting

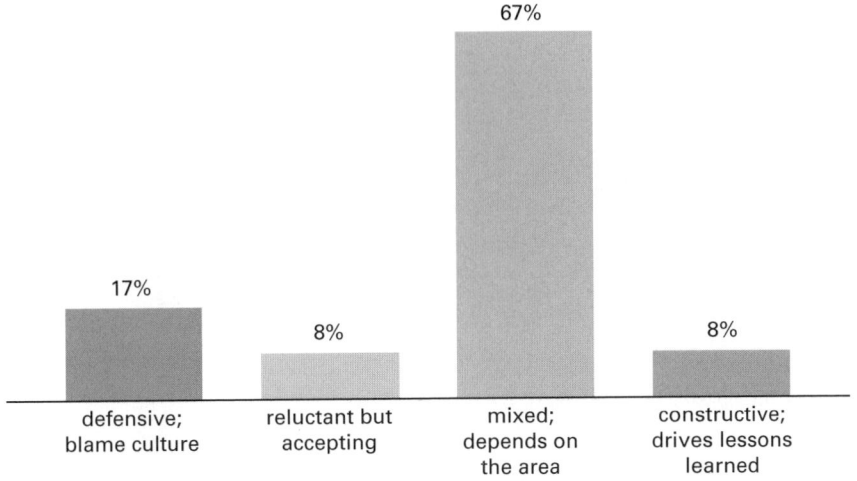

Best Practice Operational Risk Forum, 2020

concerned that their first line colleagues may feel defensive when escalating incidents, due to a sub-optimal atmosphere in the firm, and were already taking action to work with human resources and senior management to encourage a more positive approach.

Completeness of loss event reporting

Operational risk practitioners responding to the survey admitted that the completeness of ORE identification and reporting remains a challenge, as articulated by the graph in Figure 4.4. Only 18 per cent of respondents exhibited high confidence that over 90 per cent of incidents are identified and escalated, enabling the firm to derive valuable learnings from the events. The rest acknowledged the need for continuous education to maintain employee awareness. Fear of reprisal may be one of the contributing factors to sub-optimal event capture.

Reporting thresholds

One other factor potentially impacting confidence in the completeness of the dataset is the established amount, or threshold, above which events have to be collected. Less than half of the group were satisfied with the threshold, making

FIGURE 4.4   Industry poll: confidence in ORE reporting

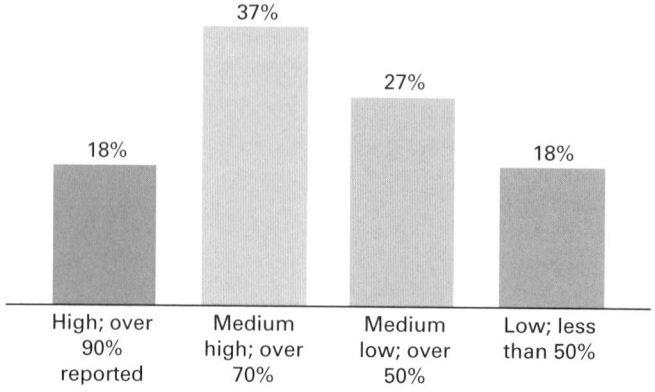

Best Practice Operational Risk Forum, 2020

FIGURE 4.5   Industry poll: ORE threshold

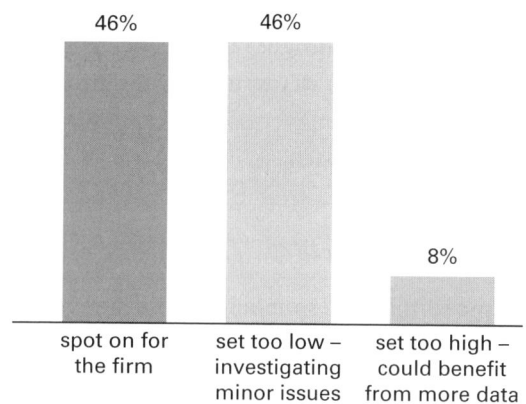

Best Practice Operational Risk Forum, 2020

it an area of much needed focus. As seen from the Figure 4.5, 46 per cent felt that the limit is set too low, generating a cottage industry of busy first line employees filling in the templates, with other second line colleagues chasing them for the status of completion and following up on actions. Over half of surveyed firms had a zero reporting threshold.

Increasing the limit helps to turn risk administration into risk management, thereby enabling focus on what is truly important to the organization.

Practical workplace exercise

Reflecting on the content of this chapter, examine a sample of operational risk events recorded within your organization over the last year, and consider the following questions:

1 Have a scope and thresholds been set for OREs and are they fit for purpose?

2 What analysis has been undertaken to support the scope and thresholds?

3 Is there evidence of active risk management of events, with analysis of the root cause and actions to prevent reoccurrence?

4 Is the culture of the firm conducive to employees speaking up and logging incidents without fear of reprisal?

5 What are the strengths of the process?

6 What can be improved? Note down possible enhancements.

MAKE A DIFFERENCE (MAD) ACTION

Please outline the learnings and note down one action that you will take after reading this chapter to enhance your existing practices related to operational risk events.

In summary, this chapter addressed operational risk events, historically the first tool deployed by organizations, where many challenges still remain; from complex ones such as getting the culture right, to more simple ones such as setting the correct threshold.

Moving on, the next chapter will focus on forward-looking risk identification.

Notes

1   Basel Committee on Banking Supervision (2014) *Review of the Principles for the Sound Management of Operational Risk*, www.bis.org/publ/bcbs292.pdf (archived at https://perma.cc/X9UQ-5ZAB)

2   European Banking Authority (2008) *Compendium of Supplementary Guidelines on Implementation Issues of Operational Risk (CP21)*, www.eba. europa.eu/sites/default/documents/files/documents/10180/37070/8bfec18c-2de6-4436-ae28-2f1b044bd385/CEBS%202008%20230%20Final.pdf? (archived at https://perma.cc/F2V4-B35T)

3   Basel Committee on Banking Supervision (2014) *Review of the Principles for the Sound Management of Operational Risk*, www.bis.org/publ/bcbs292.pdf (archived at https://perma.cc/XBW2-27EM)

4   Basel Committee on Banking Supervision (2009) *Results from the 2008 Loss Data Collection Exercise for Operational Risk*, www.bis.org/publ/bcbs160.pdf (archived at https://perma.cc/24GS-MXYN)

5   George, ML, Maxey, J, Rowlands, D and Price, M (2004) *The Lean Six Sigma Pocket Toolbook: A quick reference guide to 100 tools for improving quality and speed*, McGraw-Hill

6   George, ML, Maxey, J, Rowlands, D and Price, M (2004) *The Lean Six Sigma Pocket Toolbook: A quick reference guide to 100 tools for improving quality and speed*, McGraw-Hill

7   Basel Committee on Banking Supervision, Basel Framework, www.bis.org/ basel_framework/ (archived at https://perma.cc/3JNV-5BB8)

8   UK Parliament (2018) IT failures in the financial services sector inquiry launched, committees.parliament.uk/committee/158/treasury-committee/ news/98937/it-failures-in-the-financial-services-sector-inquiry-launched/ (archived at https://perma.cc/2QSS-N33L)

9   Operational Riskdata eXchange Association (ORX) (2020) *Capturing Operational Risk Impacts of Coronavirus*, managingrisktogether.orx.org/ coronavirus/capturing-operational-risk-impacts-coronavirus (archived at https://perma.cc/2F77-9MSJ)

10 Basel Committee on Banking Supervision, Basel Framework, www.bis.org/ basel_framework/ (archived at https://perma.cc/LX8E-UKUF)

05

Risk and control self-assessments

What this chapter covers: Risk and Control Self-Assessments (RCSAs) are used by many organizations, yet the instrument attracts its fair share of criticism. This chapter draws attention to methodologies that have proven effective over time; suggests an approach to risk identification based on three simple questions; and emphasizes the importance of engaging with stakeholders via personable and meaningful conversations (Figure 5.1). While covering the main fundamental concepts, it also focusses on overcoming pitfalls and proposing measures of success that help evaluate whether the RCSA has delivered desired outcomes. The chapter contains case studies, examples and an industry benchmark.

FURTHER READING

- Committee of Sponsoring Organizations of the Treadway Commission (2017) *Enterprise Risk Management: Integrating with strategy and performance*
  Why recommended: One of the many strengths of the COSO approach is its emphasis on the value of enterprise risk management in relation to the setting and carrying out of strategy, positioning it in the context of the firm's performance rather than as an isolated exercise. This useful guide aids in building a business case when considering RCSA roll-out.

- Theodore Zeldin (1998) *Conversation: How talk can change your life*, The Harvill Press
  Why recommended: Perhaps a rather unusual choice for the chapter, this book brings out the art of conversations. The aim of including it is to stress the fact that RCSA is not a checklist or a mechanical task, but a meaningful – and potentially even enjoyable – interaction of minds.

FIGURE 5.1   Focus of Chapter 5: risk assessments

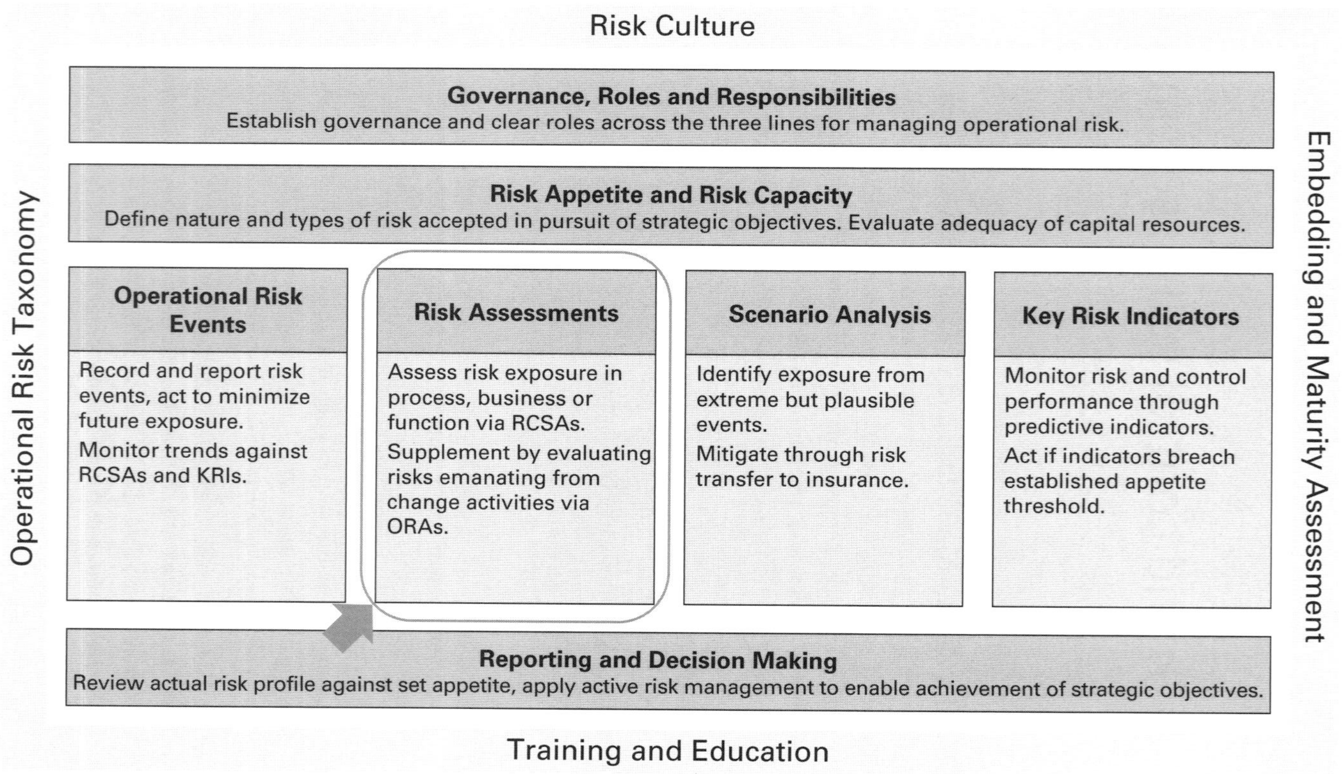

Embedding and Maturity Assessment

Risk Culture

Governance, Roles and Responsibilities

Establish governance and clear roles across the three lines for managing operational risk.

Risk Appetite and Risk Capacity

Define nature and types of risk accepted in pursuit of strategic objectives. Evaluate adequacy of capital resources.

Operational Risk Events

Record and report risk events, act to minimize future exposure.

Monitor trends against RCSAs and KRIs.

Risk Assessments

Assess risk exposure in process, business or function via RCSAs.

Supplement by evaluating risks emanating from change activities via ORAs.

Scenario Analysis

Identify exposure from extreme but plausible events.

Mitigate through risk transfer to insurance.

Key Risk Indicators

Monitor risk and control performance through predictive indicators.

Act if indicators breach established appetite threshold.

Reporting and Decision Making

Review actual risk profile against set appetite, apply active risk management to enable achievement of strategic objectives.

Training and Education

Operational Risk Taxonomy

Rethinking the approach: essential ingredients of the perfect recipe

Risk and Control Self-Assessments (RCSAs) are a key forward-looking component of the operational risk framework, and one of the most interactive and engaging tools available to risk practitioners. While widely used by many firms in financial services, RCSAs typically generate a mixed response, not only from business stakeholders but also from practitioners themselves. Sceptics question whether they bring any benefits; critics suggest that they are a waste of time. A study of industry practices published by the Operational Riskdata eXchange Association (ORX) in 2020 reflected the view that RCSAs were seen as simply not delivering enough value, and were perceived as a tick-box exercise rather than truly influencing business decisions.[1]

By this stage of evolution of the RCSA tool, firms are likely to have developed detailed procedures, predefined templates for what needs to be captured in a software or spreadsheet solution, and a library of commonly phrased risks and controls. Could it be that the methodology has become too prescriptive and that the process has trumped the business value-add? Whether starting from scratch or rethinking an existing approach, it is important to bear in mind that the essential ingredients of the perfect RCSA recipe are quite basic: the right stakeholders participating in the process, personal and meaningful engagement, a high degree of preparedness and an expert facilitator.

Heightened focus on proactive risk identification

Firms are subject to growing interest in their operational risk profile, as demonstrated by the large number of supervisory requests to articulate *top operational risks*, in addition to well-established requirements for routine loss reporting. Regulators nowadays are frequently asking:

- What are the top 10 operational risks your firm faces?
- What are your top 5 emerging risks?

As an example, in 2014, the Prudential Regulation Authority in the UK performed a thematic review on risk identification. Several participating banks were asked to submit their most significant past operational risk events. The supervisors then conducted interviews of senior management, discussing for each reported event:

- Was the risk associated with the event identified *before* the event occurred?
- If so, was it escalated to executive management before the event occurred?
- If it was identified, how was this done?

These questions explore the strength of firms' forward-looking risk identification: was the organization aware that an operational risk event (ORE) could happen, or did it occur without warning? They also address the cultural aspect of escalating risks openly and transparently.

As highlighted in previous chapters, these developments demonstrate very effectively the shift of focus in the industry: from being merely an operational risk regulatory capital calculation towards more active risk management. To this end, RCSA is an important tool that encourages proactive thinking, provides boards and management with a detailed view of the firm's risk and control environment, and leads to prudent decision-making. Coupled with the big regulatory drive towards increased personal accountability, RCSAs are instrumental in helping senior management to demonstrate and evidence that they have taken reasonable steps in understanding and managing their risk and control environment. There are plenty of reasons to make the most of the exercise.

Top-down and bottom-up assessments and their features

Defining RCSAs

In Chapter 4 we discussed OREs, the events of the past. RCSAs, in contrast, encourage firms to consider the areas where they are exposed and where things *could* potentially go wrong for them in the future; thereby enabling them to invest in preventative as well as detective measures.

Terminology varies widely between firms. The risk assessments may also be called Risk and Control Assessments (RACAs), Control Self-Assessments (CSAs), or Own Risk Self-Assessments (ORSAs). Going forward, throughout this chapter and the rest of the book, we will refer to these assessments collectively as risk and control self-assessments, or RCSAs.

> RCSA is a process of the identification and assessment of risks faced by the firm and review of the control environment, in order to highlight areas where controls are ineffective or insufficient to mitigate the risk and take appropriate action.

Despite the RCSA concept being rather straightforward and necessarily simplistic, it generates multiple questions that all require answers. As with any process, one of the fundamental steps in carrying out a successful RCSA is deciding on the right way of doing it. With no standard industry design, it is imperative that each firm selects an appropriate methodology and approach, process and level of granularity that is suitable given its own circumstances.

Methodological questions that need to be considered include:

- How to structure a *bottom-up* approach, gathering intelligence from the employees at the coal face as well as how to obtain a *top-down* view from the senior stakeholders; *both sets of discussions* are needed;
- What assessment scales should be adopted;
- Whether controls will undergo judgemental evaluation or need to be actively tested;
- How to add value and measure the success – or failure – of the exercise.

Presented below are examples of selected RCSA approaches, their key features, advantages and weaknesses.

Granular assessments

Detailed bottom-up assessments help a firm to achieve greater understanding of its risk and control profile. One methodology in this category is process risk self-assessment (PRSA) which aims to map a particular process end-to-end, and to identify the key risks and controls within it. Activities are selected based on certain criteria. For example, if the driver is Sarbanes–Oxley (SoX), a regulation which historically gave rise to many internal control evaluation programmes, the focus would be on the processes that impact the company's most significant general ledger accounts.[2]

Where the driver is operational resilience – as has been the case more recently – the organization identifies the business services which are most important for its clients or the financial markets it operates in.

Organizations that have historically applied a PRSA methodology driven by SoX are also better positioned when it comes to satisfying operational resilience demands. This is because the fundamental yet very time-consuming task of mapping the process, and understanding its interdependencies, would have already been accomplished in the first stage of analysis. (See also Chapter 14, Operational Resilience).

A PRSA schematic is described in Figure 5.2.

FIGURE 5.2 Process risk self-assessment

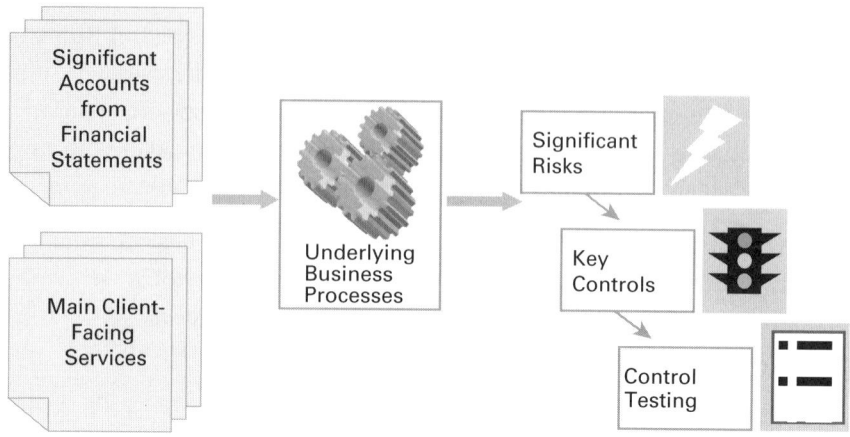

Examples of processes or services that may be selected for PRSA include:

- Client deposits: these are mapped end-to-end, from the point of establishing a client relationship and performing due diligence checks, through to the client depositing the money which results in accounting entries on the balance sheet.

- Foreign exchange: similarly this process is mapped from the point of a new corporate/institutional client being set up, to agreeing the deal with the trader, confirmation, settlement and general ledger accounting entries.

PRSA is a *bottom-up* assessment, resulting in relatively granular risk identification, for example:

- risk of money laundering resulting from missed or poorly executed client due diligence at the account opening stage;

- risk of incorrect foreign exchange transactions due to trader 'fat finger' error.

Key features of this approach are outlined below:

- Advantages:
  - o Process mapping is a robust technique which in itself generates immediate benefits, including process optimization, as redundant steps are identified and eliminated.

- o A cross-functional methodology brings together participants from the front office, operations, finance, technology and other functions, encouraging fruitful dialogue and increasing overall understanding of the risk and control environment; and improving collaboration between business units and support functions.

- o Due to end-to-end mapping, the impact of failure on the external customer becomes transparent and measurable. This is essential learning for non-client facing departments and a key differentiator of the approach.

- o Often process controls are actively tested (rather than judgementally evaluated), making the assessment more factual and objective.

- Challenges:

- o It takes a lot of thought, and sometimes some trial and error, to set the right boundaries around the process; and to obtain agreement on where it starts and ends and what is (and is not) included. It may be equally challenging to find an owner for a particular process, due to its cross-functional nature. Organizations are rarely structured *by process*, but usually rather by department.

- o The approach is labour intensive and requires rigorous work creating maps and keeping them up to date; it is most likely to succeed where a firm is already in the habit of process mapping as part of its culture.

- o The approach requires consideration of how the broader risks of, for example, poor governance or conduct can be addressed; as well as how the granular results are aggregated and presented to the board and senior management at the top of the house.

An alternative detailed form of assessment is the *departmental* RCSA, focussing on the risk and control environment of a particular department, business or function. This approach fits well with firms' organizational structure, with clear *units of measure* – departments – already established and operating, and an obvious RCSA owner, the respective unit head. It also aligns closely to senior management accountability and therefore can be used in personal attestations to satisfy certification and accountability regimes where they exist. The approach is, however, siloed by nature as each business unit is evaluating its own setting without considering interdependencies and reflecting on the overall impact of the risk or control on the client or the balance sheet. Overall, therefore, PRSA is a stronger and more rewarding approach. But if you are conducting the assessments at departmental level, aim to maximize the exploration of linkages and interdependencies.

High-level assessments

Top-down assessments are essential for engaging with senior management and arriving at an enterprise-wide view. Strategic risk assessment (SRA) focusses on the identification of risks which may prevent the firm from achieving its strategic objectives, and the formulation of controls to mitigate those risks. The starting point is the high-level business plan, which usually translates into the goals of business heads. This gives rise to an immediate value proposition: the conversation starts with an offer from the risk practitioner to help the business identify and mitigate the risks that could impede the successful realization of *their own* objectives and business plan. It sounds so much better than a bald statement of the type 'You need to complete your RCSA'.

Operational risk practitioners often complain that they are not invited to the strategy table. In this context the SRA is a sound tool which not only generates value but also elevates the brand and profile of risk professionals. The assessment is best conducted at the start of the year, to *coincide with strategy setting*, arriving at robust objectives given risks that have been well understood and evaluated. This timing is important to ensure that the SRA does not represent an isolated exercise but is linked to the need to *make a decision* – namely to discuss and adopt the strategy given the risks to it. As noted by COSO, enterprise risk management and these kinds of exercises enrich the 'dialogue by adding perspective to the strengths and weaknesses of a strategy'; and allow management 'to feel more confident that they've examined alternative strategies'.[3] This is described in schematic form in Figure 5.3.

FIGURE 5.3   Strategic risk assessment

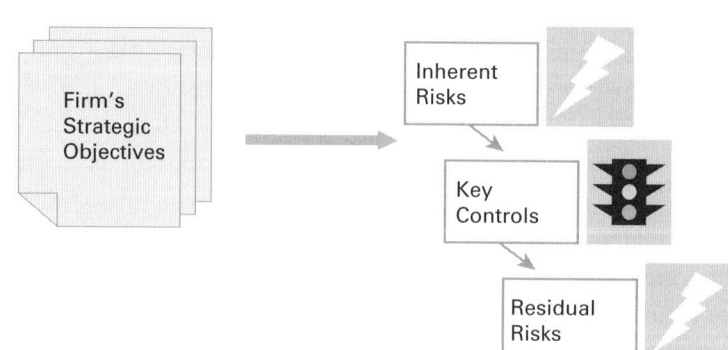

SRA is a top-down assessment resulting in the identification of high-level risks which stretch beyond purely operational, actually entering into enterprise risk territory.

CASE STUDY 5.1

An investment bank sets one of its objectives as being 'to create an extensive range of competitive products that meet client requirements', with a plan to significantly increase its client value proposition during the coming year. During the SRA, in discussing what issues might prevent the business heads from executing on this objective, three risks are identified:

- inadequate product design leading to poor customer outcomes;
- inability to identify and implement new regulatory requirements on a timely basis;
- new product approval process too slow.

The last risk is considered a real blocker to delivering on the strategy. A multimillion improvement programme is launched, to recruit additional resources in support functions and invest in a parallel system testing environment. Metrics are agreed as to what constitutes an acceptable new product review and approval time frame, and each new product is measured against the timeline.

Arguably, reasoning such as this ('new product approval process too slow') does not belong in the operational risk domain. In the above example, however, this is clearly a very important risk for the business; and the methodology needs to be flexible enough to accommodate what truly matters to stakeholders, rather than what can be neatly fitted into the standard taxonomy.

The key features of the SRA approach are presented below:

- Advantages:
  - SRA is a vital tool for understanding the most significant risks that underlie the business. This is an essential step for subsequently setting the firm's risk appetite (see Operational Risk Appetite, Chapter 9).
  - The exercise is directly relevant to business heads as it is closely linked to their goals and strategic objectives. This kind of value proposition helps to build a convincing case for participants.

o SRA promotes *risk conversations* at the senior management level, increases awareness, elevates the value of the risk assessment process and drives the need and appreciation for resulting management information and reporting.

o By its nature, SRA is broader than operational risk and evaluates the risk and control environment on a holistic basis, considering both gaps and areas that might be overcontrolled.

- Challenges:

o By design, the SRA does not delve deep into the details of individual controls.

o It is not easy to organize and requires robust planning given the busy diaries and preoccupations of the participants.

o Controls are evaluated judgementally, not tested, making the assessment less factual.

The organization needs to conduct assessments that are both granular and high level. They complement each other, enabling a deep dive as well as considering the firm-wide profile, which cannot be arrived at via mere aggregation. The risks are *key* at the level where they are raised; so a PRSA will capture process-related risks, but is not expected to reflect executive committee concerns (for example, around failed governance arrangements or strategic business risks).

Whichever approach is applied, an RCSA has a number of distinct steps that need to be followed.

Risk identification and assessment

Identifying risks

Risk identification aims to highlight material risks for the area covered by the RCSA, potential failures that may impact key business activities and prevent respective business unit or support functions from meeting *their objectives*.

To achieve a robust outcome, it is essential to involve the right stakeholders – usually the heads of the respective departments, their direct reports and selected subject matter experts – and for strategic risk assessment, the chief executive and their management team.

FIGURE 5.4 Three questions for risk assessments

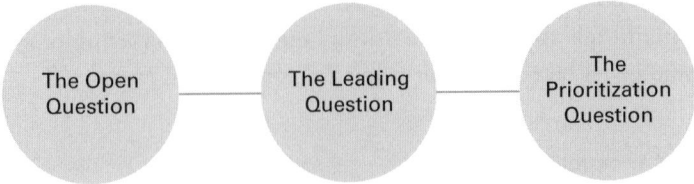

While there is no agreed universal approach, risk identification lends itself well to individual interviews with the appropriate participants, facilitated by an experienced operational risk practitioner. This can be followed by a follow-up workshop, discussed later in the chapter. One-to-one discussions allow inputs to be gathered effectively and efficiently. A good start can be achieved via a conversation centred around three basic questions, described in Figure 5.4.

THE OPEN QUESTION

Open questions explore participants' concerns about the area in scope, to obtain an understanding of *what keeps them awake at night*. The question is broad and posed in the language of the participant (rather than risk-type language such as 'what are your inherent risks?'). Stakeholders understand their business; the answer should provide a good feel for their key areas of focus.

Various elements may arise from this process which are not necessarily risks; the aim is to listen, probe and turn the information into desired output. Many accomplished operational risk managers see themselves as *translators*, interpreting regulation into day-to-day practices, converting stakeholders' input into risk language and complexity into simplicity.

Slightly digressing from the discipline of operational risk into the art of leading a conversation: to quote Theodore Zeldin, 'Real conversation catches fire. It involves more than sending and receiving information.'[4] A risk practitioner is not an administrative note-taker, but a knowledgeable and equal partner in the dialogue, orchestrating the conversation. A relationship of mutual trust helps bring about a good debate.

Back to risk identification, an alternative open question might explore *what could go wrong, or what might prevent stakeholders from achieving their annual objectives?* Linking every risk assessment to objectives brings much needed connection to the business plan and what needs to be achieved.

Or, *if they were building this process from scratch, what would they be concerned about?*

The intention is to talk about risk in language the stakeholder can easily understand, even better without using the actual word *risk* itself.

Failure of a control is *not* a risk.

Potential hurdles to watch out for include participants raising, for example, *failure of account reconciliation* as one of their concerns. Account reconciliation is a control that detects occurrences of multiple risks, including the risk of transactional error or internal fraud, as highlighted in Figure 5.5. In this case the facilitator needs to bring the focus back to the risk: one way of achieving this is via the use of the bow-tie model outlined in Chapter 1. This model, yet again, helps us to visually differentiate between materialized risks (events) and their causes and impacts, as well as the controls discussed later in this chapter. Skilled operational risk practitioners operate the bow-tie model subconsciously, automatically converting inputs into the right formulation of risks.

Often the answers to the open question will cover most of the necessary ground, but a few remaining risks will emerge from the second question.

THE LEADING QUESTION

The second, follow-on question is about completeness. Simply put, it comes down to what else *should* be keeping the stakeholder awake at night. This is

FIGURE 5.5 Use of the bow-tie model in RCSA process: risks

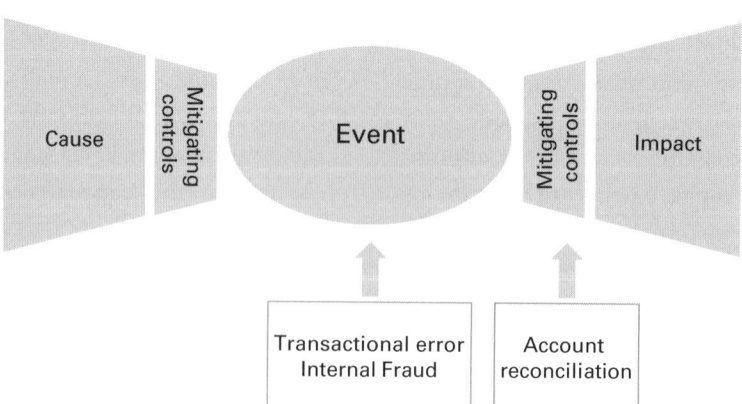

where the risk taxonomy – whether the Basel version or internally developed – is particularly handy, helping the discussion to become leading, or 'menu-based'. The risk practitioner encourages the stakeholder to consider relevant topics not brought up previously; for example, considering the possibility of future technology failures and their impact on the business; probing whether their exposure to money laundering is increasing; or whether internal fraud is more or less likely to happen than previously.

Facilitating free-flowing stakeholder conversations does not mean arriving at the meeting unprepared. On the contrary, the more skilled and equipped with information the risk expert is, the more confidently they will hold their ground at the session.

Before the meeting, the risk professional must have formed their own view on what risks they expect to come up, based on their understanding of the business and its environment. A pre-reading pack with supplementary information is an essential aid for the assessment. Pack materials might include:

- strategy and business plan, financials, minutes of governance committee meetings, planned material change programmes;
- operational risk data, including a history of operational risk events, key risk indicators, and outputs from previous RCSAs if they exist (note: these are certainly useful, but it is important not to allow them to limit the scope of the current assessment);
- output from other control disciplines, for example, compliance assessments and internal audit reports;
- data from external sources, including external loss data for peer firms, information on the regulatory landscape and priority areas for home and host state regulators.

Detailed preparatory work, including close examination of the pack, enables the risk practitioner to be an equal partner in the discussion, effectively providing *oversight and challenge*.

THE PRIORITIZATION QUESTION
The third part of the conversation needs to concentrate on *how much* the raised concern is keeping the stakeholder awake at night. In practical terms, what monetary loss do they expect to sustain next year as a result of the concern? What level of customer harm, reputational damage or regulatory censure is anticipated? This line of questioning helps to evaluate the risks

relative to each other; some being more significant than others in terms of impact. Which brings us neatly to risk assessment.

Assessing risks

Risk assessment needs to be carried out on both an inherent and a residual basis.

RESIDUAL RISK

Residual risk is the risk remaining after the application of controls, and is quite intuitive. Stakeholders are asked to articulate – even given the current control environment – what still *keeps them awake at night*. This kind of questioning reflects the existing state of the environment, 'as is', and participants are usually easily able to perform the assessment.

INHERENT RISK

Inherent risk is the risk before the effect of the existing controls. It is a less intuitive concept, as it can be very challenging for business units to try to imagine their environment without controls. It is also a very specific form of risk jargon, whether expressed in English or other languages. Depending on the maturity and level of risk knowledge of the audience, at times it may be best, therefore, to start the risk assessment by evaluating the level of residual risk first, followed by inherent risk; perhaps using the more intuitive wording *how much worse could it be if the primary controls failed?*

Risks are commonly assessed in two dimensions: the likelihood of their occurrence and their impact.

Likelihood means the possibility of the risk materializing in the future, expressed using a range of values. While the methods used by organizations to articulate likelihood vary considerably – with time horizons that may stretch from 12 months out to 100 years – RCSAs are typically confined to the current business cycle and thus focus primarily on the near term (1–5 years). The tool is not intended to analyse worst-case or catastrophic events – for example, a 1-in-100-year flood. Those are generally addressed through a separate scenario analysis, as discussed in Chapter 8. Some firms do, however, find it useful to highlight extreme risks as part of the RCSA exercise; noting them down as *potential candidates* for scenario analysis and developing them further at a later stage.

The second dimension, risk *impact*, evaluates the consequences, both financial and non-financial, of risk materializing. The unified impact rating grid has already been introduced in Chapter 4, in Figure 4.2.

FIGURE 5.6 Risk grading matrix

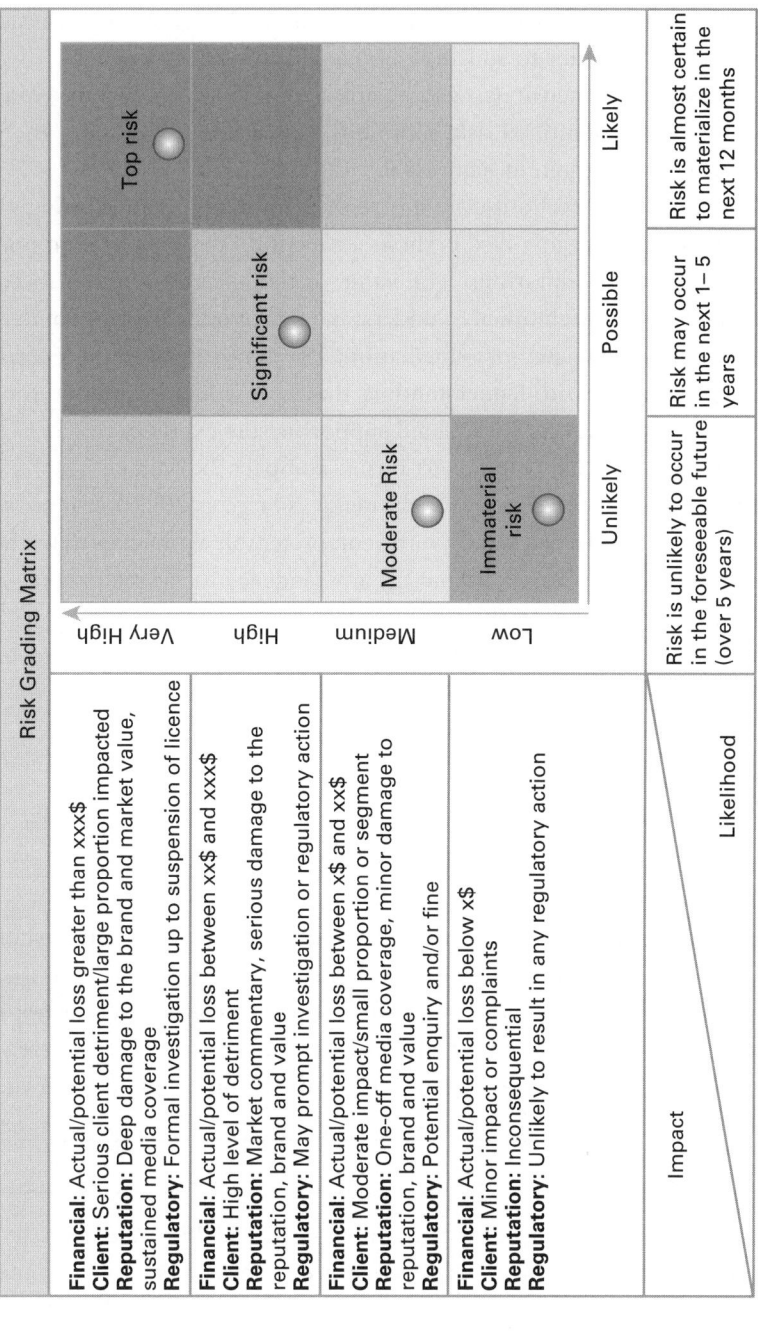

Risk Grading Matrix

	Unlikely	Possible	Likely
Very High			Top risk
High		Significant risk	
Medium	Moderate Risk		
Low	Immaterial risk		

Financial: Actual/potential loss greater than xxx$
Client: Serious client detriment/large proportion impacted
Reputation: Deep damage to the brand and market value, sustained media coverage
Regulatory: Formal investigation up to suspension of licence

Financial: Actual/potential loss between xx$ and xxx$
Client: High level of detriment
Reputation: Market commentary, serious damage to the reputation, brand and value
Regulatory: May prompt investigation or regulatory action

Financial: Actual/potential loss between x$ and xx$
Client: Moderate impact/small proportion or segment
Reputation: One-off media coverage, minor damage to reputation, brand and value
Regulatory: Potential enquiry and/or fine

Financial: Actual/potential loss below x$
Client: Minor impact or complaints
Reputation: Inconsequential
Regulatory: Unlikely to result in any regulatory action

Impact	Likelihood	Risk is unlikely to occur in the foreseeable future (over 5 years)	Risk may occur in the next 1–5 years	Risk is almost certain to materialize in the next 12 months

While the most common non-financial impacts consist of client, regulatory and reputational consequences, firms may also add other categories; for example *people* impact – perhaps evaluating the scope for physical and psychological injury to staff – as well as other types of impact.

These two dimensions, when combined, reflect the overall exposure of the firm to the identified risk. This finds its place on a *heat map*, an example of which is presented in Figure 5.6.

Heat maps attract criticism due to their imprecision and the high level of human judgement involved in the assessment process. And it is important to recognize these limitations. The value of the exercise is more to compare risks relative to each other, to understand which ones are more material and need to be prioritized for remediation. The aim is not to find a *perfect risk position* on the grid. Understanding these constraints helps the tool to be used appropriately as a visual aid supporting the exercise.

Assessment scales often start out as compact 3×3 dimensional matrices, with some more extensive versions being as large as 20×20. A more sensibly sized matrix of 4×4 is usually sufficient, preferably with an even (rather than odd) number of cells, to discourage any tendency for participants to aim for a mid-point and 'sit on the fence'.

Potential methodological enhancements for the risk grading tool are described below.

More on risks: velocity, killer risks, emerging risks

Risk velocity

An additional third dimension, *risk velocity*, is useful to understand how quickly a given risk is expected to change its position on the matrix. Some risks may develop rapidly and start posing a threat which was not evident before, and therefore require more focus at an earlier stage. Where velocity is not used, *risk direction* (eg increasing, decreasing) can be outlined.

Killer risks

One of the key learnings that came out of the Covid-19 pandemic is the danger of deprioritizing material risks which are deemed *unlikely* to happen. The threat of infectious diseases was in fact identified in the January edition of the 2020 global risk report by the World Economic Forum, rated as significant but with relatively low likelihood.[5] This was an interesting finding which has been extensively discussed by the risk community, including questions as to what the risk profession could have done better to ensure pandemic preparedness. One possibility, therefore, for enhancing the risk matrix is to take the probability out of the equation for risks with a *very high* impact. As a result, the *entire row of very high* risks can be viewed as *top* or *killer risks* as described in Figure 5.7; prompting to concentrate on their mitigation regardless of the likelihood score.

Escalation, acceptance, appetite

Heat maps are very useful in helping to guide end-users on subsequent action. For example, the level of *escalation* required for residual risks, depending on their magnitude, can be articulated with the help of the heat map, with more material risks needing to be brought to the attention of the board and senior committees. Rules can also be set around *risk acceptance*, determining what authority is required to accept each risk level; as well as defining what risks lie outside the firm's appetite, will not be tolerated and require mitigation.

FIGURE 5.7   Risk grading matrix: extending top risks

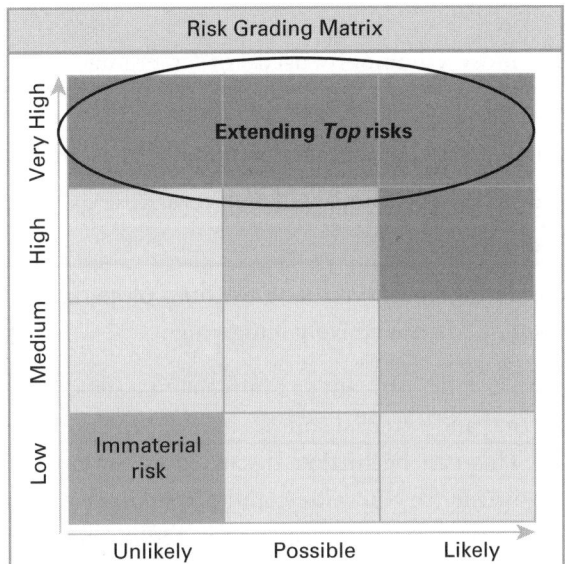

Emerging risks

In addition to the existing risk environment, it is good practice to apply a structured approach to the identification of *emerging risks*. The insurance industry is more advanced in this area compared to banking and asset management, as insurers typically seek to understand as much as possible about the emerging risks potentially impacting their portfolios. These emerging risks have the characteristic of being less familiar than the existing risk portfolio, not fully understood but still perceived to be potentially significant. Various definitions have been provided, for example by the International Risk Governance Council and Lloyds of London.[6, 7]

This is a very interesting subject in its own right, and not just for insurers. Public-sector bodies have a considerable interest in emerging risks, while a number of think tanks and scientific academies have produced research and guidance on the topic. Management consultants meanwhile continue to develop tools aimed at detecting and responding to emerging risks.

In the operational risk context, *emerging risk* can be defined as a new or increasing operational risk which has the potential to become a *top risk*.

Top risks are those inherent risks which, if not well controlled, will result in the most significant impact to the firm.

Tools that are most commonly used for emerging risk identification include:

- horizon scanning, a scan of characteristics and changes in the environment;
- scenario analysis or workshops with subject matter experts;
- metrics or indicators;
- surveys, considering questions along the lines of, perhaps, 'risks you are aware of that you are not actively mitigating'.

The Operational Risk department can implement a structured approach of monitoring internal and external sources in order to develop a watchlist of emerging risks. This can be further discussed at the operational risk or other relevant governance committee, and *candidates* can subsequently be selected for further scenario analysis, as discussed in Chapter 8. Potentially these candidate risks could be *promoted* to top risks, depending on the outcomes.

Documenting risks

What is the right way to document risks, and how prescriptive should the format be? The documentation methodology will vary depending on the type of the exercise:

- Allow stakeholders, aided by risk practitioners, to phrase their risks in their own language (free style). This approach is suitable for strategic risk assessments with a senior audience.

- Provide guidance language, based on the premise that risk is a negative statement. This approach will typically make use of words such as *inability, inadequate* and *failure of.* For example: *Inability to identify and implement new regulatory requirements on a timely basis, resulting in fines, regulatory censure and reputational damage.* This approach is not overly prescriptive hence appropriate for most assessments.

- Establish a format along the lines *there is a risk of... due to... resulting in... .* For example: *There is a risk of data breaches due to inappropriate data usage by staff, leading to fines, client harm and reputational damage.* This is a sensible structure but should be used with caution. The *due to* element can inadvertently lead to a proliferation of identified risks, by exploring multiple causes which all lead to the same risk materializing.

- Develop a library of risks, where the stakeholders can select pre-populated risks that specifically relate to them.

The more prescriptive the approach, the more consistent the documentation of the risks. However, some of the nuances and real concerns may be lost, and the value of the exercise diminished accordingly. After all, when elaborating the firm's strategy, the chief executive and their team do not select strategic objectives from a predefined list of objectives. It is better for the risk practitioner to help the stakeholders articulate their risks in the required format while capturing as closely as possible the true meaning of what was said.

Identified risks need to be mapped to the firm's taxonomy, which allows for cross-comparison with other framework elements. Usually, RCSAs in the operational risk space lead to the identification of risks aligned to the Basel categorizations or the firm's internal classification. However, high-level strategic RCSAs – dealing with the risks that may prevent the firm from achieving its objectives – will usually highlight a broader spectrum of risks, including strategic and business risks.

Control identification, categorization and assessment

A control is an activity or process established to mitigate the risk and, as noted by COSO, is 'designed to provide reasonable assurance regarding the achievement of objectives'.[8]

Every risk is typically mitigated by a multitude of controls. For RCSA purposes we are looking for *key* controls, or the controls which mitigate the risk *the most effectively* – and thus cannot be left out of the assessment. In arriving at the determination of whether or not a control is *key*, it is useful to consider what the impact would be if the control was removed.

There is no prescribed number of controls to mitigate each risk. But the suggestion is to identify at least one primary control, and no more than three to five in total.

Control identification

In a similar way to risk identification, controls can be defined during one-to-one interviews with subject matter experts.

As with risks, approaches vary when it comes to documenting controls and deciding on how rigid the format should be:

- Provide minimum guidance to ensure the process referred to is known and understood, for example, *account reconciliation*, *client due diligence*, *employee recruitment*; this approach should certainly be used in high-level assessments.

- Prescribe the format, requesting a description of both the process and its results, and noting, at minimum, *what*, *who* and *when*. [what?] Pre-employment screening is conducted for all staff [by whom?] by HR [when?] prior to employment. This is a useful format which results in controls being described quite specifically, with allocated accountability for control performance and a defined *control owner*.

- Develop a library of controls, where participants can select existing controls that mitigate their risk.

A helpful way of thinking about controls is by categorizing them into *Preventative*, *Directive*, *Detective* and *Corrective* types, as described in Figure 5.8.

- *Preventative* and *Directive* controls reduce the likelihood of risk materializing, by establishing processes which preclude the threat from happening, and clearly instructing employees to do the right things.

FIGURE 5.8   Control categorization

PREVENTATIVE	DETECTIVE
Prevent risk from happening **Examples:** Segregation of duties User access rights Client due diligence	Help to identify if risk has materialized **Examples:** Reconciliation Control testing & assurance Reviews
DIRECTIVE	**CORRECTIVE**
Provide guidance and direction on tasks and duties **Examples:** Policies Procedures Training	Ensure continuous improvement **Examples:** Implementation of Internal Audit recommendations Actions from OREs

Reduce Likelihood

Reduce Impact

FIGURE 5.9   Use of the bow-tie in RCSA process: controls

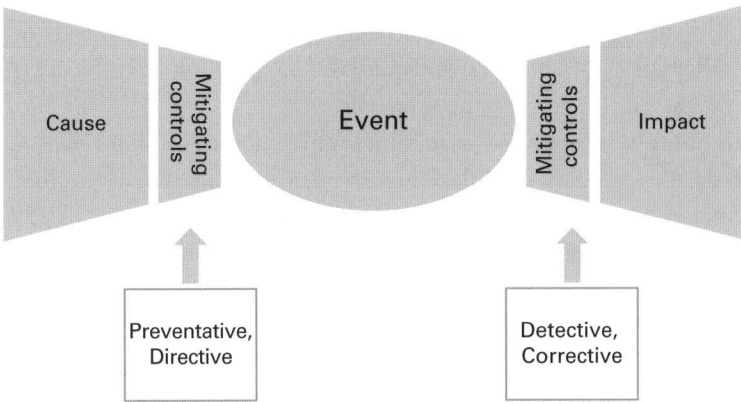

- *Detective* and *Corrective* controls decrease the impact, via prompt identification of deficiencies and speedy remediation, not allowing the impact to spread.

The distinction described above is reflected pictorially in Figure 5.9.

There is a clear relationship between the inherent and residual risk levels, which is directly dependent on the controls in place. If an inherent risk (say Risk 1, as depicted in Figure 5.10) is mitigated only by preventative or directive

FIGURE 5.10   Residual risk dependency on controls

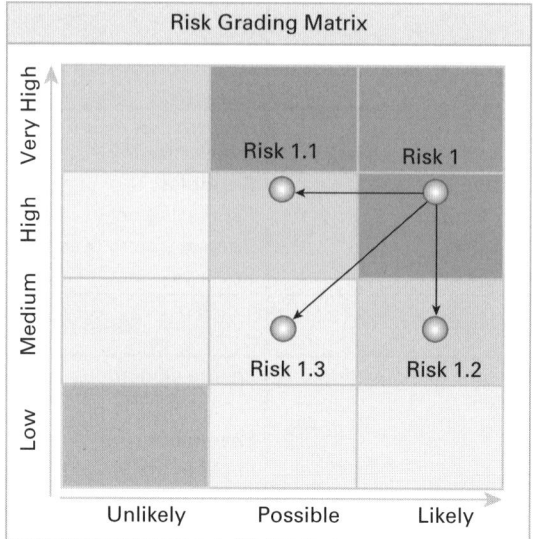

controls, that will reduce the likelihood of its occurrence, ie move the risk hori-zontally (left) along the heat map to assume residual position 1.1. Conversely, controls which are solely detective or corrective will only allow the risk to move vertically (downwards), decreasing its impact to a residual level of 1.2.

In order for the risk to move diagonally (to position 1.3), both types of controls have to be present and effective.

This point is important as sometimes inherent and residual risk levels are assessed independently and placed on the heat map in almost random posi-tions; not substantiated by mitigating controls.

RCSA encourages users to directly evaluate the controls that they oper-ate. If one of the key controls is owned by another function, it can still be included and relied on (with the agreement of the respective function). This is a good practice which prompts employees to collaborate and explore risk and control interconnectedness. For example, a business may own the risk of *inability to identify and implement new regulatory requirements on a timely basis*; and include its own controls as well as an additional regulatory horizon scanning control owned by the compliance function.

Control assessment

Assessment of controls establishes how effectively they are being imple-mented in practice, and therefore to what extent they reduce the level of inherent risk. There are two main methodologies for this form of assessment: either judgemental evaluation or factual testing.

JUDGEMENTAL EVALUATION

Evaluation involves subject matter experts opining on control effectiveness based on their knowledge and experience. The rating can be one-dimensional, for example 'effective', 'somewhat effective' or 'ineffective'. Or it can be carried out on a two-dimensional scale:

- *Control design*: this considers how well the control has been built to mitigate the risk; is it automated or manual, and does it mitigate the risk fully?

- *Control performance*: this considers how the control operates in practice, including the human element; whether employees are appropriately skilled and execute the task correctly, on the required frequency and to the expected quality standard.

Following evaluation of each control individually, it is beneficial to assess the *overall suite* of controls, considering whether in aggregate they provide a sufficient level of risk reduction. An ineffective overall control suite may reveal a missing control which needs to be considered in addition.

TESTING

Testing is a process which involves selecting a representative sample of control performances to establish how effectively the control is operating.

CASE STUDY 5.2

A private bank develops a control testing programme to periodically check the key controls that mitigate its most significant inherent risks. An example test programme plan is created, describing the risk, the control, the test plan and its frequency.

RISK TO APPROPRIATENESS AND SUITABILITY

Selling products that do not fit clients' risk appetite or investment profile, resulting in sales-related complaints.

CONTROL

Prior to conducting any trading or investments on a client's behalf, an investment risk profile is established, reflecting the client's investment objectives and risk appetite. This is agreed with the client and updated with the frequency required by policy.

TEST PLAN

Select a sample of 25 accounts opened during the last quarter, and ascertain the date of the first investment transaction from the system:

- review whether or not the investment risk profile is present in the client file and has been approved by the appropriate investment specialist;

- check that investment specialist's sign-off precedes the date of the first transaction, as identified above;

- select a sample of 15 existing customer account relationships and confirm that their investment profiles have been updated according to the frequency established by policy.

TEST FREQUENCY: QUARTERLY

The testing programme is approved and operated effectively by the institution. Use of test scripts with clear control objectives and defined sample sizes allow staff with no audit or risk background to perform effective testing in line with internal audit practices.

RCSA WORKSHOPS

RCSAs lend themselves well to workshops, which provide an opportunity to build on collective intelligence, debate ideas and challenge assessments. Workshops are usually arranged as a follow-up to individual interviews, where participants have already considered their risks and controls, thus laying a foundation for the joint meeting. They are, however, an expensive tool as they collect multiple senior people in the room for a period of time. Consequently, they require maximum preparedness, with clear messages on what is expected to be achieved, how the meeting will be run, and how long it will take. Good workshop organization includes inviting the respective *risk owners* for the whole duration of the meeting, while allocating specific time slots to discuss particular controls. Using this approach, *control owners* or subject matter experts (SMEs) – such as Human Resources for people-related controls or Technology for information technology-related matters – need only join for their allocated time slot. This saves SMEs time, makes the meeting more focussed and moves it along. Facilitation is a key skill which needs to be mastered by the workshop leader; this is discussed further in Chapter 11. Short, targeted meetings facilitated by expert operational risk teams are typically well received by attendees and this helps to achieve the desired outcomes.

RCSA life cycle and measures of success

The RCSA life cycle is presented below: the first two components, identification and assessment, have already been covered in this chapter:

- **Identify:** significant risks which may prevent the achievement of objectives are identified, together with the controls that mitigate them.

- **Assess:** risks and controls are evaluated using a defined methodology.

- **Conclude and act:** results are presented to achieve formal sign-off and agreement of action plans for any areas where controls are ineffective or insufficient to mitigate the risks.

- **Refresh:** RCSA is updated periodically or based on particular trigger events.

CONCLUDE AND ACT

To finalize the exercise, the executive owner is required to sign off that the RCSA is a true and fair reflection of the risk and control profile of their respective area; and most importantly, to consider the 'so what?' question, confirming actions and next steps. Presenting the results in a clear manner, with key messages and actions outlined, supports the conclusion. A meaningful report will contain an executive summary explaining the overall risk profile, whether it is elevated, has decreased or remained stable. It will also articulate key changes since the last assessment, outline the most significant risks, point out ineffective controls and articulate any necessary actions. This summary needs to be supported by additional data which has already been analysed in the preparatory pack as described earlier in the chapter: OREs, issues, audit and compliance findings need to correlate to key messages in the summary.

The main part of the report needs to contain a narrative which tells a story. This narrative can be supported by visual aids: for example, a heat map drawing attention to the most significant risks, or radar charts which are effective in pointing out risk and control relationships, highlighting risks as well as areas that may be overcontrolled. (See also Chapter 10, Operational Risk Reporting, for further ideas on meaningful, effective reporting.)

REFRESH

RCSA is a living document which needs to be kept current. This has historically been a challenge, and remains so. As noted by the ORX industry study, 'RCSAs are often out of date'.[9] Usually a periodic – eg semi-annual – refresh is combined with trigger-based updates. The trigger can be a material change to the business model, product set or organizational structure; anything that creates impetus to revisit an area's capability to continue delivering on its objectives given the change. A significant ORE that raises a question on control effectiveness, an external event or a major regulatory change can also serve as triggers. In the periodic refresh, it is worth following the same structure adopted in the main RCSA process: three questions, starting with seeking an understanding of what keeps the stakeholder *awake at night* at any given moment; aiming to elicit material changes since the last update.

The usual risk management life cycle is comprised of the components identify–assess–manage–report. So the valid question may arise: what about reporting? Monitoring and reporting of *top risks* is undertaken via Key Risk Indicators (KRIs), which are a suitable way to address these key components of the overall life cycle. This is discussed further in Chapter 7.

Measures of success

A continuous debate is under way in the industry on the effectiveness of RCSAs and whether they represent a truly useful tool or merely a tick-box exercise. Known benefits of a well-executed RCSA programme include the following:

- process optimization, enhanced operational resilience and a well-developed business-service mentality (where the PRSA methodology is used);
- sound strategy setting with a good understanding of risks (where SRA is used);
- evidenced support for senior management certifications and attestations;
- an improved control environment, through the identification of weaknesses and implementation of adequate corrective actions;
- documented agreement where risk is accepted and no further action is needed;
- positive cultural impacts: *risk conversations* encouraging risk thinking and elevating risk and control consciousness at all levels of the firm.

To support the value proposition of RCSA, it is a good practice to develop specific *measures of success*. These can include:

- RCSA as a driver of change: any actions emanating from the RCSA – ideally with the monetary value of any improvement projects initiated as a result of the programme – are good measures of how useful the exercise has been.

- RCSA as a driver of transparency around the risk and control environment. RCSA should minimize surprises in subsequent internal or external audit reviews, as material risks are already known and addressed. In view of this, the number of new or unknown significant risks identified by internal audit (perhaps as a percentage of the total number of risks), can be used as a tangible measure of RCSA effectiveness. Some firms use a Management Awareness Rating System (MARS), where internal audit provides two ratings, one on the audit result and a separate one on the effectiveness of self-identification of risks and issues.

- RCSA as a robust risk management tool: surveys can be used to gauge stakeholders' feedback, especially after the RCSA is introduced for the first time or following a change in approach. The questions can be centred around the value RCSA delivered, asking for an outline of the most significant benefit. They can also enquire about the overall stakeholder experience, as well as collect views on what has worked and what can be improved.

An industry study I conducted in 2018 demonstrated that very few organizations explicitly measure the success of their RCSAs, as outlined in Table 5.1.

TABLE 5.1 Industry study: measuring success of RCSAs

RCSA Measures of success	% Firms
No formal measures of success	72%
Actionability (number of emanating actions)	10%
Risk awareness (no surprises in audits)	22%
Other measures	5%

Institute of Operational Risk (IOR), 2018, webinar

Roles and responsibilities

The role of the second line Operational Risk department is key to the success of the RCSA programme. The department is responsible for developing the approach and methodology; educating stakeholders on the process and expected benefits; completing pre-work and being fully conversant with the area's environment; mastering facilitation skills; as well as providing the usual oversight and challenge on whether the outcome reflects and correctly represents the environment. Ultimately, the operational risk team is largely responsible for the success (or failure) of the initiative.

As *risk and control owners*, first line business units and support functions are accountable for the robust identification and management of risk. It is to their benefit to ensure that the exercise is taken seriously, that the right stakeholders are at the table and that the RCSA generates meaningful results. First line functions must develop action plans to address weak controls, and track them through to resolution. Where business units have embedded operational risk coordinators, they can take on the role of risk experts, interviewers and workshop facilitators – leading the whole RCSA exercise – as long as the right level of knowledge and skills have been transferred to them by the second line team.

Below is a risk coordinator checklist.

FIRST LINE RISK COORDINATOR CHECKLIST: RCSAs

✓ Management and staff can consistently articulate top risks of their area.

✓ OREs and other relevant data are used to inform RCSA.

✓ Action is taken to manage the risks and improve poor controls.

✓ There is process and governance around decision making. (What level of risk can be accepted? By whom?)

✓ RCSA is a living document and is refreshed with frequency set per policy and upon major change.

✓ RCSA results are used in decision making.

Common challenges and good practices

Common challenges

Challenges that may be encountered when designing and deploying risk and control self-assessments are outlined below.

STAKEHOLDERS NOT ENGAGED

RCSA is an up-front investment in understanding and improving the control environment to prevent potential risks materializing in the future. It is not always obvious to stakeholders why they should spend time *now* when nothing bad has happened (and may never happen). It is somewhat easier to spearhead the remediation of operational risk events, where the firm has already experienced unpleasant consequences; but more challenging to achieve the same level of engagement and interest in risk assessments. It is essential to have senior management, who are personally accountable for failures, fully involved in the process and fully conversant with the value proposition and the time commitment required. They should also ensure the scope of the exercise is explicitly agreed at the appropriate governance committee.

UNDERINVESTMENT IN RISK EXPERTISE

As can be seen from this chapter, it is the author's opinion that risk teams play a crucial role in the whole RCSA process. Although RCSA has the word *self* in its name, business units rarely, if at all, have the maturity and understanding to conduct self-assessments on their own, without expert support. They need guidance on the level of granularity to adopt; the correct formulation of what is a risk (and what is *not* a risk); assistance on how to approach impact-likelihood assessment; and a general understanding of what good looks like. Forms, questionnaires and requests to complete Excel spreadsheets are not effective: RCSA needs to be *facilitated by a knowledgeable individual*. Perhaps the tool needs to be renamed to RCFA, risk and control *facilitated* assessment.

To provide the required level of support, risk teams, both second and first line, should have extensive experience not only in the risk discipline itself but also in the softer skill of facilitation. Underinvestment in this skillset will lead to a situation where neither the leaders nor the followers really know what they are doing. The whole enterprise will undergo an expensive exercise that only results in sub-optimal outcomes.

DISPROPORTIONATE EFFORT

If the methodology is not fit for purpose, RCSAs may end up with hundreds and sometimes thousands of entries – emphasizing *quantity over quality* and quickly leading to organizational fatigue. While there is no accepted standard number of risks, a good RCSA will probably generate a range of 10 to 30 risks, with three key controls per risk. Not all risks need to be recorded; the focus should be on material items. It is good practice to work this guidance into the assessment, for example, recommending the capture of only *top* and *significant* inherent risks (see Figure 5.6) and carving out less important entries.

RCSA NOT ACTIONABLE

The RCSA is completed and filed, but no action emanates from the exercise due to an inability to draw conclusions, apathy or poor communication of the results. A study of industry practices conducted by ORX concluded that RCSA is 'not sufficiently influencing business decisions' and 'not enabling institutions to be as proactive on risk management as intended'.[10] A lack of tangible outcomes leads to questions about the value of the programme, and major effort should be put in to deriving clear, well-worded actions and next steps.

Good practices

CORRECT METHODOLOGY

RCSAs are typically applied across the whole organization and remain the most demanding, laborious and time-consuming of all the tools in the operational risk framework. Therefore, it is worth investing time and thought up-front into developing the right approach. It is recommended that the exercise only commences after a detailed research review of relevant literature; benchmarking against the industry; and discussion with fellow practitioners to draw out good practices. Allocating enough budget to obtain external advice and provide the necessary training for facilitators helps considerably in achieving the right outcomes.

IDENTIFICATION OF OVERCONTROLLED AREAS

As part of the RCSA exercise, it is good practice to focus on any areas that might be overcontrolled, in addition to searching for gaps and weaknesses. This not only provides a more balanced view on the control environment but also results in potential cost savings where unnecessary controls can be reduced or eliminated. This is a valuable activity that is not undertaken enough in the industry; control reduction may be an uncomfortable subject for both senior executives as well as for some risk practitioners.

REFLECTION OF OUTSOURCED ACTIVITIES

In cases where the organization outsources activities to a third party or another group entity, the risk is still owned by the entity and this should be fully recognized in the RCSA. For example, if the process of developing and maintaining credit models is performed by a third-party provider, the organization will need to reflect *outsourcing risk* (including third-party failure and inadequate oversight) as well as *model risk* (inaccurate design or implementation of models).

AGGREGATION

One of the common questions around RCSAs relates to aggregation. As articulated in this chapter, both *bottom-up* and *high-level* assessments are needed. High-level assessments are, effectively, judgemental summaries of more detailed results, using the collective intelligence of senior leaders across the organization. Executives arriving at the top-down workshops may take their existing granular RCSAs into consideration, enabling them to arrive at the entity- or firm-wide view, which will inevitably be more elevated and thematic. If the firm is not in the habit of conducting high-level assessments, the second line Operational Risk department can take on the role of aggregating RCSA outcomes itself. This process also needs to be judgemental, with due consideration of key themes and using the firm's taxonomy to report on the results.

ADDRESSING CULTURAL ASPECTS

Organizations with a good risk culture recognize the value of early identification and escalation of material risks and encourage transparency. Where it is perceived that assessments are overly positive – perhaps due to employees' fear of reprisals – oversight and challenge by the Operational Risk department can help to ensure the RCSA is calibrated correctly and that it delivers difficult messages if needed. Celebrating success – by sharing examples where action was taken to mitigate the risk – draws attention to the positive aspects of the RCSA and really reinforces and emphasizes the value of risk management.

EMBEDDING RISK THINKING

To ensure that risk assessments are properly embedded, business units and support functions can be encouraged to add a quick 'top of mind' risk identification exercise as part of their periodic departmental meetings. This can be accomplished by splitting employees into groups, with each group being asked to use a heat map to discuss what *keeps them awake at night* and comparing notes afterwards. Not only does this highlight true concerns, it also generates good risk conversations and exchanges of knowledge between employees. Similarly, an important activity that I lead every year via the Best Practice Operational Risk Forum is to benchmark top and emerging operational risks across the financial services industry. Practitioners from various firms are split in groups and use a simple heat map which invariably generates a lively debate and important outcomes.

Industry benchmark, 2019

'There's a way to do it better – find it': a quote attributed to Thomas Edison, the famous US inventor, when searching for his next discovery. It seems fitting to apply this philosophy to the perpetual topic of RCSAs, in line with the conclusions of the Best Practice Operational Risk Forum. The majority of practitioners participating in the live poll believe that their RCSA methodology could be improved (64 per cent, Figure 5.11), although some are in a better place, with the current methodology deemed either 'adequate' (12 per cent) or 'spot on' (12 per cent).

First line perception: value-add or time wasted?

First line business units and support functions seem to have embraced RCSAs and accepted that they are a necessity (45 per cent, see Figure 5.12): they help to manage risks, create transparency and demonstrate that reasonable steps have been taken to understand and control the environment.

How, though, to move people from the 'time-consuming' camp to 'value-add'? The success of this transition depends on the chosen approach, cultural

FIGURE 5.11   Industry poll: satisfaction with RCSA methodology

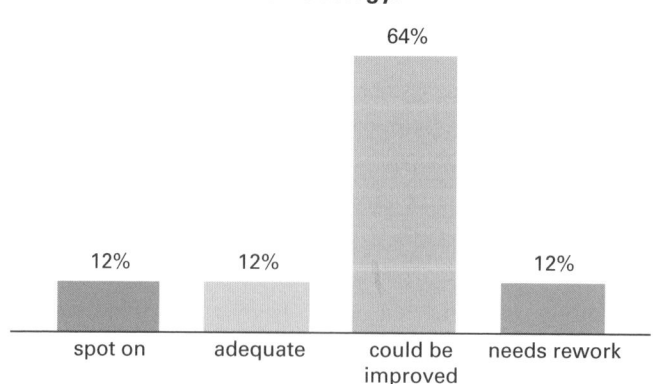

Satisfied with RCSA methodology?

Best Practice Operational Risk Forum, 2019

FIGURE 5.12 Industry poll: first line perception of RCSAs

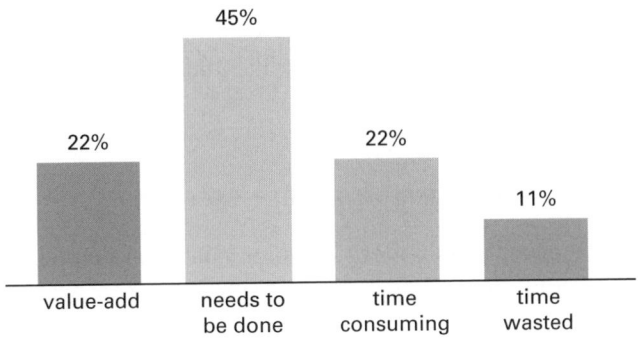

1st Line perceives RCSAs as

Best Practice Operational Risk Forum, 2019

aspects and organizational maturity. While there is no simple recipe, more positive outcomes can be delivered by creating a more effective value proposition, replacing templates with facilitated discussions, and focussing more clearly on actionability.

A favourite tool despite criticism?

Even so, RCSAs were the favourite pick out of all operational risk tools when it came to value-add, as seen in Figure 5.13. Practitioners ranked framework components in order of 'usefulness', and RCSAs were deemed the most impactful, interactive and engaging.

FIGURE 5.13 Industry poll: most valuable operational risk tools

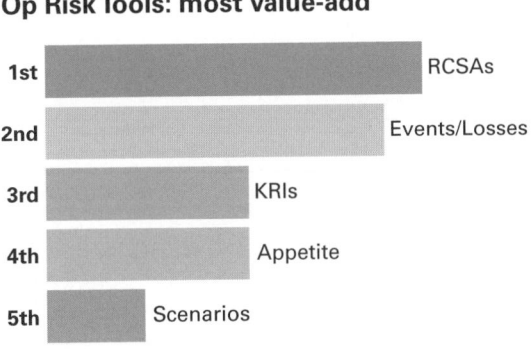

Op Risk Tools: most value-add

Best Practice Operational Risk Forum, 2019

In conclusion, while most firms have by now established an RCSA, according to the Basel Committee's findings, 'the tool was currently undergoing some form of change or enhancement'.[11] It is a process of trial and error. Hopefully, not too many attempts and methodological amendments will be needed before we collectively, as an industry, arrive at a way of conducting RCSAs that deliver both real value and positive stakeholder feedback.

Practical workplace exercise

Consider key concepts and ideas examined in this chapter. Obtain an example of the firm's RCSA, and review it, considering:

1 Is the organization conducting both top-down strategic and more granular assessments?

2 Considering the most significant operational risk events of the past year, were the risks that the event may occur identified *before* the event?

3 If risks were identified, were they documented in the RCSA?

4 How is the exercise perceived by stakeholders and are there formal measures of success in place for the RCSA exercise?

5 Make notes of RCSA features that you particularly like.

6 What can be improved? Note down potential enhancements.

MAKE A DIFFERENCE (MAD) ACTION

Please outline key learnings and note down one specific action you will take after reading this chapter, to enhance risk and control self-assessments within your organization.

In summary, this chapter introduced RCSAs, a forward-looking tool for identifying and assessing risks that may prevent threats to the achievement of the firm's objectives.

The next chapter will focus on a supplementary assessment methodology for change initiatives.

Notes

1 Operational Riskdata eXchange Association (ORX) (2020) *Optimizing Risk and Control Self-Assessment*, managingrisktogether.orx.org/sites/default/files/public/downloads/2020/01/orx_rcsa_practice_benchmark_summary_report.pdf (archived at https://perma.cc/8G3N-2HNG)

2 The Sarbanes–Oxley Act of 2002, www.sec.gov/about/laws/soa2002.pdf (archived at https://perma.cc/CK4A-P6K3)

3 Committee of Sponsoring Organizations of the Treadway Commission (2017) *Enterprise Risk Management: Integrating with strategy and performance*, www.coso.org (archived at https://perma.cc/L86L-5J2X) www.coso.org/Pages/ERM-Framework-Purchase.aspx (archived at https://perma.cc/6326-EM95)

4 Zeldin, T (1998) *Conversation: How talk can change your life*, The Harvill Press

5 World Economic Forum (2020) *The Global Risk Report 2020*, www.weforum.org (archived at https://perma.cc/WF89-74DD) www.weforum.org/reports/the-global-risks-report-2020 (archived at https://perma.cc/7JAY-YYWB)

6 The International Risk Governance Council (IRGC) *IRGC Guidelines for Emerging Risk Governance* (2015), irgc.org/risk-governance/emerging-risk/a-protocol-for-dealing-with-emerging-risks/ (archived at https://perma.cc/RCX9-CNGV)

7 Lloyds of London, www.lloyds.com/news-and-insights/risk-reports/emerging-risks-team/ (archived at https://perma.cc/T2K4-C2E3)

8 Committee of Sponsoring Organizations of the Treadway Commission (2013) *Internal Control: Integrated framework*, www.coso.org/Pages/ic.aspx (archived at https://perma.cc/34DH-P3SA)

9 Operational Riskdata eXchange Association (ORX) (2020) *Optimizing Risk and Control Self-Assessment*, managingrisktogether.orx.org/sites/default/files/public/downloads/2020/01/orx_rcsa_practice_benchmark_summary_report.pdf (archived at https://perma.cc/XA3P-W9DA)

10 Operational Riskdata eXchange Association (ORX) (2020) *Optimizing Risk and Control Self-Assessment*, managingrisktogether.orx.org/sites/default/files/public/downloads/2020/01/orx_rcsa_practice_benchmark_summary_report.pdf (archived at https://perma.cc/4ZGR-SKKS)

11 Basel Committee on Banking Supervision (2014) *Review of the Principles for the Sound Management of Operational Risk*, www.bis.org/publ/bcbs292.pdf (archived at https://perma.cc/JV6W-4CHQ)

06

Operational risk assessment
of change initiatives

What this chapter covers: This chapter continues discussion on the topic of risk assessments, outlining an approach to evaluating the risks associated with change initiatives (Figure 6.1). It is centred on the *Scope–Methodology–Integration* trilogy: defining the range of activities that benefit from further scrutiny; presenting techniques for conducting a *risks* and *opportunities* assessment; and considering how to effectively transition residual risks to a 'business-as-usual' (BAU) environment. The chapter analyses specific features of new product and system launches, projects and regulatory programmes; and highlights the value of post-implementation reviews. It includes examples, case studies and an industry benchmark.

FURTHER READING

- Helen Winter (2019) *The Business Analysis Handbook: Techniques and questions to deliver better business outcomes*, Kogan Page
  Why recommended: This book is valuable for learning about project management, including tools and techniques such as RAIDs (risks, assumptions, issues, dependencies) and process mapping, as well as waterfall/agile methodologies, in language that is engaging and easy to understand.

- Dr Spencer Johnson (1999) *Who Moved My Cheese? An amazing way to deal with change in your work and in your life*, Ebury Publishing
  Why recommended: An old-time favourite, this entertaining book on the crux of change management is a must-read for every risk practitioner. It is still widely read, by both individuals and teams, and especially during major corporate transformations.

FIGURE 6.1 Focus of Chapter 6: risk assessments

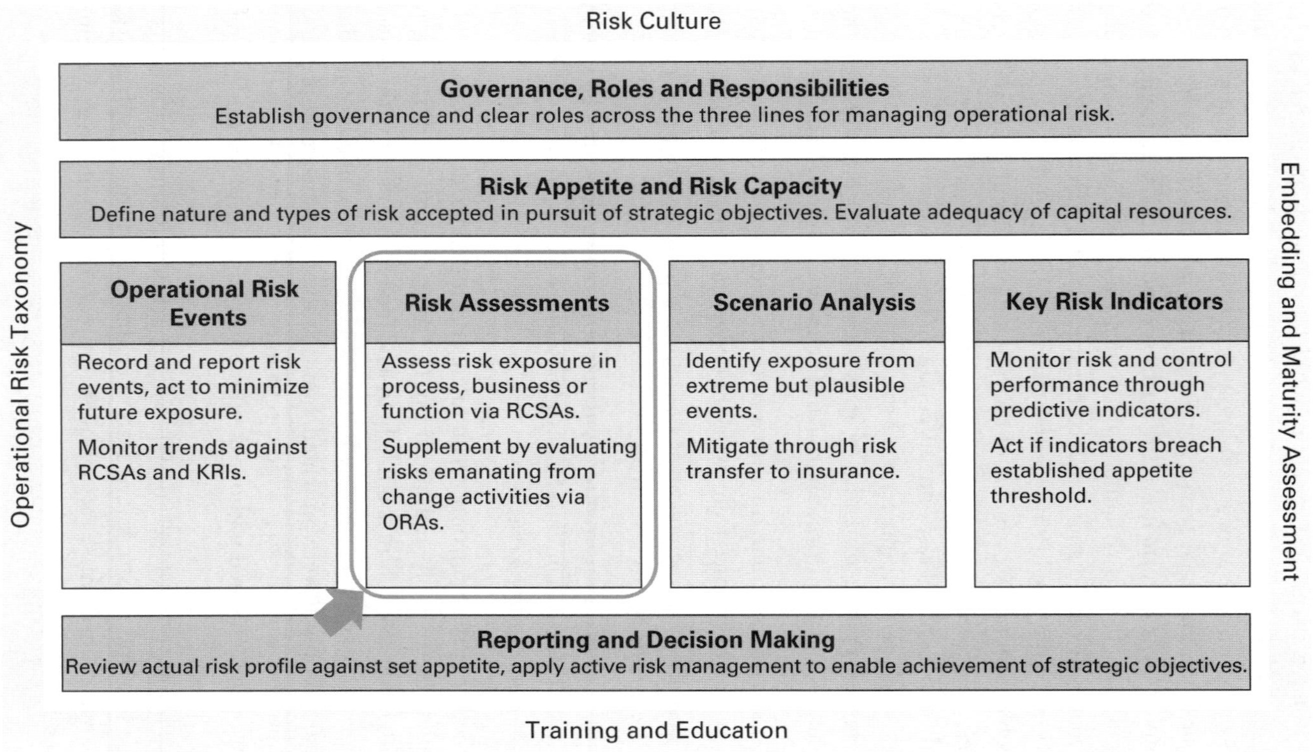

Embedding and Maturity Assessment

Governance, Roles and Responsibilities
Establish governance and clear roles across the three lines for managing operational risk.

Risk Appetite and Risk Capacity
Define nature and types of risk accepted in pursuit of strategic objectives. Evaluate adequacy of capital resources.

Operational Risk Events	Risk Assessments	Scenario Analysis	Key Risk Indicators
Record and report risk events, act to minimize future exposure.	Assess risk exposure in process, business or function via RCSAs.	Identify exposure from extreme but plausible events.	Monitor risk and control performance through predictive indicators.
Monitor trends against RCSAs and KRIs.	Supplement by evaluating risks emanating from change activities via ORAs.	Mitigate through risk transfer to insurance.	Act if indicators breach established appetite threshold.

Reporting and Decision Making
Review actual risk profile against set appetite, apply active risk management to enable achievement of strategic objectives.

Risk Culture

Operational Risk Taxonomy

Training and Education

Trilogy: Scope–Methodology–Integration

'Nothing is permanent except change.' This quote is attributed to Heraclitus, a Greek philosopher famous for proclaiming that change is the essence of the universe, and author of a well-known saying about not stepping into the same river twice. Financial services as an industry is characterized by an enormous amount of transformation, driven by technological advancements and new regulation. In this dynamic environment, are the risks inherent in change activities identified and managed consistently and effectively?

One of the Basel Principles for the sound management of operational risk evolves around assessments of operational risks for all 'new products, activities, processes and systems'.[1] According to the Basel Committee's survey, only two-thirds of respondents conducted such assessments; a rather meagre uptake given the importance of this principle.[2]

Indeed, the sheer breadth of firms' change agenda often hinders the implementation of a uniform approach. The most common challenges include:

- a struggle to come up with a *holistic definition* of change, which results in the governance framework not covering all types of initiatives;

- decentralized management of change activities, resulting in *inconsistent treatment* across initiatives;

- sub-optimal transition to a *business-as-usual* state, with a lack of monitoring of risks emanating from the initiatives and an absence of formal *post-implementation reviews.*

Whether challenging or not, conducting operational risk assessment of change initiatives is simply and intuitively the right thing to do. Drawing parallels with credit risk, a firm is unlikely to lend money to a client without evaluating their creditworthiness: any governance committee would look in disbelief if such a proposal were presented. Similarly, major change to a process, system or product is prone to a wide spectrum of operational risks, and simply must not be implemented without the full understanding of the underlying risks it may pose.

The role of the Operational Risk department in this area is instrumental. The function must take the lead in enabling the firm to apply a risk lens to change programmes, raising questions centred around three main topics, presented in Figure 6.2.

FIGURE 6.2 Trilogy: Scope–Methodology–Integration

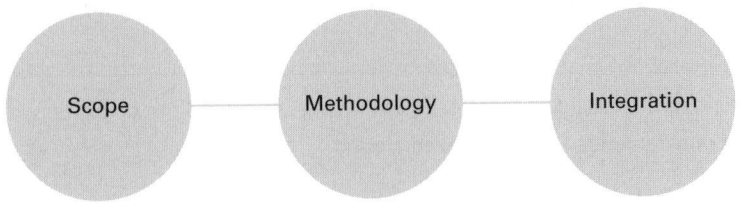

OPERATIONAL RISK FOCUS ON CHANGE INITIATIVES INCLUDES:

- *scope:* how to identify those activities that require an operational risk assessment (ORA);
- *methodology:* what tools are best suited to assess the risks emanating from the initiative; and
- *integration:* how to transition risks and their ownership into a business-as-usual environment on completion of the programme.

Identifying risky change activities

Change activities consist of a vast variety of events, including, for example:

- new product launches;
- system upgrades;
- relocation to a new building;
- payments process optimization;
- reorganization leading to offshoring of tasks to another location;
- implementation of a new regulatory requirement.

Every business/function within an organization will inevitably be managing a pipeline of projects. Among this sea of initiatives there could be a handful of potentially *riskier* programmes which could have significant impact outside the firm's appetite, and therefore would really benefit from increased scrutiny.

The role of the operational risk team is to develop criteria that enable a wide net to be cast to capture those activities that are more material and potentially more risky, ensuring that they undergo an ORA. This process is more powerful if done in close collaboration with project management functions (where they exist), to jointly agree on the most suitable approach.

Criteria for material and therefore *riskier* change initiatives can be expressed via a set of parameters that are centred around:

- *criticality* of business processes impacted by the change (see Chapter 14, Operational Resilience);

- *novelty*, eg whether the activity is business-as-usual or a new market or product; the less familiar the territory, the higher the risk;

- *scale/magnitude*, eg duration, resources, spend, number of impacted areas;

- *urgency*, considering whether implementation is being rushed through and therefore poses higher risk; and

- *complexity* of requirements, eg a new regulatory directive.

As an alternative, the determination can be also made using a more guided scorecard approach. This consists of developing a set of questions with predefined responses that have a score assigned to them. The overall sum of individual scores serves as a guide to suggest what category the change falls under – whether minor or material – thereby providing a triage mechanism. Examples of questions that can appear in the scorecard are presented in Table 6.1.

TABLE 6.1 Scorecard approach for assessing materiality of change initiative

Theme	Criteria	Score
Operational Resilience	Will the change pose a threat to operational resilience?	Score 1: No new system development; a minor process or people change in a non-critical business process
		Score 3: Limited system development, use of spreadsheets or other user-developed applications (also called *end-user computing* (EUC) applications); moderate process or organizational change in a non-critical business process
		Score 5: Significant system development, reorganization or process transformation; any change activity impacting a critical business process; or one requiring new or amended business continuity arrangements in a non-critical business.

(continued)

TABLE 6.1 (Continued)

Theme	Criteria	Score
Outsourcing	Does the change involve outsourcing of all or part of the activities?	Score 1: No outsourcing Score 3: Limited change to the scope of existing outsourcing arrangement Score 5: Material new third-party or inter-group relationship
Data	Does the change involve processing of personal or sensitive information?	Score 1: No change to data processing Score 3: Moderate impact to a limited scope of internal use data only Score 5: A change to processing personal and/or sensitive information
Regulatory Compliance	Is there a risk of regulatory non-compliance?	Score 1: No regulatory impact Score 3: Potential limited fines for non-conformance Score 5: Regulatory-driven initiative with substantial fines or other penalties for non-compliance

In any approach, it is not possible to cover all the idiosyncrasies of every change. Business units and support functions need to apply common sense to identify activities that may have material impact on the risk profile of the organization.

Methodology: risks and opportunities assessment

ORA DEFINITION

The operational risk assessment (ORA) of change activity evaluates the risks emanating from the activity; which enables the relevant governance committee to take an informed Go/No-Go decision on its implementation.

Unlike RCSAs, as discussed in Chapter 5, ORAs are temporary and valid only for the duration of the initiative, leading to its implementation. After this they cease to exist, with any remaining risks being transitioned to business-as-usual. They are also linked directly to a specific decision requiring action. Therefore, while ORAs have some similarities with RCSAs, they also possess distinct features, as discussed in this chapter.

ORA IS A SHORTENED FORM OF RCSA:

- inherent risks are identified and evaluated in a similar manner;

- no control assessment takes place due to the activity being in a *transitional/ project* mode; instead, actions to reduce the level of inherent risk throughout the duration of the programme are noted; and

- residual risk levels, anticipated after the completion of intended actions, are recorded.

Analogously to the RCSA, the ORA is ideally conducted via a cross-functional workshop with subject matter experts, facilitated by a skilled operational risk professional. The facilitator leads the discussion, drawing out the significant risks of the change activity. To ensure a consistent approach across the organization, the same risk grading matrix introduced for RCSAs (see Chapter 5, Figure 5.6) should also be applied for ORAs. This familiar matrix prompts consideration of impact and likelihood, providing uniformity not only to the approach, but also to the meaning of the risk levels, from *low* to *high*.

Two potential methodological enhancements are described below:

1 First, some initiatives, for example new products, are prone to credit, market, strategic, business and other risks. The coverage of the assessment can be *expanded* to a broader universe of threats, beyond operational, providing a rounded, all-encompassing view. This provides a perfect opportunity for operational risk professionals to exhibit their facilitation skills and, at the same time, increase their exposure to a wider universe of risks.

2 Second, the evaluation can be enriched by supplementing the 'risks' view with the mirror view of 'opportunities'.

Risks and Opportunities assessment aims to create a balanced view of threats and benefits, emphasizing the positive aspects of risk management.

EXAMPLE ORA

The firm is evaluating a new proposition which includes the use of artificial intelligence (AI) for providing personalized insights to clients based on their transactional history.

Identified risks include:

- AI displacing workforce;
- software failure or glitches impacting performance;
- risk of poor machine conduct, resulting in inadequate or discriminatory advice;
- inappropriate use of data leading to potential privacy breaches;
- cyber risk: the probability of cyber incidents occurring and their impact.

Opportunities include:

- speed and efficiency;
- availability of advice 24/7;
- enhanced quality of insight based on data analysis;
- cost reduction.

Risks and opportunities are plotted on a double-sided heat map (see Figure 6.3) for an assessment of the threats and opportunities landscape and to help prioritize areas of focus. Can opportunities be maximized? Risks reduced? The purpose of the workshop with subject matter experts is to establish a consistent approach to the risk assessment and build on combined knowledge.

Following the exercise, detailed focus groups are established to further explore material risks, as well as opportunities.

FIGURE 6.3 Risks and opportunities matrix

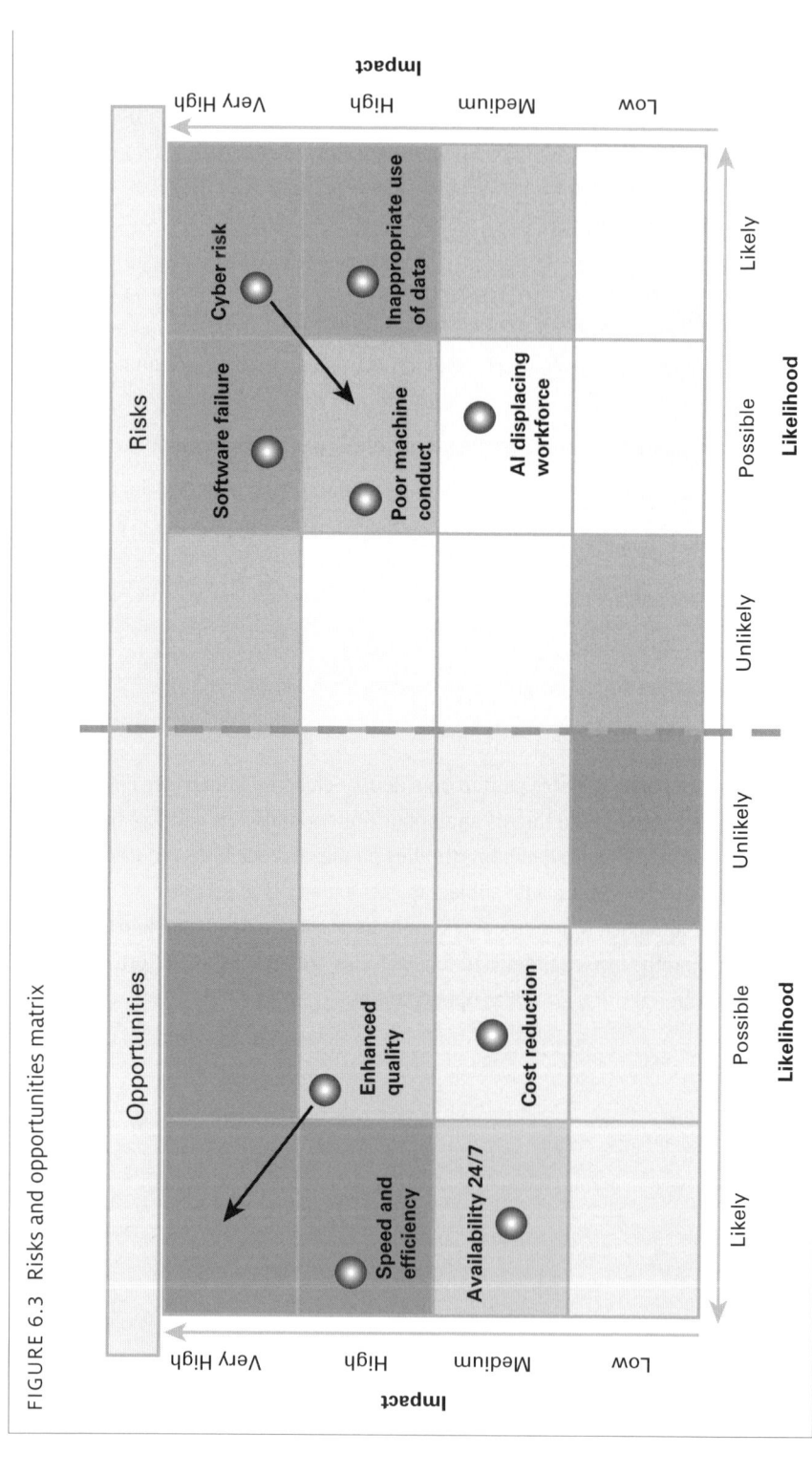

The opportunity assessment can be undertaken when evaluating business prospects, products, ventures and processes. In fact, it is suitable for a balanced appraisal of any change activity. It reinforces *positive risk management*, an enabler not a show stopper, assisting business units to arrive at an honest picture of threats and benefits in order to weigh them up and take a prudent, risk-aware decision. In reality, the view that recognizes both risks and opportunities is not given enough airtime. The Risk department, like a gloomy critic, is often in the habit of highlighting the negatives and missing the positives. In a live poll conducted by the Best Practice Operational Risk Forum in 2020, less than half of respondents admitted to having a structured approach to identifying and evaluating the upside of risk.

When is the best time to perform an ORA? Ideally, at the inception of the product/process development, enabling valuable conversations around risks and opportunities to take place in a structured manner. This remains an industry challenge. On occasions, business units work on a new proposition for months before reaching a decision, with the operational risk function neither aware of the proposal nor present at the table. The risk assessment is then hastily completed at the end, to satisfy governance requirements, which devalues the process.

What steps should be followed to enact the ORA more meaningfully, ensuring that it takes place at the right time and in a disciplined manner?:

- Start with senior management education: outline the value of a clear articulation of risks and opportunities to help them reach a Go/No-Go decision.
- Provide broader education for relevant staff and first line champions: to help embed the use of the ORA tool, list examples and illustrate successful programmes where evaluation helped to identify significant risks.
- Where change activity is overseen by a central governance committee, work in close partnership with the secretariat responsible for assembling committee papers; this will ensure that requests submitted without a completed ORA are caught on a timely basis and returned to the respective business/ function.
- For decentralized activities – for example, process changes and reorganizations – collaborate with first line champions to facilitate implementation within their respective areas.

It is also useful to understand the overall landscape of change activities within the organization. The result can be documented in an inventory, an example of which is presented in Table 6.2.

TABLE 6.2 Example change landscape

No	Type of Change Activity	Materiality threshold?	Governance Committee?	Committee name	Policy in place?	Policy name
1	New Products	Yes	Yes	NPA Committee	Yes	NPA Policy
2	System Changes	Yes	Yes	IT Change	Yes	IT Change Management
3	Projects	No	No	–	Yes	Project Management
4	Regulatory Programmes	No	Yes	Regulatory Programmes Oversight Committee	No	–
5	Process Changes	No	No	–	No	–

This inventory will demonstrate that some initiatives, for example, new products, may already have set criteria to define *new* or *materially different* products, and are executed in a structured manner, with a dedicated policy and a governance committee. Others, for example, process changes, do not apply any notion of materiality, and are completely decentralized and implemented by each department in its own way.

To further illustrate the point, various types of change activities and their specific features are analysed below. (Note, the final part of the trilogy Scope–Methodology–Integration is covered later in the chapter as part of the change life cycle.)

Change activities and their features

New products

New Product Approval (NPA) is a process through which an organization channels new products or customer propositions, ensuring that rigorous review and sign-off take place prior to the product launch. In many organizations this process is relatively well-established and contains the following features:

- *Clear scope:* a definition of what constitutes a *new* and/or *significantly modified* product, thus capturing all initiatives that fall under the policy and providing a perfect trigger for an operational risk assessment. Where this is the case, no additional criteria or scoring are needed.
- *Central governance committee* that ultimately makes a Go/No-Go decision.
- *Defined roles* of product sponsor and *cross-functional reviewers* from operations, technology, finance, compliance and other functions, enabling a comprehensive and multifaceted product evaluation.

Compared to other change activities, NPA usually works like a well-oiled machine, with propositions going through defined steps, one of which is an ORA. Stakeholders are bound and energized by the same goal of getting the product launched. They have interest in achieving success, and a risk assessment to help the team identify and mitigate the risks of their *own* initiative is usually well received. A real measure of success is to have product owners *want* their projects to be evaluated, demonstrating their understanding of the value and benefits of prudent risk management.

System changes

System enhancements deserve special attention because of the fact that change management is cited as the number one root cause of technology outages and a threat to operational resilience.[3]

Information Technology (IT) departments commonly have their own change management processes and categorizations of activities. The challenge is one of alignment. It is imperative for operational risk experts to work closely with IT colleagues to agree on what constitutes a material change. The criteria should not be skewed towards purely system considerations but should also extend to financial, client, regulatory and reputational impacts.

In contrast to new products, system enhancements employ a fair amount of technical jargon; this can result in stakeholders who are less IT-savvy becoming disengaged and the change being typically assessed and implemented by the Technology department itself. In contrast to NPA governance, this means that at times there is either no or minimal cross-functional review and sign-off of IT changes, despite the undoubted value in involving business units and support functions – the actual users of the technological solutions. Successful IT functions present their initiatives in simple language, explaining potential implications, encouraging dialogue and maximizing input from other departments.

CASE STUDY 6.1

In close collaboration with a business unit, the IT department is planning a system upgrade which will result in superior product features to the benefit of the clients. The change is regarded as *material* and triggers an ORA.

The operational risk team is facilitating a cross-functional workshop, and in addition to more common risks of *significant system failure* and *inadequate business continuity arrangements*, the risk of *unfair customer treatment* is raised. This emanates from an exception included in the small print of the product documentation. A particular customer segment has been excluded from the proposition, and the group questions whether as a result these customers may unfairly lose out on the service. This scenario has simply not been considered: the main reason provided is the clients' accounts of the excluded segment reside on a different, older platform which is becoming obsolete and therefore any upgrades are out of scope.

As a result of the discussion, the programme objective is amended to find appropriate solutions and make the offer available to all client groups.

This case study demonstrates the value of proper cross-functional risk conversations. Accomplished operational risk practitioners thrive on facilitating workshops with varied audiences, thinking out of the box and pulling out key risks, including the less obvious risks as well as the more common ones. Workshop facilitation is also addressed in Chapter 11, Operational Risk Training and Education.

Additional challenges with system changes are related to the firm's culture, especially in matrix organizations where the IT department is set goals on a different basis than the rest of the organization. In an agile environment, this translates into IT work prioritization being at variance with the project manager's needs and expectations. Operational Risk has a role to play in ensuring that the ordering principles applied in the technology pipeline are appropriate; and that there is adequate governance in prioritizing, for example, regulatory requirements and business growth initiatives. Where the ranking of IT change activity conflicts with project requirements, it is important that the organization has effective conflict resolution mechanisms, with quick escalation so that decisions can be made by senior management.

Emergency upgrades deserve a special mention. In these cases, urgency is already embedded in the name, and consequently these implementations are risky by nature. There may not be time for a fully documented ORA, but a formal recognition of material risks, followed by a post-upgrade review, is essential for emergency upgrades. This ensures that the Technology department will not flick the switch without citing approvals from the key stakeholders.

Projects

Project managers may argue that they are already managing risks by using the RAIDs (risks, assumptions, issues and dependencies) concept which is a core part of project management methodology. However, operational risk management can still bring distinct value to this domain. The two disciplines are complementary. Experts running change initiatives are, naturally, mostly focussed on the risks to the programme itself: the risks of not being on time or within budget, or of not delivering to the required specification. This is consistent with the definition of project risk used by the Project Management Institute: 'An uncertain event or condition that, if it occurs, has a positive or negative effect on one or more project objectives such as scope, schedule, cost and quality'.[4]

ORA will supplement this by bringing out the operational risks *inherent in the programmes*.

CASE STUDY 6.2

Due to a change in its business model, a corporate bank is planning to transition multiple customer accounts from one entity to another. A multi-year project is initiated, led by the central Programme Office.

Throughout the duration of the project, the risks of not delivering on time, on budget, or failing to execute client transition seamlessly are rigorously identified and tracked via a central RAID log. Due to the magnitude of the programme, an ORA is also carried out and facilitated by the Operational Risk department. The assessment examines a range of risks and highlights an increased risk of external as well as internal fraud. Clients may be targeted by fraudsters during a mass change in account numbers; while employees may find the environment prime for unauthorized activity.

The ORA triggers further examination of these risks and a review of the overall internal control environment.

This case study reflects the complementary nature of the ORA and project RAIDs. And yet again, it highlights the significance of risk conversations facilitated by expert facilitators.

The traditional project methodology, also sometimes known as a water-fall approach, involves a sequential process of 'defining requirements before design starts, then design being completed before development starts'.[5] From a risk management perspective, these projects are easier to manage due to the fact that they involve robust governance, impact assessment and sign-offs at each stage prior to proceeding to the next stage.

More and more organizations are however moving to an agile environment. Agile projects apply an iterative approach, with teams working in parallel, delivering in increments and collaborating to evolve the design over time. This flexible methodology is based on self-organized teams, motivated individuals and face-to-face conversations, welcoming 'changing requirements, even late in development'.[6] From an operational risk perspective, agile projects pose more challenge compared to waterfall projects, simply due to their fluidity.

> Embedding operational risk specialists into agile teams is the ideal way of ensuring that *risk conversations* take place throughout an agile programme.

This does, however, place a high demand on risk resource, be it first or second line.

Agile environments also embrace the concept of a Minimum Viable Product (MVP), a product which meets the basic design features and requirements but does not have all the bells and whistles that may be developed subsequently. By definition, an MVP may have limitations which create risks. It is essential that these risks are appropriately assessed to determine whether the limitation is acceptable against the overall risk appetite. For example, perhaps an MVP does not have a reporting capability which limits the performance management of a product; or regulatory reporting must be completed manually, leading to impacts (including errors and penalties) which are potentially outside the firm's appetite.

Regulatory programmes

JWG, a pioneering market intelligence company, performed the interesting exercise of counting the total number of pages of new regulation and estimating the height of the pile if they were stacked on top of each other. They noted that 'since the financial crisis, we have been gifted over two Eiffel

Towers high worth of complex and costly financial regulation, ever increasing in quantity and intricacy'.[7] Needless to say, then, a large proportion of transformation is driven by regulation.

These regulatory change programmes are inherently risky. Countless examples of substantial supervisory fines demonstrate how easy it is to end up with inadequate implementation.

The key challenge of regulatory programmes evolves around the interpretation of voluminous technical texts, spanning hundreds of pages, into practical implementation. Among other things this interpretation process needs to point out which specific field in the system needs to be amended and how. Is the organization crystal clear on who is taking this decision? It may be assumed that this is the role of the compliance function. Compliance, however, will argue that they can recite the letter and the spirit of the regulation, but that it is up to business users, with their in-depth knowledge of the business process, to take the right decision. Assumptions will be made, and the best judgement of project participants will be accepted as the way forward. In these situations, ORAs are needed more than ever, to articulate the risks, including any uncertainty around the correctness of the application together with an assessment of the magnitude of its impact. However, this requires a level of maturity where *all* employees are sufficiently conversant with risk management concepts and tools to pause the discussion at the right point, in order to recognize and document the risks. Rarely is an organization this advanced. The path to success is in firm-wide education; and in the meantime, yet again, in embedding operational risk practitioners into major regulatory programmes, to facilitate *risk conversations*. Even this is often challenging, due to the scarcity of resource.

As an example, the Markets in Financial Instruments Directive (MiFID II), a complex piece of legislation, led to big changes in the structure and operating model for trading, treasury and support functions, and involved significant decisions being taken by project teams. In 2017, prior to the directive going live, I led an industry study to understand the extent to which operational risk professionals were party to the programme. This study revealed that in the majority of firms the project was run by compliance; and over half of operational risk practitioners admitted to having little or no involvement. A third of the group were members of the relevant governance committees, providing oversight at a high level; but only a minority were actively engaged facilitating ORAs. As part of the study, the group concluded that it was key for operational risk staff to get more involved in major initiatives of this kind; however, this inevitably clashed with other priorities.

For complex regulatory directives, multiple ORAs may be executed for logical sub-parts of the programme. As an example, MiFID II and the Global Data Protection Regulation (GDPR) generated a range of 10 to 20 separate ORAs, allowing the assessments to cover a wide range of the programme. In complex cases the process is iterative for each ORA, with an assessment conducted at inception and subsequently amended in the event of significant change to any of the parameters.

Process changes

This is the least homogeneous of all the change areas, and the one where clear criteria on what constitutes a *material* change is most needed. One way of handling process transformations is by extending existing governance – for example, NPA – to accommodate a broader set of initiatives, thereby ensuring the same rigour is applied to process changes, organizational changes, restructuring and others. In this way the NPA committee upgrades itself to NPCA – the New Product and *Change* Approval committee. In other cases, organizations create a separate material change committee. Most firms, however, do not apply consistent governance in this area. The lead from the Operational Risk department is absolutely essential, initiating the development of a set of parameters and embedding the discipline of risk assessing process changes.

Change assessment life cycle

The change risk assessment process life cycle is described below:

- **Scope:** a clear set of parameters is agreed in order to capture activities that require an operational risk assessment.
- **Assess:** a practice of risk assessing material change initiatives is adopted firm-wide.
- **Integrate:** a hand-over process is set up to transition residual risks into the BAU environment.
- **Check:** post-implementation reviews are conducted to evaluate success and derive lessons learned.
- **Aggregate** and **Monitor:** the overall impact of multiple transformations on the risk profile of the firm is assessed and monitored via Key Risk Indicators.

The first stage (scope), describing the parameters which differentiate significant initiatives, was covered at the beginning of this chapter.

Assess

As outlined earlier, ORA is a simple yet effective way of evaluating the risks of change initiatives, using the already-familiar risk grading matrix. Are there alternatives to ORAs, and what other approaches exist for dealing with change risks?:

- Where ORA is not used, the change may serve as a trigger to revisit an existing risk and control self-assessment. While this approach is plausible, it does not lend itself well to the transient nature of the change.

- Scenario analysis can be conducted to examine extreme outcomes. This tool is supplementary rather than primary as it does not deal with volume – it is neither feasible nor necessary to run scenarios for each material change.

- There may be no specific assessment, but instead stepped governance, implemented based on the scale of the activity. This increases the level of scrutiny, but does not provide a structured approach to identifying and assessing risks.

Integrate

Integration is another key step in the *Scope–Methodology–Integration* trilogy. While change programmes are live, they attract attention, energy and rigour. We have all witnessed the decline that is triggered when project teams are disbanded, people leave and in-depth knowledge departs with them. It is vital to ensure transition not only of the relevant expertise, but also of any residual risks that have been flagged and not closed during the risk assessment stage.

Material residual risks not mitigated during the change programme must be formally handed over to the new business-as-usual owner, with the transfer being cemented by a sign-off from the recipient. The change activity cannot be considered complete without this sign-off.

The hand-over of risks is executed via transitioning a completed ORA to the now-accountable head of the business unit or support function. Challenges may arise at this stage if, during the programme, identified risks were assigned to a project resource – potentially not the owner who is best placed to understand, mitigate and treat them holistically. It is always advisable to involve BAU usual teams in the change activity from the beginning. Engagement and regular updates will ensure full proficiency in and agreement with the amended processes and controls; as well as the risks that the BAU team may need to manage in the future.

One possible solution is for the BAU risk owner to formally accept the residual risks of the initiative prior to going live, thereby acknowledging that these risks will now be managed as part of the business's overall portfolio of risks.

Check

Post-implementation reviews (PIRs) have multiple aims. Firstly, a PIR evaluates how effectively the project, programme or activity was run and what lessons can be derived for the future. Secondly, it determines whether initial objectives were met; for example, for new products, it allows comparison of actual volumes to forecasts, and an assessment of profitability and customer feedback. And finally, PIRs provide a great opportunity to do a *deep dive* into the control environment. If significant risks were identified during the initial risk assessment, the reviewer can cast a critical eye over the performance and quality of the controls that mitigate these risks. The latter element is rarely in scope and not considered nearly enough; yet, for regulatory programmes, for example, it provides an opportunity to ensure that controls are still operating as originally intended and that the operating environment has not deteriorated subsequently.

Post-implementation reviews are commonly conducted within three to nine months of the change. Sometimes they can be followed by an additional long-term review, within two years of completion of the change. PIRs can also be triggered by an increased incidence of operational risk events, signalling that transition to a BAU state has not been smooth.

Not all activities require a PIR. New products and regulatory programmes, however, are among those that most benefit from the look-back and re-evaluation that a PIR provides. It is also worth testing a sample of change initiatives that were not in scope of the initial risk assessment, to determine whether they actually should have been included. This acts as a deterrent against change owners understating the scale of the change to avoid review.

Aggregate and monitor

The aggregation step aims to assess the overall impact of multiple simultaneous initiatives and to evaluate whether the firm's *change risk* is elevated beyond its appetite. Various approaches are possible to achieve this:

- The most common consolidation is based on an inventory of initiatives in flight, prepared by a central change management function (if such a function exists within the organization). An appropriate governance committee reviews the list noting pressure points, including dependencies on key personnel, to weigh up whether the firm can cope effectively with the change portfolio. This results in a judgemental assessment of whether the overall impact of multiple transformations is tolerable.

- Another option is to add a *change risk* category into the operational risk taxonomy. As discussed in Chapter 1, the question of whether *change risk* is a distinct risk type or a cause of other risks crystallizing is an active debate, which has split opinion in the industry. If a separate category is used, functions can highlight the raised risk levels in their respective RCSAs, which can then be aggregated later.

- A final option is to perform a trigger-based review, via analysis of operational risk events and their root causes. An increase in the number and/or value of risk events with the same root cause (ie an excessive change agenda) will signal that immediate focus is required. While this kind of review is somewhat beneficial, it is a rather reactive approach.

Presented below are examples of key risk indicators that can be useful for evaluating various aspects of change:

KRI1: *Change risk* – the percentage of overdue and at-risk projects within the active project portfolio. The KRI reflects on the overall health of the portfolio, monitoring the ratio of struggling programmes vs those that are on track.

KRI2: *Transition to business-as-usual* – the number of change activities where post-implementation reviews highlighted material issues. PIRs are used to measure the success of project discipline and the metric tracks unsuccessful and poorly implemented projects.

KRI3: *Risk assessments* – the number of material change activities in scope without a completed ORA. This metric is related to cultural aspects of the firm, and monitors compliance with the set process to ensure that change projects undergo a risk assessment.

Further KRI examples are discussed in Chapter 7, Key Risk Indicators.

Roles and responsibilities

Second line Operational Risk departments are the masterminds behind the change risk assessment methodology, working closely with relevant stakeholders – be they project, product or other teams – to ensure that ORA is integrated into business practices. Effective collaboration enables a firm to find the right solutions that are appropriate to the size, nature and culture of the organization. Operational Risk department provides training and education for first line business units and support functions, and facilitates workshops. It is also the role of the department to oversee and challenge material initiatives, ensuring that the level of risk is commensurate with the activity, and reporting on the aggregate level of change risk to the relevant governance committees.

First line business units and support functions own the risks and are ultimately accountable for the success or failure of their initiatives. They are responsible for identifying material projects and programmes that fall within the set criteria, and for conducting ORAs as required. Where there are embedded first line operational risk champions, they help considerably in spreading knowledge and can serve as advisors and facilitators when it comes to ORAs.

A first line risk coordinator checklist can be found in the following box.

FIRST LINE RISK COORDINATOR CHECKLIST: ORAs

✓ Staff are aware of policy and governance for change activities.

✓ Change initiatives are evaluated according to the set criteria to define their materiality.

✓ ORA is completed for *material* change initiatives.

✓ Risks and opportunities are considered to arrive at a balanced view.

✓ Upon completion, remaining residual risks are transitioned to business-as-usual state in a disciplined manner.

✓ Post-implementation reviews are conducted.

Common challenges and good practices

Common challenges

Potential hurdles when dealing with change risk assessments are presented below.

UNBALANCED GOALS AND OBJECTIVES

Cultural challenges may arise when business goals are weighted so heavily towards growth and efficiency that product and change owners are not incentivized to ensure that the control environment is appropriate to the risk that is being taken on. They may not necessarily see the review process as beneficial, rather as a necessary stage or even a hindrance to their project, and may refuse to jump through the approval hoops. The right tone at the top and balanced business goals that reflect the risk appetite of the organization help to address this challenge.

LACK OF TRANSPARENCY FROM CHANGE SPONSOR

By the same token, if a risk-based approach is adopted for conducting ORAs for *riskier* initiatives, it is important to ensure that the sponsor provides a full perspective on the proposition so that it is not understated and as a result falls below the review threshold. This is a concern particularly if the owner does not see the review as beneficial or adding value.

RELUCTANCE TO COMPLETE THE ORA

Business units and support functions may be reluctant to complete an ORA, reasoning that they do not have capacity and in any case that the review is a bureaucratic step which will not highlight anything new. The best way to convert the sceptics is to identify true risks that were missed or not thought of. Presenting past success stories, demonstrating that the Operational Risk department can skilfully lead discussions, facilitating workshops and lending your own expertise also help to change sceptical attitudes.

INCORRECT ROLES AND RESPONSIBILITIES

It is widely deemed to be the role of the operational risk team to complete the ORA. The Basel Committee noted this paradox in its survey,[8] emphasizing that actually first line business units and support functions are responsible for identifying and managing their *own* risks. Operational risk is a powerful facilitation partner but is not the owner (see also Chapter 3 highlighting roles and responsibilities of the three lines).

CRITERIA NOT FIT FOR PURPOSE

When the criteria for what constitutes a *material* change initiative are set too low, the exercise becomes a formality, a tick-box template. This can cause the business, as well as the Operational Risk department, to be overwhelmed by numerous unnecessary assessments. Using sound judgement helps to correctly calibrate the parameters and align the ORAs with the risk appetite of the organization.

SUB-OPTIMAL TRANSITION TO BUSINESS-AS-USUAL

Sometimes, transition from the programme to a BAU state is sub-optimal; the project is closed without formally transferring the remaining risks, or the newly identified owner is not willing to accept accountability. Involving the right stakeholders and teams from the start – and ensuring they are part of the risk conversation – helps avoid failures down the line.

LACK OF OPERATIONAL RISK INVOLVEMENT

There are instances of major change activities with no participation or involvement from either first or second line operational risk employees. This creates a gap in understanding of the overall risk profile of the change; as well as missed opportunities for operational risk professionals to be at the decision table and help implement a structured approach to evaluating risks and opportunities. It is recommended that first and second line operational risk functions hold periodic catch-ups to ensure adequate coverage and awareness of the most material change activities.

Good practices

EMBEDDED USE OF ORAs

Organizations with a well-embedded risk culture recognize the value of risk assessments. Executive committees and boards rely on ORAs accompanying material change initiatives, because a clear picture of risks and opportunities is simply indispensable for decision making. They will reject a new business proposition without an ORA; this is a sign of maturity and sends a powerful message in support of robust risk management practices.

RISKS AND OPPORTUNITIES ASSESSMENT

Use of a *risks and opportunities* matrix brings a positive sentiment to risk management and enhances the brand of the operational risk function. In developing approaches and leading conversations, it is important to balance out the words that have a negative connotation – *losses, threats, risks* – with more optimistic and upbeat terminology – *opportunities, benefits, lessons learned.*

FINDING THE RIGHT APPROACH

If a template is used for conducting ORAs, it is good practice to have the operational risk taxonomy built into the template, as a reminder of areas that need to be covered. The sponsor can then select relevant risks from the menu and add commentary, evaluate estimated inherent and residual risk levels, and outline known mitigating actions at an early stage of the programme. However, to the points raised in Chapter 5 on RCSAs, while templates do provide a framework to encourage consideration of a full range of risk pillars, they can also limit the risk identification mindset. In this case the template becomes a tick-box exercise. Often assembling a meeting with the right stakeholders and starting with a blank page asking *what are the risks here?* can draw out top-of-mind themes more effectively. The template can then be used as a basis for documenting the discussion in a disciplined way.

USING SYSTEM OR SOFTWARE

Unlike RCSAs, risk assessments of change initiatives are short-lived (and even, for longer regulatory programmes or projects, have an end of life). They are usually documented via manual Word or Excel documents. If operational risk software has a *change* module, it enables the loading, tracking and storage of ORAs in one place. Evaluating how many live ORAs exist at any point in time, and what their risk level is, helps operational risk to oversee the overall transformation landscape and increases transparency. As highlighted in the industry benchmark further on, this technique is rarely used, and only by a minority of organizations.

CELEBRATING SUCCESS

The Operational Risk department commonly has a preview of all ORAs, given their role in facilitation, review and challenge. Consequently, operational risk staff gain an enormous amount of experience and insight, and can use that knowledge to draw out relevant lessons learned and share them with business units and support functions. Celebrating success is once again an important topic. Discussions that focus on cases where assessments were particularly impactful really reinforce the value of risk management.

RETAINING EVIDENCE

In the age of evidence, it is important to retain solid documentation of ORAs, demonstrating how risk decisions were taken. Assessments can be referred to in the future, especially in cases where personnel have moved roles or left the organization.

Industry benchmark, 2018

Results from the live poll conducted at an industry meeting of operational risk practitioners showed that 93 per cent of respondents were positive that at least *some* change initiatives were risk assessed; a sound practice which enables increased levels of scrutiny and sign-off where needed (see Figure 6.4). But only 40 per cent of professionals were confident that the parameters were correctly defined to capture all *significant* or *riskier* activities in order to evaluate them.

Few firms are using a change risk assessment module within their operational risk system, allowing them to take an aggregate view of the firm's change profile. This tool does not seem to be widely used, with only 19 per cent of respondents benefitting from it (see Figure 6.5).

Practitioners described how change is managed in their organization; many used expressions such as *in silos* and *ad hoc.* Some institutions

FIGURE 6.4 Industry poll: risk assessment of change initiatives

Do you define and risk assess 'significant' change initiatives?

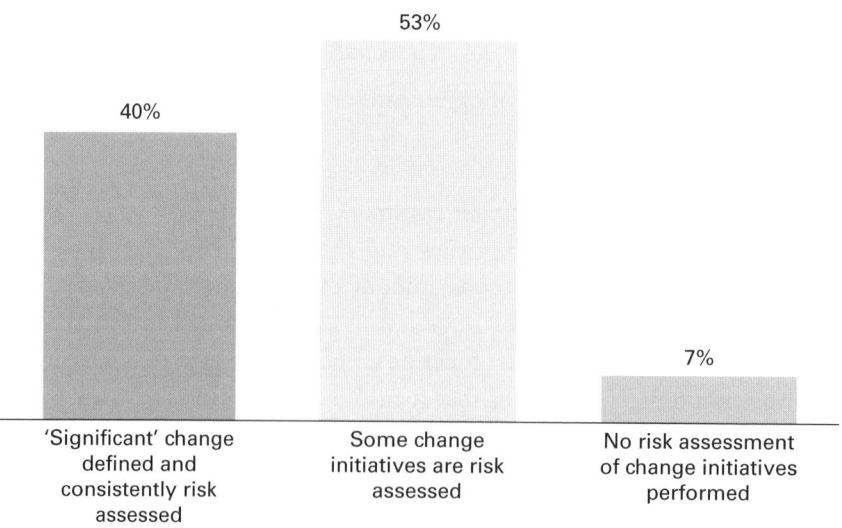

'Significant' change defined and consistently risk assessed — 40%
Some change initiatives are risk assessed — 53%
No risk assessment of change initiatives performed — 7%

Operational Risk Workshop, PSD

FIGURE 6.5 Industry poll: change software

Does your Operational Risk system/software include a 'Change' module?

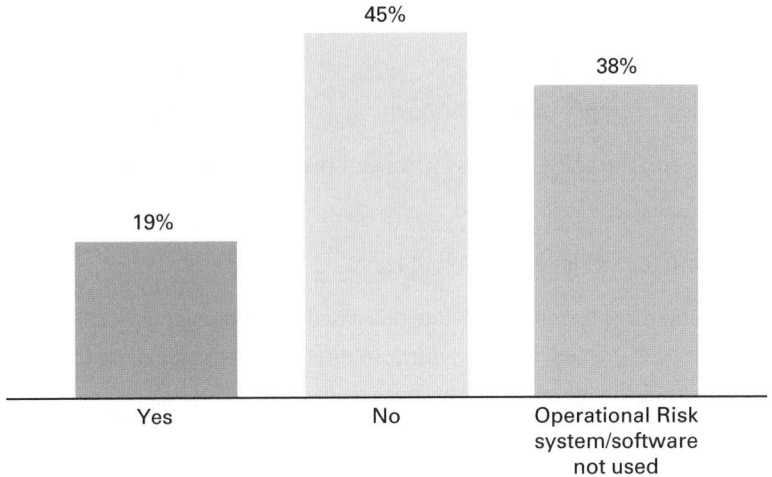

Operational Risk Workshop, PSD

exhibited more confidence in their practices, managing transformations *collaboratively*, in a *timely manner*, *proactively*, and in accordance with established *risk appetite*. In contracts, others brought up the challenges of change processes perceived as *poor*, *disjointed* or *reactive*.

Overall, operational risk professionals agreed that they need to spend more time in developing the scope and methodology for risk assessments of change initiatives. In particular, the approach to implementing IT system changes was deemed to be worthy of revision, by teaming up with technology colleagues to jointly review how the change process can produce better outcomes.

Practical workplace exercise

Obtain a sample of various change initiatives completed within the last year, and consider the following questions:

1 Are there set criteria for defining *material* change activities that would benefit from an ORA?

2 Is there an ORA process; or if not, how are the risks emanating from change initiatives identified, assessed and managed?

3 What is the role of the Operational Risk department in the change process?

4 What is working well?

5 What can be improved? Note down possible enhancements.

A template for the ORA process has been provided in Appendix 3.

MAKE **A D**IFFERENCE (MAD) **A**CTION

Please outline key learnings and note down one specific action you will take after reading this chapter, to enhance your existing practices relating to the risk assessment of change initiatives in your organization.

In summary, this chapter discussed the approach to identifying and assessing risks in change initiatives, supplementing Chapter 5, RCSAs.

Now that risk identification is complete, the next topic is dedicated to risk monitoring via key risk indicators.

Notes

1 Basel Committee on Banking Supervision (2020) Consultative document, *Revisions to the Principles for the Sound Management of Operational Risk*, www.bis.org/bcbs/publ/d508.pdf (archived at https://perma.cc/U4VE-BMG6)

2 Basel Committee on Banking Supervision (2014) *Review of the Principles for the Sound Management of Operational Risk*, www.bis.org/publ/bcbs292.pdf (archived at https://perma.cc/3V88-VK6R)

3 Financial Conduct Authority (2018) *Cyber and Technology Resilience: Themes from cross-sector survey 2017–18*, www.fca.org.uk/publication/research/technology-cyber-resilience-questionnaire-cross-sector-report.pdf (archived at https://perma.cc/LUV7-G6FZ)

4 Project Management Institute (2013) *A Guide to the Project Management Body of Knowledge*, 5th edn, Project Management Institute (PMI)

5 Winter, H (2019) *The Business Analysis Handbook: Techniques and questions to deliver better business outcomes*, Kogan Page

6 Manifesto for Agile Software Development, agilemanifesto.org/principles.html (archived at https://perma.cc/9LYB-K57R)

7 JWG (2017) Preparing for the regulatory flood: standards getting us to high ground!, jwg-it.eu/article/preparing-for-the-regulatory-flood-standards-getting-us-to-high-ground/ (archived at https://perma.cc/8UUS-XAHV)

8 Basel Committee on Banking Supervision (2014) *Review of the Principles for the Sound Management of Operational Risk*, www.bis.org/publ/bcbs292.pdf (archived at https://perma.cc/N6YE-95JV)

07

Key risk indicators

What this chapter covers: Key Risk Indicators (KRIs) score the lowest rating in operational risk implementation surveys, and remain a big challenge for practitioners. This chapter examines KRIs from a practical perspective, focussing on their purpose, design and benefit to the business (Figure 7.1). It discusses what is really important when implementing KRIs; provides a framework for assessing whether a metric is *useful* or *useless*; and reviews examples of effective (and not so effective) indicators. It also includes an industry benchmark and a list of 50 suggested KRIs (Appendix 4).

FURTHER READING

- Institute of Operational Risk (2021) *Operational Key Risk Indicators*
  Why recommended: A short supplementary read, containing several examples of key risk indicators.

- Michael George, John Maxey, David Rowlands and Mark Price (2004)
  The Lean Six Sigma Pocket Toolbook: A quick reference guide to 100 tools for improving quality and speed, McGraw-Hill
  Why recommended: This excellent handbook is one of many on Six Sigma methodology and is useful for those wishing to obtain a broader perspective on the importance of measurement and how it fits into the overall process improvement cycle.

FIGURE 7.1 Focus of Chapter 7: key risk indicators

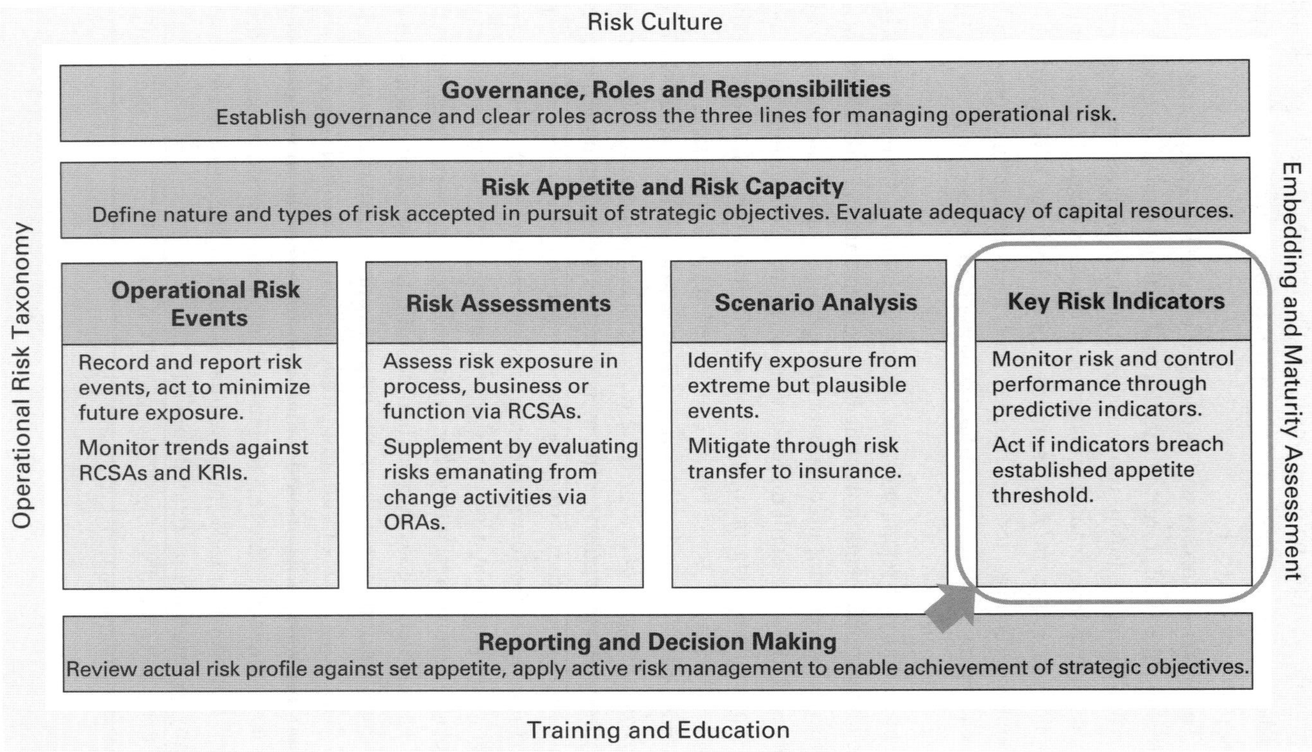

Risk Culture

Embedding and Maturity Assessment

Governance, Roles and Responsibilities

Establish governance and clear roles across the three lines for managing operational risk.

Risk Appetite and Risk Capacity

Define nature and types of risk accepted in pursuit of strategic objectives. Evaluate adequacy of capital resources.

Operational Risk Events	Risk Assessments	Scenario Analysis	Key Risk Indicators
Record and report risk events, act to minimize future exposure.	Assess risk exposure in process, business or function via RCSAs.	Identify exposure from extreme but plausible events.	Monitor risk and control performance through predictive indicators.
Monitor trends against RCSAs and KRIs.	Supplement by evaluating risks emanating from change activities via ORAs.	Mitigate through risk transfer to insurance.	Act if indicators breach established appetite threshold.

Reporting and Decision Making

Review actual risk profile against set appetite, apply active risk management to enable achievement of strategic objectives.

Training and Education

Operational Risk Taxonomy

Definition, examples and key attributes

A primary monitoring mechanism, usually referred to as Key Risk Indicators (KRIs), is a core component of the operational risk framework and a powerful risk management tool.

The secret of success with KRIs is in channelling energy and thought into designing the right, targeted metrics and setting suitable thresholds, without overburdening the business or support functions with terminology and definitions: for example, leading vs lagging, or cause vs effect. In terms of practical application, the *usefulness* test matters most: have the KRIs resulted in better business decisions? First line business units and support functions would prioritize deriving real value from the use of the KRIs to becoming crystal clear on their categorization.

In a survey of regulated banks, Basel Committee found that KRIs scored the lowest implementation rating out of all operational risk framework tools.[1] Either they were not used as part of the framework at all; or, in most banks surveyed, they were still under development and not yet fully implemented.

The challenge starts right at the outset, from the definition. As the Basel Committee noted, some banks considered *key risk indicators* and *key performance indicators* to be the same set of metrics; while others differentiated between *key risk indicators* (metrics designed to measure inherent risk) and *key performance indicators* (focussing on the adequacy of underlying processes and controls). Other firms use *key control indicators* for controls and *key performance indicators* to measure business performance. It is not surprising, then, that confusion arises; or that, for simplicity, some firms find it easier to replace the term KRI altogether, with the label *monitoring metrics*.

The challenge goes deeper than definition, however. It extends to the role of the KRIs and their place in the broader operational risk framework. In my 15-year experience of running public and in-house training courses, it has often been the KRI module that has attracted the most discussion and debate – and sometimes even light-bulb moments. Furthermore, at the end of each course when I ask participants to call out the most useful takeaways, many mention points related to KRIs.

Let's start by defining KRIs and discussing their role and place in the broader operational risk framework.

KRI DEFINITION

- A key risk indicator (KRI) is a metric or measure used to monitor the state of a *key* risk, indicating whether it is increasing or reducing.

- The KRI can be linked to the risk itself or to a key control that mitigates the risk.

- The KRI should be a well-chosen, targeted metric that helps the firm to take decisions (*usefulness test*).

In Chapter 5, we covered Risk and Control Self-Assessments (RCSAs). An RCSA is effectively a snapshot, at a point in time, of the firm's risk and control environment. The assessment is true and valid on the day it takes place; but what can happen tomorrow, next month or next quarter? The control environment may deteriorate due to, for example, experienced members of staff, with knowledge of information technology systems, leaving the firm. Inherent risk may increase due to the firm starting to trade new products. While it is important to periodically refresh RCSAs, it is not cost-effective to do this on a continuous basis.

That is where KRIs come in.

Once the most important (*top* or *key*) risks have been identified, the purpose of KRIs is to monitor them. As part of the RCSA process, business units or support functions have already agreed that the key risks are more significant than other risks; and therefore, they are now selected for special treatment. They are worthy of the time and effort involved in monitoring them and KRIs are defined for each *key* risk, to allow us to keep an eye on its behaviour.

The word *key* in 'key risk indicators' relates to the risk and signifies the *risk* being key, not the *indicator*.

When KRIs are selected to monitor key risks, the advantages include:

- clarity on why the metric is being collected – it monitors the behaviour of a risk which is known to be significant to the firm;

- reduced number of indicators – it enables a small sub-set of key risks to be monitored, which is more efficient and ensures focus on what is important.

CASE STUDY 7.1

A medium-sized firm acquired by a larger organization identifies one of its key risks as *Loss of staff, causing inability to meet business requirements.* During the 12 months of integration after the acquisition, senior management has to ensure continuity of high-value, high-volume transaction services, while recognizing that inevitably, there will be attrition. Management decides that in this situation it is crucial to monitor the risk via a KRI, *Predicted attrition* – defined as the number of employees expected to leave in the next month, as a percentage of the total number of staff. Each leader is requested to maintain an honest dialogue with their staff discussing future plans, and report the *Predicted attrition* KRI on a monthly basis.

While accepted to be not very scientific, this KRI, based on the leader's knowledge and informal estimates, proves very useful. It provides a basis for management to act, proactively recruiting temporary workers and a consultancy firm to fill identified potential gaps, and the integration is successfully completed.

Attributes of the *Predicted Attrition* KRI:

- It is directly relevant to the risk *Loss of staff causing inability to meet business requirements.*

- It measures the level of risk, indicating whether that is increasing or reducing, and is helpful in decision making.

- Although not precise, it is at least measurable: to quote the British philosopher and logician Carveth Read, 'It's better to be approximately right than exactly wrong.'

In normal circumstances, though, the practice of asking employees whether they are planning to resign in the near future is neither feasible nor recommended. So, what are the alternatives?

Risk: loss of staff causing inability to meet business requirements

KRI1: *Absenteeism* – this can be narrowed down by cause, eg stress-related absenteeism; an increase may be a sign of poor staff health, leading to future attrition. The opposite – *Presenteeism* – equally became a concern during the Covid-19 pandemic, where working hours have stretched with employees moving to home working environment; this led to fatigue and burnout.

KRI2: *Use of employee helpline* – if this kind of facility is available, spikes in usage may signal a broader issue and require investigation.

KRI3: *Employee satisfaction survey rate* – decreased staff satisfaction with the role, manager or the company may lead to resignations.

KRI4: *Exit interview analysis: number of identified concerns* – if the Human Resources department interviews leavers and analyses trends (a very valuable activity), they will be able to flag if there is a recurring theme or concern.

KRI5: *Salary benchmark*, showing the number or percentage of positions not benchmarked or below the industry benchmark – uncompetitive pay may prompt employees to look elsewhere.

KRI6: *Key staff without succession plan* – this will not prevent employees from leaving, but will reflect how well the impact can be mitigated if they do.

Depending on particular aspects of risk that are of concern to the firm, additional indicators can be designed, for example, ones that help understand *who* is leaving:

KRI7: *High performance (regretted) turnover* – highly rated leavers as a percentage of total number of leavers.

Or *how quickly* people are leaving:

KRI8: *Permanent staff leavers* – left within six months of joining.

CASE STUDY 7.2

In a highly dynamic start-up firm, indicator *Permanent staff leavers, left within six months of joining was* instrumental in helping management to monitor a pattern whereby employees either stayed for a long time, or joined and left very quickly. Following further investigation, it was revealed that the vibrant and entrepreneurial environment was either loved or hated by the members of staff. As a consequence, Human Resources enhanced the employee on-boarding process to explain the culture to prospective new joiners at the interview stage, allowing them to decide up-front whether it suited them, and reducing the number of speedy departures.

What attributes are we looking for when selecting KRIs?

ATTRIBUTES OF GOOD KRIs

☐ relevant, targeted – specific to the risk or control;

☐ predictive, forward-looking – provide an early warning;

☐ useful – help the firm to take decisions;

☐ available for collection;

☐ measurable.

Some organizations use the KRI *Staff attrition rate*. While factual, this KRI is backward-looking (ie employees have already left); and it provides no insight into why the departures happened or whether people are more or less likely to leave in the future. It is difficult for management to act on the information and therefore, from a risk management perspective, the KRI is not very helpful. The recommendation is to select more predictive and targeted metrics that can provide an early warning when the level of risk is increasing.

Another example of risk worth reviewing is the *Unauthorized/rogue trading*, which is a key risk for firms with markets or trading business. Direct measures of the risk (in this case, the number of employees expected to turn rogue in the next month) rarely exist, if at all. If there are no risk indicators as such, KRIs can be set to monitor the control environment in order to alert management to any deterioration, thus allowing them to promptly implement corrective measures.

Indicators can be established for a *risk* as well as for a *control* that mitigates the risk.

Risk: Unauthorized/rogue trading

Example of a KRI dashboard for the risk of Unauthorized/rogue trading, containing control indicators.

KRI1: *Unconfirmed deals over 20 days* – highlighting aged trades that have not been agreed to by the trade counterparty for a long time (eg over 20 days), flagging a potentially erroneous or fraudulent deal.

KRI2: *Trades executed at off-market rates* – identifying 'unusual' trades that require further explanation.

KRI3: *Late deals* – counting exceptions where trades have been concluded after the close of the business day.

KRI4: *Unresolved profit & loss (P&L) differences as of month-end over the threshold* – monitoring discrepancies between a trader's position and the books and records of the firm.

KRI5: *Cancel & amends* – showing the number of deals that were cancelled and/or amended after being agreed with the counterparty, potentially requiring further investigation.

KRI6: *Trader mandate breaches* – monitoring instances where trades were executed outside of the prescribed mandate, either due to an error or deliberate non-compliance.

Risk: Money laundering/financial crime

Finally, examining the risk of *Money laundering/financial crime*, which can be measured using a combination of risk and control indicators:

KRI1: Percentage of *high risk accounts vs overall accounts* – a risk indicator which provides a view of the overall portfolio.

KRI2: *Client due diligence (CDD) reviews past due over 30 days* – highlights delay and/or non-completion of CDD refresh, a control indicator.

KRI3: *Open activity monitoring alerts not properly actioned* – monitors investigation and resolution of alerts of suspicious activity, a control indicator.

Market abuse and financial crime are growing concerns in the financial services industry, with firms moving to automated real-time trader surveillance to detect manipulation, and use of artificial intelligence to identify suspicious patterns. This is an area of continuing enhancements and a great opportunity for operational risk practitioners to lead the way in transforming manual KRI monitoring into state-of-the art real-time indicator dashboards.

Defining thresholds and mastering aggregation

Once KRIs have been identified, thresholds (or tolerance levels) need to be established for each indicator. The levels define tolerance for error or failure with respect to the specific risk or control that the KRI is intended to monitor, effectively outlining what is acceptable and what will not be tolerated.

Thresholds are essential for escalation and action, and are commonly set on a Red/Amber/Green (RAG) basis:

Red: Unacceptable: immediate action needed

Amber: Tolerable: attention, explanation, monitoring and/or plan to bring to green

Green: Acceptable: no action needed

RAG status may also be defined in more detail. For example, red metrics may require escalation to an appropriate governance or a board-level committee.

The following steps are recommended when setting the thresholds.

SETTING RAG THRESHOLDS

✓ Establish data collection process.

✓ Observe values internally.

✓ Benchmark with industry (if available).

✓ Present a proposal to the governance committee.

Thresholds outline what the firm considers acceptable, effectively establishing the firm's operational risk appetite (see Chapter 9, Operational Risk Appetite). They need to be approached with a high level of rigour, including review and approval by the relevant governance committee(s). Group-wide or *top of the house* indicators and their thresholds are usually approved by the board.

Collecting the data and observing current values helps greatly in understanding the existing risk and control environment, although should not be used for guidance in setting the thresholds. External benchmarks are rarely available in financial services, but are worth checking if a relevant study has been published.

EXAMPLE 1

Risk: Payment errors/poor transaction execution, leading to customer detriment, financial loss and reputational damage.

KRI: *Number of aged reconciliation breaks* – a control indicator, monitoring volume of discrepancies and speed of resolution.

Thresholds:

> Green: Less than 20 breaks outstanding >30 days at month-end AND zero
> breaks outstanding >60 days
> Amber: Less than 50 breaks outstanding >30 days at month-end AND zero
> breaks outstanding >60 days
> Red: Over 50 breaks outstanding >30 days at month-end OR any breaks
> outstanding >60 days

The same KRI can be turned into a composite measure, combining both
volume and the monetary value of reconciliation breaks,

KRI: *Strength of reconciliation process* – combining volume and value.

> Green: Less than 20 breaks outstanding >30 days at month-end AND zero
> breaks outstanding >60 days AND overall value of unresolved discrepancies
> <$50,000

Some indicators can be binary, turning from *acceptable* directly to *unacceptable*, ie by-passing the *tolerable* level.

EXAMPLE 2

Risk: Incorrect financial/regulatory reporting, resulting in penalties and
regulatory censure.

KRI: Number of high-risk spreadsheets or end-user computing (EUC)
applications with policy exceptions – a control indicator, already narrowed
down to critical spreadsheets/EUC applications where the firm has no tolerance
for exceptions to policy requirements (protecting the content, restricting
access, performing back-ups and validating the formulas).

Thresholds:

> Green: zero
>
> Red: >= 1

Aggregation

At both group-wide and business unit level, there are usually multiple KRIs,
each reported with its own RAG rating. Hence the need arises for aggregation of the measures, to enable an understanding of whether the risk overall
is within or outside the firm's risk appetite.

Aggregation can be rule- or judgement-based. In rule-based aggregation:

- Conservative/cautious: the overall rating is based on the worst value KRI, ie if at least one indicator is at an *unacceptable* level, the overall RAG rating becomes *unacceptable*.

- Moderate/modest: the result is *unacceptable* if a set percentage of KRIs is flagging red (eg over 20 per cent).

In judgement-based aggregation, the KRI owner – namely the responsible first line head of business unit or support function who owns the KRI – decides on the overall rating using their expert knowledge. To ensure the process is robust and avoids gaming, the reasons for the rating need to be articulated in writing, which enables the second line operational risk function and respective governance committees to provide effective challenge.

CASE STUDY 7.3

A global financial markets business unit, trading out of multiple locations, is monitoring the risk of *Unauthorized/rogue trading*. One KRI (*Unconfirmed deals > 20 days*) is flagging Red in one location (Figure 7.2). When presenting the dashboard to the risk committee, the head of financial markets confirms that an investigation into the Red KRI has commenced and argues that, overall, the risk is within the elevated but tolerable Amber level. This is due to the good performance of mitigating controls in place (namely other KRIs flagging Green), which were recently reviewed and tested by the Quality Assurance function.

The committee accepts this argument but requests to see the results of the investigation. On further analysis, it transpires that all unconfirmed trades are with the same small-size corporate client, with a single authorized signatory whose frequent business travels result in a significant backlog of unsigned confirmations.

Given the increased risk of fraudulent and erroneous trades that this represents, the firm decides it has no appetite to continue dealing with the client unless they appoint an additional signatory and regularize the backlog. The client complies and the KRI returns to Green within two months.

In the above example, judgement-based aggregation was used. If a rule-based conservative/cautious approach was applied, the overall RAG rating would have turned Red, flagging that the overall risk of *Unauthorized/rogue trading* for the global financial markets business is outside the firm's risk appetite.

FIGURE 7.2 Example key risk indicators dashboard

Operational Risk Dashboard	WHEM		EMEA	APAC		Global Financial Markets
KEY RISK INDICATORS	NY	Miami	UK	Sing	HK	
RISK of ROGUE TRADING						
1: Unconfirmed Deals > 20 Days	○	● Red	● Red	○	○	
2: Trades Executed at 'Off-Market' Rates	○	○	○	○	○	
3: 'Late Deals'	○	○	○	○	○	
4: Unresolved P&L Differences as of Month-end>Threshold	○	○	◐ Amber	◐ Amber	○	◐ Amber
5: Cancel&Amends	○	◐ Amber	◐ Amber	○	○	
6: Mandate breaches	○	○	○	○	○	

● = Red   ◐ = AMBER   ○ = GREEN

KRI life cycle and checklist: useful or useless?

The KRI process cycle is described below:

- **Select:** A key risk that requires monitoring is selected (from RCSA);
- **Design:** A workshop is run with subject matter experts to define KRIs;
- **Collect:** A data collection process is established;
- **Propose thresholds:** Subject matter experts conduct the study to propose thresholds;
- **Approve thresholds:** KRI and thresholds are presented to the relevant governance committee for approval;
- **Monitor:** KRI is monitored with agreed frequency; actions are taken if the level becomes 'unacceptable';
- **Validate:** Data accuracy is periodically reviewed (eg by Internal Audit).

Selection

KRIs are commonly established at multiple levels throughout the organization, including at group-wide and individual business or support function level. Respectively, the starting points are key risks at the top of the house which are most significant to the firm; and more granular individual business- or function-level risks. The selection process involves deciding on what constitutes key risks that require monitoring. These can be, for example, inherent risks with the highest impact and likelihood rating; or residual risks that are outside the firm's risk appetite; or a combination of both. Less is more – narrowing down is important to ensure that reviewing the KRI dashboard is manageable.

Design

This stage is best achieved via a workshop with respective subject matter experts from the business or support functions, led by operational risk. Design is a creative, stimulating and enjoyable process, where participants collectively define the best metrics that possess the right attributes – relevant, targeted, predictive, useful, measurable and available for collection – for each of the key risks. Business units and support functions are already engaged as the value proposition is clear – let's find ways to monitor those significant risks that may prevent the *business* from achieving its *own* objectives.

In preparation for the workshop it is worth examining existing metrics, as some may already be collected. If this stage proves difficult, and the team is running out of ideas, external help is also available. Some organizations provide a library of key risk indicators (via a paid subscription service), as well as guidance on where and how each indicator can be used.[2] A collaborative approach of second line operational risk professionals, who have a solid understanding of the framework and desired outcomes, working together with business units and support functions, ensures that identified metrics will provide an insight into the level of risk and present a true and fair reflection of the risk profile of each unit or function.

Data collection

This stage is usually manual, because KRIs are the most manually intensive of all operational risk tools. Data accuracy is key, and KRI owners need to establish verification procedures to ensure the correctness of information which is used for decision making. This may involve review and sign-off by department heads.

Thresholds

These were discussed in the previous section.

Monitoring and mitigation using KRIs

Breaches of KRI thresholds need to be explained, acted upon and notified to the appropriate governance committees. Especially the unacceptable Red level, if correctly calibrated, cannot be ignored. The firm has already agreed what outcomes would not be tolerated and needs to follow through with investigation, resolution and if needed, monetary investment. Clear accountability helps to achieve desired results, so it is good practice to have an owner for every KRI. This may be the respective risk or control owner, who takes the lead in resolving the breach and bringing the metric back to acceptable level.

Validation

As highlighted in the data collection step, beware errors in the dataset. Many organizations end up having to go back to the risk committee and/or the board explaining why the KRI was mis-reported for the previous month(s). Maintain data quality with spot checks, period assurance and internal audit reviews.

Periodic updates

KRIs should be subject to periodic review following the RCSA refresh, triggered by a major change or significant operational risk event, or at least annually. During the review, it is recommended to consider the *usefulness test* (see box below).

KRI USEFUL

✓ clearly linked to a *key* risk;

✓ targeted, relevant metric;

✓ demonstrable decisions;

✓ drives improvement, replaced with a better KRI.

In many instances, once KRIs become visible and continuously monitored, they lead to enhancements. To quote H James Harrington, the US performance and quality guru, 'Measurement is the first step that leads to control and eventually to improvement.'

Six Sigma, an effective problem-solving methodology for improving business performance, is centred on the DMAIC concept: Define, Measure, Analyse, Improve and Control.[3] In my career I have been fortunate to manage Six Sigma green and black belts, working with the methodology and seeing first-hand evidence of the value that the projects delivered. Robust key risk indicators fit into this overall improvement cycle; and if used correctly can take a firm a long way towards advancing its processes and performance.

CASE STUDY 7.4

A medium-sized firm experiences a moderate technology failure and decides to proactively revisit its disaster recovery capabilities. A programme of work commences to categorize systems into critical and non-critical in terms of client impact; and to establish recovery time objectives (RTO), determining a target time frame for bringing the system back up following an incident. Management selects two indicators to monitor the risk *Inability to promptly recover from a significant system failure.*

The first KRI *Number of systems not yet categorized* reflects the progress of the programme; and measures the remaining unknown population and potential areas of risk. The second KRI *Critical Systems without RTO* counts the number of systems with the most significant impact where RTO have not yet been agreed and tested.

The firm sets a zero tolerance for both KRIs, resulting in *unacceptable* Red RAG ratings for the duration of the project. Stringent governance is thus required, with updates from the head of Information Technology to the governance committees and the board.

Following project completion, both KRIs become redundant and are replaced by a better indicator – *Number of critical systems that failed RTO* – for continuous monitoring of the results of the scheduled quarterly disaster recovery tests.

> **KRI NOT USEFUL**
>
> ✓ not linked to a *key* risk;
>
> ✓ difficult to explain why collected;
>
> ✓ no decisions taken;
>
> ✓ constant Green;
>
> ✓ if it turns Red, it is argued that it is not a real Red: no action needed.

In some firms, KRIs are not linked to any particular risk. A dashboard is created from scratch (perhaps based on the question *what shall we monitor?*) or assembled using data that is already being gathered. KRIs are subsequently monitored in case they collectively flag a developing risk. While this approach is feasible, it is also laborious and ineffective, as the firm ends up collecting more indicators than it needs (not all related to *key* risks), and struggles to justify why a particular metric is being monitored. When working with clients, I always recommend identifying the *key* risks first, and selecting the KRIs subsequently.

In terms of decision-making, examples of less useful KRIs include those backward-looking, or lagging, indicators that reflect risk having already materialized. Among them is the earlier-mentioned *Staff attrition rate* (employees have already left) as well as *Number of system failures*, *Number of cases of internal fraud*, and *Number of reported operational risk losses*.

In short, it is good practice to select predictive, rather than backward-looking metrics where possible. (Note: as mentioned in the introduction, while specific terminology such as *leading* and *lagging* is widely used by the risk community, it is best to avoid overloading business units with these labels.)

KRIs – and their thresholds – may also need to be examined in case they persistently report *Green* for a prolonged period of time (eg over a year), including in periods of stress. This pattern may signify that the department is overstaffed or has extra capacity, or that the threshold has been set incorrectly.

Even worse is when KRI turns *Red* and the importance of the event is downplayed. For example, an explanation is provided that it is not a true exception and that there is no reason to be concerned. This situation warrants a review. The threshold may have been incorrectly set, or, more likely, it is recognized that investment is required to resolve the issue, but there is neither budget nor appetite among management to progress this further.

Appendix 4 provides some example KRIs.

Roles and responsibilities

First line business units or support functions are responsible for most of the KRI cycle: developing indicators which monitor their risk and control environment; proposing the thresholds; establishing a data collection process; monitoring and providing commentary; and then acting when indicators breach the threshold. This is common sense risk management, and if indicators are correctly selected to monitor significant risks that may prevent the business or support function from achieving *their own* objectives, there should be no pushback.

The traditional role of the second line Operational Risk department is to provide oversight and challenge. In reality, Operational Risk works in partnership with first line functions, facilitating KRI workshops and adding its expertise and knowledge of the KRI tool and the desired outcomes. The challenge piece can be provided as part of the discussion at the KRI workshop. The second line usually has the right to add or alter indicators or thresholds (see Chapter 3, Three Lines of Defence). If the firm has first line coordinators embedded into its business units or support functions, those individuals will play a crucial role in achieving the right outcomes.

Below is an example checklist for a first line risk coordinator.

FIRST LINE RISK COORDINATOR CHECKLIST: KRIs

✓ KRIs are set to monitor *key* (top) operational risks.

✓ Collected data is accurate and reliable; data quality is validated.

✓ KRI thresholds are defined and approved by the relevant governance
committee.

✓ Dashboard is used in decision making – if KRI breaches the threshold, action
is taken.

✓ KRI outputs are compared and contrasted against other core operational
risk tools.

Common challenges and good practices

The following challenges may be encountered when designing and deploying
key risk indicators.

Common challenges

BUSINESS UNITS DISENGAGED

At times, employees may perceive KRIs as a pointless exercise and refuse to
engage in their design. It is crucial to build a value proposition and make a
case for monitoring what is important to the *business*, namely those significant risks that may prevent the business from achieving *their own* objectives.

THRESHOLD MANIPULATION

Business units or support functions may attempt to game the threshold, proposing ranges that will always exhibit a Green KRI (in particular in firms which
are characterized by a blame culture, ie to avoid the consequences of being
Red); or, on the contrary, purposely setting a threshold to display Red in order
to substantiate a request for more people or better systems. Independent second
line operational risk opinions (referred to earlier as *challenge*) can be helpful in
resolving these tendencies.

LACK OF ACTION

A dashboard with Red flashing indicators is presented month-on-month but
with no action taken to resolve the matter and bring the metric within the

tolerable level. This pattern should be avoided at all costs, as it simply devalues the whole process.

MANUAL DATA COLLECTION

KRIs are the most manual tool in the operational risk framework. When starting the project, allow sufficient time and resource not only for the design phase but for the future manual and possibly labour-intensive collection process. Consider automation where possible – firms investing in technological solutions are ahead of the game, using the best practice of inviting IT and data specialists to the initial KRI workshop and thus ensuring that potential automation is considered from the outset.

TOO MANY KRIs

It can be challenging to identify the correct number of KRIs for a given firm: usually there are too many (the challenge is rarely in the opposite direction, namely too few). Some organizations monitor hundreds (or even thousands) of indicators. I am frequently asked what is the right number. While there is no absolute correct answer, a range of around 30 good KRIs at the top of the house and for each business/function is appropriate.

Good practices

REVIEW WHAT ALREADY EXISTS

While it is unrealistic to rapidly turn existing departmental metrics straight into a KRI dashboard, it is valuable to review what is already being collected. Frequently, current indicators serve as a base for the conversation. Business units and support functions naturally manage their people, systems and processes and will often have a good set of measures that help them take decisions. This can be supplemented by blue-sky thinking, to consider what KRIs should ideally be used, and if felt important, time and technical capabilities invested to put them in place. If risks are the starting point, that narrows down the scope and creates a much better case for agreeing what is essential to monitor.

DEFINE A HEALTHY PORTFOLIO

Evaluate the proportion of predictive metrics vs backward-looking measures in the overall portfolio. A healthy set of indicators will contain predominantly predictive measures that aid in decision-making. Use operational risk taxonomy as a checkpoint for completeness purposes, to ensure metrics for key taxonomy categories have been developed.

TRANSLATE KRIs INTO A STORY

Ensure KRIs tell a story to the governance committees and especially when presented at board level. The context helps in escalating Red KRIs and ensuring they are acted upon. Measure and highlight the length of persistency of Red KRIs, which demonstrates apathy and unwillingness to deal with issues.

APPLY THE USEFULNESS TEST

Apply the *usefulness* test and revisit KRIs after major changes, aiming to continuously evolve them. Review KRIs in search of better, more targeted metrics, avoiding stale indicators. Additionally, review the thresholds periodically to make sure that they are still appropriate and fit for purpose.

SHARE LEARNINGS AND CELEBRATE SUCCESS

Share good examples of KRIs between first line risk coordinators. It is good practice to run periodic workshops where coordinators present their best indicator of the year, substantiated with reasons why. Group discussions and the exchange of practical hints and tips injects positive energy into risk management. Report on cases where KRI monitoring has resulted in improvements, emphasizing the value of risk management. This practice is not done nearly enough.

APPRECIATE THE BIGGER PICTURE

The operational risk team needs to be involved and fully on-board with the firm's strategy and business objectives, to ensure that the data collected and monitored aligns with the bigger picture and is truly important to the firm.

Industry benchmark, 2019

Operational risk practitioners participated in a live poll to examine the use of key risk indicators. Starting from the number of KRIs used for monitoring and reporting at the top of the house, only a few firms had under 30 KRIs; while 47 per cent of respondents used hundreds of metrics, ranging from 100-plus to more than 700 (see Figure 7.3).

Regular updates were seen as important: firms are constantly searching for targeted, predictive and useful indicators, with over 70 per cent of respondents planning to enhance their KRI set, as presented in Figure 7.4. Around 8 per cent were working to decrease their number of KRIs (especially

FIGURE 7.3 Industry poll: number of key risk indicators

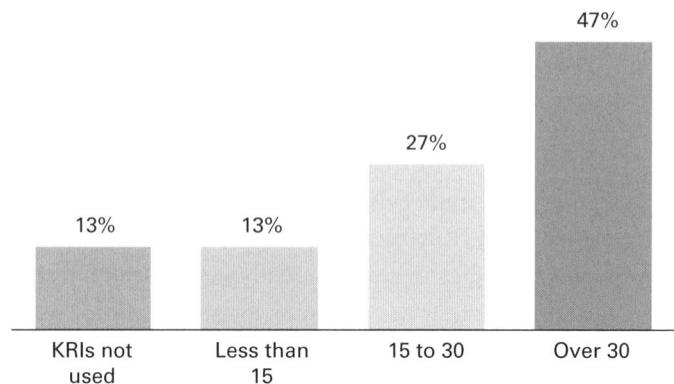

How many KRIs are at the 'top of the house'?

Best Practice Operational Risk Forum, 2019

FIGURE 7.4 Industry poll: next steps for key risk indicators

What are your plans/next steps for KRIs?

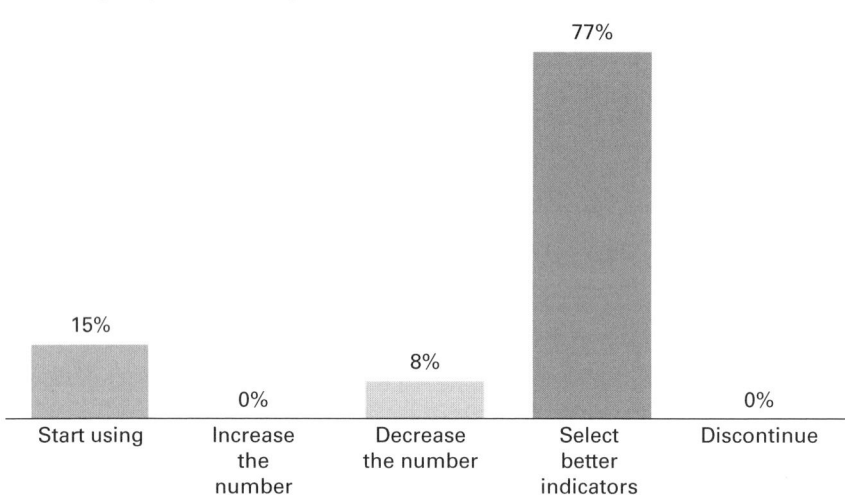

Best Practice Operational Risk Forum, 2019

if the number ran to hundreds), while others were intending to start KRI reporting. No respondents planned to increase their number of KRIs or to completely discontinue use of the tool.

It was encouraging to see the *usefulness* score increasing (1 being the lowest and 5 the highest, Figure 7.5), with KRIs being deemed a helpful tool

FIGURE 7.5 Industry poll: usefulness of key risk indicators

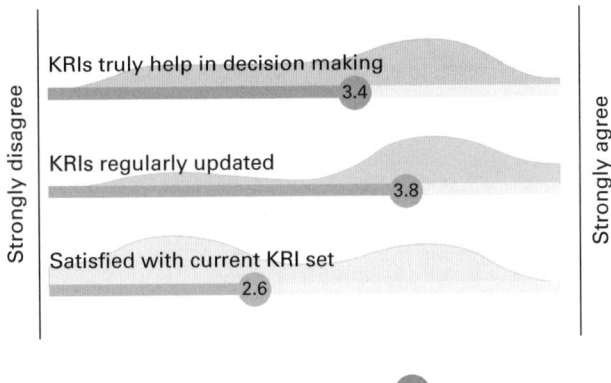

1 = strongly disagree, 5 = strongly agree ⬤ = average rating

Best Practice Operational Risk Forum, 2019

in decision-making. Despite not yet scoring full marks, this represented a good picture overall, and very good progress since 2014, when – as mentioned at the start of this chapter – KRIs received the lowest implementation rating out of all the operational risk tools in the Basel Committee's review of the Principles for the Sound Management of Operational Risk.

Practical workplace exercise

Reflect on the content of this chapter. Obtain a copy of the RCSA or a list of your firm's top/key risks. Select three risks and practise creating three or four key risk indicators for each risk, taking into account the attributes of good KRIs.

Obtain a copy of your firm's KRI dashboard. Review it, considering the following questions:

1 Are the KRIs clearly linked to a key risk? Are they reported together with the risk?

2 Do they have the right attributes?

3 Are decisions taken when the KRI breaches the threshold?

4 Which KRIs are most useful? Make notes of the features that you particularly like.

5 Which ones are less useful and can be replaced? Note down potential 'better' KRIs.

MAKE A DIFFERENCE (MAD) ACTION

Please outline the key learnings and note down one specific action you will take after reading this chapter, to enhance your existing practices relating to key risk indicators.

In summary, this chapter discussed the ultimate monitoring tool, KRIs, used for observing the behaviour of *key* risks and aiding in decision making.

The next topic is dedicated to the final core tool of the operational risk toolbox – Scenario Analysis.

Notes

1 Basel Committee on Banking Supervision (2014) *Review of the Principles for the Sound Management of Operational Risk*, www.bis.org/publ/bcbs292.pdf (archived at https://perma.cc/ECZ3-KB9N)

2 RiskBusiness, www.riskbusiness.com/brochures/content-kri-library.pdf (archived at https://perma.cc/A2X3-M4CT)

3 George, ML, Maxey, J, Rowlands, D and Price, M (2004) *The Lean Six Sigma Pocket Toolbook: A quick reference guide to 100 tools for improving quality and speed*, McGraw-Hill

08

Scenario analysis

What this chapter covers: This chapter explores Scenario Analysis, a tool that historically was used solely for risk measurement purposes; and advocates for the strengthening of its use, given its benefits for risk management (Figure 8.1). The chapter provides an overview of the process by exploring three different scenario workshop case studies. The chapter outlines examples of good practices, lists common pitfalls and provides suggestions on how to avoid them. It also includes an industry benchmark containing the results of a live poll with industry practitioners.

FURTHER READING

- Basel Committee on Banking Supervision (2009) *Observed range of practice in key elements of Advanced Measurement Approaches*
  Why recommended: The document contains a valuable benchmark on the various aspects of scenario analysis, for those interested in exploring a wide range of practices.

- Nassim Nicholas Taleb (2008) *The Black Swan: The impact of the highly improbable,* Penguin Books
  Why recommended: Simply the best book on the subject of the unpredictable.

FIGURE 8.1 Focus of Chapter 8: scenario analysis

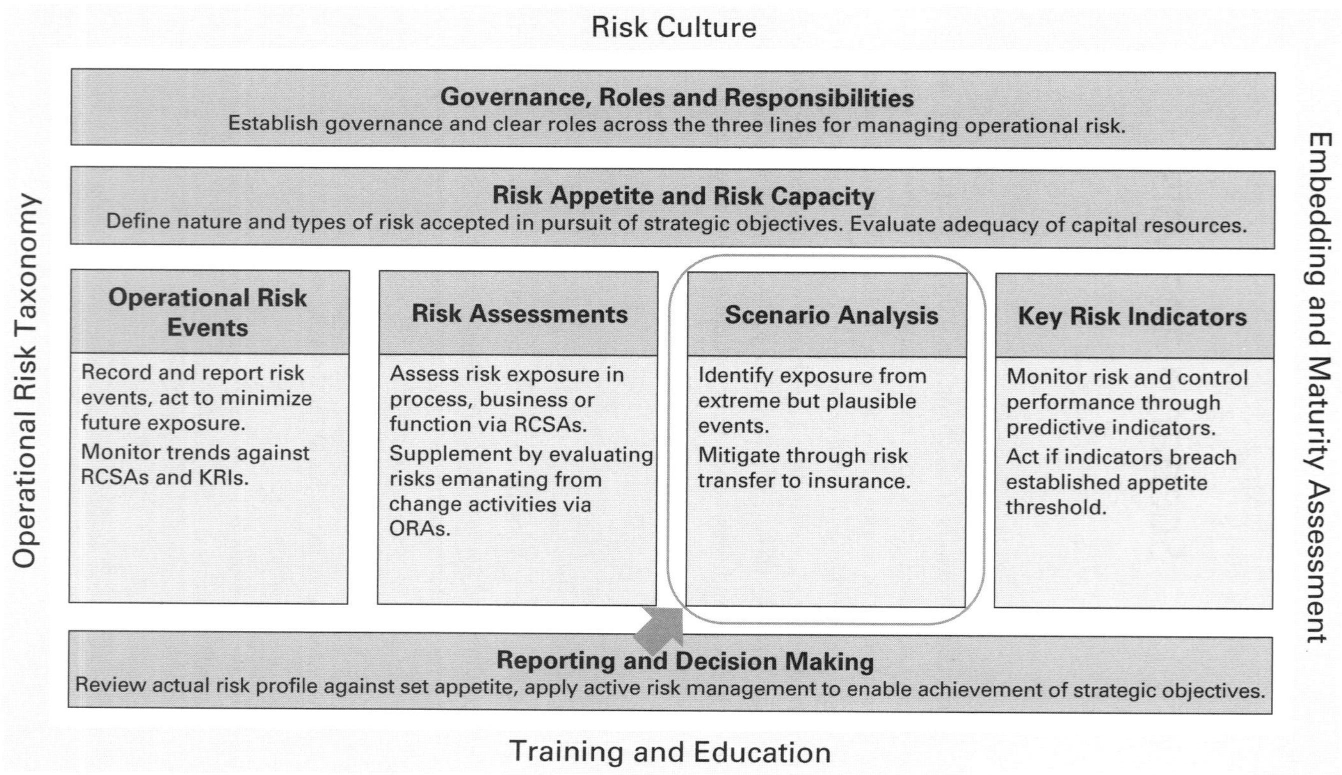

Embedding and Maturity Assessment

Risk Culture

Governance, Roles and Responsibilities

Establish governance and clear roles across the three lines for managing operational risk.

Risk Appetite and Risk Capacity

Define nature and types of risk accepted in pursuit of strategic objectives. Evaluate adequacy of capital resources.

Operational Risk Events	**Risk Assessments**	**Scenario Analysis**	**Key Risk Indicators**
Record and report risk events, act to minimize future exposure. Monitor trends against RCSAs and KRIs.	Assess risk exposure in process, business or function via RCSAs. Supplement by evaluating risks emanating from change activities via ORAs.	Identify exposure from extreme but plausible events. Mitigate through risk transfer to insurance.	Monitor risk and control performance through predictive indicators. Act if indicators breach established appetite threshold.

Reporting and Decision Making

Review actual risk profile against set appetite, apply active risk management to enable achievement of strategic objectives.

Training and Education

Operational Risk Taxonomy

Definition and purpose: for risk management and measurement

As mentioned in the Preface to this book, in my role as chair of various industry bodies I regularly lead operational risk meetings with practitioners. For these meetings, we typically select a topic and conduct a study of how it is being addressed by member firms. Risk and Control Self-Assessments (RCSAs) and Key Risk Indicators (KRIs) are among the most popular subjects, and usually manage to create engagement with all participants.

In contrast, whenever Scenario Analysis (SA) comes up as the study topic, a third of the audience will invariably skip the meeting. The reasons given often include the fact that the tool is too quantitative, and that many operational risk practitioners – especially if working in a foreign branch of an international organization – are not closely involved in the process. The tool is usually administered by a select group of experts in the organization's head office, where scenarios are run for capital calculation purposes – often for subsidiaries required to compute their own regulatory capital. Scenarios are also widely used by publicly rated firms, as rating agencies invariably require them; and by insurance industry practitioners who generally favour quantitative approaches.

In a similar way to operational risk losses, scenarios were historically required and used primarily for risk *measurement* purposes.

The tool was utilized with a single intent – to come up with numbers which could be put into a statistical model in order to produce a capital charge. The overall dataset for the model was reasonably solid. Many firms made significant progress in collecting internal loss events (usual, or *expected losses*), and additionally many subscribed to external loss data consortia to supplement their internal data. However, at the end (or tail) of the impact scale – covering rare, severe or *unexpected losses* – the loss data was sparse, as over time the industry simply had not experienced that many extreme operational events, as described in Figure 8.2.

> That was where scenario analysis came in: a tool for generating synthetic data not yet observed, by imagining hypothetical events and estimating their corresponding impact.

FIGURE 8.2 Loss distribution curve

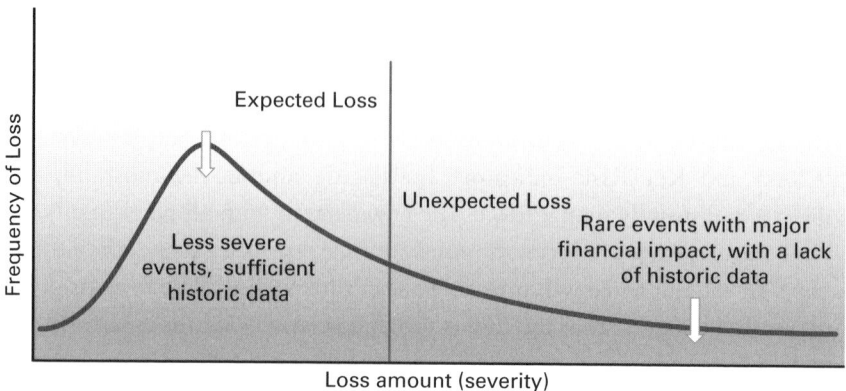

Putting aside the need to satisfy a regulatory objective – deriving numbers for capital calculation purposes – the design and examination of scenarios is actually one of the most interesting, interactive and intellectually challenging activities in the operational risk toolset. It is also great fun. Scenario analysis is as useful for risk *management* as it is for risk *measurement*; it can be used for both, or for risk *management* only (also see Chapter 14 for articulation of *operational resilience* scenarios).

The chapter aims to illustrate practical ways in which a firm can establish and maintain scenario analysis as part of its overall operational risk framework.

Aim of scenario analysis

> Scenario analysis is the continuation of risk assessment, as pointed out in Figure 8.3, with a specific focus on events at the more extreme end of the spectrum. Each scenario is also a deep dive into a particular theme, allowing focus on a detailed story line.

FIGURE 8.3 OREs, RCSAs and scenario analysis horizon

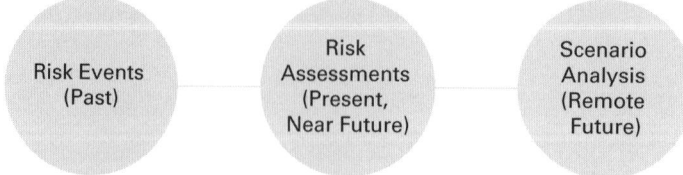

The two main differences between scenario analysis and RCSAs, described in Chapter 5, are the time horizon and the magnitude of considered events. While RCSAs concentrate on the business cycle and business-as-usual risks (high frequency, low severity), scenarios focus on rare but major occurrences (low frequency, high severity). The two tools are complementary in helping to build the overall risk profile of the firm. Some organizations have separate RCSA and SA processes; while others combine them by stretching the time horizon of the risk assessment matrix (discussed in Chapter 5) to a lengthy period, for example up to 100 years. The firm can adopt either approach, as long as they are fully integrated into the risk management framework and serve to enable the best decision making.

A note on terminology. In previous chapters, we discussed *impact* and *likelihood*:

- When working with scenarios, the terms *impact* and *severity* are often used interchangeably. The term *severity* has been historically applied by quants to model severity distribution – a statistical distribution of the amount of loss incurred in each risk event. But the word also handily emphasizes the extreme nature of scenarios and their position on the impact scale.

- *Frequency* reflects how often the event occurs – as opposed to how large it is – and is used when talking about modelling *frequency distribution* – a statistical distribution that displays how often (ie frequently) various outcomes occur.

Terms such as severity, frequency and probability are mathematical concepts that are common in scenario analysis; where often we are asked to estimate a 1 in X years event – an event which has both a defined impact (ie 'severity') and a 'frequency' that it will only occur once in every X years. But for most audiences it is advisable to use the softer, more intuitive terms and language, as described in the good practices section on page 204, and a simplified way of approaching these mathematical concepts.

The main aims of scenario analysis are to:

- consider the worst outcomes of risks materializing and evaluate their impact on the organization;

- examine the control environment and the firm's preparedness for extreme events;

- create a consolidated, forward-looking view of the firm's most material exposures by examining a portfolio of scenarios;

- enable the firm to develop a horizon-scanning capability based on an understanding of the drivers of potential extreme, low-probability events;

- raise awareness among senior management of the severe, but plausible types of events they could experience;

- use the outcome for operational risk management and reduction;

- review the adequacy of the firm's insurance coverage and identify whether any specific form of insurance is needed; and

- calculate regulatory and economic capital, and support the internal capital adequacy assessment process.

Scenario selection process

Examples of scenarios are significant events such as major cyber attacks or rogue trading, extreme weather leading to a flood in the data centre, sustained regulatory non-compliance resulting in a supervisory intervention and fine, an employment discrimination lawsuit or a pandemic. While these are relatively common story lines, the exact scenarios depend on the nature of the firm, its business model and risk profile.

The strategic RCSA (at the top of the house, reflecting risks for the whole entity or a business line) is a good starting point for thinking about scenarios, as the firm has already used this tool to consider its key, strategic level risks. Story lines can then be developed for each of the *most significant inherent risks*, pushed to their extreme. Or several risks can be assumed to have *simultaneously materialized*. The firm's taxonomy categories provide a helpful reminder of the whole range of themes to be addressed via scenarios.

External newspaper articles describing significant operational risk events – along with industry *top operational risks* surveys – can be also used to generate ideas. External events are incredibly powerful to counteract the inevitable challenge from participants that *this could never happen to us* and *this could never cost that much*. Keeping in touch with the industry and leveraging incidents also reflects very well on the organization.

Alternatively, it is possible to start from a blank page and just think the unthinkable, contemplating for example, a complete destruction of the data centre. The firm's operational risk taxonomy provides a useful checkpoint of the completeness of coverage, ensuring that scenarios have been considered for the key categories of the taxonomy.

FIGURE 8.4 Scenario analysis spectrum

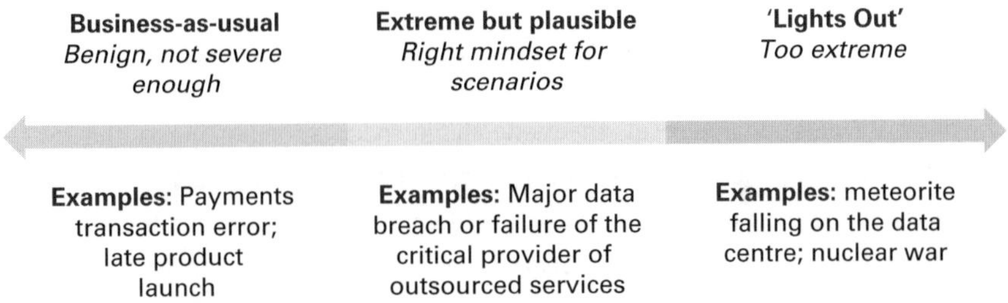

Business-as-usual	Extreme but plausible	'Lights Out'
Benign, not severe enough	*Right mindset for scenarios*	*Too extreme*

Examples: Payments transaction error; late product launch	Examples: Major data breach or failure of the critical provider of outsourced services	Examples: meteorite falling on the data centre; nuclear war

For the scenario to materialize, controls – sometimes several of them – are assumed to have failed. This is a challenging aspect for those participants who operate the daily controls and may have high confidence (and a vested interest) in their performance. But in extreme scenarios, business-as-usual controls may turn out to be less effective simply because the environment prevents one or more component, such as people or systems, from functioning properly.

As described in Figure 8.4, scenarios usually bounce between business-as-usual known experiences and *lights-out, end-of-the-world* thinking. The hard part is developing and cultivating an *extreme but plausible* mindset that the firm can actually work with as a basis for credible testing.

Scenarios in practice: three case studies

Let's review three case study examples of different scenario approaches, to articulate the range of practices used in the financial services industry, and highlight their strong points and areas for improvement.

CASE STUDY 8.1

A newly-established financial markets equities and fixed income business examines a *Rogue Trader* scenario, which it sees as its most significant potential risk. This is done via a workshop with the following participants:

- head of Operational Risk (workshop *facilitator*);
- head of Trading (scenario *owner*), joined by a trader;
- chief risk officer;
- head of Market Risk;

- head of Operations;

- head of Finance;

- representatives from Compliance and middle office/product control.

The head of Operational Risk sets the scene and introduces the purpose of the workshop. Given the business line is newly established, the specific aim is to deliberate exactly *how* a dishonest trader might approach unauthorized trading and what strategies they may adopt. It is also to evaluate the firm's control environment, and to test its resilience and ability to withstand a worst-case event. The outcomes will also feed into the firm's capital adequacy process, though this objective is secondary.

The trader describes three potential rogue trading strategies, which are reviewed in detail by the participants:

- *deliberate skimming*, including collusion between the trader and their counterparty (to share the profits);

- *excessive intra-day position taking*, a foolish bet whereby the trader believes they can make major profits during the day and establishes large positions which they subsequently liquidate by the end of the day; and

- *concealing positions*, whereby large positions are created by over-the-counter (OTC) deals being intentionally not entered into the trading system.

The group scrutinizes key preventative and detective controls:

1 Trader supervision, relying on the head of Trading to be constantly aware of all traders' dealing activities. It is assumed that this control fails and fraudulent activity is overlooked.

2 The confirmations process, administered independently by Operations. This is a primary detective control ensuring that each deal is matched with a corresponding counterparty's trade. Upon close examination, a gap is identified. It transpires that the process involves several counterparties signing a short form confirmation which is received by the trader rather than an independent operations unit. An action to remediate the deficiency is taken jointly by the head of Trading and head of Operations; this should include re-evaluation of the relevant risks and controls set out in the RCSA.

During the workshop, the overall maximum amount of loss for each of the three scenarios is estimated by reviewing trading volumes, considering the nature and number of counterparties, and external limitations set by exchanges and correspondent banks.

Following the meeting, the head of Operations and head of Finance state that they found the study very useful, and ask Operational Risk to facilitate similar workshops within their respective areas. Their request is to replicate the thought process of the rogue trading workshop, examining possible ways in which unauthorized or fraudulent payments can be executed, and trying to find potential loopholes. These workshops are subsequently run for risk *management* purposes only – it is known a priori that the financial outcomes will be lower than *rogue trading* and therefore are unlikely to be used for capital assessment purposes.

What are the positive features of this process?

- An approach with a strong sense of purpose, which engages the participants and establishes scenario analysis as a valuable risk management tool that subsequently becomes in demand.
- An explicitly defined executive level scenario owner (the head of Trading).
- A value-added control review leading to remedial actions.

What can be improved?

- The estimation of the amount at risk, considering different elements that might contribute to a loss; including, for example, regulatory fines and remediation costs.

CASE STUDY 8.2

A medium-sized regulated subsidiary is subjected to a review of its internal capital adequacy assessment process (ICAAP), with unsatisfactory results. One of the regulator's criticisms is around scenarios, which are deemed too benign and not sufficiently extreme. As part of the remediation, senior management agrees to start running multifactor scenario analysis. Despite the process being regulatory driven, the head of Operational Risk is aiming to derive maximum value out of the exercise.

The 10 most significant (top) inherent risks are extracted from the subsidiary's risk and control self-assessment and noted down on post-it notes, one risk on each note. Five members of the senior executive team consisting of the CEO, head of Corporate Banking, head of Risk, chief operations officer and head of Finance are asked to each pick two post-it notes at random and to come up with a scenario where their two chosen risks materialize at the same time. This approach is useful because in real life an extreme unexpected loss often arises from a combination of unrelated events which, when combined, place intolerable stress on the control environment.

The head of Finance selects *Poor change management process* and *Significant data breach* and develops a plausible story line combining two failures:

- the subsidiary is planning to migrate customer accounts to a new system;

- the deadline is fast approaching and corners are cut in the testing phase;

- once the transition goes live, a major issue is highlighted, and migration has to be stopped and rolled back to the pre-transition stage;

- an employee participating in the project, who has worked significant overtime over several months, is frustrated with this result and uses the opportunity to print out and anonymously leak confidential details of multiple client accounts;

- the leak is not discovered until later due to key personnel being occupied with the roll-back.

Other participants introduce their respective scenarios before the two-hour workshop concludes. The workshop generates lively debate among senior management participants, resulting in agreement about several areas that need further exploration and possible enhancement of processes and controls. Proposed story lines are subsequently supplemented by a study of relevant internal and external loss data, and a financial value for each scenario is estimated at follow-up meetings with a broader audience of subject matter experts.

What are the positive features of this process?

- Multifactor scenarios, assuming that multiple risks crystallize at once.

- Senior stakeholder engagement.

- Several improvement projects emanating from the workshop.

What can be improved?

- A disciplined approach to the creation of a preparatory pack; this should contain supporting materials with internal and external loss data and other information to facilitate the assessment of scenario amounts.

CASE STUDY 8.3

An institution using a statistical model to calculate its operational risk capital is running a scenario analysis workshop. (Note: the firms in the earlier case studies were not using statistical models.) The workshop is led by the first line operational risk coordinator, with middle management from relevant business lines in attendance. The operational risk coordinator explains that scenarios need to be created due to key gaps in the relevant loss data. In the future, these scenarios could be decommissioned if they are replaced by real events, either internally or externally sourced.

As preparatory work, operational risk has distributed a reading pack containing internal loss data, external loss data and an analysis of the risk and control environment relevant to the story line. A training session has also been offered to participants prior to the workshop, which some of the attendees have opted to take.

The scenario story line is a major regulatory breach. The group discuss the cause, the event itself and its consequences, using the already familiar bow-tie approach, as per Figure 8.5.

Causal factors include prior regulatory criticism of the lack of first line ownership, poor change management and rushed implementation of a new regulatory initiative. Assumptions are documented around a generally deteriorating business environment and a series of minor reportable breaches which preceded the main event. This combination of factors then culminates in a major regulatory non-compliance incident, whereby the firm fails to identify, understand and implement an important new regulatory directive before its effective date.

The consequences of the event include a fine and investigation, disciplinary actions against the firm and its managers, and a loss of client business due to damaged brand and reputation.

FIGURE 8.5 Cause–Event–Impact approach to scenario analysis

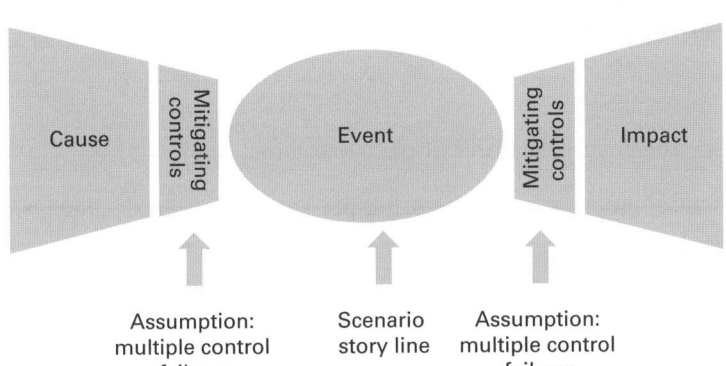

TABLE 8.1 Scenario quantification

Loss category	Description	Applicable? Yes/No	Amount
Direct loss	Impact of the loss on the P&L account		
Fines and penalties	Regulatory, compliance, taxation or other penalties as a result of non-compliance		
Expenses	Consultancy costs or other unbudgeted expenses		
Legal liability	Legal fees, legal judgement and/or settlement		
Indirect costs	Overtime paid to staff due to extra hours worked in resolving the loss, short-term rental of additional premises, travel and other indirect expenses		
Risk of life	Danger or loss of life of an employee		
Reputational impact	Reduced sales and lost revenue due to brand damage		

To assist scenario quantification, participants use the checklist in Table 8.1 which contains different categories of possible impacts.

The overall loss amount is estimated as a sum of applicable sub-components. Participants are asked to consider three scenario frequencies – a 1 in 10-year event, 1 in 25 and 1 in 40 – and to come up with an estimated loss number in each category, giving rise to three points to model as the basis of a loss curve.

The workshop lasts for one and a half hours and concludes with no further actions.

What are the positive features of the workshop?

- Structured approach to generating pre-reading materials and providing training.

- Consistent format for estimating the amount, resulting in well-reasoned evaluations.

- First line operational risk in the lead.

What can be improved?

- The value proposition, use of a workshop for *risk management* purposes, ownership and agreement of actions, senior stakeholder engagement.

Life cycle: from pre-reading packs to mitigating bias

The scenario process life cycle is described below:

- **Define:** A theme or topic for a scenario and a detailed story line are developed.
- **Prepare:** Relevant data is researched and assembled into a pre-reading pack.
- **Explore and Assess:** A workshop is run with subject matter experts to discuss the scenario and arrive at the estimated numbers.
- **Extract Learnings and Actions:** Identified control gaps and actions are noted down, with owners and target dates.
- **Validate:** Scenario outcomes are scrutinized by relevant subject matter experts and governance committees.

Define

As mentioned above, the most significant inherent risks from RCSAs can be a good starting point to generate scenario ideas. It is good practice to examine simultaneous multiple failures, for example, by combining two to three *top* risks from the RCSAs, for example *Significant system failure* and *Internal fraud*. In the event that the firm is anticipating an acquisition or expansion into a new market, this kind of strategic initiative also needs to be taken into consideration.

> When defining story lines, it is important to ensure that scenarios are *forward looking* and correspond to the organization's strategy. Scenarios can examine plausible events that may crystallize as a result of a chosen strategic direction, thus aiding good decision-making.

Scenarios can be established at multiple levels of the organization, including at group-wide and individual business or entity level. The selection process involves deciding on what constitutes a key risk which would benefit from further exploration. There may be a need to run the same scenario – for example *internal fraud* – several times to ensure all business units are included. Systemic risks impacting any number of control processes operating in business units also need to be considered.

It is good practice to agree an *executive sponsor* at the outset, a senior executive who owns and is accountable for the content and the story line. The owner plays a key role in the whole life cycle, from defining the story line to providing sign-off as part of the later validation stage, and finally ensuring any follow-up actions are actually completed.

Prepare

Pre-reading packs help to structure the workshops. Typically, the operational risk team researches, prepares and analyses relevant materials. These will often include internal losses, a selection of pertinent external events experienced by peer firms, and RCSA data reflecting the firm's risk and control environment, as well as the results of compliance monitoring and internal audit reviews. Applicable operational and financial data, containing transaction volumes, values and profitability, help to make the discussion more factual and to arrive at accurate loss estimates. It is useful to outline the inherent risk exposure from the RCSAs up-front; as well as noting if the scenario involves breaches of the firm's appetite. A consistent and uniform approach to the preparatory packs helps to achieve reliable outcomes.

Generally, the more time spent in preparation, the shorter the required length of the workshop. Foundational activity may involve working with the scenario owner and relevant business experts to define a story line. The workshop can then be used, in effect, as a validation activity.

Alternatively, a shorter preparation time can result in a longer workshop where the story line itself is debated and developed in detail. This can be done using, for example, a technique such as a Bayesian tree scenario, commonly used in the insurance industry. In simple terms, this approach allows a mapping of the scenario journey by workshop participants all working together. This might involve a starting point: for example, the new normal of *working from home* which has emanated from the Covid-19 pandemic. The story line is then progressively developed, exploring potential for a data loss, cyber attack and internal fraud. The strength of this approach is its ability to explore the interconnectivity between various different causes.

Explore and assess

The Basel Committee notes four possible approaches to scenario analysis, namely workshops, individual interviews, questionnaires and voting.[1] In the 2020 poll I ran with industry experts, 100 per cent of respondents were using workshops: no other mechanism was deemed nearly as effective, though the duration of workshops differed sharply, as illustrated in Table 8.2.

As part of the workshop, an estimation should be made as to the frequency and severity of the losses occurring in different timelines; usually in normal situations as well as worst or stressed cases. The quantification is then completed by business experts based on their subjective judgement. This process involves a risk of partiality or unfairness (bias) in the assessment; driven by common bias factors such as overconfidence, motivational bias, availability or anchoring. Consequently the firm needs to have measures in place to address those biases, for example as described in Table 8.3.

TABLE 8.2 Industry study: scenario workshop duration

Workshop duration	% Respondents
1 hour	30%
1.5–2 hours	20%
3–4 hours	30%
Half-day or longer	20%

Best Practice Operational Risk Forum, 2020

TABLE 8.3 Mitigating bias

Bias	Explanation	Mitigation
Overconfidence	Attendees overestimate the robustness of controls	Pre-reading pack containing factual data on past internal events Stress testing controls: exploring what will make them fail
Motivational	Participant is conflicted/ interested in influencing the outcome of the workshop (to, for example, reduce the estimated loss amount)	Consistent and robust facilitation to manage conflicting interests Use of anonymous voting polls or obtaining estimated numbers beforehand Challenge and validation by subject matter experts

(continued)

TABLE 8.3 (Continued)

Bias	Explanation	Mitigation
Availability	Increased focus on recent events as they can be easily recalled	Pre-reading pack containing factual external event data Encouragement to think about possible events that have not yet occurred
Anchoring	Different starting points (anchors) will yield different results	Use of neutral open questions Avoidance of leading questions containing a number (anchor) Training for participants to explain different terms; and what should or should not be included into estimates Request to submit quantifications ahead of the workshop Use of ranges instead of specific values

Based on the 2020 industry study mentioned earlier, only 50 per cent of respondents explicitly addressed biases in their scenario analysis process.

Extract learnings and actions

This is a critical part of SA, which in practice is underemphasized or entirely overlooked. The workshops need to answer both questions: *how much?* (capital calculation, or a risk *measurement* question) and *so what?* (a risk *management* question). A key aim of scenario analysis is to use the outcomes for risk reduction. Risk mitigating measures need to be considered when:

- a specific control weakness is identified as a result of the exercise; or

- assessment reveals that insurance cover is insufficient or inadequate; or

- the measurement results of the analysis exceed a certain threshold level, bringing it outside the firm's appetite (also see Chapter 9, Operational Risk Appetite). This may happen when a specific scenario highlights significant risk exposure and consequences that are deemed unacceptable for the organization.

The actions need to contain a target date and an owner, and the Operational Risk department usually monitors progress until they have been fully implemented.

At times, the purchase of insurance is a standalone activity which is not coordinated with the firm's risk management efforts. Evaluating the degree and scope of insurance coverage is a great opportunity for operational risk to work closely with the department responsible for procuring the firm's insurance: for example, assessing proposals obtained in the market, considering the types of cover offered, and analysing whether they are appropriate. This is the opportunity to consider gaps in cover as well as any ambiguity on whether a particular loss is or is not included in the policy. Insurance needs to be both commensurate with identified exposure and in sync with the story lines examined in the workshops. Furthermore, given the nature of the insurance market, both corporate insurance buying functions and external brokers can be good sources of credible but extreme scenario suggestions.

Finally, the scenario workshop can also trigger a revision of RCSAs, to sense check the inherent risk assessment; as well as amendments to/introductions of new key risk indicators, discussed in Chapter 7.

Validate

Based on the Basel Committee study, four challenge functions are used to maintain the integrity of scenario analysis: review by a risk control function (93 per cent); review by internal/external audit (83 per cent); comparisons by experienced or expert staff (76 per cent); and comparisons with other data elements (62 per cent).[2]

The second line Operational Risk department is usually the first point of validation. To enable this to occur, it is critical that the team does not contribute to the quantification, to avoid marking its own homework.

Scenarios can be assessed for consistency of outcomes, ensuring that:

- the scenario is correctly classified using the firm's usual operational risk taxonomy;
- financial impact is not lower than that experienced from internal loss events;
- if different frequencies are used, the financial impact with the lower frequency is smaller than the higher-frequency event;
- story lines and related assumptions are comparable with related external events;
- there is consistency in the documentation and rationale around the outcomes, to ensure 'a clearly defined and repeatable process'.[3]

Further evaluation is usually undertaken by a wider group of stakeholders, either at the risk committee or the capital and stress testing committee; or by the appropriate governance committee responsible for the operational risk capital calculation.

How are the reviewers determining whether the story lines are extreme enough and the amounts plausible?

The construct and extremity of scenarios is in part a cultural matter, reflecting how cautious and well capitalized the firm aspires to be. The approach is often tested in practice at times of crisis, resulting in some conservative firms having sufficient reserves while others find themselves operating to the wire and perhaps in need of external help. During the early stages of the Covid-19 pandemic, Nassim Taleb relayed thoughts on this topic when discussing the concept of bail-out, stipulating that bail-out (of banks in particular) is encouraging the wrong behaviour, favouring those firms that do not have an adequate buffer, and pointing out that 'not having a buffer is irresponsible'.[4]

Therefore, in practice, scenario validation can be a tenuous activity. By definition, scenarios are made-up events with imaginary story lines that have been allocated a potential loss amount by workshop participants. The cultural element in firms often manifests itself in haggling over the numbers. One of three things can happen: reduce the estimate, increase the estimate, or enhance controls.

CALL TO REDUCE THE ESTIMATE

Reviewers will state that estimated amount is abnormally high, resulting in a greater than expected capital requirement; workshop participants must go back and re-evaluate the amount, ideally bringing it lower. This eventuality can be due to incorrect workshop attendees, poor methodology or excessive confidence in the ability of the control regime to respond to the event. However in many cases there is an additional cultural aspect: a refusal to tolerate any buffer that increases the cost of running the business (this links back to motivational bias). This attitude also creates a danger of losing the operational value of the risk management points raised by the scenario, simply due to over-consideration of the costs of the final number.

CALL TO INCREASE THE ESTIMATE

The estimated amount can also be perceived as too low, with a similar request to re-work it. This, again, can occur because of procedural elements, but in most senses is a positive sign: the firm would rather be too cautious than overly optimistic. This happens far more rarely and is a credit to any firm whose leaders raise this kind of challenge.

CALL TO ENHANCE CONTROLS

The scenario amount is assessed as unacceptably high; however rather than changing the number, there is a request to improve the control environment, so that if the scenario materializes, the impact is reduced. Participants walk away from the process committing to develop, agree and implement mitigating actions. This is the preferred outcome, which not only demonstrates the use test but also does not devalue the efforts of workshop participants and does not over-ride their judgement. A sign of risk maturity is to learn from the expertise in the room but as a consequence of the scenario analysis to seek to reduce its impact or likelihood.

Periodic updates

Many organizations factor trigger-based scenario updates into their policies. In practice, however, where scenarios are run mainly for risk measurement purposes, they are more usually updated annually, to coincide with the update of the ICAAP. Ideally, scenarios are management's first choice when it comes to exploring or anticipating the impact of major changes or disruptions to the firm's business. These can include:

- changes in business model, including a new line of business, service or geography, acquisition, or divestiture;
- material changes in the external environment, be it the pandemic, new regulations, a material external loss event, or wider social or political behaviour;
- a large unexpected internal loss or significant deterioration in the internal control environment.

The outbreaks of avian flu in 2003 and Covid-19 during 2020 prompted many organizations to run a pandemic scenario, exploring the readiness of the firm and considering actions (risk *management*) as well as evaluating their potential impact on the capital position (risk *measurement*). Similarly, large industry rogue trading events served as a trigger for scenario revision. If a scenario owner is engaged and has enjoyed a good experience with the workshop, they will be more inclined to rely on the tool as a first point of call in the event of a major shift in the day-to-day environment – as a way to explore the consequences of the event. This can be one of the clearest measures of the success of the tool: to have the owners *want* to use the SA process.

Other softer factors are also recognized as a foundation for good decision making; including situational awareness, which refers to perceptions about the wider environment and a good comprehension of the meaning and projection of the future state. Indeed, what transpired during Covid-19 is that while most firms had the scenario analysis tool at their disposal, it was those firms with a situational awareness mindset who promptly applied it in practice and showed maximum responsiveness.

Roles and responsibilities

The second line operational risk team sets the tone and determines whether the SA exercise will be used for measurement and regulatory compliance purposes only, or whether it will have a true value proposition. It goes without saying that key building blocks need to be in place. These include robust policy and guidance for participants; close oversight, ensuring that story lines are clearly defined with sufficient level of detail; the right stakeholders being involved; a strong validation and challenge process; and, last but not least, a trigger-based refresh process. It is far more difficult, and yet at the same time essential, to invest time and effort in turning the scenario exercise into a tool that stakeholders are truly keen to use; because of its clear benefits to them. The actions and behaviours of the second line, whether consciously or subconsciously, define the brand and reputation of scenario analysis. How will it be seen? Is it 'this needs to be done for capital purposes; but apart from that it's not very useful'? Or is it 'a valuable exploratory exercise; our first point of call when considering significant internal and external changes which also, by the way, generates inputs into the capital calculation'?

First line business units and support functions own and operate the controls and therefore, the scenario process examines *their* exposure to extreme risks. They are responsible for owning the story lines, evaluating the environment, identifying and agreeing actions and following them up until resolution.

Below is an example checklist for a first line risk coordinator.

FIRST LINE RISK COORDINATOR CHECKLIST: SCENARIO ANALYSIS

✓ Staff are aware of the SA tool and its benefits.

✓ There is a nominated senior executive, *the scenario owner*, for each scenario owned by the department.

✓ Material change in the environment triggers a consideration of scenario refresh or a need for a new one.

✓ Actions emanating from the SA are followed up until resolution.

✓ Post-SA, other core tools, including RCSAs, KRIs, OREs and where separately used, *emerging risks*, are considered for revision.

Common challenges and good practices

Common challenges

The following challenges may be encountered when dealing with scenario analysis.

CHALLENGES OF THE OPERATIONAL RISK DISCIPLINE

Within the operational risk discipline, historically there existed a disconnect between the quantitative community: of modellers who designed statistical models for the capital calculation, and generalists who focussed more on the qualitative aspects of embeddedness, helping to implement good practices within, for example, the Human Resources or IT departments. Modellers and generalists not working together often led to risk *measurement* and *management* not being in sync. This is a very specific challenge to operational risk. In contrast, credit and market risk disciplines are more homogeneously quantitative – they do not have to work hand-in-hand with, say, Human Resources. On the other side, the compliance function – which is perhaps akin to operational risk in that it works with all the different units across the firm – does not typically design or run its own statistical models. It is crucial for both communities to work together. The generalists who have a natural curiosity about the quantitative aspects and take the time to understand the model assumptions and limitations, often play a key role in bridging the gap between the quants and the business.

PARTICIPANTS DISMISSIVE OF THE STORY LINE

Workshop participants are dismissive of the scenario, taking the viewpoint that *this can never happen to us*. This is a common challenge from attendees who operate controls and understandably take pride in their robustness. Participants need to be pushed to think outside their comfort zone, by being educated and informed about the purpose of the SA process. It should be emphasized that it is not a test of the BAU control environment but a stressed, extreme environment enabling the firm to build shock-proof controls; and bringing to the fore relevant case studies of external events which prompted failures.

TERMS HARD TO UNDERSTAND

Attendees struggle to understand the notion of frequency, questioning what exactly do the statements *1 in 40 years* or *1 in 100 years* actually mean. Operational risk team needs to provide an explanation, comparing it more intuitively to, for example, a *once in a career event* or a *once in a lifetime event*. Some practitioners run workshops using softer terminology, keeping the probability numbers and concept in the background. One approach that should definitely be avoided is to invite attendees to *assess the 95th percentile loss amount*, or other similar statistical measures; as these are mathematical concepts which may take considerable time to explain. (Note: another common misunderstanding is that a *1 in 40 years* event will not occur with the prescribed impact for the next 40 years; while it could happen tomorrow!)

DIFFICULTY IN ARRIVING AT A NUMBER

From a *measurement* viewpoint, scenario analysis relies heavily on expert judgement to produce a rather extreme number. It is important to recognize that participants from business and support functions, as knowledgeable as they are in their areas, are not really experts in predicting the future, and consequently may be only partially effective in providing loss estimates. It often helps to allow people to express ranges, even for a single event or component of it.

LACK OF ACTION

A rather bureaucratic exercise is run and quickly forgotten. After the numbers are obtained, no actions emanate from the workshop and its value rapidly diminishes. It is essential to acknowledge the value of SME inputs; to share outcomes with senior management; to keep participants informed on uses of the output, and to highlight real-life internal and external events when they happen (helping to demonstrate the reality of the scenarios); as well as to ensure that the SA exercise includes a thorough control examination. All these features should be a mandatory part of the process.

OVERALL NUMBER OF SCENARIOS

The number of scenarios varies significantly from firm to firm. Similar to KRIs, some organizations design and run way too many scenarios, running to hundreds, purely for *risk measurement* purposes. While there is no right target number and it is often determined by the firm's risk taxonomy and footprint, a range of around 15–30 scenarios with solid *risk management* outcomes is appropriate. This comes with a caveat, however, of what is meant by scenario and what value is derived from the process. For management purposes, cyber war games, crisis management and incident response table-top exercises are also labelled as scenarios by some organizations, even though they do not generate a capital number. Some firms differentiate 'big S' Scenarios used for capital calculation purposes and 'small s' scenarios run to identify and remedy control weaknesses.

MODELS DRIVE THE EXERCISE

Sometimes organizations applying less quantitative, formula-based approaches to capital calculation are not driven and *constrained* by the statistical model and consequently do better with scenario analysis from the value proposition point of view. This, however, does not have to be the case; business benefits need to come first regardless of the approach, with regulatory compliance a secondary, not primary outcome.

Good practices

ENSURING VALUE PROPOSITION

The secret of success with scenario analysis is in ensuring it has a clear value proposition *for the attendees* and does not become an operational risk number-generating exercise. When running workshops, it is important to consider what benefits *participants* will derive from the meeting. A clear purpose ensures that the scenario process is integrated with business decisions. The purpose can be, for example, to examine preparedness for a particular event that is relevant to the business owner and keeps them awake at night; to assess the impact of a major change, including a new product, service or geography, or wider social and political shifts. Scenarios are there to help first line business units and support functions to examine *their own* exposure to extreme risks, and to mitigate them so eventually they are able to meet *their own* objectives.

WORKSHOP FACILITATION

Good workshop facilitation, discussed in Chapter 5, is even more critical for scenarios. The Basel Committee notes the need for 'qualified and experienced facilitators with consistency in the facilitation process'.[5] This is important for the brand and value proposition of the exercise as well as for achieving reliable outcomes. Facilitation can include the use of aids such as live polls which can help mitigate, for example, motivational bias by requesting participants to anonymously vote on a scenario estimate. Expert guest speakers, YouTube clips and functional presentations also make the workshop more engaging for the attendees.

STRESS TESTING CONTROLS

It is good practice to challenge each control in turn, finding ever more extreme situations in which a control may fail. This can be thought of as *stress testing* each control. In real-life situations one or more controls fail to operate due to what are often unforeseen circumstances, thus proving that the improbable is actually more probable in practice than in theory.

RIGOUR AND DOCUMENTATION

Regulatory focus is often on the rigour of the process used to obtain inputs into any capital model. That process needs to be systematic and to generate good-quality documentation. The output pack needs to contain the scenario description and rationale for its selection, assumptions, a chronology of events, and robust loss estimates with justification of the amounts; as well as any other scenarios considered and discounted. Scenarios are sometimes loaded into the operational risk system/software, where other risk modules or scenario data relevant to the risk may exist. Where the evidence is kept in an Excel or Word format, maintaining the library to a good standard ensures accessibility and evidenced decision making. Actions emanating from the workshops can be uploaded into an *action* module, to enable tracking of progress until full resolution.

MEASURES OF SUCCESS

One of the measures of success is the number of actions that emanate from scenario workshops; even better if they lead to monetary investments in improving the control environment. This outcome is, unfortunately, underused.

The Basel Committee notes that 'overall, few banks develop action plans from their scenario analyses.'[6]

Industry benchmark, 2020

Operational risk practitioners from various financial services firms participated in a live poll to examine the use of scenario analysis in operational risk management. Overall, the meeting revealed a positive story. Despite the historic use of SA for risk *measurement* purposes only, gone are the days of pure number generation; the industry seems to have tackled the challenge, with the majority (76 per cent) using the tool for both risk *management* and *measurement* purposes, as seen in Figure 8.6.

How many operational risk scenarios do firms have? The range varies between 10 and 40, with organizations generally planning to reduce the number if they have over 30 (Figure 8.7).

Finally, while scenarios are not considered the most valuable tool in the operational risk framework, they are deemed to generate significant business value (36 per cent, per Figure 8.8). This is the area of focus for the future: how to move from 'moderate' and 'minor', with no actions emanating from the exercise, to bringing significant benefits.

FIGURE 8.6 Industry poll: use of scenario analysis

Scenario Analysis (SA) is used for

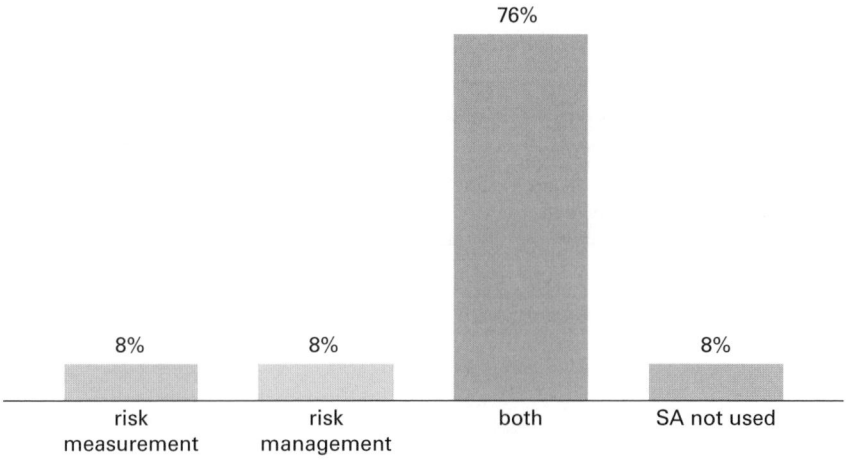

Best Practice Operational Risk Forum, 2020

FIGURE 8.7 Industry poll: number of scenarios considered

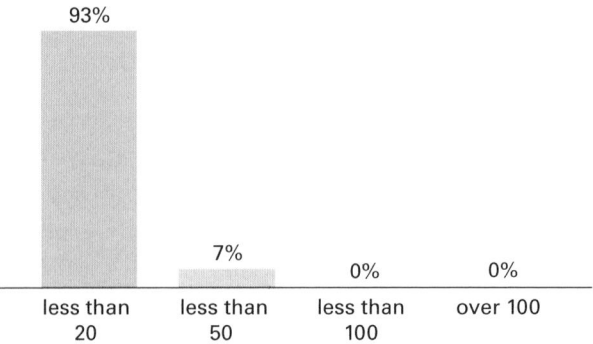

Best Practice Operational Risk Forum, 2020

FIGURE 8.8 Industry poll: value of scenarios relative to other tools

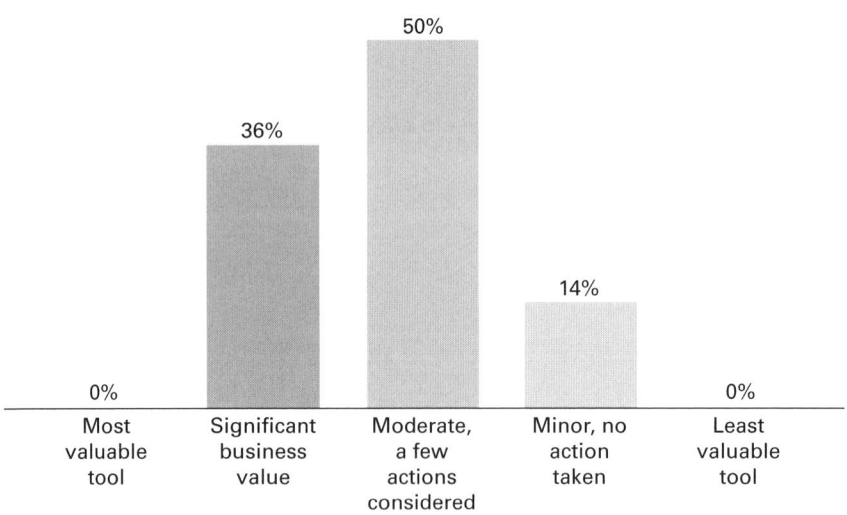

Best Practice Operational Risk Forum, 2020

Practical workplace exercise

Obtain a copy of the firm's set of scenarios from the scenario library. Review it, considering the following questions:

1   What is the firm's approach to scenario analysis? Is it driven by capital considerations and run primarily for risk measurement purposes, or risk management, or both?

2   Are scenarios clearly defined? Is the story line documented and does the documentation contain assumptions, a clearly described workshop rationale and justification of the resulting loss amount?

3   What actions have been considered following the workshop? Did the scenarios covered include an examination of the control environment and did any improvements result from the process?

4   Is there a comparison of scenarios with the firm's insurance coverage?

5   What works well? Outline the strength of the process.

6   What could be improved? Note down potential areas of enhancement.

MAKE A DIFFERENCE (MAD) ACTION

Outline the key learnings and note down one specific action you will take after reading this chapter, to enhance your existing practices relating to scenario analysis.

In summary, this chapter discussed scenario analysis, an instrument that utilizes proactive risk assessment thinking and applies it to extreme but plausible circumstances.

Now that all the core tools of the operational risk toolbox have been examined, the next chapter considers mechanisms that converges the core elements, commencing with the operational risk appetite.

Notes

1   Basel Committee on Banking Supervision (2009) *Observed Range of Practice in Key Elements of Advanced Measurement Approaches*, www.bis.org/publ/ bcbs160b.pdf (archived at https://perma.cc/338U-X5GQ)

2   Basel Committee on Banking Supervision (2009) *Observed Range of Practice in Key Elements of Advanced Measurement Approaches*, www.bis.org/publ/ bcbs160b.pdf (archived at https://perma.cc/KHM8-9Q66)

3   Basel Committee on Banking Supervision (2009) *Observed Range of Practice in Key Elements of Advanced Measurement Approaches*, www.bis.org/publ/ bcbs160b.pdf (archived at https://perma.cc/5FBU-QM9S)

4   Bloomberg (2020) Interview with Nassim Nicholas Taleb, www.bloomberg. com/news/videos/2020-03-31/nassim-taleb-says-white-swan-coronavirus- pandemic-was-preventable-video (archived at https://perma.cc/F6PJ-WXWH)

5   Basel Committee on Banking Supervision (2011) *Operational Risk: Supervisory guidelines for the advanced measurement approaches*, www.bis.org/publ/ bcbs196.pdf (archived at https://perma.cc/66QD-MLSQ)

6   Basel Committee on Banking Supervision (2014) *Review of the Principles for the Sound Management of Operational Risk*, https://www.bis.org/publ/bcbs292. pdf (archived at https://perma.cc/7BT6-HPFU)

09

Operational risk appetite

What this chapter covers: The chapter discusses Operational Risk Appetite, a topic which continues to pose challenges for firms due to its essentially qualitative nature (Figure 9.1). The chapter considers two divergent opinions, examining whether operational risk is consciously taken for reward or is merely mitigated downwards. It then proceeds to practical implementation, proposing a three-stage process to developing a risk appetite that is meaningful and used for decision making. It goes on to present an approach for the expression of risk appetite using particular tools, and provides an assessment scale to help analyse the maturity of the approach. The chapter also provides examples and contains an industry benchmark.

FURTHER READING

- Financial Stability Board (2013) *Principles for an Effective Risk Appetite Framework*
  Why recommended: Although slightly dated, this is an essential guide covering the risk appetite framework and definitions of capacity, tolerance and profile.

Risk reward equation and its application to operational risk

Financial services firms are in the business of taking risk and have been doing so for hundreds of years. When it comes to the neighbouring disciplines of credit and market risk, the risk–reward equation is well understood: conservative lending is less profitable while loans to riskier sectors attract higher interest rates and generate better returns. This is described in Figure 9.2.

FIGURE 9.1 Focus of Chapter 9: operational risk appetite

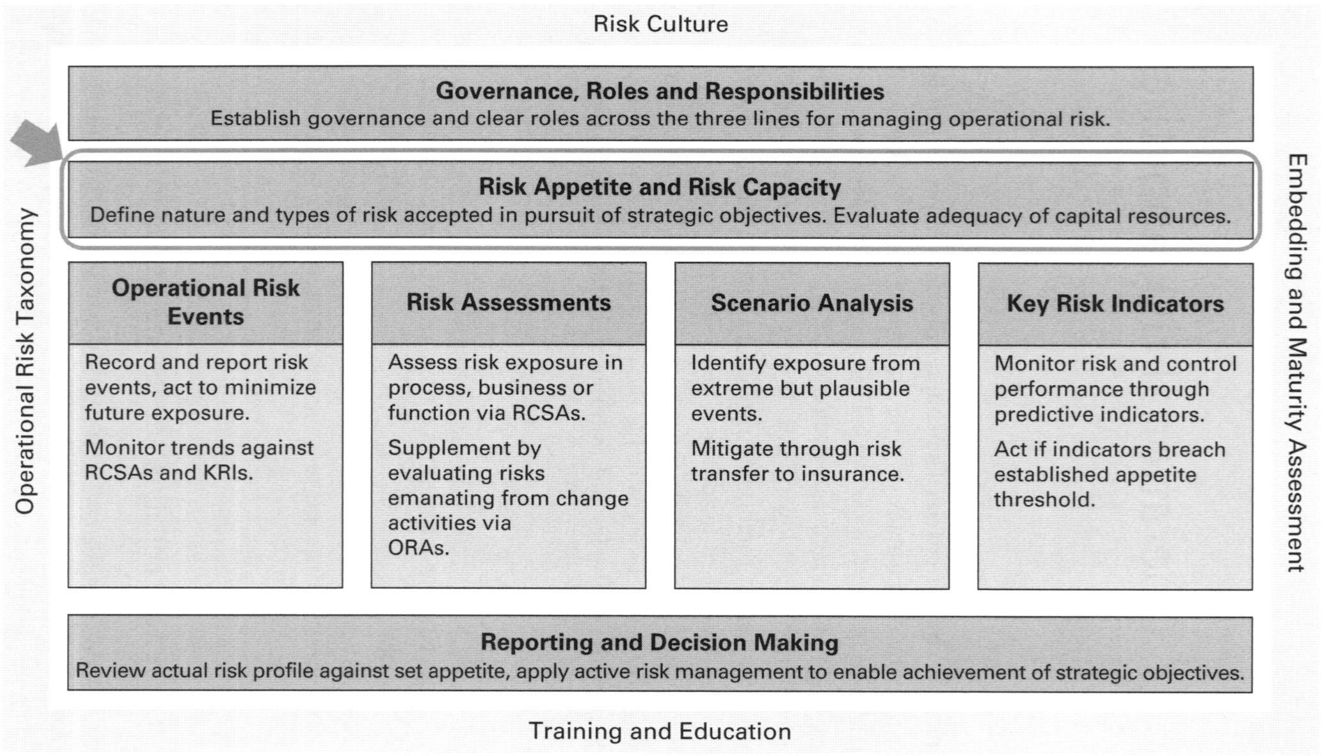

Embedding and Maturity Assessment

Risk Culture

Governance, Roles and Responsibilities

Establish governance and clear roles across the three lines for managing operational risk.

Risk Appetite and Risk Capacity

Define nature and types of risk accepted in pursuit of strategic objectives. Evaluate adequacy of capital resources.

Operational Risk Events	Risk Assessments	Scenario Analysis	Key Risk Indicators
Record and report risk events, act to minimize future exposure. Monitor trends against RCSAs and KRIs.	Assess risk exposure in process, business or function via RCSAs. Supplement by evaluating risks emanating from change activities via ORAs.	Identify exposure from extreme but plausible events. Mitigate through risk transfer to insurance.	Monitor risk and control performance through predictive indicators. Act if indicators breach established appetite threshold.

Reporting and Decision Making

Review actual risk profile against set appetite, apply active risk management to enable achievement of strategic objectives.

Training and Education

Operational Risk Taxonomy

FIGURE 9.2   Risk–reward relationship

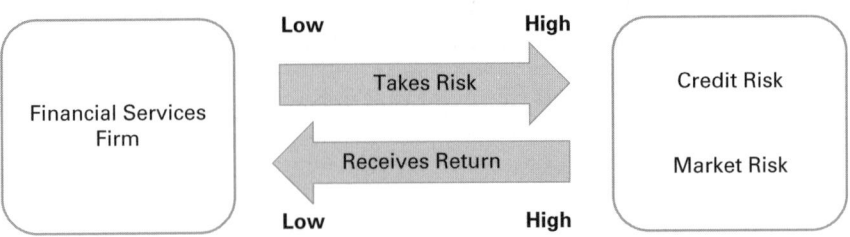

The same formula becomes less obvious when applied to operational risk. There are two main schools of thought on this subject.

The first one differentiates operational risk from credit and market risks, using the word *contrary* in explaining its nature.

Contrary to credit and market risk, operational risk:

- has no material upside in terms of return or income generation;
- cannot be capped; and therefore
- must be mitigated downwards.

This view is somewhat echoed by the European Banking Authority, who wrote that operational risk is by nature 'unavoidable and it is neither willingly incurred nor is revenue driven. Moreover, it is not diversifiable and thus it cannot be fully eliminated.'[1]

This attitude of risk mitigation can be illustrated by examining sub-category 4 of the Basel operational risk taxonomy *clients, products and business practices*:

- Events in this contentious sub-category include unlicensed activity, breaches of regulation, inappropriate sales practices and unsuitable products.
- There is no upside in consciously choosing to contravene the regulation or offer ill-designed products. In fact, it is unethical and unlawful.
- The risk will inevitably materialize into incidents as a result of human errors, poor training or wilful misconduct. It is not possible to put a hard limit on the level of risk in terms of the number and value of losses as they cannot be completely eradicated – unless the firm chooses to exit the business altogether.

- Consequently, organizations revert to a risk reduction approach, implementing policies, providing training and enhancing detective mechanisms for early identification of non-compliance.

There is, however, a second viewpoint that uses the word *similar* instead of *contrary*.

In a *similar* way to credit and market risk:

- operational risk has to be looked at on a risk–reward basis;
- the reward aspect may include revenue from engaging in specific activities or cost reductions; and therefore
- the right level of risk is consciously taken in pursuit of strategic objectives.

When running training courses, I usually ask the audience to come up with examples where operational risk is taken for return. This commonly proves to be less familiar territory for participants, and it is typically more difficult for them to contemplate the 'risk–reward' concept compared to 'risk mitigation'.

CASE STUDY 9.1

A client of an investment bank makes a request to trade a new product. To satisfy this demand, the bank develops a value proposition and carries out an operational risk assessment (ORA). While credit and market risks are within the firm's appetite, product booking and accounting cannot be accommodated systematically and will need to be processed via manual workarounds. The firm acknowledges that the level of operational risk is high; but so is the reward being offered by the client. The proposal is discussed further in the light of the firm's appetite, and is agreed with acceptance of the risk commensurate with the return.

The risk–reward philosophy applied to operational risk leads to a more commercially astute position, balancing the risk with just the right amount of mitigation. Too few controls will result in fines, client detriment and reputational damage; but overdoing them, introducing excessive processes and procedures may render the proposal non-viable. The latter reasoning is generally underused by firms; not only senior managers but even some risk practitioners themselves can feel quite uncomfortable talking about 'letting go of controls' and accepting even a small level of errors and losses. This is an area where the operational risk function can increasingly add value, introducing a risk–reward equation to assist in arriving at balanced, sensible decisions. As discussed in Chapter 6, with the Risks and Opportunities assessment, this approach reinforces positive risk management, encouraging appropriate risk taking while protecting the firm from an overly aggressive attitude.

This more entrepreneurial style also reflects the position expressed in the Financial Stability Board (FSB)'s guidelines on risk appetite; and therefore will serve as a base for the definition of operational risk appetite: [2]

DEFINITION: OPERATIONAL RISK APPETITE

Operational risk appetite represents an aggregate *level* and different *types* of operational risk that 'a financial institution is willing to assume in order to achieve its strategic objectives and business plan'.[3]

The FSB document is a helpful guide for any risk practitioner. It nevertheless recognizes that operational risk appetite is a more difficult summit to conquer due to the qualitative nature of the topic, and therefore goes no further into outlining what good looks like for this particular area.

Deliberations of this kind, on the nature of operational risk and the chosen attitude, be it *mitigated downwards* or *taken for reward*, are important. They define the firm's overall stance towards risk, and the language that will be used to describe it. They also stretch into more cultural aspects, namely whether the firm perceives itself as rather conservative or more entrepreneurial.

Three steps for developing an effective appetite statement

As is the case with most operational risk tools, there is no prescriptive or universally accepted operational risk appetite framework which perfectly suits every organization, sector or jurisdiction. In fact, it is perhaps the most embryonic element in the entire operational risk discipline.

Risk appetite is inextricably linked to *measurement*, which in itself remains a process that is still to be fully mastered by the industry. Those in favour of quantitative approaches – and thus seeking a definitive number to

FIGURE 9.3 Three steps for developing an operational risk appetite

express the appetite – may find that a risk appetite framework does not lend itself well to purely numeric limits and thresholds. In fact, as we will see from this chapter, many descriptors are primarily qualitative.

Also, creating an appetite is not about merely writing a set of statements: it involves providing a decision-making tool to enable prioritization and the deployment of resources, and to drive considered, risk-based decisions. The hardest part of it is fulfilling the *use test* and achieving *embeddedness* throughout the organization. Appetite development is an iterative process where less is more; it is better to have an unsophisticated framework which is well embedded and understood, than a state-of-the-art appetite statement which does not translate into actions and behaviours.

Proposed below is a three-stage process for building an operational risk appetite, outlined in Figure 9.3.

It is suggested that the three steps below are followed when implementing an operational risk appetite:

- define the desirable risk level on a spectrum – both overall and for principal operational risk sub-types;
- develop qualitative statements at an aggregate operational risk level and for each principal risk sub-type;
- establish qualitative and quantitative limits and triggers.

Step 1: Defining desirable risk level on a spectrum

In the first instance, it is valuable to understand the overall types and levels of risk the organization is willing to take in pursuit of its objectives. In simple terms, this step explains how the company intends to remain profitable (ie by taking a given level of risk or accepting a particular level of reward), considering return requirements and the specific idiosyncrasies of the firm's business model. This is an enterprise risk exercise which should be led by Operational Risk, jointly with other risk colleagues, to encompass all risk categories and create a consolidated framework. Desired risk levels can be expressed with the help of a qualitative scale, which provides a useful point of reference for future discussions. The scales can be absolute or relative.

An example of an absolute four-point scale is presented in Figure 9.4 below:

FIGURE 9.4   Risk appetite: absolute scale example

Minimal	**Low**	**Moderate**	**High**
Avoid; take as little risk as possible	Reduce; adopt conservative approach	Take risk commensurate with return	Actively accept exposure to risk to maximize reward

The risk range can be also expressed using a relative scale. An example of a four-point scale is included in Table 9.1:

TABLE 9.1   Risk appetite: relative scale example

Risk-averse	Avoid or minimize risk; the firm is willing to accept below market risk return/incur losses significantly lower than peers
Neutral	Adopt a balanced approach; control risk to achieve returns/incur losses in line with industry norms
Risk-tolerant	Take a measured amount of risk; the firm is willing to accept some risk if the circumstances include reward in line with or above industry norms
Expansionary	Actively pursue risk; the firm is willing to accept superior risk-adjusted reward/accept losses if reward is significantly above industry norm

The use of ranges and postures such as these enables a sensible conversation with the board; summarizing in a nutshell what kinds of risk the firm will actively pursue vs the ones it will aim to control or avoid. For example:

Risk Type	Risk Appetite
Strategic risk	high – actively accept exposure to risk to maximize reward
Operational risk	moderate – take risk commensurate with return
Market risk	low – reduce; adopt conservative approach
Credit risk	low – reduce; adopt conservative approach

And positioned on the scale (Figure 9.5):

FIGURE 9.5   Positioning principal enterprise risks on the scale

Credit Risk Market Risk	Operational risk	Strategic risk

Minimal	Low	Moderate	High
Avoid; take as little risk as possible	*Reduce; adopt conservative approach*	*Take risk commensurate with return*	*Actively accept exposure to risk to maximize reward*

The attitude to operational risk taking, whether *mitigated downwards* or *taken for reward*, will define the position it occupies on the scale.

Ancillary to this discussion is the concept of risk tolerance; the words *appetite* and *tolerance* are often used interchangeably when applied to operational risk. Organizations that adopt a *mitigate downwards* attitude towards operational risk frequently give preference to the term *tolerance*, signifying that the risk has to be (unwillingly) endured as it cannot be eliminated.

However, approaches vary:

- Tolerance in some firms can be *greater* than appetite. To use an example, the police's appetite for speeding is set by the speed limit assigned to a road (30mph, for example) but the officers will often tolerate a higher speed (which may be 33mph) before they prosecute.

- Other firms adopt a stance that tolerance is *lower* than appetite. For instance, appetite will be set at a 33mph limit which should not be exceeded at any cost; consequently, tolerance is set below the appetite at 30mph to provide an early warning sign.

Once the principal risk types have been placed on the appetite range, the same exercise needs to be conducted for the next level *top* or *principal* operational risks, which were discussed in Chapters 1 and 5. *Top* or *principal* risks are those inherent risks which, if not well controlled, will result in the most significant impact to the firm.

> Due to the huge variety of possible risk sub-categories, considering risk appetite solely at an aggregate operational risk level – for example, lumping together *financial crime, outsourcing, people* and other risk sub-types of an entirely different nature – is simply inadequate.
>
> It is better to elaborate appetite statements for each principal operational risk sub-type that underlies the firm's business thus addressing 'the nature, types and levels' of operational risk the firm is willing to assume.[4]

FIGURE 9.6   Positioning principal operational risks on the scale

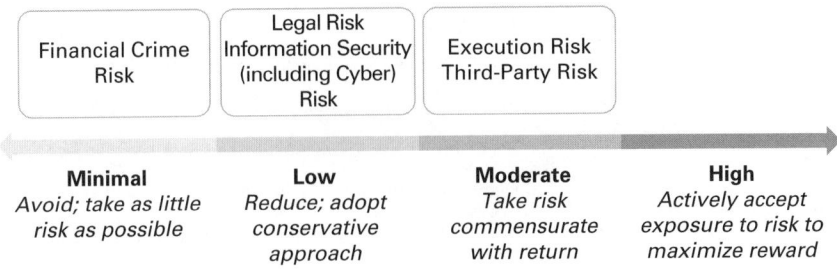

Figure 9.6 provides an example of a firm that identifies five principal operational risk sub-types and expresses their desired risk level on a spectrum.

Figures 9.5 and 9.6, presented to the board simultaneously, should generate some discussion. If the firm has a *high* appetite for strategic risk and is planning to significantly expand, on-boarding clients from new businesses and geographies, how does this tie in with the fact that it accepts only a *minimal* level of financial crime risk? This may be more suitable for a conservative, mature organization which is mostly maintaining an existing client base; since it has to be recognized that growth will inevitably generate an increased level of exposure to financial crime. If the board is not comfortable with that formulation, perhaps the firm's strategic aspirations and business plans need some revision. Alternatively, maybe the firm needs to double its investment in controlling financial crime risk, to maintain its minimal appetite level given expansion. Is the money on the table? This is the exact purpose of the scales, to generate debate on anticipated risk levels and the relationship between different elements of risk.

A question that frequently arises when working with risk ranges evolves around the exact meaning of terms, eg *minimal, risk-averse, expansionary*. To provide more colour and help define boundaries, the scale can broadly be based on the operational risk unified impact rating grid discussed in previous chapters. Accordingly, as illustrated in Figure 9.7, risk-averse appetite translates into tolerating low financial, client, regulatory and reputational impacts; while an expansionary stance assumes acceptance of at least one (usually *financial*) of the stated *very high* consequences.

Some firms prefer to use the ALARP principle as an alternative to appetite ranges.

FIGURE 9.7   Aligning appetite scale with the unified impact rating grid

	Impact	Description
Expansionary *Actively pursue risk for superior reward*	Very High	**Financial:** Actual/potential loss greater than $xxx **Client:** Serious client detriment/large proportion impacted **Reputation:** Deep damage to the brand and market value, sustained media coverage **Regulatory:** Formal investigation resulting in action and fines
Risk Tolerant *Take a measured amount of risk*	High	**Financial:** Actual/potential loss between $xx and $xxx **Client:** High level of detriment **Reputation:** Market commentary, serious damage to the reputation, brand and value **Regulatory:** May prompt investigation or regulatory action
Neutral *Adopt a balanced approach*	Moderate	**Financial:** Actual/potential loss between $x and $xx **Client:** Moderate impact/small proportion or segment **Reputation:** One-off media coverage, minor damage to reputation, brand and value **Regulatory:** Potential enquiry or one-off fine
Risk-Averse *Avoid or minimize the risk*	Low	**Financial:** Actual/potential loss below $x **Client:** Minor impact or complaints **Reputation:** Inconsequential **Regulatory:** Unlikely to result in any regulatory action

The ALARP Principle – *As Low As Reasonably Practicable* – encourages the mitigation of identified risks by balancing the cost of mitigation with the benefits, and formally enabling acceptance of the residual operational risk.

ALARP is applied as a decentralized decision-making model and operates by placing accountability on individual senior managers and executives. They assume risks and defend the position of what is practicable in terms of mitigation in each individual case. This can generate inconsistencies in application. If this thinking is adopted, it is important that the second line operational risk function reviews and challenges decisions, to ensure process reliability and robustness of outcomes. It is also recommended to supplement the ALARP approach with clear direction on desired appetite levels, via the use of qualitative ranges.

In summary, while qualitative scales are somewhat imprecise, they help to set the scene and provide soft guidance for better understanding the approach to risk taking within the organization. These scales are widely used by non-financial services firms, as they explain the appetite, at a high level, in pictures and language that are easy to comprehend. At times financial services firms, especially those applying more quantitative approaches to the operational risk capital calculation, favour numerical expressions and statistical probabilities – perhaps losing the softer explanatory element as well as the opportunity for honest board discussions. Perhaps this is something that can be learned from non-financial services industries?

Step 2: Qualitative appetite statements

The second stage of the process involves assigning a qualitative risk appetite statement for operational risk overall and for principal risk sub-types.

The statement is a more detailed explanation, in written form, supporting the position of each risk on the spectrum. It aims to rationalize whether the risk will be actively pursued, controlled or avoided; and provides the reasons for the chosen approach. Yet again, due to the qualitative nature of operational risk, descriptive statements are essential, and may include cultural and behavioural nuances, which cannot be measured in numbers.

Starting from the overall level, the attitude to operational risk taking, *mitigated downwards* or *taken for reward*, will be explained further. Compare the following statements:

EXAMPLE 1

The firm's tolerance for operational risk is minimal. It is not possible to eliminate operational risk, but the firm aims to reduce it. Operational risk tolerance is defined via a limit of $25 million on aggregate operational losses, which is then broken down to lower limits across sub-categories of operational risk including, among others, fraud, legal, compliance and money laundering.

This is a very basic outline which nevertheless appears in the annual reports of many financial services firms in some form or another. It is good practice to develop more elaborate statements; and challenge whether the firm indeed intends to apply a *risk avoidance* attitude to the entirety of its operational risk, as a blanket approach, or whether it is prepared to differentiate between sub-categories. Note, the term *tolerance* is used here, instead of *appetite*, to emphasize the desire to mitigate the risk downwards.

EXAMPLE 2

The firm takes operational risk consciously in pursuit of its strategic objectives. It believes that risk acceptance is often necessary to foster innovation and that it is neither possible nor necessarily desirable to eliminate all the operational risks inherent in its activities. The firm's overall appetite is neutral, with a maximum loss appetite threshold of $10 million. For certain sub-categories, such as *financial crime*, *conduct* and *regulatory compliance*, the firm assumes a more conservative risk-averse attitude. Eight principal risk categories have been identified, namely *financial crime, technology and information security, execution, conduct, regulatory compliance, change, people* and *third party* and each has been assigned a qualitative risk appetite statement supplemented by various risk metrics. Each principal risk is owned by a named senior executive, who is accountable for devising appropriate controls and presenting the overall level of risk to the board. The board is ultimately responsible for agreeing the appetite for each risk. Breaches to the risk appetite must be escalated and actioned.

FEATURES OF OPERATIONAL RISK APPETITE STATEMENTS

✓ Easy to understand; this is crucial for subsequent embedding of risk appetite in the organization.

✓ Provide a definition of the risk sub-type; important to avoid second-guessing of what is included.

✓ Contain a link to strategic objectives; this sounds like an obvious point, but unfortunately it is still rare that operational risk statements are displayed with direct reference to strategy and business plans.

✓ Outline accountability, which may include a risk owner, subject matter expert or relevant committee.

✓ Contain a response framework, stating the consequences of breaching the appetite.

This expanded statement has several helpful attributes; specifically, it refers to accountability and response. Further features are outlined in the box below.

Considering these features, an example of an appetite statement for a sub-type of operational risk is provided in Table 9.2.

TABLE 9.2 Example operational risk appetite statement

Principal Operational Risk Sub-type	Definition	Linked to Strategic Objective	Risk Owner	Risk Appetite	Risk Appetite Statement
Third-Party Risk (Outsourcing & Supplier)	The risk emanating from reliance on third parties, including incidents or failures of third parties to deliver on their obligations.	Confident customer experience	Chief Operating Officer (COO)	Moderate	The firm relies on third parties in delivering core business activities and services to its clients. It is willing to accept moderate level of risk working with contracted third parties to gain access to new technological platforms, improve flexibility and efficiency. Clients and regulators expect the firm to manage these arrangements effectively. The firm aims to limit disruptions by conducting robust third-party due diligence and performing monitoring and oversight by a dedicated outsourcing team. The firm has identified single points of failure and where feasible, developed a substitution plan in case of critical provider failure or unavailability. Where substitution is not viable, the firm has enhanced oversight and actively takes part in third parties' testing of their resilience and recovery capabilities. Elevated level of risk and breaches to appetite are escalated to the board and require action according to the firm's Response Framework. The firm accepts that occasional minor disruptions may occur.

This statement for the *third-party* sub-type of operational risk follows the recommended format. It provides a definition, outlines the link to strategy, and points to the executive owner as well as delivering an explanatory narrative. Similar statements need to be developed for the remaining top/principal operational risk sub-types.

Let us expand on two rather challenging aspects: accountability and response frameworks.

ACCOUNTABILITY FRAMEWORK

Accountability assumes that each of the key risk areas has clear ownership; either by a dedicated senior executive or a joint group or committee (depending on the governance arrangements) responsible for devising appropriate controls and risk mitigation activities. This is challenging to achieve in practice as it requires a well-defined allocation of responsibilities within senior executive teams. Also, some risks span across multiple business lines and geographies.

As an example, *technology risk* is usually the responsibility of the chief technology officer (CTO) as the majority of controls reside with the IT function; alternatively it can be co-owned by the heads of the business, the primary users and drivers of technological solutions, and the CTO. *Financial crime risk* is *not* owned by Compliance, despite the fact that compliance is usually tasked with designing and owning the framework. Rather, it is the duty of each and every employee and hence all senior executives to instil appropriate practices and behaviours within the organization to combat fraud and crime. Similarly, accountability for *People risk* is shared across all business units and support functions, while Human Resources provides policies and guidance. These kinds of risks should typically have joint owners in the first line, being the heads of major business units; or alternatively, the firm's chief executive.

Discussions on ownership can be heated and contentious; to the extent that the *risk owner* column is sometimes removed altogether. Cultural aspects play a significant part in this area, and firms that have a collaborative, honest and risk-aware ethos commonly excel in agreeing their accountability framework. With increasing supervisory focus on culture and conduct, and the introduction of personal accountability and certification regimes, the ownership of risks at the top of the house should align and conform to the broader accountability statements.

RESPONSE FRAMEWORK

In turn, the response framework deals with mechanisms to treat appetite breaches seriously and trigger robust action. One way of bringing this framework to life is by ensuring that significant breaches result in monetary penalties for the responsible owner or senior executive who is accountable to keep the risk within the limit; or perhaps a shared penalty for the whole senior executive team if they are jointly accountable for the risk sub-type which has caused the breach. This approach makes the instrument tangible and less of a theoretical exercise; but its success depends significantly on the firm's ability to agree on the accountability framework described above. It is worth noting the Basel Committee's view that 'compensation policies should be aligned to the bank's statement of risk appetite and tolerance.'[5]

Step 3: Limits and triggers

The final step consists of translating the appetite statements into limits and triggers that will help to measure actual risk exposure against established levels, indicating when the appetite has been – or is about to be – breached.

What tools are used to measure the appetite?

Common tools to measure operational risk appetite include:

- qualitative and quantitative – key risk indicators;
- quantitative – losses and scenarios.

We have already examined these instruments in their respective chapters. Let's review them in more detail in the context of the operational risk appetite.

KEY RISK INDICATORS

KRI metrics are important because they define what is acceptable (and, respectively, unacceptable), thus setting standards and guiding behaviours. They are inextricably linked to the culture of the organization. As described in Chapter 7, indicators are developed for the *key/top* risks, which is exactly what we have at hand when it comes to the expression of appetite.

Quantitative measures are equally significant as they warn about potential capital erosion. The firm is only able to assume any given amount of risk *within its risk capacity*.

Capacity is the overall resource or, in other words, *the budget*, that the firm has at hand reflecting the maximum level of risk it is able to assume; and is inseparably linked to economic capital. The firm will not be able to sustain losses beyond its capacity, as it will become insolvent.

The FSB definition of risk appetite includes risk taking within the firm's *capacity*,[6] which – in the context of financial risk types such as credit and market risk – is represented by an amount of capital. For operational risk, strictly speaking, the definition is broader and includes, for example, the supply of people and systems; meaning that the firm will not be able to process more transactions than humanly possible given the number of employees it recruits and the systems it operates. These factors are harder to incorporate into appetite considerations; therefore, where the term *capacity* is used, it usually refers purely to financial resource.

OPERATIONAL RISK LOSSES

Actual operational risk losses reflect the instances where risk has materialized. Organizations would not be able to absorb an unlimited amount of losses; and therefore, a threshold on the *expected* annual amount is an adequate and the most commonly used quantitative measure. Its purpose is to signal when the level of crystallized events may pose a threat to the broader corporate objective of remaining profitable.

This threshold can be absolute or relative, as illustrated in the following examples:

- absolute: the losses must not exceed $5 million;
- relative: the firm is prepared to tolerate a potential loss of 1 per cent of recurring revenue.

It is important to note that these measures do not put a cap on losses; even if the firm is not willing to exceed a set amount, that may still happen. Rather, they serve as triggers for action. When the appetite is breached – or even better, before the breach, when approaching the limit – this warrants an immediate review and investigation of why the negative financial impact has exceeded the level that was agreed as acceptable; and requires the relevant risk owner to come up with a plan of action. This may, at times, include drastic measures, for example having to discontinue a product or exit a business line/geography if it is not a viable, cost-effective proposition.

SCENARIO ANALYSIS

Scenarios supplement the loss threshold by measuring the level of *unexpected* operational risk losses that the organization is able to withstand. As discussed in Chapter 8, scenarios help a firm to explore and anticipate the impact of major changes or disruptions to its business. Setting an appetite for scenario outcomes – which in truth is rarely explicitly defined by firms – can help to guide the enterprise during, for example, a major change to its business model. It could signal, for instance, that the level of unexpected losses incurred from a given scenario may be above the acceptable level. In the case of outsourcing and supplier risk cited in Table 9.2, this could happen if, for example, further critical activities were outsourced to the same service provider, creating an intolerable dependency on a single third party.

Limits and triggers are a double-edged sword: while they are essential, they can also drive inappropriate behaviours. If an executive is set a quantitative loss and/or scenario limit for which they are personally accountable, this could result in the executive being incentivized to hide or under-report losses, or to wilfully underestimate scenario outcomes. In a similar way, as described in Chapter 7, business units may attempt to game KRI thresholds in order to present a more positive picture.

Continuing to build on the example in Table 9.2, appetite measures for a sample sub-category of operational risk are presented in Table 9.3.

TABLE 9.3 Example: defining appetite measures

Principal Operational Risk Sub-type	Appetite Measures	Board Approved Threshold: AMBER – elevated; define path to GREEN	Board Approved Threshold: RED – unacceptable; immediate action needed
Third-Party Risk (Outsourcing & Supplier)	**Losses:** maximum total financial loss from third-party failures	> $1.5 million	>$2 million
	Scenario Analysis maximum estimate	>$25 million	>$30 million
	KRI1: Percentage of critical providers with service below expected SLA levels for 2 consecutive months, without an action plan	>1%	>5%

(continued)

TABLE 9.3 (Continued)

Principal Operational Risk Sub-type	Appetite Measures	Board Approved Threshold: AMBER – elevated; define path to GREEN	Board Approved Threshold: RED – unacceptable; immediate action needed
	KRI2: Percentage of critical providers without resilience arrangements or with material failures identified during testing	> 5%	> 10%
	KRI3: Percentage of critical providers without defined succession plan / not easily substitutable	> 20%	> 30%

The measures highlighted above are used to monitor the level of risk in the following dimensions:

- actual amount of materialized losses, a backward-looking but factual measure;

- scenario estimate, a forward-looking metric;

- predictive *control* indicators (KRI1 and KRI2), which closely monitor performance levels against service level agreements (SLAs) and resilience capabilities; and

- a predictive *risk* indicator (KRI3), reflecting the level of exposure to critical suppliers which have no identified alternative and therefore may in future represent a single point of failure.

The same process of designing and agreeing limits and triggers needs to be repeated for the remainder of top/principal operational risk sub-types.

A simple scale to assess the quality and maturity of the operational risk appetite is presented in Figure 9.8.

FIGURE 9.8   Appetite maturity ladder

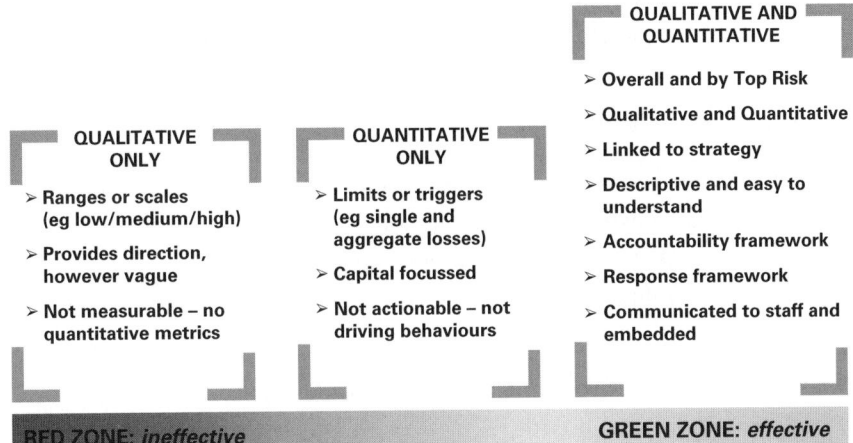

QUALITATIVE ONLY
- Ranges or scales (eg low/medium/high)
- Provides direction, however vague
- Not measurable – no quantitative metrics

QUANTITATIVE ONLY
- Limits or triggers (eg single and aggregate losses)
- Capital focussed
- Not actionable – not driving behaviours

QUALITATIVE AND QUANTITATIVE
- Overall and by Top Risk
- Qualitative and Quantitative
- Linked to strategy
- Descriptive and easy to understand
- Accountability framework
- Response framework
- Communicated to staff and embedded

RED ZONE: *ineffective*   GREEN ZONE: *effective*

Monitoring risk profile and taking action

Risk appetite expresses the *desired* level of risk that an organization should be taking in pursuit of its objectives. In reality, the firm may be assuming less or more risk than intended; hence the need to monitor the actual exposure, or the firm's *risk profile*, against the pre-agreed parameters.

FIGURE 9.9   Monitoring risk profile against the appetite

Principal Operational Risk Sub-type	Definition	Risk Owner	Risk Appetite	Risk Level relative to Appetite	Trend
Third-Party Risk (Outsourcing & Supplier)	The risk emanating from reliance on third parties, including incidents or failures of third parties to deliver on their obligations.	Chief Operating Officer (COO)	Moderate	○ Elevated, define path to GREEN	⬆

Expected Losses	Unexpected Losses	Key Risk Indicators
○ GREEN	○ GREEN	○ AMBER

This assessment is performed on a monthly or quarterly basis at the respective governance committees, where actual values are reported against the appetite. An example of a risk profile report is presented in Figure 9.9.

Embedding the appetite

The risk appetite needs to be 'used as a tool to promote robust discussions on risk', and as a basis for decision making.[7] Undoubtedly, though, embedding it is often difficult to achieve in practice.

The appetite is first developed at a corporate, firm-wide level. To enable it to really be used effectively, appetite needs to:

- be understood, debated and approved by the appropriate governance body, commonly the board;

- have regular and formal monitoring arrangements, via, for example, monthly or quarterly reviews by the risk committee and the board, where the actual risk profile is evaluated against the desired appetite levels;

- have effective limits and trigger points enabling escalation and action;

- have assigned owners at the executive level, ensuring accountability and requiring them to act;

- be appropriately documented and reviewed on a periodic basis.

For small to medium-sized organizations where the same senior executives sit at the table taking most of the relevant business and operational decisions, a single top-of-the-house appetite is sufficient. For larger international firms with multiple lines of hierarchy, the appetite needs to be disseminated and translated at lower levels of the organization, or strata; for example, based on entity or business line:

- Business lines, usually at a global level, require an appetite statement which is cascaded from the corporate statement. Quantitative limits are then *allocated* to the business based on various parameters including their revenue share. For example, the threshold for the overall expected loss amount can be split into lower sub-component limits attributed to various businesses. Qualitative indicators may apply in exactly the same way (for example, conduct, people, or fraud-related indicators); with business units being given identical or more restrictive thresholds. Some measures may be relevant to a specific area only; for instance, rogue trading metrics will be monitored by the markets business only and will not apply to other business lines.

- Material group entities, in particular, subsidiaries or legal entities that operate with their own board of directors, will also need to develop their own appetite, for approval by their board. The entity's appetite statement will represent a hybrid cross-over between the business lines operating out of that entity alongside a cascade of the corporate statement.

- Statements need to operate consistently at a consolidated level and at sub-strata level.

- A response framework needs to be in place within both the business lines and the entities.

The ultimate responsibility for approving the appetite lies with the board of directors of the organization. The second line operational risk team plays a crucial role in developing the approach; articulating the firm's position; working with subject matter experts and risk owners to make sense of the framework; and proposing statements and thresholds. It is an exciting opportunity to work with risk owners and senior executives to arrive at a meaningful appetite framework.

Common challenges and good practices

Common challenges

Challenges that practitioners may experience when developing and embedding an operational risk appetite are as follows.

LOSSES ONLY

A decade ago, operational risk appetite was defined via a limit on aggregate losses; sometimes additionally broken down to lower limits across principal sub-categories. While this is a good start, quantitative measures alone are insufficient as they are backward-looking (ie the losses have already crystallized) and do not provide guidance on behaviours. They need to be supplemented, as discussed in this chapter, with descriptive statements and qualitative key risk indicators.

ZERO TOLERANCE

A declaration of *zero tolerance* frequently features in the narrative. While this may work well in internal policies developed by Human Resources that articulate the firm's position towards, for example, internal fraud committed by employees, it does not work well when applied to the appetite. If the firm has *zero tolerance for fraud*, it may as well consider exiting the business, because some instances of fraud will inevitably occur. While a 'zero fraud' expression may be tempting to use, a better approach to the language would be to state that the firm has a risk-averse approach to financial crime, and aims to mitigate the risk by maintaining a robust control environment, while recognizing that occasional instances of fraud may occur.

USE OF DISTRIBUTIONS AND PERCENTILES

Bringing statistics into this domain is not always helpful either. Poor examples include statements that 'operational risk appetite is defined by the operational risk loss value using a 99.5 per cent confidence level on the statistical aggregate loss distribution'. Such statements will not be easily understood by all staff, are not actionable and – similarly to *zero tolerance* – should be avoided.

STAKEHOLDERS NOT ENGAGED

At times, operational risk faces lack of engagement from business units and subject matter experts, to the extent that it becomes, as articulated by one frustrated risk practitioner, like *getting blood out of a stone*. The best way forward is to find the correct *risk owner*, to whom the management of relevant risk, and therefore its appetite, matter. This is not easy in organizations with vague accountability frameworks. The challenge may also arise at the board of directors' level if the directors do not think they have any responsibility for or involvement in the risk appetite process, which is a rather worrying sign. Director education and executive briefings can somewhat mitigate the challenge.

WORDSMITHING EXERCISE

Appetite may be approached as an exercise to contribute to the annual report. Statements are developed by report writers in risk management or finance teams, in silos, without collaboration, discussion or agreement. In this case the stated appetites do not carry weight and are not embedded in the organization. It is important that the whole appetite cycle is followed, including essential value-add board conversations.

SIGNIFICANT EFFORT

Operational risk appetite, although not an embryonic topic, is still not studied carefully enough in most firms. Because of the difficulty deriving a meaningful statement and metrics, people may give up on the effort. It is better to approach the topic as an iterative process, starting with simple statements and measures and enhancing them over time and as experience is gained, not aiming for perfection up-front.

Good practices

OVERALL AND BY TOP RISK

As discussed in the chapter, operational risk appetite needs to be established at the overall operational risk level as well as for sub-categories of risk. The correct taxonomy plays a critical role and helps with the definition of the sub-categories. If the organization is using the Basel Committee taxonomy, it can make this process somewhat more difficult – for example the *execution, delivery and process management* risk sub-type – due to the sheer breadth of the category. It is good practice to develop more intuitive and fit-for-purpose categorizations as described in Chapter 1. The taxonomy will split the risk universe into principal risk sub-types for which appetite statements can then be developed.

BENCHMARK WITH INDUSTRY PEERS

In addition to developing appetite frameworks, every year I research and analyse the appetite statements of both financial and non-financial services firms, to observe industry progress in this nascent area and extract good examples. These statements are publicly available as part of firms' annual reports and can be easily located on the internet. This is a very useful exercise, recommended for all those working on developing an appetite framework. The research proves that, overall, steady progress is being made in this area, despite drastic divergence in the chosen approaches and the variable quality of outputs.

LANGUAGE EASY TO UNDERSTAND

As mentioned earlier, firms outside the financial services industry commonly achieve more clarity using simply worded statements, compared to financial services firms, some of which are *constrained* by statistical models, appear to favour probability-based measures, and underestimate the importance of qualitative aspects. Statements do not have to be over-complicated; on the contrary, if they can be explained simply enough for every employee to understand, then the employees *may* in fact read them. It is even better if highlights of the appetite can be presented to all staff as part of management town halls or educational campaigns, helping larger numbers of staff to better understand their own organization.

Industry benchmark, 2019

Simply, operational risk appetite is not easy to get right: the industry continues to make progress while challenges remain. This is a relevant and exciting subject for discussion, and one where the quote by French philosopher Michel de Montaigne – 'there is no conversation more boring than the one where everybody agrees' – is very pertinent. Whenever the topic comes up, it invariably ends in debate and split opinions over what constitutes an effective appetite statement.

Presented below is a snapshot of the current landscape from the industry meeting of operational risk practitioners from financial and non-financial services firms.

Nature of operational risk: similar or different to other risk disciplines?

From Figure 9.10, 28 per cent of participants perceived operational risk as distinctly opposed to credit and market risks, which are likely to be *encouraged up* to the stated appetite level. Operational risk on the contrary was expected to be *mitigated downwards*. On a positive note, 72 per cent of respondents were prepared to adopt a more entrepreneurial approach and to embrace risk–reward thinking for at least some of the sub-categories of operational risk in their firms, enabling more balanced conversations to occur.

Expression of appetite

It is encouraging to see 39 per cent of practitioners, as demonstrated in Figure 9.11, expressing their risk appetite via both qualitative and quantitative measures; both are needed given the complex and broad nature of operational risk. The others, however, were either still in the process of developing a statement or had just one type of metric in place.

FIGURE 9.10   Industry poll: approach to operational risk

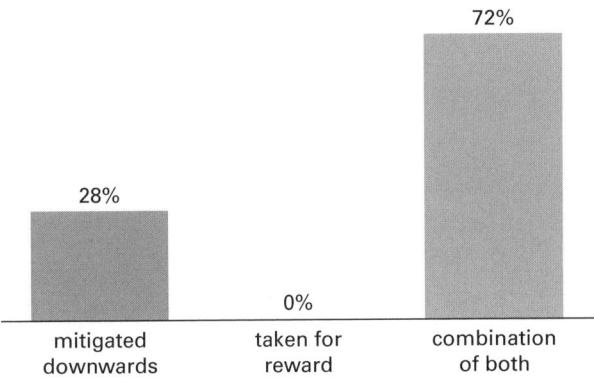

Operational Risk Workshop, PSD

FIGURE 9.11   Industry poll: expression of appetite (qualitative vs quantitative)

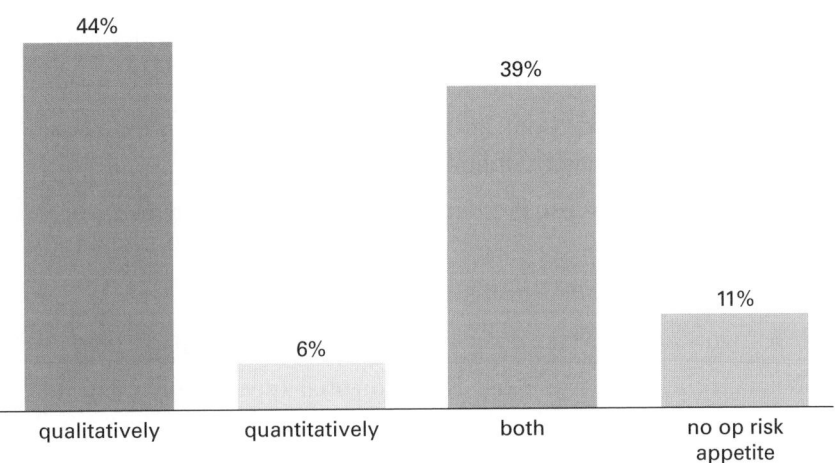

Operational Risk Workshop, PSD

Tools to express the appetite

Key risk indicators were voted to be the preferred appetite measure, followed by more quantitative scenarios and losses, while RCSAs were perceived as more of a day-to-day management tool (see Figure 9.12).

FIGURE 9.12 Industry poll: operational risk tools to express the appetite

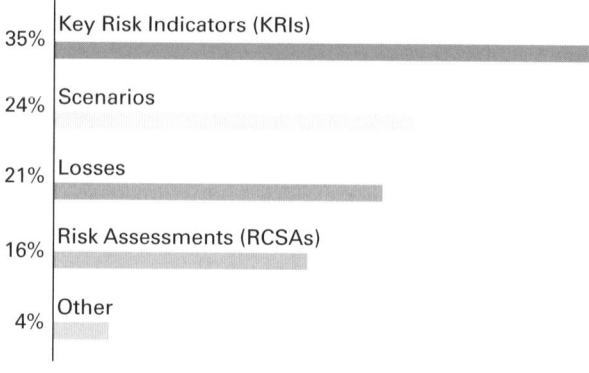

Most effective tools for expressing the appetite

35% Key Risk Indicators (KRIs)

24% Scenarios

21% Losses

16% Risk Assessments (RCSAs)

4%   Other

Operational Risk Workshop, PSD

Practical workplace exercise

Reflecting on the content of this chapter, obtain a copy of the firm's operational risk appetite and review it, considering:

1 Is the appetite easy to understand and does it articulate the *types* and *levels* of risk the firm is willing to accept?

2 What approach has been adopted, *mitigated downwards*, *taken for reward* or a combination of both?

3 Are principal risk sub-types distinguished and have statements been set for them?

4 What qualitative and quantitative measures are used?

5 What works well? Make notes of the features that you particularly like.

6 What can be improved? Note down potential appetite enhancements.

MAKE A DIFFERENCE (MAD) ACTION

Please note down one action that you will take after reading this chapter that will make a positive difference to the development of operational risk appetite.

In summary, this chapter proposed an approach to creating an operational risk appetite framework and statement, defining measures, and ensuring it remains a useful tool for decision making.

Moving on, the next chapter focusses on operational risk reporting and combines elements from all the tools examined in previous chapters.

Notes

1 European Banking Authority (2019) *The EBA Methodological Guide: Risk indicators and detailed risk analysis tools*, www.eba.europa.eu/sites/default/documents/files/documents/10180/1380571/343e01d7-0c8f-4d7f-b59e-cc23a7b9dd9d/Revised%20EBA%20Methodological%20Guide%20%20Risk%20Indicators%20and%20DRAT%20%2820%20March%202019%29.pdf (archived at https://perma.cc/6LFW-9GV5)

2 Financial Stability Board (2013) *Principles for an Effective Risk Appetite Framework*, www.fsb.org/wp-content/uploads/r_131118.pdf (archived at https://perma.cc/E9S4-F5KZ)

3 Financial Stability Board (2013) *Principles for an Effective Risk Appetite Framework*, www.fsb.org/wp-content/uploads/r_131118.pdf (archived at https://perma.cc/9XFB-46D5)

4 Basel Committee on Banking Supervision (2020) Consultative document, *Revisions to the Principles for the Sound Management of Operational Risk*, www.bis.org/bcbs/publ/d508.pdf (archived at https://perma.cc/5BD5-RAGH)

5 Basel Committee on Banking Supervision (2020) Consultative document, *Revisions to the Principles for the Sound Management of Operational Risk*, www.bis.org/bcbs/publ/d508.pdf (archived at https://perma.cc/9ZM3-P5M5)

6 Financial Stability Board (2013) *Principles for an Effective Risk Appetite Framework*, www.fsb.org/wp-content/uploads/r_131118.pdf (archived at https://perma.cc/F7TL-3EKU)

7 Financial Stability Board (2013) *Principles for an Effective Risk Appetite Framework*, www.fsb.org/wp-content/uploads/r_131118.pdf (archived at https://perma.cc/2LTZ-M6DB)

10

Operational risk reporting

What this chapter covers: The chapter stresses the significance of Reporting as the window through which Operational Risk communicates with the outside world and sends important messages to stakeholders (Figure 10.1). It discusses how results from the tools and instruments examined in previous chapters can be consolidated in a meaningful way for consumption by board and senior committees, without being excessively lengthy and verbose. It highlights practical ways of presenting an operational risk profile, getting right to the point and answering the vitally important *so what?* question, making reports succinct, punchy and actionable. The chapter includes examples and an industry benchmark.

FURTHER READING

- Basel Committee on Banking Supervision (2013) *Principles for Effective Risk Data Aggregation and Risk Reporting*
  Why recommended: a key regulatory document on the subject, outlining requirements on risk aggregation and reporting.

- Trevor Bentley (2002) *Report Writing in Business: The effective communication of information*, CIMA Publishing
  Why recommended: A perfect read for those interested and willing to improve their report-writing skills.

FIGURE 10.1 Focus of Chapter 10: operational risk reporting

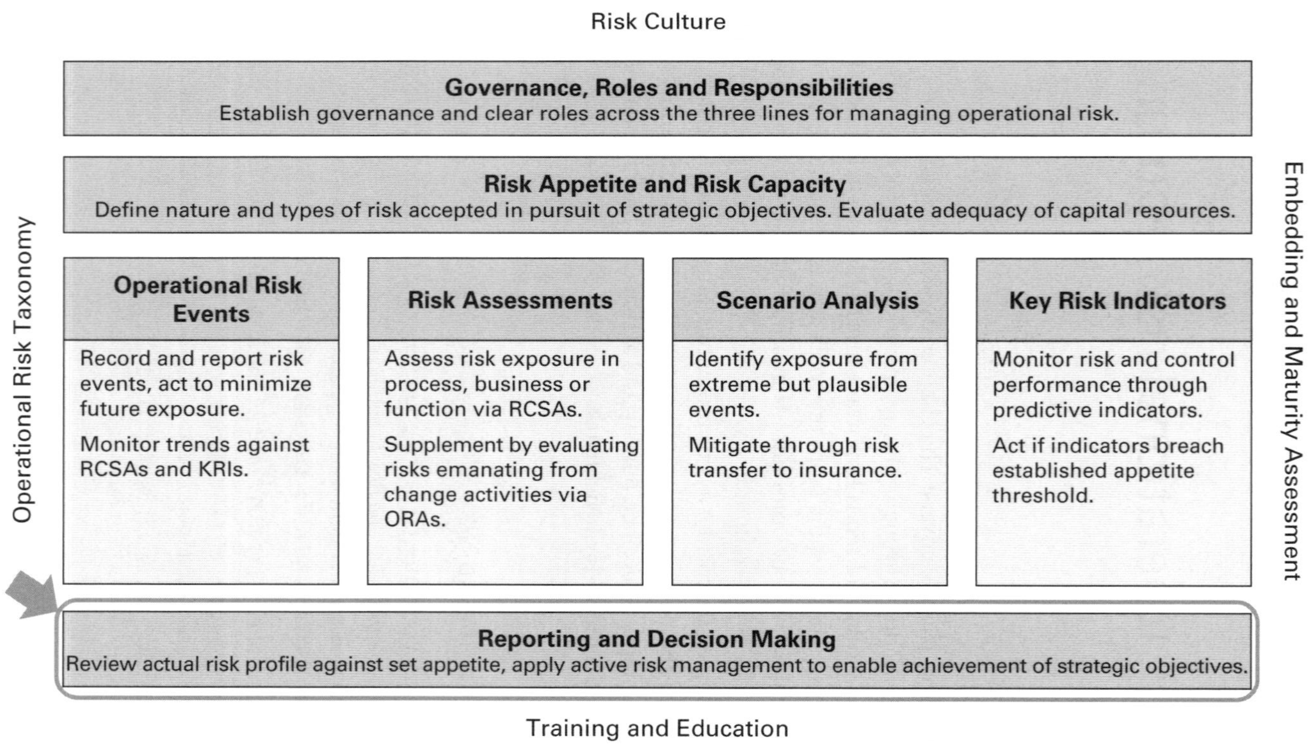

Risk Culture

Embedding and Maturity Assessment

Training and Education

Operational Risk Taxonomy

Governance, Roles and Responsibilities
Establish governance and clear roles across the three lines for managing operational risk.

Risk Appetite and Risk Capacity
Define nature and types of risk accepted in pursuit of strategic objectives. Evaluate adequacy of capital resources.

Operational Risk Events	Risk Assessments	Scenario Analysis	Key Risk Indicators
Record and report risk events, act to minimize future exposure.	Assess risk exposure in process, business or function via RCSAs.	Identify exposure from extreme but plausible events.	Monitor risk and control performance through predictive indicators.
Monitor trends against RCSAs and KRIs.	Supplement by evaluating risks emanating from change activities via ORAs.	Mitigate through risk transfer to insurance.	Act if indicators breach established appetite threshold.

Reporting and Decision Making
Review actual risk profile against set appetite, apply active risk management to enable achievement of strategic objectives.

Reporting: its role and its challenges

Operational risk reporting is a key activity. It is the culmination of all the hard work invested in designing framework tools which represent the best fit for the firm; and many days and weeks spent on embedding, training and educating the business. It is the end-result of analysis, discussions, debates and sometimes arguments with colleagues to resolve issues, find solutions and agree action owners. It is the opportunity to package up all this content, so it is well worth investing in the best quality packaging – it will reap benefits in the long term.

But caution: it also comes with a warning. Underinvestment in reporting will devalue the whole framework. Even when operational risk tools are operating effectively, if the reports are unclear, not well structured, or not actionable, the readers – mostly senior executives who only see the final product – may not appreciate or make sense of the importance of the operational risk management process and information.

When starting an assignment with a new client, I usually ask for a set of the operational risk reports that are submitted to governance committees. They provide an invaluable insight on the quality and maturity of the framework. If the reports do not meet the expected standard, I tend to investigate from the end-product back to the beginning. Does the policy mandate the use of the right tools? Are the elements of the framework calibrated correctly, embedded and generating meaningful outputs? If there are challenges, they usually lie with the design or calibration of the tools, or their embeddedness. It is a real pity if in practice everything is working well but when it comes to the last step – packaging the content – the author did not do the content proud.

From the outset, writing and structuring operational risk reports to the board and senior committees is a demanding activity. More generic hurdles on report writing are compounded by the immense challenges emanating from the breadth and complexity of the operational risk discipline.

Generic challenges

Over the years, I have participated in and led many exercises to help committees self-assess their effectiveness. This is good governance practice. Members rate important aspects of their own practice, including committee composition; the manner in which meetings are conducted; the allocation of time to various topics on the agenda; the quality of information received; and other attributes which help them to evaluate whether the committee is effectively discharging its duties. Inevitably, reporting receives its fair share of feedback. The most common criticisms from committee members – who are after all the report recipients – include:

- papers being too lengthy (board and committee packs are rarely just in the hundreds – more likely thousands – of pages in length);
- not outlining the *ask* clearly – for example, is the paper for approval, opinion or information only;
- not providing an overall perspective;
- being backward- rather than forward-looking;
- not being timely;
- being too vague and unfocussed.

And the list goes on.

When speaking to report writers – individuals or teams within departments tasked with drafting committee papers – they are also vocal on this topic, and raise plenty of reporting challenges, including:

- The absence of any brief from the board or senior executives on what they would like to see in the report. Are there any particular areas of interest? Authors frequently complain that they are writing blind, as no one has ever sat down with them to clearly explain what the recipients are looking for.
- The lack of a standard reporting template, leaving the writer to decide which style and format to use.
- A lack of training for report writers. What does good look like? How long, how detailed, structure, language, format? Word or PowerPoint?
- No feedback loop – after being written, reports usually disappear into a black hole. Authors rarely receive feedback on whether the information met recipients' expectations, whether any actions emanated from the discussion, and how they could do better next time.

Operational risk reporting challenges

All these challenges are relevant when it comes to operational risk report writing. In addition, operational risk faces some specific considerations:

- the breadth of the discipline, where every risk sub-type is important in its own right and deserves attention;

- multiple tools that generate significant output – losses, RCSAs, KRIs, scenarios – can all be presented using their own individual narratives, charts and graphs; and

- the fact that the discipline has both qualitative and quantitative components.

The objective of reporting is to present the overall operational risk profile, highlight pressure points, articulate whether the level of risk is within or outside the appetite, and drive decision making. For example, the UK Corporate Governance Code provides guidance by stating that directors should receive '*accurate, timely and clear information*', reinforcing that the board should always ensure that it has 'the policies, processes, *information, time and resources it needs in order to function effectively and efficiently.*'[1]

Or, simply put, they need to know if there is a problem; and if so, what action needs to be taken to resolve it.

What makes a good report?

Three steps for effective report writing

Three steps for effective report writing, proposed in Figure 10.2, are described in detail in this chapter.

Step 1: Data gathering

The first step in report writing consists of gathering accurate, timely and meaningful data. This involves extracting the outputs from operational risk tools – hopefully from the systems or, if not, from Excel spreadsheets or other sources – and collecting relevant inputs from first line business units. The industry faces continued focus on the quality and integrity of its data

FIGURE 10.2 Three steps for report writing

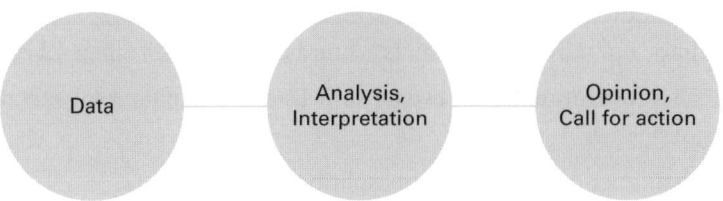

following the Basel Committee's publication of its principles on risk data aggregation and reporting: these require firms 'to generate accurate and reliable risk data' which is 'aggregated on a largely automated basis so as to minimize the probability of errors'.[2] This task is, however, mainly dependent on the firm's IT capabilities and remains a challenge, as is recognized by the Basel Committee in their 2020 progress report. While firms had clearly 'made improvements to their data architecture and IT infrastructure', there is 'still much work to do in this area'.[3]

Once the information is collected, a pause to contemplate: whose role is it to make sense of the data and interpret what it means? If the Operational Risk department perceives that it is the role of senior executives – the report recipients – to answer the *so what?* question, then the activity stops here. This is especially true if there is a fast approaching deadline for the paper to be submitted to the committee. The collected *raw data* is then pasted into the report, inviting the readers to decide for themselves what they make of it. Let's review an example of such a report.

EXAMPLE 1

Extract from an operational risk report

1   Operational risk events: This month, there have been 11 operational risk events, totalling $18 thousand. The largest loss of $9 thousand occurred in the Markets Division; further details are presented in Appendix X. There is a downward trend: overall ORE value is decreasing month on month since the beginning of the year, although the number of occurrences has increased from 7 to 11 a month in the last quarter.

2   RCSAs: There are four *high* residual risks in departmental RCSAs.

3   KRIs: There are no *Red* key risk indicators this month.

This narrative is supplemented by:

- bar chart: operational risk events – actual losses, rolling 12 months;
- bar chart: operational risk events – number of events, rolling 12 months;
- pie chart: operational risk events split by Basel (or internal taxonomy) category;
- pie chart: operational risk events split by business unit;

- RCSA results table – total number of *very high*, *high*, *moderate* and *low* risks by business unit;
- key risk indicators – a table with Green, Amber and Red indicators.

In reading this extract, inevitable questions arise. What does this mean? Is this good or bad? What, if any, action is needed? The burden of analysis is passed on to the reader. While the bare facts may be somewhat interesting, without any interpretation from subject matter experts this report is difficult to digest, is not actionable, and ultimately will not allow board or committee members to function *effectively and efficiently*.

Therefore, we move on to Step 2.

Step 2: Analysis and interpretation

Typically, a substantive manual effort – or perhaps semi-automated if systems permit – is required to review the data and translate it into a *story* that answers the *so what?* question. This is, after all, the essential value-add of the operational risk teams, who are the subject matter experts best placed to interpret the data. They need to analyse it from all perspectives, considering, for example, the following questions:

- What are the key changes in the risk profile since the last report?
- Is the level of risk within or outside the stated appetite?
- Is there any evident deterioration – an increase in OREs (value or numbers), significant risks or *Amber/Red* KRIs? If so, why?
- Are the operational risk tools telling a consistent story?
- Are there common themes across different business units or support functions?
- Is there a common root cause of various OREs?
- Are there any controls that seem to keep failing repeatedly (for OREs), or controls that are poorly assessed by multiple departments (RCSAs)?
- Are there any indicators which have been *Amber* for more than two consecutive months? If so, why?

Practitioners must search for trends, themes and a story where every piece of data is adding to the narrative. In practice, this kind of in-depth research, with a list of rigorous investigative questions, is rarely discussed or agreed among the operational risk team. Use of sophisticated data analysis tools and application of data science would be of immense help with this process. Despite being quite embryonic in operational risk space, more and more organizations are including exploration of techniques that offer future potential into the list of their priorities.

As a concept, operational risk appetite, as discussed in the previous chapter, can also assist. If well defined, it ties the various tools together, reducing the need for a separate coverage of RCSAs, OREs, KRIs and scenarios. Even so, a diligent analyst will investigate beyond the appetite considerations. Actual financial losses may be within the appetite, but could have been prompted by a common control failing in different business units – providing a great opportunity to call the problem out and discuss any necessary action.

In sizeable operational risk teams, it is essential to agree the role of the report writer relative to the rest of the department.

> The report writer is the *executive advocate,* stepping into the shoes of senior executives – the report recipients – and examining the document from their perspective.

The writer needs to challenge and refuse any raw data dumps provided by colleagues. If the data provides no insight and no story that answers the *so what?* question, the report writer should simply reject the input, explaining how it needs to be improved for subsequent submissions.

An additional important governance role is that of the report sponsor.

> The *report sponsor* is a senior executive member of the respective committee whose role is to review the paper for fitness and quality prior to its final submission.

For risk reports, the sponsor is usually the chief risk officer, who reviews credit, market, operational, liquidity and other relevant papers. This process creates another opportunity to sit down and actively challenge the material. So it is good practice to mandate this kind of sponsor review for all senior committee and board papers.

Compare the following extract from a risk report after this kind of in-depth analysis has been completed.

EXAMPLE 2

Extract from an operational risk report, after in-depth analysis

'This month there have been 11 operational risk events, totalling $18 thousand. Analysis of root causes and comparison with the RCSA and KRI data reveal that 8 out of 11 occurrences are due to the failure of the same control, namely segregation of duties. This control is rated as ineffective in three business units that use system X, due to manual workarounds required to operate it.'

After this second step, the report is likely shorter, and outputs from the ORE, RCSA and KRI frameworks have now been integrated into the analysis.

Step 3: Opinion, call for action

The third step takes us to the next level, aiming to provide an opinion and call for action. It reflects *behind the scenes* activity which happens *in between the reporting cycles*: the Operational Risk department acting on the story that emerged from the investigative analysis undertaken in the previous step. This step involves arranging meetings, discussing and agreeing actions and action owners. If applied to the earlier example, the report will be further enhanced as seen in the following example.

EXAMPLE 3

Extract from an operational risk report, after further activity

'This month, there have been 11 operational risk events, totalling $18 thousand. Analysis of root causes and comparison with the RCSA and KRI data reveal that 8 out of 11 occurrences are due to the failure of the same control, namely segregation of duties. A cross-functional working group facilitated by operational risk examined relevant cases and concluded that there is a significant risk of errors and future losses. A proposal to invest in enhancing the segregation of duties is presented for the committee's approval: see agenda item X.'

After this third step, as more time is spent on the analysis, with key messages being summarized for the recipients, the depth and quality of the paper is enhanced while the overall length is decreased; some of the individual appendices can now be removed as they have been integrated into the narrative.

The increased accountability of senior executives, as a result of the various regulatory regimes, is driving a desire to move away from ambiguous charts, graphs and appendices to succinct and clearly worded, actionable content that can be revisited, if necessary, months or even years after being written. As we will see from the industry benchmark at the end of the chapter, some operational risk reports are over 50 pages long. There is a real danger of information overflow, with directors and senior managers missing vital pieces of information hidden in the voluminous reports.

The ideal length of value-add papers is under five pages, while being able to summarize this kind of content into 1–2 pages is an outstanding feat, bordering on brilliance.

'If I had more time, I would have written a shorter letter' is a quote attributed to many, including Mark Twain and Winston Churchill. Spending more time on the analysis, key messages and storytelling increases the quality and decreases the length.

Helpful format and templates

While operational risk reporting diverges significantly across firms, a golden rule is to have an effective executive summary. Let's examine an example of a page, presented in Figure 10.3, which frequently appears in some shape or form in operational risk reports.

Positive features of this example include:

- a quick preview, in a summarized format, of what is to follow on subsequent pages;

- focus on actionability with separate sub-section dedicated to actions;

- outline of prior month status, reflecting on dynamics.

What could be improved, as discussed at the beginning of this chapter, is the integration of separate elements – RCSAs, KRIs, losses and audit issues – into one story answering the holistic *so what?* question.

Having written, read and helped to design hundreds of papers over my career, out of the many possible approaches I favour the CQC concept of good report writing, also advocated by Board Intelligence.[4]

FIGURE 10.3 Example of executive summary

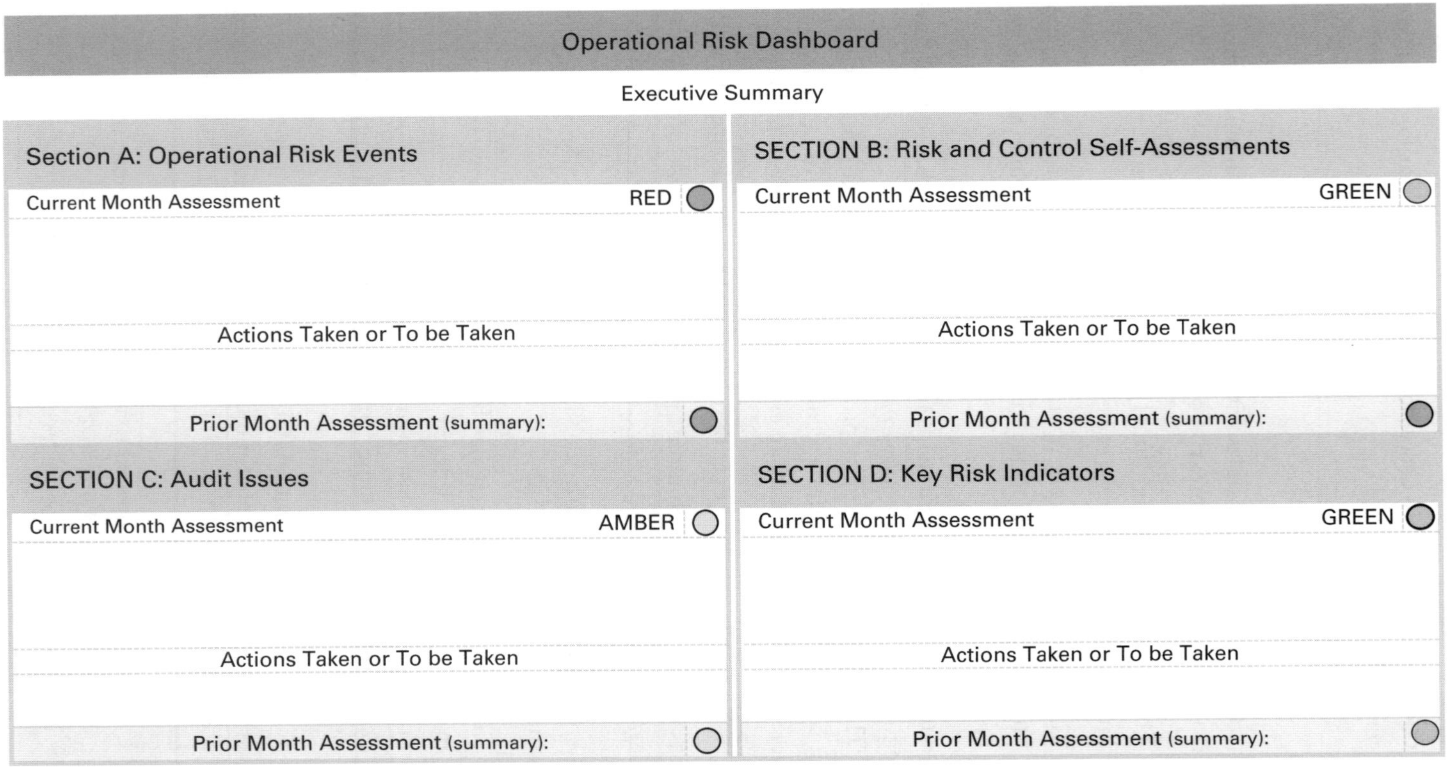

Operational Risk Dashboard

Executive Summary

Section A: Operational Risk Events

Current Month Assessment   RED ◉

Actions Taken or To be Taken

Prior Month Assessment (summary): ◉

SECTION C: Audit Issues

Current Month Assessment   AMBER ◯

Actions Taken or To be Taken

Prior Month Assessment (summary): ◯

SECTION B: Risk and Control Self-Assessments

Current Month Assessment   GREEN ◯

Actions Taken or To be Taken

Prior Month Assessment (summary): ◉

SECTION D: Key Risk Indicators

Current Month Assessment   GREEN ◯

Actions Taken or To be Taken

Prior Month Assessment (summary): ◯

> **CQC**: **C**ontext–**Q**uestions–**C**onclusions provides a solid structure for a board or committee paper.

This kind of report often starts with a short explanation of *why* the recipient is reading the paper (Context). For example:

- This is a quarterly operational risk update provided to the committee in line with its terms of reference; or
- The purpose of this ad hoc operational risk report is to brief the committee on a significant operational risk event, and outline actions taken to resolve it.

Context is important, as it helps the reader to answer the question which is frequently on their mind: *why am I reading this?*

The next phase is Questions, providing opportunity for the writer to outline the scope of the paper and articulate what issues it will be addressing. The choice of questions is key. As an example, 'good' questions include:

- What are the key changes to the operational risk profile since the last report?
- Is the level of risk within the appetite?
- What actions are proposed for the committee's approval?

The Conclusions then provide short answers to the above questions, for example:

- Since the last report there has been a moderate increase in the overall risk profile. Operational risk levels are elevated for *Technology and Information security* (same as last quarter), *Outsourcing and Supplier* (new) and *People* risk (new), resulting from the pandemic and working from home (WFH) arrangements.
- While the level of operational risk remains within the appetite, there are six new early-warning Amber indicators for the three risk categories outlined above. Actions are on track for a path to Green in *Technology and Information Security* risk.
- The committee is requested to review and agree actions proposed to mitigate the *People* and *Outsourcing and Supplier* risks, bringing exposure within the desired appetite level.

FIGURE 10.4 Example operational risk report format

Quarterly Operational Risk update for the Risk Committee of the Board, per Committee's Terms of Reference	
Prepared by: Head of Operational Risk	**Executive Sponsor: Chief Risk Officer**

Questions this paper addresses: | **Conclusions:**

1	What are the key changes to the Operational risk profile since the last report?	Conclusions:
2	Is the level of Operational risk within the stated appetite?	Conclusions:
3	What actions are proposed for Committee's approval?	Conclusions:

Input received | **Input sought**

In producing this paper input has been received from the following departments...	The committee is requested to agree proposed plan of action...

Main part of the report

Conclusions are expanded with a broader narrative, and supporting charts and graphs included. Main part of the report can be 2–3 pages long.

Summary

Previous Quarter: AMBER	●	Current Quarter: AMBER	●	Expected next quarter level: GREEN	●
Movement	⇧	Moderate increase in risk profile		Justification is included...	

Summary questions to avoid include:

- Individual questions on operational risk events, RCSA results or KRIs; analysis needs to be conducted integrating the outputs from these tools to extract a story, rather than presenting them separately.

- What is the operational risk profile? (as opposed to 'what are the key changes since the last report?'). If there are no noteworthy changes for several quarters in succession, the paper runs the risk of becoming repetitive. If the profile is stable, the opening line can say so up-front, leaving room to focus instead on a particular risk sub-type, and perhaps do a deep dive into, for instance, *legal* risk or *financial crime* risk.

- What has the Operational Risk department been doing? For obvious reasons, boards and committees are more interested in outcomes than in the specific activities of employees.

An example reporting template is provided in Figure 10.4.

Common challenges and good practices

Common challenges

Challenges that firms may encounter when compiling board or committee operational risk reports.

NEVER-ENDING REPORTING CYCLE

Significant effort goes into the preparation of reporting documents, with hours spent compiling, drafting and redrafting them. One of the rather unfortunate implications of the personal accountability and certification regimes is an even longer set of reports to boards and senior committees, prompted by a desire on the part of accountable individuals to document everything to the nth degree. By the time the reviews have been completed and approvals obtained, the next reporting cycle has already commenced and papers are due again. To avoid being caught up in a never-ending reporting saga, provide shorter updates on a monthly basis, and more complete reports with detailed deep dives quarterly or semi-annually.

DISCIPLINE TOO BROAD

As described earlier in the chapter, every operational risk sub-type is significant in its own right and deserves attention. This makes it challenging to cover a broad spectrum of sub-categories succinctly in a single report. It is good practice to spread deep dives into different risk sub-types throughout the course of the year; covering, for example, *Outsourcing and Supplier* risk in the first quarter, followed by *Technology and Information Security* risk in the second. The schedule can be discussed with the committee chair, and dates for the presentations agreed in advance. This planning provides ample time to develop a value-added paper, after engaging with relevant subject matter experts. It also shortens the regular operational risk report and makes it less repetitive. This approach can also help to address the perpetual topic of various reports not being integrated. Often the Compliance function presents on financial crime, Information Security develops its own set of papers and the Legal department reports on legal risk. Additionally, the operational risk function presents on all of the above topics, given that they are also sub-sets of operational risk. This can create duplication or even confusion if there are discrepancies between two datasets. Working in collaboration and producing a joint report is an excellent initiative, though rarely done in practice.

REPORT WRITER REMOVED FROM THE FRONT LINE

In larger operational risk departments, the reporting unit is usually separate from the framework and oversight teams, who are in the front line talking to business units and support functions. This creates a challenge for report writers who do not have the full picture themselves and are dependent on colleagues to submit intelligent insights. In this kind of structure, reporting team members need to take it upon themselves to educate their colleagues on what good looks like, and to push back on inputs of sub-optimal quality.

SOFTWARE NOT PRODUCING EXPECTED OUTCOMES

Whether off-the-shelf or developed in-house, operational risk software is unlikely to deliver a finalized committee paper at the touch of a button. It can be very useful in the analysis and interpretation stage, allowing interrogation of the data from different angles. But expert knowledge, time and effort is still required to produce the report, so it is best to avoid expectations of the software that are unrealistic.

REPORTS INTERNALLY FOCUSSED

Most organizations are largely internally focussed and do not provide enough external perspective. It is good practice to actively engage with industry forums and trade associations, and to read external and regulatory reports to obtain a view of how the firm compares with its peers and the industry more broadly. What emerging risks are on the horizon? What are your peers focussing on? In this context another good question to add to the set of Questions highlighted earlier is 'How does the firm's profile compare to industry peers/external trends?'.

DATA LACKS INTEGRITY

As highlighted by the Basel Committee, data integrity remains a challenge for most firms.[5] Many of the standard operational risk instruments are manual, or even where software is used the outputs are not easy to aggregate. Some pieces of data quickly become out of date. Self-assessment of data quality, integrity and timeliness, with follow-up actions if needed, is a robust practice.

Good practices

CREATE A REFERENCE LIBRARY

We have all been on the receiving end of a report that is poor and does not answer the *so what?* question. Generally, these will go straight into the bin, allowing us to move onto the next urgent task on our list. On the other hand, every time we come across a clear, concise report – where every piece of data is adding to the narrative – we can add it to a reporting 'reference library', to store ideas and give us a head start when producing the next document.

KNOW YOUR AUDIENCE

Knowing your audience helps greatly in delivering reports that are fit for purpose. For example, some recipients may be colour blind; worldwide there are approximately 300 million people with colour blindness.[6] For these people, a typical risk heatmap, filled with Red, Amber and Green KRIs, will not be well received and is better replaced with descriptive narrative. Alternatively, both colour and a descriptor (eg the word *Amber*) can be used simultaneously. Furthermore some senior executives may favour high-level summaries while others will be highly detail orientated and will want to search for supporting data. To manage this problem effectively, aim to solicit feedback proactively, initiating a dialogue with the committee or board to really understand their expectations and discuss what went well in the last report and what might be improved. This kind of feedback is rarely forthcoming if not asked for; it is best to take the initiative and seek it out.

ADDRESS REPORT WRITING BASICS

As obvious as it sounds, it is important to address generic report-writing challenges, including developing a template, and providing training to report writers and other team members who are tasked with submitting inputs. Ideally, appoint a person with excellent language skills in addition to operational risk expertise. Ensure that all graphs are annotated with explanatory notes, so the audience is not left guessing as to their meaning.

APPEND OPINION TO FIRST LINE BUSINESS UNITS' REPORTS

First line business units and support functions should also produce or contribute to committee and board papers. It is good practice to ask the risk owner in the first line to present on their own risk profile. This approach is especially effective in cases where the first line is asking for investment to mitigate a material risk. It is also beneficial for celebrating success; if, for example, an area has been found to have significant flaws and subsequently took remedial actions, deriving meaningful lessons learned which are worth sharing.

When first line business units and support functions are authoring reports, the second line Operational Risk department can append its independent opinion to the first line reports. This is a powerful technique that allows senior committees and the board to have the benefit of both sets of views.

ADD VALUE

Reporting is a start of the process, not the end of it. Every paper has its purpose, be it, for example, to *initiate further action or request input*. When producing a document, ask yourself the question 'Is it adding value?' Inevitably, committee and board meetings run out of time, and papers *for noting* are usually taken as read and therefore skipped. This makes it even more important to develop reports that appear at the front of the pile, generating discussion and helping in decision making. Some firms actively prohibit papers that are *for information only* or *for noting*.

Industry benchmark, 2019

Operational risk practitioners from multiple financial services firms of different sizes and geographical spread participated in a live poll to examine various aspects of operational risk reporting.

FIGURE 10.5 Industry poll: length of operational risk report

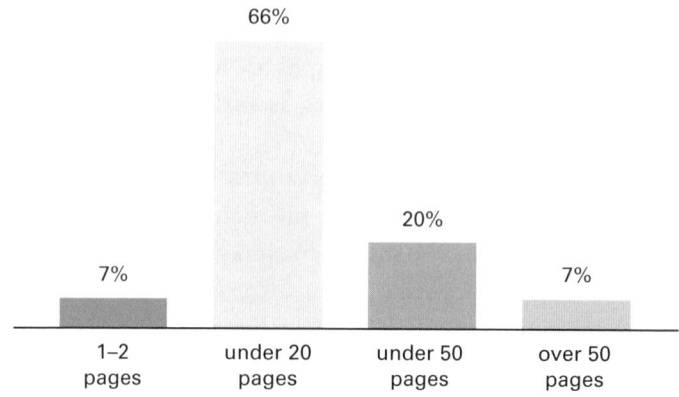

What is the length of Op Risk Report?

Best Practice Operational Risk Forum, 2019

How long are operational risk reports?

Voluminous operational risk reports are commonly presented to risk committees, executive committees and the board. The industry benchmark indicated that 67 per cent of packs are about 20 pages long, 20 per cent are nearing 50 pages, and 7 per cent are over 50 pages long, as seen from Figure 10.5.

What do operational risk reports usually contain?

The usual reporting cycle is monthly and the most common aspects of the packs are:

- an executive summary covering highlights, issues, the status of action plans and updates on ongoing initiatives;

- a view of the firm's risk profile, via a heatmap and/or a supporting narrative;

- overall trends and details of selected material operational risk events that are above the established threshold;

- key risk indicators;

- although aiming to report regularly against the appetite, not all firms are there yet, and some are still developing this feature.

FIGURE 10.6 Industry poll: aspects of operational risk report ranked by importance

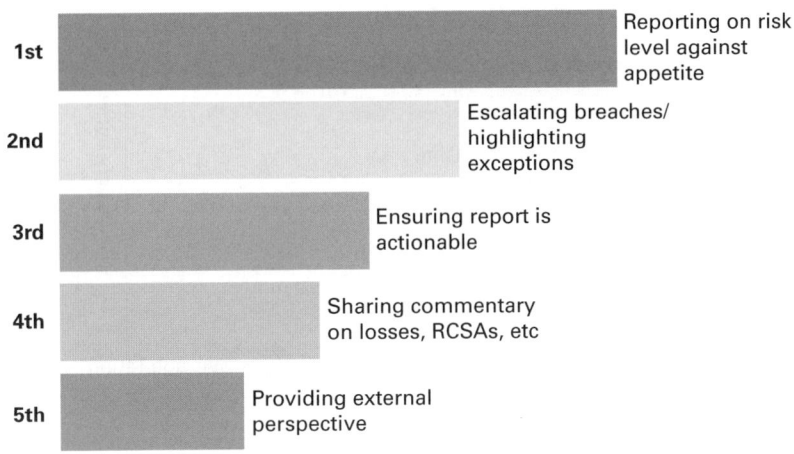

Rank aspects of Op Risk Reporting in order of importance

1st — Reporting on risk level against appetite

2nd — Escalating breaches/ highlighting exceptions

3rd — Ensuring report is actionable

4th — Sharing commentary on losses, RCSAs, etc

5th — Providing external perspective

Best Practice Operational Risk Forum, 2019

What are the most important aspects of operational risk reporting?

In ranking order, reporting on the level of operational risk against the set appetite was considered the most important feature, followed by ensuring that paper is actionable and really focusses on the *so what?* question (see Figure 10.6). Providing an external perspective was deemed of less significance. This is perhaps debatable, given the benefits that an external view can bring on how the firm's internal risk profile compares with the rest of the industry.

Have we mastered operational risk reporting or are we still on a journey?

Reports may be longer than desired but, most importantly, they prompt debate and help in decision making, as seen from Figure 10.7. Good practices include being selective by concentrating on specific themes, including good insights on what the data means and focussing on actionability. Some firms report by exception only, outlining problem zones with material risks and significant events, and listing emanating actions via a RED report (**Risks, Events, Decisions**). While this approach will clearly shorten the paper, it may also send an alarmist message. Most agree that including a balanced view of *Red* and *Green* provides a more holistic perspective.

FIGURE 10.7 Industry poll: value of operational risk reporting

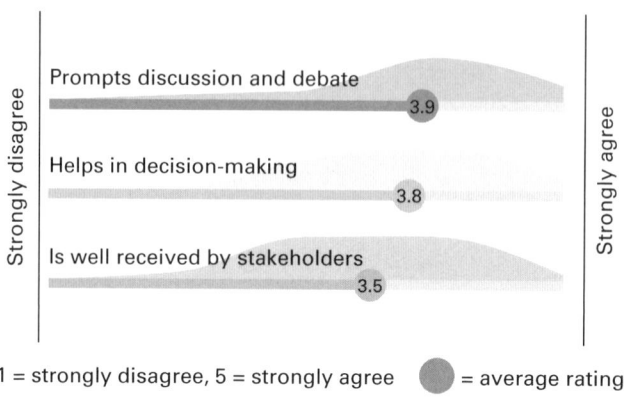

Operational Risk reporting

1 = strongly disagree, 5 = strongly agree   ● = average rating

Best Practice Operational Risk Forum, 2019

Generic good practices also help, including having a clear brief from the board and senior committees on what they would like to see in the reports; using a standard report template; and providing timely and regular feedback to the authors on how the report was received by the stakeholders.

The financial services industry is on a positive journey with regard to its reporting capability; and, given more time, firms will continue to evolve their ability to create shorter, punchier operational risk reports which help boards and committees to take the right decisions.

Practical workplace exercise

Reflecting on the content of this chapter, obtain copies of operational risk reports submitted to the risk committee, board or other governance committee over the last year, selecting at least three reports for comparison purposes. Review the reports, considering:

1 Has the report writer followed all the three steps outlined in this chapter?

2 Is there an opinion and call for action?

3 Is the report clear and well structured?

4 What works well? Make notes of the features that you particularly like.

5 What can be improved? Note down potential improvements for future reports.

MAKE A DIFFERENCE (MAD) ACTION

Please outline the learnings and note down one action that you will take after reading this chapter that will make a positive difference to operational risk reporting practices in your workplace.

In summary, this chapter discussed the crucial role of operational risk reporting, proposing an approach for developing concise, actionable and value-add reports.

Now that we have covered the core elements of the operational risk framework, subsequent chapters move to describing supplementary aspects, starting with training and education.

Notes

1 Financial Reporting Council (2018) *The UK Corporate Governance Code*, www.frc.org.uk/getattachment/88bd8c45-50ea-4841-95b0-d2f4f48069a2/2018-UK-Corporate-Governance-Code-FINAL.pdf (archived at https://perma.cc/47XG-5UUA)

2 Basel Committee on Banking Supervision (2013) *Principles for Effective Risk Data Aggregation and Risk Reporting*, www.bis.org/publ/bcbs239.pdf (archived at https://perma.cc/Q3XQ-467P)

3 Basel Committee on Banking Supervision (2020) *Progress in Adopting the Principles for Effective Risk Data Aggregation and Risk Reporting*, www.bis.org/bcbs/publ/d501.pdf (archived at https://perma.cc/F9BM-7FXA)

4 Board Intelligence, www.boardintelligence.com/product (archived at https://perma.cc/MET9-MZM7)

5 Basel Committee on Banking Supervision (2020) *Progress in Adopting the Principles for Effective Risk Data Aggregation and Risk Reporting*, www.bis.org/bcbs/publ/d501.pdf (archived at https://perma.cc/F9BM-7FXA)

6 Colour Blind Awareness, www.colourblindawareness.org/colour-blindness/ (archived at https://perma.cc/KA7G-M8C4)

11

Operational risk training
and education

What this chapter covers: The chapter focusses on the importance of investing in upskilling colleagues across the organization on operational risk; and embedding further knowledge about the responsibilities across the firm (Figure 11.1). In an age of training fatigue – when employees can easily be overwhelmed by the number of mandatory training courses they need to complete – the chapter suggests useful hints and tips for deploying best-in-class training programmes that employees will find educational, engaging and memorable.

FURTHER READING

- Robert Pike (2003) *Creative Training Techniques Handbook: Tips and how to's for delivering effective training*
  Why recommended: This practical book is packed with brilliant ideas on designing and developing high-impact training programmes. It can be supplemented by excellent books on specific topics:

  - Facilitation:
    Bob Pike and Dave Arch (1997) *Dealing with Difficult Participants: 127 practical strategies for minimizing resistance and maximizing results in your presentations*, Pfeiffer

  - Public speaking:
    Viv Groskop (2018) *How to Own The Room: Women and the art of brilliant speaking*, Bantam Press

  - Influencing:
    Thomas Harris (2012) *I'm OK, You're OK: A practical guide to transactional analysis*, Arrow;
    Eric Berne (2016) *Games People Play: The psychology of human relationships*, Penguin Life

FIGURE 11.1 Focus of Chapter 11: training and education

Embedding and Maturity Assessment

Risk Culture

Governance, Roles and Responsibilities
Establish governance and clear roles across the three lines for managing operational risk.

Risk Appetite and Risk Capacity
Define nature and types of risk accepted in pursuit of strategic objectives. Evaluate adequacy of capital resources.

Operational Risk Events

Record and report risk events, act to minimize future exposure.

Monitor trends against RCSAs and KRIs.

Risk Assessments

Assess risk exposure in process, business or function via RCSAs.

Supplement by evaluating risks emanating from change activities via ORAs.

Scenario Analysis

Identify exposure from extreme but plausible events.

Mitigate through risk transfer to insurance.

Key Risk Indicators

Monitor risk and control performance through predictive indicators.

Act if indicators breach established appetite threshold.

Reporting and Decision Making
Review actual risk profile against set appetite, apply active risk management to enable achievement of strategic objectives.

Training and Education

Operational Risk Taxonomy

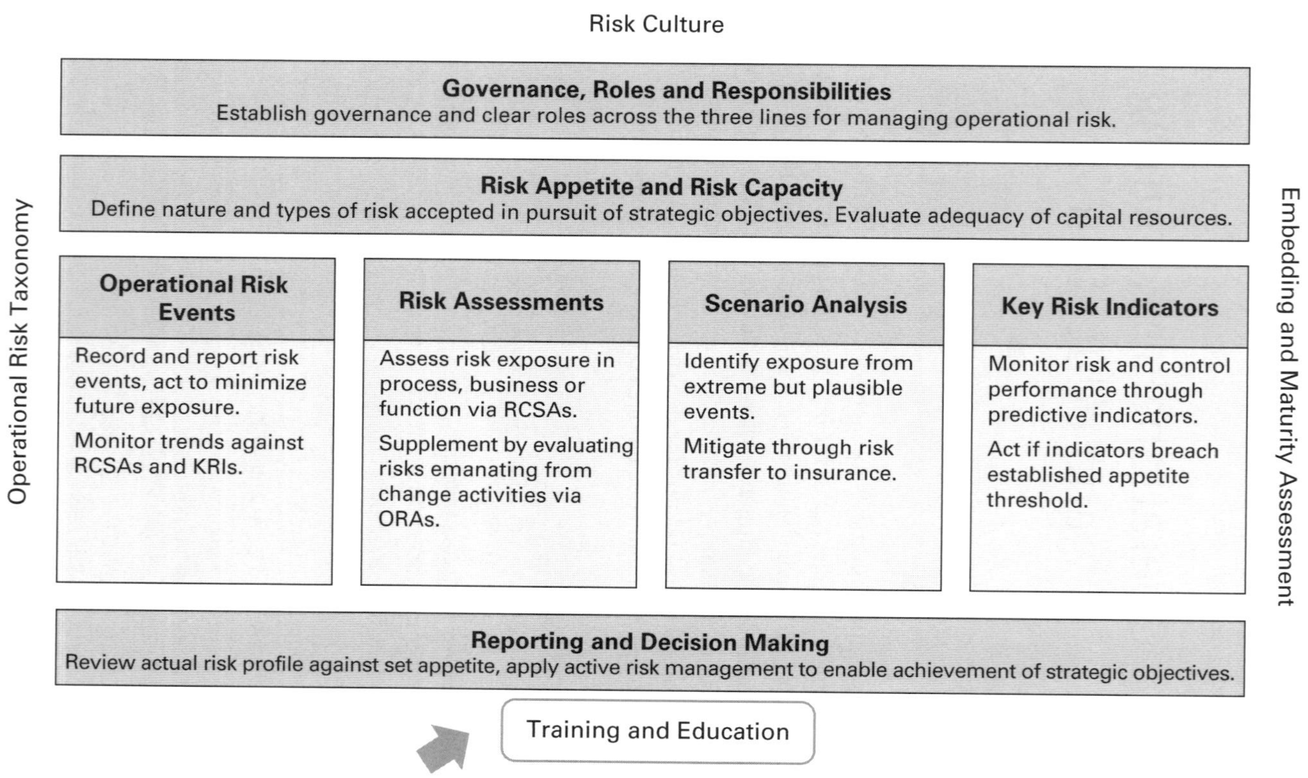

Advocating for risk education

This chapter discusses education at all levels of the organization; it starts with an outline of relevant training for second line operational risk personnel, and ends with some suggestions on the design of all-staff sessions.

Education is one of the most powerful things in life. As a professional trainer with over 20 years' experience in delivering public and in-house courses, I feel passionate about this subject and always advocate for profound investment in learning. Education is particularly important when it comes to operational risk management as it is vital for embedding the practices in the organization. The discipline is still relatively young and has not yet fully bedded down; therefore, there is a continuous need for managers and practitioners to keep constantly raising awareness, delivering impactful and relevant messages to ensure that all employees are conversant with and apply key risk management principles and concepts. A review conducted by the Basel Committee in 2014 confirms that firms recognize this need, as most 'indicated that some form of operational risk training has been established but had plans to enhance existing training'.[1] Update to the sound practices issued by the Basel Committee in 2020 since strengthened the educational requirements, directing organizations to implement training programmes that are '*mandatory* for specific roles, such as heads of business units, heads of internal controls and senior managers'.[2]

Building blocks for upskilling risk professionals

The educational journey must begin with the second line operational risk function. As discussed in Chapter 3, second line *multipliers* are tasked not only with engaging with the first line *champions* but also with passing on their own knowledge and inspiring the entire organization. Consequently, the skills and abilities of the second line team are a core factor in successfully implementing risk management tools and processes across the firm. The development of deep second line expertise leads to the department being perceived as a centre of excellence and each team member becoming an ambassador of good practices.

While specific training requirements may arise based on individual need assessments, there are several key skills that all team members should possess in order for them to become all-round role models. This key skillset consists of three essential building blocks proposed in Figure 11.2, and a number of bonus add-ons.

FIGURE 11.2 Three educational building blocks for the second line teams

Operational risk framework and tools

The first learning objective is to achieve full proficiency with the framework and tools. It is difficult to educate others when one's own knowledge is only partial. To excel, every second line employee needs to master all individual components of the framework – RCSAs, KRIs, appetite and others – as well as having a clear grasp of how the components relate to each other. In larger teams, employees may be split into sub-units, focussing on a particular aspect of operational risk management which they are practising continuously and in which they consequently develop deep expertise. These focussed employees can (and should) be requested to routinely share their knowledge with the rest of the group. Instil the discipline of dedicating part of regular departmental meetings to an overview by one of these specialists, covering their particular subject. Over time every component of the framework can be covered in a series of sessions, increasing everyone's familiarity with the multifaceted framework and equipping the whole team with broad and cohesive knowledge. After this process personnel will be well positioned to transfer skills to the rest of the organization. In fact, for staff working in the Operational Risk department there is simply no excuse for operating in silos or displaying limited know-how.

External perspective and industry acumen

Integrated framework knowledge allows employees to answer the *how* question: how do we manage operational risk in our organization? Practitioners also need to be able to articulate *why* the tools have been designed in a particular way. This is a more difficult challenge to surmount. Ideally it requires heuristic experience of working in multiple companies, enabling the practitioner to compare practices first hand, to reflect on what works and tailor the appropriate solutions. Knowledge of the *why* can, however, also be acquired by consciously seeking a perspective on how the firm's operational risk management compares with industry best practices. As discussed in previous chapters, these practices are not set in stone; there is great divergence among financial services institutions in the use of the different framework elements. Successful professionals have their finger on the pulse. They are perceptive about where the industry is headed, conversant with regulatory priorities and areas of focus, and aware of how their own tools and processes relate to the benchmark.

Practical suggestions on how this wider perspective can be achieved are listed below:

- Researching, finding and joining practitioners' forums. Nothing replaces the value of conversations between fellow professionals, performing comparative analysis and sharing real life successes and challenges.

- Subscribing to news feeds and magazines. Plenty of free subscriptions are available, including Operational Riskdata eXchange Association (ORX)[3] and Risk Channel[4] which provide thoughtful insights that anyone can benefit from. Examples of paid platforms include: Thomson Reuters,[5] an industry leader in regulatory intelligence; Risk.net,[6] which includes events, conferences and a magazine; and Risk Spotlight,[7] which offers a horizon scanning portal.

- Obtaining membership in professional organizations such as the Institute of Risk Management which enables access to seminars, a network of practitioners and an opportunity to obtain a qualification (Certificate in Operational Risk Management – CORM).[8,9]

- Attending external operational risk training courses. These are run by multiple organizations, the London Stock Exchange Academy being one good example.[10]

- Inviting external guest speakers or trainers to share their views on particular topics.

- Asking first line colleagues to attend second line team meetings and talk about their risks.

Use all the means available to you to continuously gather and share intelligence and stay abreast of industry developments.

Interpersonal: facilitation, speaking, influencing

Even with exceptional framework and industry knowledge, practitioners will not be successful if they are unable to relay it effectively. Consequently, enhancing the ability of employees to communicate, engage with an audience and energize their stakeholders is crucial.

Operational risk *multipliers* should be already spending a significant proportion of their time out there talking to their audience; whether educating, making presentations, or facilitating RCSAs, KRIs or scenario workshops.

FACILITATION

> Workshop facilitation involves leading a group of participants to success and providing them with the necessary resources and opportunities; it is the art of making meetings more effective.

Facilitation is a key skill which needs to be practised and mastered. It can be mistakenly assumed that anyone can step in and competently lead a workshop with any type of audience, instantly achieving the desired outcome. On the contrary, sufficient thought and planning is needed on the prerequisites and capabilities required by the facilitator. Audiences can be unruly; and trying to a facilitate a meeting or workshop without sufficient know-how or dexterity in handling problems can be a recipe for disaster. So important is this attribute that the outcome of a group session often depends significantly on the talents of its leader. At the other end of the spectrum, regrettably, I have witnessed poor workshop management being a major contributor to a sub-optimal RCSA programme.

Facilitation training prior to leading any RCSA, KRI or scenario workshop needs to include:

- The basics, covering organizational matters such as creating an agenda, setting expectations, managing time, and delivering an outcome.
- Advanced components, including various workshop structures, agreeing ground rules, use of tools (post-its, flipcharts and others) and a range of approaches to engaging participants and shaping group discussions.
- Core and vital – but nevertheless frequently omitted – is an understanding of the different types of personalities attending the workshop, and a range of tactics for managing them. Tailored approaches can be used to handle disruptive participants such as *the domineering*, who overrules everything that is said; *the sceptic*, who constantly questions the value of the meeting and doubts whether anything useful will come of it; and *the introvert*, who holds valuable information but never speaks; among many others.

- Additional useful techniques for dealing with latecomers and distractions (for example, phones and laptops), managing conflicts and drawing on the collective intelligence of the room.

If budget permits, invest in external facilitation masterclasses and/or certifications. Alternatively, assemble a library of essential books as recommended in the beginning of the chapter.

CASE STUDY 11.1

A large international financial services firm launches operational risk assessments which it plans to execute via a series of workshops. Over the years, the company has successfully applied a Six Sigma process improvement methodology, making it compulsory for every employee who commences a project to complete a masterclass covering methodological as well as leadership and facilitation aspects. Using this model as an example, Group Operational Risk decides to adopt the same proven tactic and mandates facilitation training for any member of staff expected to direct a workshop. This training consists of two half-day sessions and contains basic and advanced components of facilitation. It prepares participants administratively, mentally and emotionally for the task ahead and ensures uniformity in the firm's approach to the workshops.

PUBLIC SPEAKING

Public speaking deserves a special mention. A large number of candidates working in operational risk have an accounting, audit or operations background. These professions are by nature more introverted than, for example, sales and marketing. Public speaking may not be a natural strength of employees with this kind of background; so a conscious investment needs to be made in developing them to be dynamic, engaging and enthusiastic presenters. This is a valuable and transferrable skill: employees who master the art of public speaking are in great demand in any industry and will likely go further in their careers. Furthermore proficiency in public speaking is also immensely helpful in facilitation.

Build teams that excel by:

- starting with basics, training and coaching internally;
- having an observer sitting in and providing feedback to the presenter post-meeting;

- working with a coach to film the speech or presentation and then play it back, focussing on both content and delivery;
- exploring external public speaking courses;
- adding to the library of essential books, as suggested in the section on further reading.

INFLUENCING

Those interested in psychology will acknowledge that not only is it a captivating subject, but also very useful in the corporate world. The modus operandi of operational risk employees is by *influencing*; they do not directly manage business units or support functions, but are expected to be the *change agents* of culture, transforming risk management thinking and the practices of the organization. Thus, any additional knowledge on how to improve influencing skills is most welcome.

A specific area where reading the dynamics is particularly beneficial is the relationship between a second line operational risk *multiplier* overseeing a first line operational risk *champion*. This multiplier–champion pair can be dysfunctional without anyone realizing it. For example, you may have encountered a first line coordinator who, like a disobedient *child*, is chronically late in completing RCSA refresh, tardy with loss event reporting, and continually missing the deadline for providing commentary on their risk profile. The second line multiplier, however, acts in a *parent* capacity, always stepping in and helping their colleague out. This pair is locked in a *parent–child* relationship; with the first line getting away with murder and the second line constantly going above and beyond the call of duty. They need to recognize this dysfunction and take the relationship to a new *adult–adult* level, rebalancing their roles and responsibilities.

Another potential example is a *parent* in the first line speaking down to a *child* in the second line; perhaps scolding them for not having sufficient understanding of all the intricacies of the first line business; or maybe even asking them to come back only when they have read all the relevant policies and procedures.

A number of excellent books explore *transactional analysis* and the famous *parent–adult–child* theory; two books have been recommended in the beginning of this chapter.

Additional areas for development

The breadth of the operational risk discipline leads to grand expectations around the general level of knowledge and skill of operational risk practitioners. Whether realistic or not, all aspects of people, systems, processes and external environment are presumed to have been mastered by the risk practitioner. Therefore, increasing the general level of knowledge of operational risk professionals will invariably bear fruit. Useful areas employees are encouraged to assimilate via internal (and where possible, external) courses include:

- areas of regulatory focus; for example, operational resilience, outsourcing and cyber;
- skills and processes helping employees to be more entrepreneurial and business-savvy, eg decision making, project management and Six Sigma process improvement;
- topical know-how in the field of data, automation and artificial intelligence; and
- business-specific knowledge (this is particularly important).

Encouraging employee self-development

Learning is a joint responsibility of the employee and their leader. While managing large international teams I always aimed to motivate staff to invest in their self-development. I found it useful to outline clear pointers on what 'good' looks like, encouraging staff to use their initiative to progress on their educational journey. Table 11.1 is an example of a rating scale agreed at the beginning of the year, which is subsequently incorporated into the broader performance evaluation process at year end.

TABLE 11.1 Self-development objectives for second line operational risk practitioners

Rating	Activities
Achieved Expectation	Keeps up to date on operational risk topics by reading relevant press/ magazines, participating in external conferences and meetings. Researches, prepares and delivers at least one educational presentation to the team on a chosen operational risk topic.

(continued)

TABLE 11.1 (Continued)

Rating	Activities
Achieved Plus	Enrols into and successfully obtains a recognized operational risk qualification or certification. Joins a relevant market industry body or group. Researches, prepares and delivers a series of educational presentations to the team and first line business units support functions.
Exceeded Expectation	Authors an article published in a recognized professional/industry magazine. Delivers a presentation at a public forum or external conference. Is recognized as an industry expert, takes on a role as chair of a panel, forum or committee. Designs and develops train-the-trainer presentations to the team and first line business units/support functions. Mentors a team member on public speaking/facilitation.

Cultivating first line risk coordinators

In Chapter 3, we discussed the importance of developing a network of champions in the first line of defence. Champions, once appointed and in situ, need to be kept continuously energized and motivated, and education plays a crucial role in achieving this objective.

What do champions need to know? Essentially, they are an extension of the second line operational risk function, so the same kinds of educational resource and opportunity should be offered to them also.

In cases where the champion is a part-time role and they have more limited time, a more concise tuition programme can be developed:

- Training on operational risk framework and tools. It is particularly powerful when this training can be delivered by the organization's second line experts, either in its entirety or in a combination with external trainers; as this explicitly reinforces the department's position as a centre of excellence. This training can cover key framework components such as losses and near misses, RCSAs, KRIs and scenarios.

- Encouraging further studying to obtain a recognized operational risk qualification.

- Providing opportunities to join external training, offering tickets to operational risk conferences (where budget permits), or extending invitations to participate in industry forums.

- Facilitation training. If the firm is already running a good programme, it is beneficial to offer it to the first line champions who inevitably will end up leading meetings and workshops.

The second line can assist by developing minimum skillset requirements for first line coordinators; and undertaking a training needs analysis, to identify gaps between the skills held and knowledge required.

CASE STUDY 11.2

A two-day training programme is developed by the second line Operational Risk department, with the aim of raising the general standard of education on operational risk and making it more comprehensive. This programme contains an overview of all framework components and how they are implemented in the organization. The team works together to add interactive elements including group work, case studies and quizzes, which all enhance the participants' experience. The course, piloted on first line champions, is delivered face-to-face, with each topic presented by a different speaker from the second line.

It receives excellent feedback. Delivery by internal personnel is praised and perceived as a strong point which immediately boosts the department's reputation. Based on this experience, subsequent sessions are scheduled regularly in various locations across the country, allowing the maximum number of attendees to benefit from the training being offered.

The educational journey: three steps towards memorable risk training

Once the second line is fully equipped with knowledge and first line champions have been well trained, it is time to launch a firm-wide campaign.

Training for the wider population of staff usually involves a combination of online modules and face-to-face sessions, since classroom-led training is widely recognized as being far more impactful than online tutorials. It is strongly recommended to include a programme for all new joiners as part of their overall induction, as well as periodic refresher sessions.

Outlined in Figure 11.3 are three suggested steps to deliver effective, memorable operational risk training.

FIGURE 11.3 Three steps for developing all-staff education

Step 1: Design phase – high-quality materials and a theme

Education does not have to be boring, and there are many good alternatives to a set of dull training slides which merely recite Basel Committee guidelines on operational risk management. All firms have professionals whose job is to produce sleek and colourful promotional materials, ads and client presentations. Commonly, Marketing and Communications departments employ creative people full of ideas of what 'good' looks like when it comes to capturing an audience's attention. When developing operational risk training programmes, partner with experts and request their advice and help to design presentations for internal personnel that are not only impactful but visually appealing. This resource is not utilized nearly enough – Operational Risk departments need to reach out and speak much more to marketing, communications or other equivalent functions to take advantage of their skills and expertise.

To strengthen the message, it is beneficial to find a meaningful theme which resonates with the firm's strategy, objectives and aspirations. This makes the training more engaging, vivid and real.

CASE STUDY 11.3

An all-staff operational risk training programme is being developed in a start-up firm. The chief executive understands and embraces the value of operational risk, eloquently comparing the organization with a newly built airplane: proper management of people, systems, processes and the external environment will all support a smooth journey. The Operational Risk department partners with Marketing and agrees on an aircraft theme for the programme, with a photo of the chief executive in the cockpit and key messages from the pilot. Each training participant receives a key ring in the form of a plane as a free gift. Employees understand the analogy and connect with the theme, and the training manages to achieve its objective of reaching out with simple messages and raising awareness.

Step 2: Delivery – interactive and with a sense of humour

Once the training materials have been developed, it is important to focus on the excellence of delivery. Consider various learning styles, be they visual, auditory or kinaesthetic (learning by doing), and design a programme which incorporates a mixture of approaches. Chinese philosopher Confucius is reputed to have said: 'I hear and I forget. I see and I remember. I do and I understand.' Interactive sessions where participants apply their learning in practice maximize the degree to which the material is absorbed. Reflecting on many years of my own teaching, the delegates always quote engagement and the doing part as a very enjoyable feature of the courses I have run.

For longer one- or two-day training sessions, it is effective to use group work, splitting participants into teams. Engaging exercises can be designed for each component of the framework:

- OREs – reviewing internal or external case studies of major operational risk failures;
- RCSAs – having a go at identifying *top operational risks* and plotting them on a *heat map* to practise risk identification;
- KRIs – creating indicators for a select *top operational risk* and setting thresholds, or sharing the best metrics currently used to manage risks and discussing their attributes;
- reporting – to reinforce the message that reporting should be succinct – selecting a film or a book and summarizing it in six words.

There is still time for attendee interaction even in shorter sessions. When introducing operational risk events, ask the audience to come up with an example of a recent event for all relevant categories of the taxonomy. At the end, running a short quiz with a few simple questions on definitions, thresholds for loss reporting, roles and responsibilities works quite well.

Training should be fun, so light-hearted delivery works best. People like to laugh, and it is up to the trainer to find relevant yet humorous examples which reinforce the need for risk management. Clever use of personal stories, cartoons and images can be powerful. One video clip has two Australian comedians talking about the BP oil spill in the Gulf of Mexico; this conveys exceptionally well the need to think about risk proactively, and most participants seem to find it very amusing.

Trainers inevitably bring examples of industry disasters when talking about operational risk events. Instead of citing ordinary cases of technology failures or fines for money laundering, do some research and find more unusual events. There is a rather interesting case of a teenager taking revenge on former bosses by sending some five million emails quoting a warning from a horror film, *The Ring*, which eventually led to the collapse of the firm's servers under the weight of the email traffic.[11] I always ask the audience to guess what was in the quote.

Step 3: Feedback and continuous evolution

A training module is only as good as the audience thinks it is. It is valuable to solicit feedback after each session, via a paper form or an online survey. Key questions to consider may include:

- Was the session useful and well delivered?
- Did the training provide learnings that you can apply in your daily job?
- Do you understand your role in managing operational risk?

It is useful to leave some room for free format comments and suggestions on how to improve the training. Attendees can then come up with creative ideas and fair criticism, which should be studiously examined with the aim to continuously improve the training offering.

Tailoring the content to the audience

What about training content? While there is no universal answer and the agenda depends on each firm's individual circumstances, the emphasis should be on the relevance of the learning. Employees need to come out of the session equipped with knowledge that they can directly apply in practice.

At its simplest level, all employees need to know:

- What is operational risk?
- How is it managed?
- What is my role in the process, and what should I be doing?

All staff should be able to recognize and report operational risk events (OREs); therefore the training must provide examples of what those are and guide employees on how to do those things. If the session is delivered to a particular business or function, the content can be tailored to suit the audience, with relevant discussion around losses and near misses that can potentially happen in their area. Chapter 4 articulated such examples for Human Resources and Trading.

Training covering RCSAs, KRIs, scenarios and ORAs is more targeted to those who are taking part in these exercises, and should be carried out in a timely manner, shortly before the workshops or even as part of them.

It is imperative to incorporate executive briefings for senior management. The same concept of relevance applies, in a similar way to employees, to assist senior executives to absorb the key information while also applying the concepts. Therefore, the best learning happens when executives:

- carry out a strategic risk assessment (see Chapter 5), identifying and evaluating risks that may prevent them from achieving their objectives;
- review their departmental RCSA, outlining what keeps them awake at night and debating mitigating actions for significant risks;
- act on the operational risk assessment of a new product which has highlighted a material risk area.

An introductory methodological presentation is beneficial, especially when it is followed immediately by a participation exercise.

Online training

It may not be possible to run ongoing face-to-face sessions for all staff. Web-based refresher training can play a supportive role in delivering key messages to a larger target audience. However, a word of caution. We have all been there and done that – clicking through the pages quickly to get to the end in record time ('phew, mandatory training completed'). So it takes twice as much creativity to design an online module that stands a chance of attracting attention:

- Use the same first step as in face-to-face training, aiming for high-quality materials and a theme, to enhance attendees' visual learning experience.
- Supplement the training materials with an auditory learning element, by including personal and impactful recorded video messages. These can be from senior leaders on the importance of risk management, or from employees on what risk management means to them in their daily jobs.
- Add questions and quizzes to incorporate the *doing* part. This is one of the few advantages of online modules, where tests are easy to administer. Well-designed activities help to engage the learners, prompting them to maintain focus and participate actively in the training.

- Place the evaluation up-front, rather than at the end of the course. A session which starts with a test of current knowledge recognizes that some employees will already have a good grasp of core material. If they pass, they do not need to proceed with the full course, thus saving them time and retaining their goodwill.

- To add variety, consider embedding pointers and/or links to the internal company website. These could contain, for example, names and (ideally) photos of second line *multipliers* and first line *champions*, making them more personal and accessible; or a template for logging operational risk losses; or other relevant information.

- Develop a sequential progressive modular training programme, which builds on the knowledge imparted during previous modules.

- If an online module is re-used as refresher, ensure that materials and evaluations are significantly amended to reflect advances in both internal processes and the external environment. Integrate new recorded messages. There is nothing worse than the same training module being offered as a refresher year after year. If staff become over-familiar with the offering they will simply switch off. In this event not only is the training called into question but also the wider reputation of the Operational Risk department.

In conclusion, training in itself will not do the job of embedding operational risk management. It needs to be supported by a robust framework with meaningful tools and the right tone from the top. Education, however, can take the firm a long way forward in achieving this objective.

Common challenges and good practices

Common challenges

Challenges that may arise when designing and delivering educational programmes are outlined below.

LIMITED BUDGET
Training has cost implications. While a lot can be achieved via internal means, there are undeniable benefits from investing in targeted external courses, where relevant. Operational risk courses and conferences, as well as facilitation and public speaking programmes, can significantly enhance employee skillsets. A clear articulation of the investment being sought and the expected

outcomes of the training, to help achieve senior level buy-in and approval, are therefore required.

EMPLOYEES PUSHING BACK

Often, the challenge around training and education is *'why do I need to do this?'* type of comeback from staff. The training aids in embedding further knowledge about the responsibilities of colleagues across the firm and draws out the consequences of poor operational risk management. Understanding and managing firm's risks is an enabler to meeting strategic objectives while remaining within defined risk appetite.

TRAINING FATIGUE

While in the past end-users would be responsible for seeking out their own relevant training, the ever-increasing tsunami of regulation means that many other people are out there trying to achieve mandatory training objectives for everyone in the firm. Commonly folk are now chased by Compliance (to attend new conduct and culture training), Financial Crime (it's time for your mandatory anti-money laundering refresh), Information Security (cyber risk update), Data Protection (the obligatory Global Data Protection Regulation education session), Health and Safety, and many others. Operational risk is thus only part of a rather long queue. This makes it all the more important to stand out, with well-designed, memorable, engaging and meaningful learning that employees can truly benefit from. In addition, where possible, avoid organizational silos and look for synergies, developing joint modules where possible to relieve pressure on the end-user.

APATHY

At times, training workshops can be marred by apathy and/or poor attendance on the part of business units or support functions. I always believe that leading by engagement is more powerful than via punishment or penalty. Persevere and continue to deliver excellent educational programmes. Through word of mouth, employees will get to hear about them, tag along and join in.

MISSED OPPORTUNITIES

Over the years, I have interviewed multiple second line operational risk professionals. While many came across as all-round experts, quite a few actually had experience of dealing with only one specific framework component, for example losses and near misses. They were not always proficient with other tools and could not always articulate how all the elements of the framework fitted together. When working in operational risk as an employee, be curious and strive to acquire a holistic understanding of the discipline and the surrounding business and regulatory environment. As a leader, be sure to always provide opportunities for cross-training and aim to develop a comprehensive pool of knowledge across all team members.

Good practices

ADOPT ENTREPRENEURIAL APPROACH

Second line *multipliers* are key to the success of operational risk management in the organization. To encourage a more entrepreneurial approach in the second line, it is beneficial to think of it as a consultancy firm which is rewarded based on the quality of its people. Could the operational risk function take off and branch out today, if it were hypothetically to start up as an independent company? Will the level of knowledge and interpersonal skills make it profitable? Would you hire them? If not, consider what further skill development is needed.

APPOINT A TRAINING COORDINATOR

Recognizing the importance of education, appoint a training coordinator within the second line. This is usually not a full-time role, but rather giving someone responsibility for thinking about the firm-wide training strategy and leading its implementation.

EMBRACE VIRTUAL LEARNING

Covid-19 has taught us some valuable lessons about the effective use of virtual classrooms. What was previously an instructor-led session can now be delivered both face-to-face and virtually. Online platforms such as Zoom have excellent functionality, including live polls, whiteboards and break-out rooms. Other brilliant apps are available to facilitate brainstorming and group work, for example, Klaxoon and Mentimeter. During the pandemic, all my courses switched to virtual platforms, be it on Zoom, Microsoft Teams or GoToWebinar. It took some time to explore the features but I am really impressed with the varied offerings and online tools now available in the market.

EXPLORE WHAT IS AVAILABLE ON THE MARKET

When designing online training modules, it is beneficial to explore what is available off-the-shelf. Some suppliers, especially in compliance and financial crime, also develop operational risk training programmes. Because there is no standard application of the framework elements, however, any purchased solution will need to be tailored, and supplemented by relevant examples, links and policy requirements. Still, providers such as Brainshark offer platforms on which unique, tailor-made training can be developed, offering a range of excellent features to help make the module more interactive and engaging.[12]

RETAIN EVIDENCE

Nowadays, evidencing is key. Online modules store evidence of attendance and pass rates, making them very effective for audit and control purposes.

CELEBRATE SUCCESS

And lastly, celebrating success. Perseverance in training will continue to increase the overall level of knowledge in the organization. This in turn reinforces the correct use of the different framework components, embeds the right practices and strengthens the risk culture of the firm. The progress, reflected in the maturity assessment (as described in Chapter 13), needs to be actively publicized and celebrated, to help embed operational risk management even further.

Industry benchmark, 2020

Practitioners from a range of financial services firms of different sizes and geographical spread joined a Best Practice Forum to participate in a live poll examining various aspects of operational risk training.

Participants acknowledged that firm-wide operational risk training is not yet at its point of destination. The Basel Committee's conclusion on firms needing more comprehensive education, reached in 2014, remains valid six years later. The majority of respondents rated education as ad hoc and in need of further improvement, as seen in Figure 11.4. Increasing risk training became even more paramount during the Covid-19 pandemic and working from home environment.

FIGURE 11.4 Industry poll: operational risk training delivery

Firm-wide operational risk training

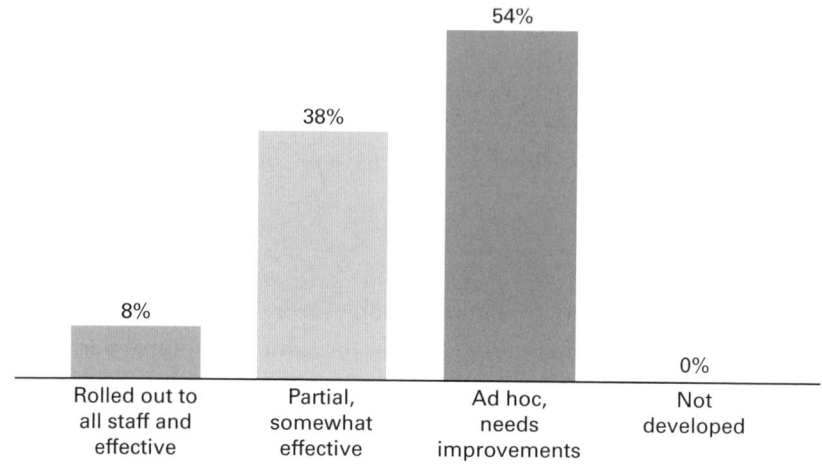

Best Practice Operational Risk Forum, 2020

FIGURE 11.5 Industry poll: operational risk training composition

Operational risk training includes

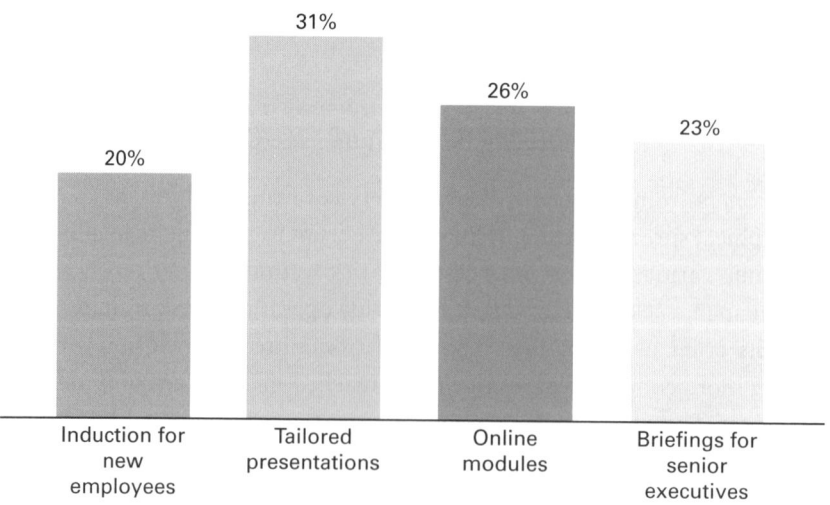

Best Practice Operational Risk Forum, 2020

FIGURE 11.6 Industry poll: operational risk second line learning

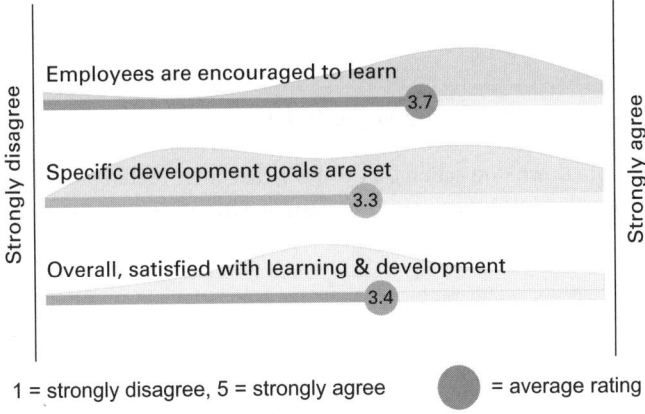

2nd Line Op Risk learning & development

Strongly disagree

Strongly agree

Employees are encouraged to learn
3.7

Specific development goals are set
3.3

Overall, satisfied with learning & development
3.4

1 = strongly disagree, 5 = strongly agree   = average rating

Best Practice Operational Risk Forum, 2020

Tailored presentations were most popular (see Figure 11.5); they are used for explaining specific framework tools, for example, RCSAs, KRIs, risk events or scenarios. By contrast, induction training for new starters was not sufficiently developed and appeared as an afterthought in some organizations.

On a positive note, second line operational risk employees feel that they are attracting continuous investment in their own learning and development, and also recognize the need for them to lead by example. Employees were confident that their firms provided good opportunities for education to enable continuous learning (see Figure 11.6).

Practical workplace exercise

Review the operational risk training offering available within your firm. Consider the following questions:

1 Does the training strategy achieve the goal of developing the second line operational risk function into a centre of excellence?

2 Is the education sufficient to support first line champions?

3 What is the current level of staff knowledge and what can be done to increase it?

4 What works well? Make a note of the strong features of the current training programme.

5 What can be improved? Note down potential improvements to the current programme.

MAKE A DIFFERENCE (MAD) ACTION

Please note down one action that you will take after reading this chapter that will make a positive difference to operational risk training in your firm.

In summary, this chapter discussed the crucial importance of education at all levels of the organization, proposing an approach for developing second line operational risk experts and transferring knowledge throughout the firm via well-designed and well-developed training.

Moving on, the next chapter continues the discussion with the topic of risk culture.

Notes

1 Basel Committee on Banking Supervision (2014) *Review of the Principles for the Sound Management of Operational Risk*, www.bis.org/publ/bcbs292.pdf (archived at https://perma.cc/7V33-DWSF)

2 Basel Committee on Banking Supervision (2020) Consultative document, *Revisions to the Principles for the Sound Management of Operational Risk*, www.bis.org/bcbs/publ/d508.pdf (archived at https://perma.cc/MJ4S-KA4Z)

3 Operational Riskdata eXchange Association (ORX) managingrisktogether.orx. org/free-resources (archived at https://perma.cc/SWH8-VQGB)

  4 Risk Channel, www.earlymorningmedia.co.uk/risk-channel-ukeurope/p/48 (archived at https://perma.cc/2NW4-ASRF)

  5 Thomson Reuters, www.thomsonreuters.com (archived at https://perma.cc/SS2E-FBUS)

  6 Risk.net, www.risk.net (archived at https://perma.cc/24ZN-3QN7)

  7 Risk Spotlight, www.riskspotlight.com (archived at https://perma.cc/8LZ8-MW6G)

  8 Institute of Risk Management, www.theirm.org/join-our-community/about-membership/ (archived at https://perma.cc/E2P6-TK6B)

  9 Certificate in Operational Risk Management (CORM) www.ior-institute.org/education/certificate-in-operational-risk-management (archived at https://perma.cc/SUN8-QP3P)

  10 London Stock Exchange Academy, www.lseg.com/markets-products-and-services/business-services/academy/london-campus/our-course-calendar/fundamentals-operational-risk-management (archived at https://perma.cc/965Q-59AL)

  11 Metro (2006) Sacked boy's revenge emails, metro.co.uk/2006/08/24/sacked-boys-revenge-emails-211474/ (archived at https://perma.cc/Z75D-F9TL)

  12 Brainshark, www.brainshark.com/why-brainshark (archived at https://perma.cc/V65F-YNA3)

12

Risk culture

What this chapter covers: The chapter focusses on the least visible but most vital aspect of risk management – risk culture (Figure 12.1). It considers how to evaluate this key topic, and proposes ways of completing an assessment via employee focus groups and the use of metrics. The chapter outlines practical steps that can be taken to embed the right ethos and behaviours. It goes on to highlight the importance of holding meaningful risk conversations across the firm; and reflects on the implications of the *identity* of operational risk practitioners on the culture of the enterprise. The chapter also includes industry benchmark and case studies.

FURTHER READING

- Michael Power, Simon Ashby and Tommaso Palermo (2013) *Risk Culture in Financial Organizations: A research report*, London School of Economics
  Why recommended: a very insightful report which still holds true today and sheds light on the multiple pockets of risk culture which may co-exist in a single organization; my favourite culture research out of multiple books and papers on the subject.

- John Purkiss and David Royston-Lee (2012) *Brand You: Turn your unique talents into a winning formula*, Pearson
  Why recommended: in this chapter, we touch upon the personal brand and identity of an operational risk professional. There is no better guide on developing a powerful brand than this book by two acclaimed authors. I would recommend it highly to anyone interested in developing their personal brand – or enhancing the brand of their Operational Risk department.

FIGURE 12.1 Focus of Chapter 12: risk culture

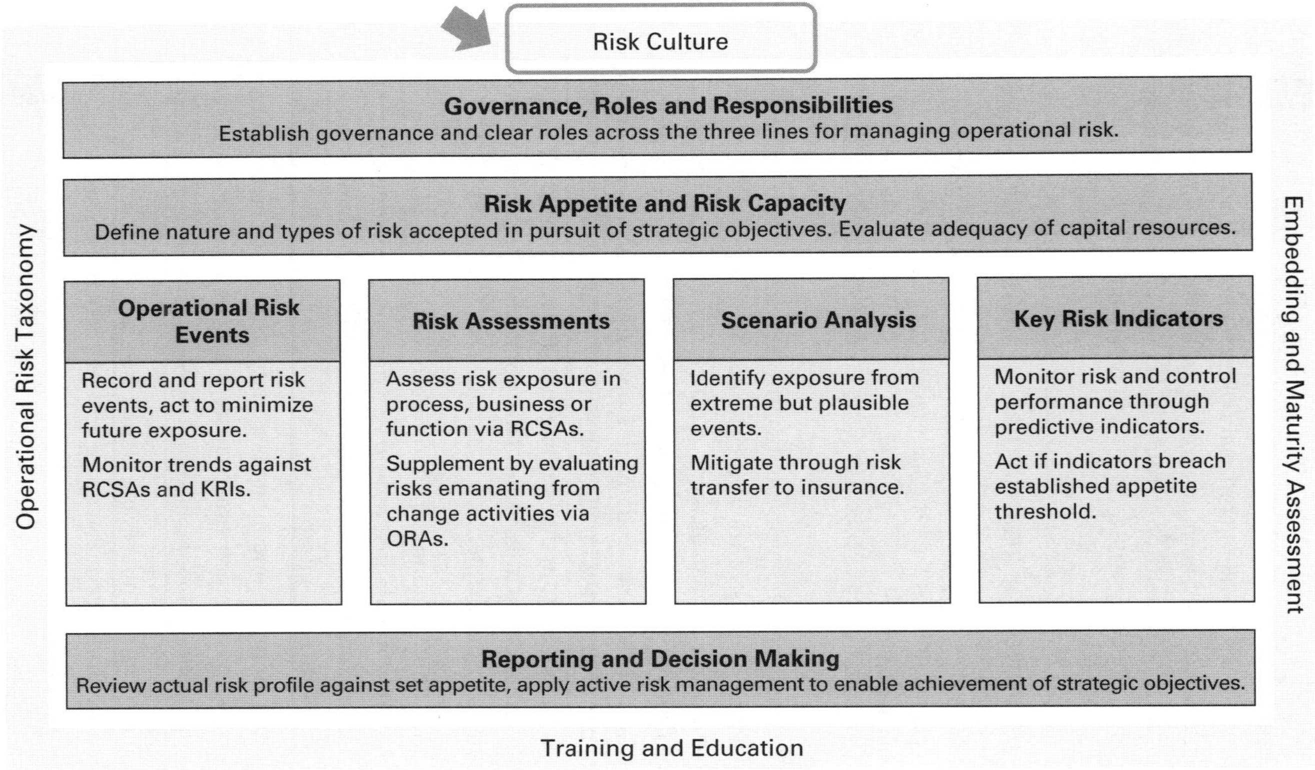

Risk Culture

Embedding and Maturity Assessment

Governance, Roles and Responsibilities
Establish governance and clear roles across the three lines for managing operational risk.

Risk Appetite and Risk Capacity
Define nature and types of risk accepted in pursuit of strategic objectives. Evaluate adequacy of capital resources.

Operational Risk Events	**Risk Assessments**	**Scenario Analysis**	**Key Risk Indicators**
Record and report risk events, act to minimize future exposure.	Assess risk exposure in process, business or function via RCSAs.	Identify exposure from extreme but plausible events.	Monitor risk and control performance through predictive indicators.
Monitor trends against RCSAs and KRIs.	Supplement by evaluating risks emanating from change activities via ORAs.	Mitigate through risk transfer to insurance.	Act if indicators breach established appetite threshold.

Reporting and Decision Making
Review actual risk profile against set appetite, apply active risk management to enable achievement of strategic objectives.

Training and Education

Operational Risk Taxonomy

Understanding and measuring risk culture

Risk culture is not a new concept for operational risk practitioners. It is an integral part of the discipline, and features in Principle One of the Basel Committee's sound operational risk practices.[1] Historically, risk professionals have not only been involved in establishing and maintaining firms' risk culture, but actually often took the lead in some organizations' efforts, positively influencing ethos, values and behaviours.

DEFINITION OF RISK CULTURE

Risk culture is a social process that can be defined as an institution's values, 'norms, attitudes and behaviours related to risk awareness, risk taking and risk management'.[2]

By design, all the elements of an operational risk framework inevitably touch on themes of transparency, accountability and no blame. The effectiveness of risk management is closely linked to and largely dependent on the firm's culture. Organizations where the right values have been embedded are less likely to suffer damaging operational risk events, and stand a better chance of dealing with them effectively if they do occur.

It is, therefore, in the best interests of operational risk practitioners to be fully engaged on this topic. Two points before we move on to the main content of the chapter:

- An ample amount of literature has been published on the subject of culture. Regulators, industry bodies and consultancy firms have issued definitions, reports and guidelines which this chapter does not intend to replicate or re-interpret.

- Risk culture is undoubtedly a complex, multifaceted topic with no 'recipe book' answer. But practical steps can be taken to instil and embed the right behaviours throughout the organization.

Some form of culture assessment has become the norm within financial services firms. Boards expect it and regulators require it. As noted, for instance, by the Australian Royal Commission, 'all financial services entities should take proper steps to assess the entity's culture'.[3] A benchmarking survey of over 50 financial services firms revealed that, in general, firms' culture was measured via employee surveys or focus groups, or alternatively metrics and dashboards.[4] Interestingly, the top three methods used by organizations consisted of:

- employee exit interviews;
- employee surveys; and
- appraisals and feedback received during the performance management process.

As demonstrated by the industry benchmark survey discussed at the end of the chapter, cultural efforts in most organizations are led by the human resources function. But it is crucial for operational risk teams to join and contribute to these programmes.

The five-aspects risk culture assessment model

Any measure of culture is somewhat imprecise due to the complex nature of the subject. While organizations may have different perspectives, the work undertaken by the Financial Stability Board (FSB) represents a good place to start.[5] The proposed *risk culture aspects model* described in Figure 12.2 takes into consideration FSB's framework and focusses on five components: *transparency*, *no blame*, *personal accountability*, *risk awareness* and *risk reward*. It can be argued that these aspects are indicative of the firm's cultural 'state of health', and influence the firm's ability to take the informed risk decisions necessary for achieving its strategic objectives. Organizations may add further factors that they feel are relevant to their firm.

The reasons why the five factors have been selected as particularly important to the enterprise are articulated below:

- *Transparency* plays a significant role in information flows. It allows the transmission of messages without them being modified. For example, if a KRI is reported as *Red*, it does not get downgraded to *Amber* or *Green* by the time it is escalated up the chain. Some senior managers, committees and boards do not deal well with *Red* indicators and other reports which raise alarms. As a result, true risks and issues can be demoted, leading to a lack of management focus or preventative action to mitigate potentially major problems.
- Cultivating *no blame* attitudes was discussed in Chapter 3 on operational risk events. A constructive approach to resolving problems, rather than pointing fingers, has a big influence on how employees act when things go wrong.

FIGURE 12.2   Risk culture aspects model

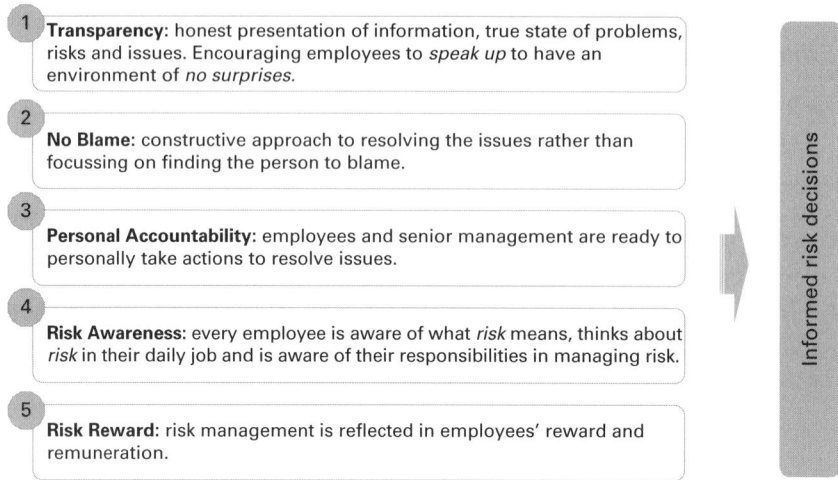

- *Personal accountability* is simply essential to move things forward and get things done. The institution can have transparent discussions around areas of concern without attributing blame, but if no one is ready to step in and act, the issues are unlikely to get resolved. This is an area of particular regulatory focus, given the introduction of formal accountability regimes over recent years.

- *Risk awareness* has been a key theme throughout this book. It measures the extent to which employees understand risk and are aware of their own roles and responsibilities in managing it.

- *Risk reward* answers the question *what's in it for me?* If actions or behaviours result in no personal impact – in the form of either an incentive for good risk management or punishment for poor practices – it is harder to articulate the case respectively for or against them.

CASE STUDY 12.1

A small-size corporate bank adopts the *risk culture aspects model* to run diagnostics around its existing culture, identifying its areas of strength and weakness. It creates cross-departmental employee focus groups, facilitated by the operational risk function, to gauge staff members' perceptions of how well or poorly the firm scores on a scale of 1 to 10 in each of the categories. The results, presented in Figure 12.3, are analysed and presented for discussion.

FIGURE 12.3   Risk culture assessment case study analysis

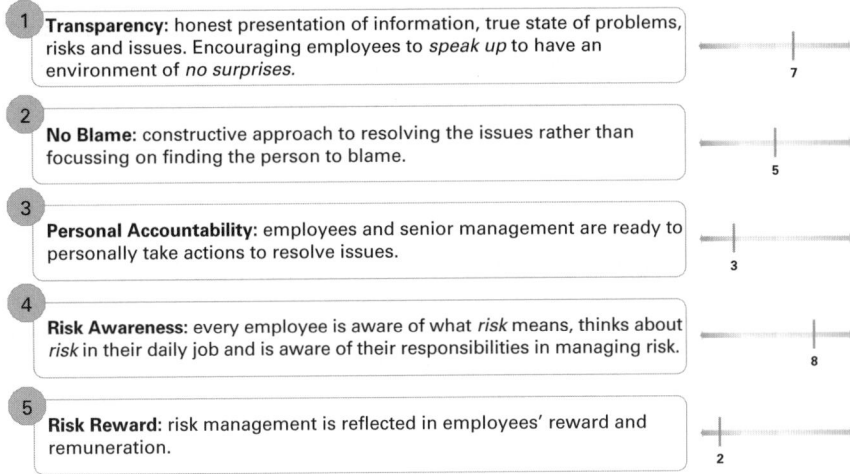

- *Risk awareness* achieves a high rating, 8 out of 10; employees recall and relate to ongoing efforts sponsored by the chief risk officer and chief executive to educate all staff on risk management. For example, via face-to-face training, led by the operational risk function, and the introduction of a popular *risk mailbox* which all employees can use to informally identify particular risks or issues. Roles are generally well understood.

- *Transparency* also scores highly; overall, management encourages and welcomes the identification and escalation of issues across the enterprise.

- *No blame* culture varies markedly by area; while there are good behaviours in many departments, it transpires that there are pockets of poor practices within Technology and Finance.

- *Personal accountability* highlights a challenge; headcount cuts have resulted in employees becoming overstretched. While staff are eager to raise issues, they are reluctant to volunteer for additional responsibilities which add extra tasks to their already full agenda.

- Finally, *Risk reward* receives the lowest score and is not deemed functional by the focus groups. While aggressive risk taking in sales and trading is penalized, the actions and behaviours of non-revenue generating functions have no similar impact. Good or poor risk management has no bearing on compensation.

The study is perceived as insightful; it results in a range of tangible actions, including adopting this kind of evaluation as a matter of practice, and continuing regular culture *health checks*, via employee focus groups, on a semi-annual basis.

In this case the Operational Risk department was able to facilitate focus groups and obtain insights into employees' honest opinions due to its good standing, earning trust and a recognition of its impartiality. As highlighted later in the chapter, the *identity* of the operational risk professional, their individual personality, has a strong contributing effect on these cultural dynamics.

Metrics: culture and conduct dashboard

Culture is still widely considered as a primary root cause of major conduct failings in financial services. Often this view focusses on a firm's broader *culture* (rather than its *risk culture*).

> Numerous credible definitions of culture exist; we will use 'habitual behaviours and mindsets that characterize an organization'.[6]

But in recent years the ancillary terms *conduct* and *conduct risk* have become more prominent in supervisory publications, speeches and discussions.

> *Conduct risk* can be defined as the risk that a firm's 'decisions and behaviours lead to detrimental or poor outcomes for their customers, and the risk that the firm fails to maintain high standards of market behaviour and integrity'.[7]

Consequently the industry is undergoing a major strengthening of employees' conduct obligations, the introduction of enhanced certification and accountability regimes, and instruments such as the legally required banker's oath.[8] The concepts of *culture*, *risk culture* and *conduct* are closely intertwined; though it would be fair to say that culture and conduct have a broader social and behavioural scope than *risk culture*. Organizations are expected to create firm-specific definitions of these key terms. Based on the industry benchmark highlighted at the end of this chapter, both the language and the focus of these efforts vary significantly depending on the jurisdiction and the terms habitually used by the firms and their supervisors.

FIGURE 12.4   Example of conduct and culture dashboard

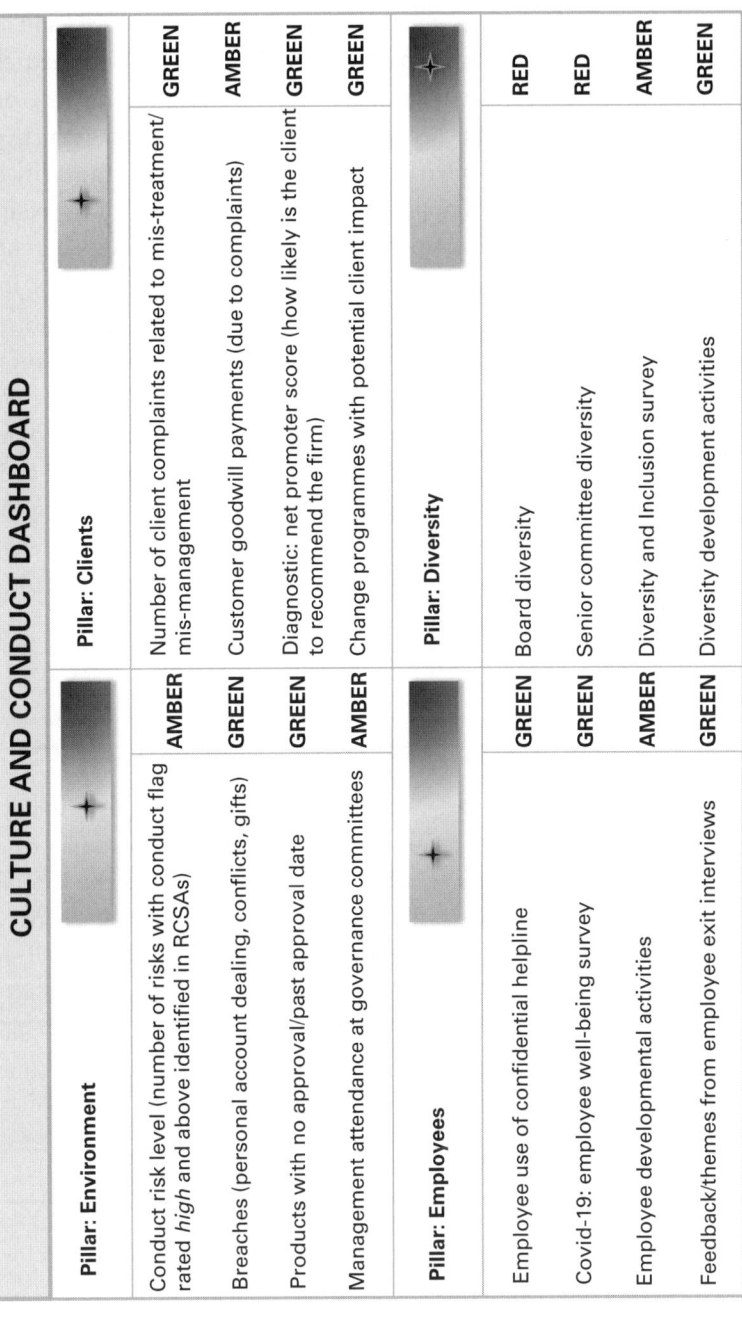

CULTURE AND CONDUCT DASHBOARD

Pillar: Environment		
Conduct risk level (number of risks with conduct flag rated *high* and above identified in RCSAs)	AMBER	
Breaches (personal account dealing, conflicts, gifts)	GREEN	
Products with no approval/past approval date	GREEN	
Management attendance at governance committees	AMBER	

Pillar: Employees		
Employee use of confidential helpline	GREEN	
Covid-19: employee well-being survey	GREEN	
Employee developmental activities	AMBER	
Feedback/themes from employee exit interviews	GREEN	

Pillar: Clients		
Number of client complaints related to mis-treatment/ mis-management	GREEN	
Customer goodwill payments (due to complaints)	AMBER	
Diagnostic: net promoter score (how likely is the client to recommend the firm)	GREEN	
Change programmes with potential client impact	GREEN	

Pillar: Diversity		
Board diversity	RED	
Senior committee diversity	RED	
Diversity and Inclusion survey	AMBER	
Diversity development activities	GREEN	

As with surveys and focus groups, operational risk practitioners need to actively join in the firm's efforts to create culture and conduct dashboards; after all, many of the metrics will be relevant to operational risk, and may even be already monitored by the department. Perhaps risk culture metrics are the future as they can deliver more value than occasional, discrete employee surveys. Organizations quickly suffer from survey fatigue which prevents them from being repeated often enough to keep track of changing risk cultures.

Figure 12.4 gives an example of such a dashboard. In this example, the dashboard measures the firm's performance against four pillars that have been designated as important to the organization. Some of these aspects, for example, diversity and inclusion, refer to core values that are broader than risk awareness, risk taking and risk management (which together represent *risk culture*). The indicators in this dashboard were selected, together with their thresholds, via a rigorous management process, as discussed in Chapter 7.

The dashboard is typically presented to a relevant governance committee, which could be an operational and conduct risk committee, the main risk committee, the board, or all of the above. This kind of metric enables the organization to continuously monitor agreed aspects of culture and constantly drive the agenda forward.

Practical steps towards embedding risk culture

From evaluation to actions, undeniably, the operational risk function plays a key role in embedding the right ethos in the firm; so it is, to a great extent, a catalyst for positive change. Ideally, a clear tone from the top and firm-wide cultural programmes will have been established, which operational risk can participate in and contribute to. Sometimes, however, firms make minimal endeavours in this area and operational risk ends up being the *sole department* pushing the heavy load up the hill. Whichever circumstances apply, practitioners can spearhead the following set of activities to influence behaviours across the organization.

Transparency

- Instituting incentives for transparency, such as *thank you* notes for reporting operational risk events.

- Via facilitation and challenge, helping first line business units to reflect the true state of risks, events and issues – neither under- nor overestimating them.

- By expressing opinions that are clear and independent, helping to transmit the right messages which consequently retain their true meaning (eg ensuring that *Red* KRIs are not diluted, when escalated upwards, by being downgraded to *Amber* or *Green*).

- Incorporating automated process workflows, for speedy dissemination and escalation of material issues to the right audience.

- Incentivizing high awareness of risks and issues.

No blame

- Developing trust with first line business units; being visible and approachable, having a known team member who serves as a liaison for every area and who can be contacted if employees have questions or doubts.

- Educating senior management on a no blame attitude; although this kind of venture does not always bear fruit, every attempt should be made.

- Setting the tone by chairing operational risk forums where issues are discussed openly and constructively.

- Documenting in policies that the firm has a no blame approach (ie a formal mechanism, although note that this can be less effective than establishing a no blame attitude more informally).

- Working with Human Resources to establish and analyse relevant metrics; for example, an increase in incidences of whistleblowing or the use of employee helplines may be indicative of potential problems that require focus.

Personal accountability

- Collaborating with Human Resources to document roles and responsibilities (for example, for first line risk owners, subject matter experts, or risk champions) and ensure they align with broader statements of accountabilities.

- Developing instruments such as an RACI matrix (**R**esponsible, **A**ccountable, **C**onsulted, **I**nformed), to outline the respective roles that first and second line functions play in a process or activity.

- Embedding risk acceptance mechanisms, to alleviate pressure on front-line functions and ensure formal agreement that no further action is needed in cases where it is not cost-effective.

- Prioritizing risks, issues and actions and focussing on what is important.

- Leading by example, stepping in to moderate any cross-functional operational risk events that have no single owner, until they are fully resolved.

Risk awareness

- Conducting employee training as discussed in the previous chapter, supplemented by other educational campaigns including social media posts, flash news, and newsletters.

- Using opportunities to present at senior management meetings and employee town halls; working with the chief executive to incorporate key messages into their internal presentations; developing key questions that a board should be asking itself on risk culture.

- Encouraging employees to participate in and use operational risk tools at the 'coal face'; working with RCSAs, KRIs and scenarios as a practical application is the best way of increasing understanding of the tools.

- Promoting the sharing and dissemination of lessons learned, tips and hints; for example, via a monthly meeting of first line operational risk coordinators.

- Highlighting interdependencies, where risks can affect others in the delivery chain. Process improvement techniques including process flow charts can be very useful in achieving this aim.

Risk reward

- Joining forces with Human Resources to incorporate risk management responsibilities into employees' objectives and the performance management process.

- Considering operational risk event data in appraisals; a punitive method is quite commonly used for front-office/sales personnel, but this can be supplemented by reward mechanisms, for example, providing formal feedback on the performance of first line operational risk champions.

- Using *compare and contrast* reviews which present, for instance, logs of incidents across all departments; timely and accurate reporting can be recognized via some kind of departmental reward (eg a shared meal);

- Celebrating success: for example, introducing employee awards for the most improved process following an operational risk event.

- Agreeing reward and punishment mechanisms when embedding the use of operational risk appetite.

Role of risk conversations

Risk experts set the tone and the language of *risk conversations*. What words come to mind when picking up the phone, switching on the webcam or walking into the meeting room with business units and support functions? What topics do operational risk professionals discuss?

Compare the two dialogues illustrated in Figure 12.5. The first box, *risk administration*, focusses on the *process* and has minimal content. It does not differentiate between low and high priority items, and focusses attention mainly on the mechanical aspects of the framework; aiming to just *get things done*, regardless of whether or not they are important. These discussions are usually brief and tend to be one-way, with operational risk chasing business units to take some kind of action or complete a form.

In contrast, *risk management* discussions evolve around the *content*. They concentrate on what is important, with more time being spent on high-priority issues that matter, because they may prevent the firm from achieving its objectives or may crystallize into major incidents. These conversations are usually longer, deeper and contain a meaningful two-way exchange of opinions.

FIGURE 12.5   Risk conversations

- Have you logged the ORE? When will you log it, it needs to be reported as soon as possible?

- Have you attached the evidence? This field is blank.

- You have seven open actions. We need to review all of them.

- Your RCSA is overdue. It needs to be completed by the end of this week.

- There are only three risks raised in your RCSA. Please ensure RCSA completeness.

- Latest ORE highlights an issue with control X. Let's discuss how it can be improved. Can this happen to other units?

- Reviewing open actions, there is one high priority item. How is your progress in obtaining the funding needed to fix the issue? How can we help to move it forward? What is the risk in the meantime?

- Based on your RCSA, X is your top risk. How is the new product/system impacting this risk? Will it increase even further? Let's discuss.

RED ZONE: Risk administration   **GREEN ZONE: Risk management**

It is important for operational risk teams to stand back and reflect on their risk conversations; as their tone and content will gradually be replicated across the enterprise. If risk practitioners lead the way using a risk *adminis-tration* approach, that is how the whole risk discipline will soon be perceived: as administrative. It also affects the culture, which develops into a bureau-cratic tick-box-type enterprise, with diminished faith in the second line risk function. By the same token, proper risk management discussions will send ripples through the business and will constantly repeat and reinforce them-selves, teaching business units what good looks like.

Impact of the identity of operational risk practitioners

As noted in the research report on risk culture in financial services mentioned earlier,[9] 'a significant aspect of the risk culture debate closely concerns the organizational position of the risk function'.

Undoubtedly, the importance of the risk profession has been increasing and the demand for practitioners is on the rise. When searching to recruit an ideal candidate, employers insist on the combination of multiple skills; includ-ing extensive experience in frameworks, knowledge of regulatory requirements, in-depth specialist knowledge, quantitative or actuarial background, and excellent communication and influencing skills. This blend makes it almost impossible to recruit the kind of superhero who possesses all the required skills and qualities. Because the operational risk discipline is still maturing, there is not yet a distinct *identity* for a typical operational risk professional.

In 2018 I conducted an industry study around this *identity* issue, to try to understand how operational risk professionals perceive themselves in their role. The results are presented in Table 12.1.

A positive result, as seen in the table, is that the majority (52 per cent) viewed themselves as consultants and trusted advisors, adopting a collabo-rative approach and working in partnership with the business. Around 25 per cent of respondents related to the identity of facilitators – influencers who spend a significant proportion of their time engaging, educating and communicating with employees and senior management, for example, facil-itating workshops and conducting road shows. These practitioners possess the traits of *multipliers* discussed in Chapter 3.

In cases where operational risk practitioners adopt a stance of *police officers* – emphasizing formal oversight, challenge and shareholder protection – they seem to lose some employees' trust. This in turn has implications for the

TABLE 12.1   Industry study: identity of operational risk practitioner

Operational risk practitioners primarily see themselves as	% Participants
Police officer	15%
Consultant	52%
Translator	8%
Facilitator	25%

TABLE 12.2   Industry study: skills of operational risk practitioners

What knowledge and skills do you see as most important?	% Firms
Knowledge of regulatory requirements	7%
Practical know-how (framework and tools)	73%
Subject matter expertise (cyber, outsourcing, other)	7%
Softer skills, influencing, facilitation	13%

interactions between risk management and the business, and ultimately, for the wider risk culture of the firm. We discussed these characters, also called *diminishers*, in Chapter 3.

Do risk practitioners possess the necessary skills to effectively perform the role of trusted advisors? The same study, the results of which are presented in Table 12.2, highlighted that operational risk employees may overestimate the importance of practical know-how at the expense of softer influencing, facilitation and negotiation skills.

CASE STUDY 12.2

An internal audit of an organization's culture gives rise to a follow-up project looking at the alignment of employees' expectations of the risk team compared to the firm's core values. Its aim is to explore how risk professionals are perceived by others. This project is completed via an enterprise-wide internal survey, supplemented by employee focus groups. The results highlight that, on a positive note, risk teams are *collaborative business partners*; however, most people express a desire for more engagement via an informal conversational approach. As a result, the Risk department restructures its routine tasks to free up more time for informal interactions, and takes an action to invest in the team's softer skillset.

Role of internal audit

Internal audit is a key partner which plays an important role in embedding sound practices and behaviours. As noted in the report entitled *Culture and the Role of Internal Audit* issued by the Chartered Institute of Internal Auditors, audit can be an essential contributor 'in giving confidence to boards that measures put in place to change culture and thus behaviour are actually working'.[10]

Good practices include:

- a clear mandate to audit the culture of the enterprise;
- integrating culture as part of every audit, as well as conducting thematic reviews;
- providing an engagement rating of how business units choose to interact with audit;
- producing a risk management engagement and effectiveness grid, showing the performance of each managing director relative to their peers;
- offering an opportunity for the business to voice unedited feedback on audits, which in itself provides a good insight into the firm's prevailing culture.

It is particularly powerful if the second and third lines, joined by HR, can all partner with each other on this complex subject, and think about what they can achieve with a joint, coordinated effort.

Common challenges and good practices

Common challenges

The following challenges may be encountered when embarking on the cultural journey.

LACK OF THE RIGHT TONE FROM THE TOP

Many regulatory and academic publications cite the right *tone from the top* and its significance to risk culture. In reality, at times the tone is either not right or not present. In these cases, the operational risk function is faced with the very difficult task of influencing behaviours by broadcasting the *tone from the side* (ie from the operational risk function itself). This is at the same time as the department is implementing framework tools, educating the units to manage risks and escalate events, to enable the firm to deal with threats that may prevent it from achieving its objectives. It is not only a challenge for the operational risk function but an inadequate substitute for the right tone from the top.

REACTIVE APPROACH

Culture work is easily forgotten as long as the organization is doing fine; when there is an unwanted trigger event, the subject is brought back into focus and becomes important again. This approach is rather reactive; proactive mechanisms such as focus groups or metrics should be adopted to keep the work constantly ongoing.

RISK ADMINISTRATION

Risk management executives may have an over-ambitious programme of work, for example enhancing risk framework tools or rolling out multiple RCSAs with tight deadlines. If this happens it raises the threat of turning the second line function into a purely administrative role, where the department concentrates on more mechanical aspects, getting things done, sometimes at the cost of quality and value-add. Conversations can easily slide into *risk administration*, affecting the risk brand and impacting the culture of the enterprise. Employees can also slip into a risk administration mindset, out of apathy or an unwillingness to focus on the content. It is important to periodically step back and listen to the words and the language being used; are the *risk conversations* good quality and adding value?

CULTURAL CHANGE PROGRAMMES

Organizations invariably display excellence as well as flaws. Some struggle with accountability because they routinely apply a philosophy of consensus which slows down decision making; others do not handle news of failures well. These vital aspects of the firm's mindset need to be understood; including the fact that the board and senior management are themselves an integral part of the culture. It is possible to drive change once the firm's existing state is analysed and it demonstrates a desire to move forward, making adjustments via small and progressive steps and recognizing that managing risk culture is for life. Aggressive change programmes that aim to move from *current* to *desired target* state are unrealistic; culture being a social process, both states keep changing during the intervention.

Good practices

WORKING WITH THE BOARD

Risk culture is the area where the board's engagement is key. It is good practice to develop a set of questions that a board should be constantly asking itself, to prompt good risk conversations. These may include, for example, how the board assesses the organization against the five *aspects of risk culture* described in this chapter; how it perceives the tone it is setting from the top; whether decisions are taken within the stated risk appetite; and what mechanisms are in place to ensure that new joiners absorb the desired values of the firm.

CONDUCTING ONGOING EVALUATION

Risk culture is 'not a static thing but a continuous process which repeats and renews itself'.[11] It is therefore good practice to conduct ongoing *health checks*, as described in the case study outlined above, where employee focus groups are run on a periodic basis rather than as a one-off effort. Changes are always occurring in the general environment in which firms operate and if the evaluation work is constant there is a better opportunity to pick them up. In general, focus groups are more useful than surveys, as they allow for more meaningful interactions and conversations around selected topics. Another powerful technique is participant observation, where, for example, an independent consultant is sitting in on risk committees, risk assessment exercises, internal audit reviews and other activities to observe behaviour at source and help the organization to conduct the assessment and interpret the results in an objective manner. This is one good reason why the help of external consultants is needed. If the organization performs and analyses the assessment, the interpretation itself is influenced by the prevailing risk culture and therefore may not be objective.

BEYOND REGULATORY FOCUS

Cultural change programmes often emerge due to a trigger event or regulatory criticism. Moving from rules to risk management to doing the 'right thing' displays the state of maturity of the firm. With the emergence of the terms *conduct* and *conduct risk*, many organizations commenced with an essentially supervision-driven approach, initially applying minimum regulatory standards; but subsequently have moved away from mere compliance to actively driving decision making and outcomes.

AUTHORITY OF RISK FUNCTION

The *authority* of the risk function has an important role to play in the cultural debate. It includes having a say at the strategy- and decision-making table, positioning the business for success while being strong and decisive; clearly expressing an opinion when the level of risk is too high and the activity may be *detrimental*. How boards and executives listen to the voice of risk reflects its brand and reputation, and influences behaviours.

Industry benchmarks, 2019 and 2020

Embedding risk culture (2019)

A positive view emerged from the industry workshop in 2019, where participants felt that overall – although more can be done – risk culture was relatively well embedded, with more efforts on the way, as seen in Figure 12.6. The three lines of defence model, which is often criticized, appears to be working well in this space. In reality, it is people who embody the model and make the three lines effective (or not); if business, risk and internal audit have a good, constructive working relationship, they will find ways of collaborating without creating gaps or tripping over each other.

The majority of internal programmes supported by the board are led by Human Resources (40 per cent of firms, as seen in Figure 12.7), followed by Risk and Compliance, or Programme Management (7 per cent) if the firm is in project mode (at least until the project is transitioned into business-as-usual).

FIGURE 12.6 Industry poll: risk culture implementation

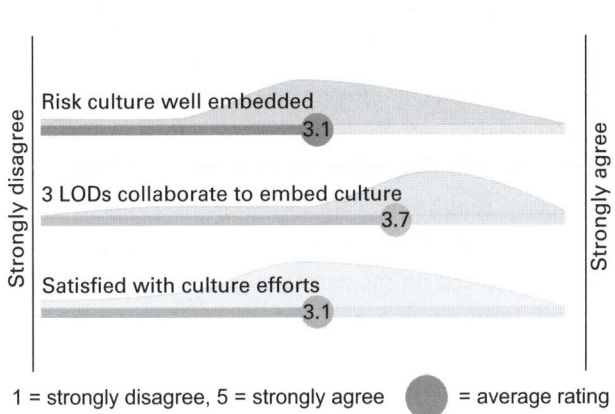

In your firm

Strongly disagree

Risk culture well embedded — 3.1

3 LODs collaborate to embed culture — 3.7

Satisfied with culture efforts — 3.1

Strongly agree

1 = strongly disagree, 5 = strongly agree   = average rating

Operational Risk Training, Risk.net

FIGURE 12.7 Industry poll: leading risk culture efforts

Who is leading culture programmes and initiatives?

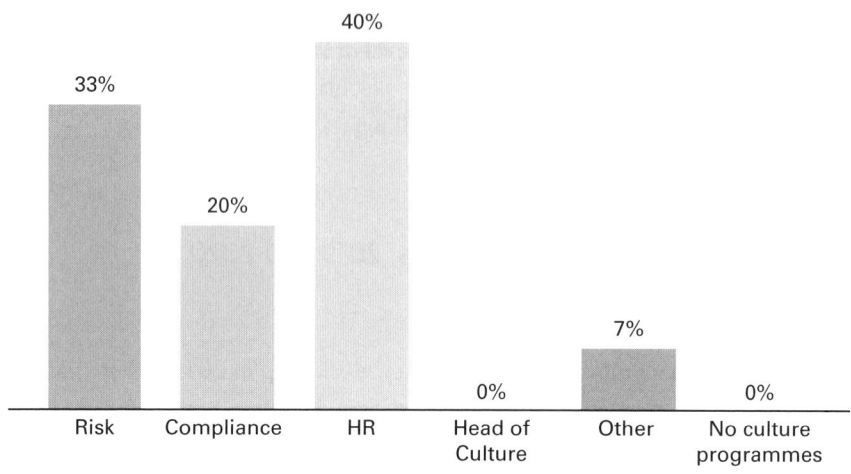

Operational Risk Training, Risk.net

Cultural programmes have a slightly different focus, depending on the geographical location of the firm and the regulatory environment – most concentrate on *culture and conduct* (69 per cent of firms), followed by *risk culture* (23 per cent) and *culture* in general (8 per cent).

Risk culture and the Covid-19 pandemic (2020)

The Covid-19 pandemic placed a strain on maintaining firms' risk culture, even for organizations that purport to have a winning set of values, attitudes and behaviours. Enforced and prolonged working from home (WFH) led to partial loss of *informal interactions*, including between risk practitioners and business units. This, in turn, eroded corporate cohesiveness – the attitude of 'we-ness' that unites employees, allowing them to remain motivated, accomplishing set goals.

The poll conducted in December 2020 at the Best Practice Operational Risk Forum reflected that 86 per cent of risk professionals believed that risk culture has somewhat deteriorated in their organizations. Supervisors around the world also commented on the perceived reduction in the effectiveness of the *second line of defence risk function itself* during working from home.

Adopting a constructive approach, practitioners discussed what activities could give a boost to firms' practices. Aspects such as *tone from the top* and *risk education* were considered the most impactful, as illustrated in Figure 12.8.

Good practices include:

- Risk function facilitating employee focus groups to consider the factors that can threaten the culture during WFH; as well as recommending to the board and senior management what behaviours should be reinforced, thus supporting and informing the tone from the top.

- Increasing and enhancing the risk education, which is relevant and personal to the end-users.

- Purposefully boosting the *informal* part of interactions, reaching out to business units with, for example, offers of *virtual coffee* discussions, to supplement more formal meetings.

Considering the risk culture aspects model described earlier in the chapter, a potential additional aspect – *situational awareness* – emerged from the Covid-19 pandemic; also referenced in Chapter 8 on Scenario Analysis. A rapid sense and response to the changing environment differentiated successful organizations and their risk teams. The winning risk teams proactively

FIGURE 12.8 Industry poll: boosting risk culture during Covid-19 pandemic

During Covid-19/WFH, what will boost risk culture the most?

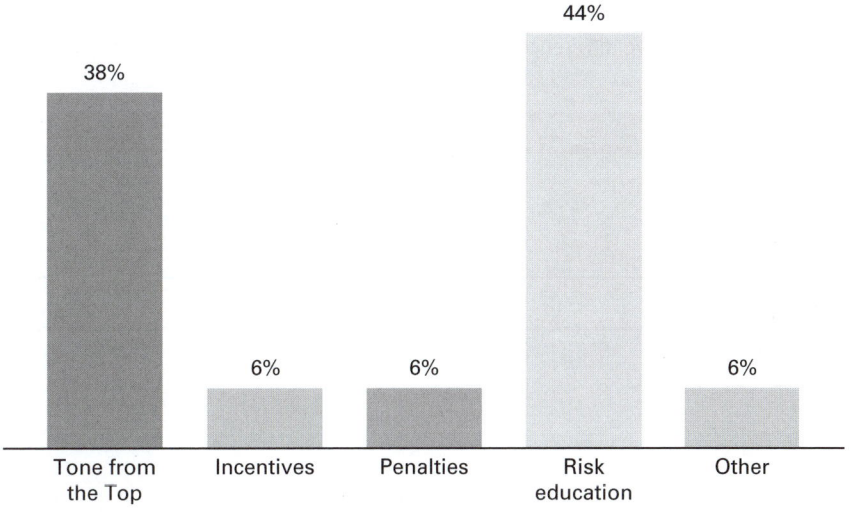

Best Practice Operational Risk Forum, 2020

reached out and collaborated with business units and support functions, to enhance risk intelligence and bolster desired behaviours.

In short, risk culture remains an exciting space, where operational risk practitioners will continue playing a crucial part, actively influencing and making a positive difference to the institution's norms, attitudes and behaviours.

Practical workplace exercise

Reflect on the topic discussed in this chapter, considering its application in your organization:

1 How has the firm defined *culture* and what efforts and programmes are in place?

2 What is the role and involvement of operational risk teams in existing programmes?

3 Considering the five aspects of risk culture described in the chapter, where would your organization score highest?

4 What works well? Make a note of the strong elements of the firm's culture.

5 What can be improved? Note down potential improvements.

MAKE A DIFFERENCE (MAD) ACTION

Please note down one action that you will take after reading this chapter that will make a positive difference to risk culture, ethos and behaviours of your organization.

In summary, this chapter discussed the role of risk culture, the least visible but most vital aspect of risk management, and proposed practical steps operational risk practitioners can take to influence ethos and behaviours.

Having examined all the tools of the operational risk framework, the penultimate chapter will focus on evaluating the maturity of operational risk management process in the organization.

Notes

1 Basel Committee on Banking Supervision (2020) Consultative document, *Revisions to the Principles for the Sound Management of Operational Risk*, www.bis.org/bcbs/publ/d508.pdf (archived at https://perma.cc/YV5H-CTGQ)

2 Financial Stability Board (2014) *Guidance on Supervisory Interaction with Financial Institutions on Risk Culture*, www.fsb.org/wp-content/uploads/140407.pdf (archived at https://perma.cc/6YJN-3N5H)

3 Royal Commission into Misconduct in the Banking, Superannuation and Financial Services Industry, www.royalcommission.gov.au/sites/default/files/2019-02/fsrc-volume-1-final-report.pdf (archived at https://perma.cc/A8DM-5P9J)

4 Financial Conduct Authority (2018) Discussion paper, *Transforming Culture in Financial Services*, www.fca.org.uk/publication/discussion/dp18-02.pdf (archived at https://perma.cc/U5PT-PR4Z)

5 Financial Stability Board (2014) *Guidance on Supervisory Interaction with Financial Institutions on Risk Culture*, www.fsb.org/wp-content/uploads/140407.pdf (archived at https://perma.cc/QJ3C-ZLA7)

6 Financial Conduct Authority (2018) Discussion paper, *Transforming Culture in Financial Services*, www.fca.org.uk/publication/discussion/dp18-02.pdf (archived at https://perma.cc/TS7L-WK3C)

7 Chartered Institute of Internal Auditors (2020) *Conduct Risk*, www.iia.org.uk/resources/fianancialservices/conductrisk

8 The banker's oath, www.tuchtrechtbanken.nl/en/code-of-conduct/ (archived at https://perma.cc/53NR-5RGR)

9 Power, M, Ashby, S and Palermo, T (2013) *Risk Culture in Financial Organizations: A research report*, London School of Economics, eprints.lse.ac.uk/67978/1/Palermo_Rsik%20culture%20research%20report_2016.pdf (archived at https://perma.cc/A8DM-5P9J)

10 Chartered Institute of Internal Auditors (2014) *Culture and the Role of Internal Audit*, www.iia.org.uk/media/598939/0805-iia-culture-report-1-7-14-final.pdf (archived at https://perma.cc/9RGM-L85N)

11 Power, M, Ashby, S and Palermo, T (2013) *Risk Culture in Financial Organizations: A research report*, London School of Economics, eprints.lse.ac.uk/67978/1/Palermo_Rsik%20culture%20research%20report_2016.pdf (archived at https://perma.cc/ZX4A-FFEH)

13

Embedding and maturity assessment

What this chapter covers: This chapter discusses the Operational Risk Implementation Journey, from its early stages to being fully implemented; describing a 'maturity ladder' for measuring progress and outlining the key characteristics of each phase (Figure 13.1). The chapter considers what *embeddedness* looks like and how it can be measured. It then goes on to introduce three pillars of embedded risk management and proposes a balanced scorecard with examples of metrics and indicators. The chapter includes results of live polls and an industry benchmark.

FURTHER READING

- Institute of Operational Risk (2020) *Embedding an Operational Risk Management Framework: Operational risk sound practice guidance*
  Why recommended: A succinct guide that examines the critical success factors involved in achieving an embedded operational risk management framework.

- Dominic Antonucci (2016) *Risk Maturity Models: How to assess risk management effectiveness*, Kogan Page
  Why recommended: An in-depth study of risk maturity models, for individuals interested to learn more about the subject.

FIGURE 13.1   Focus of Chapter 13: embedding and maturity assessment

Embedding and Maturity Assessment

Risk Culture

Governance, Roles and Responsibilities
Establish governance and clear roles across the three lines for managing operational risk.

Risk Appetite and Risk Capacity
Define nature and types of risk accepted in pursuit of strategic objectives. Evaluate adequacy of capital resources.

Operational Risk Taxonomy

Operational Risk Events	Risk Assessments	Scenario Analysis	Key Risk Indicators
Record and report risk events, act to minimize future exposure.	Assess risk exposure in process, business or function via RCSAs.	Identify exposure from extreme but plausible events.	Monitor risk and control performance through predictive indicators.
Monitor trends against RCSAs and KRIs.	Supplement by evaluating risks emanating from change activities via ORAs.	Mitigate through risk transfer to insurance.	Act if indicators breach established appetite threshold.

Reporting and Decision Making
Review actual risk profile against set appetite, apply active risk management to enable achievement of strategic objectives.

Training and Education

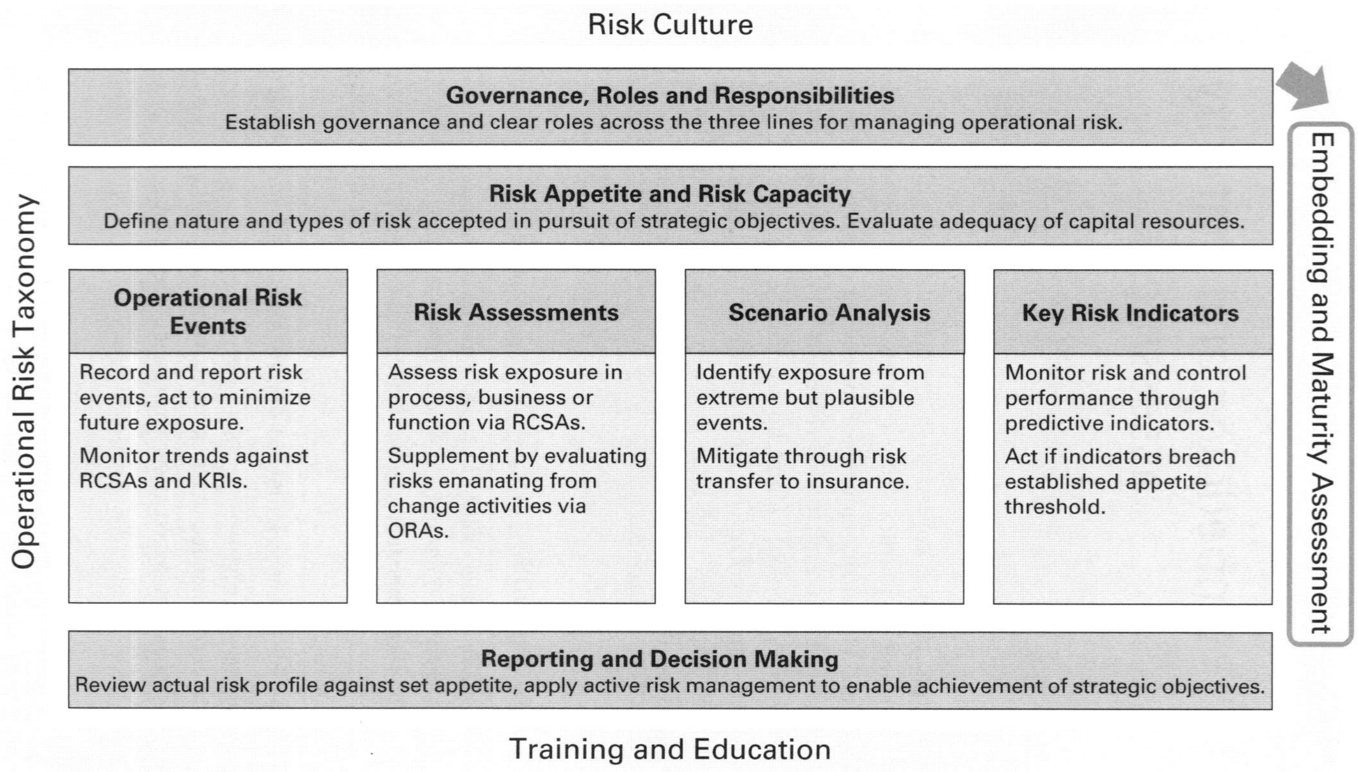

The journey to maturity: three-step maturity ladder

The journey of implementing robust operational risk management practices in an organization is as challenging as it is exciting.

At the start of the journey, the firm may be operating as a novice, experimenting in a largely ad hoc and reactive manner. In this phase business units and support functions may show a tendency to push back on the new operational risk requirements, exhibiting a natural reaction of resistance to change. They may refer to the elements of the framework as *your* processes, *your* assessments, *your* tools, implying that their role is to assist the Operational Risk department to accomplish whatever *it* requires, and consequently deprioritizing the tasks in comparison to their own activities. In turn, the operational risk function finds itself vigorously reaching out with explanations, presentations and constant follow-ups to keep the risk management ship afloat.

This initial stage is gradually replaced by an intermediate phase, which involves implementing a more structured approach and building it into the firm's routine business processes. In this phase operational risk practices are *normalized*. RCSAs, for example, become the *norm*, something that simply must be done, for multiple reasons including regulatory. This phase sees improved ownership by business units and support functions, for whom the use of the different risk framework elements – even if reluctantly at times – becomes a matter of habit.

The ultimate *embedded* stage is characterized by proactive risk management, a clear value proposition, and an enhanced risk culture in the organization. As highlighted frequently in previous chapters, the real measure of success in operational risk is when functions actively *want* to use the framework because it helps them in their decision making. While in the first phase they may have been hesitant or sceptical, business departments now complete risks and opportunities assessments for new products – because it is useful to *them*, to draw out threats and benefits. In this culture boards and governance committees rely on reports of the firm's profile against risk appetite *to take decisions*. The framework is fit for purpose. Tools are in sync. Outputs are compared and tell a coherent story. Information is actively used to achieve measurable process improvements and reduce surprises.

This progress can be reflected in a simple maturity ladder, as described in Figure 13.2. This version differentiates between three phases of maturity, but organizations can enhance and further develop the ladder as they see fit.

FIGURE 13.2 Operational risk maturity ladder

EARLY STAGES

- Basic framework
- Unbalanced roles: operational risk function is doing most of the work
- Limited value-add

MANAGED

- Developed framework and tools
- Balanced roles and responsibilities
- Demonstrable value-add
- Operational risk management becomes the *norm* within the organization

EMBEDDED

- Framework and tools are fit for purpose
- Operational risk function is a trusted advisor
- Continuous, measurable value-add
- Business units *want* to apply the tools as they aid in decision making
- Notable impact of improvements on the balance sheet

Three pillars of success: financial performance, use test, risk culture

Once a firm has embarked on its risk management implementation journey, it will want to measure its advancement across progressive levels of maturity. Measurement helps to establish a baseline, and to set targets and improvement strategies to achieve the desired stage. Maturity model can be a powerful 'diagnostic tool' and a solution for 'improving risk management system capabilities'.[1]

While firms may have widely varying views on what good risk management looks like, an approach centred around three pillars – the *financial performance*, *use test* and *risk culture* – is proposed in Figure 13.3. These three pillars work in tandem to present a coherent overall picture of *embeddedness*, defined by the Basel Framework as the level to which operational risk management practices 'have been embedded at all organizational levels'.[2] In the context of operational risk, maturity cannot be achieved without holistic engagement and use of the relevant tools by the entire enterprise. Organizations may wish to add other pillars – and even parameters within each pillar – that they feel are relevant to their firm.

Let's examine each pillar in more detail.

Financial performance

Operational risk should always be considered in the context of its impact on the firm's balance sheet and profit & loss (P&L) position. If, as discussed in Chapter 1, risk practitioners aim to sit at the strategy table and contribute to strategic decisions, P&L is often the mutual language used for these conversations. Operational risk becomes much more difficult to dismiss when it is presented in terms of hard numbers and not as 'just a risk'.

Consequently – alas, there is no avoiding it – actual operational risk losses are an indicator of embedded risk management (or the lack of it).

FIGURE 13.3   Three pillars of embedded operational risk management

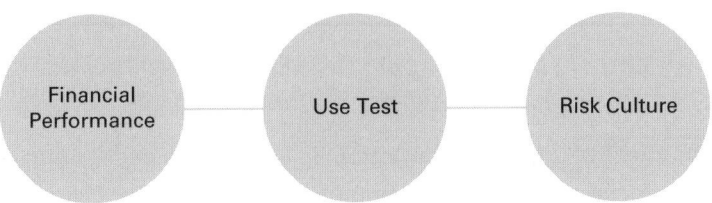

Simply put, if there is a steady upward trend in losses year-on-year, whether in growth or during periods of business stagnation and decline, the firm should be questioning its risk management capabilities.

By the same token, the upside of risk (or positive P&L benefit emanating from good operational risk management) also has to be quantified.

The following metrics can be useful to characterize both dimensions, losses and savings:

KRI1: Operational risk losses as a percentage of revenue, operating income or operating expense.

KRI2: Actual operational risk losses compared to appetite.

KRI3: Trend, number, value of losses in new products or investments relative to product/investment performance.

KRI4: Value of financial penalties (capital add-on, fines imposed for mismanagement of risk).

KRI5: Value of any savings, including reduction in cost due to process optimization, that emanate from operational risk initiatives (measure of the upside).

These measures need to be interpreted with caution; while an increase in losses is worrying, a sharp drop also needs to be investigated, as highlighted in Chapter 4. It may be providing a false comfort and could instead be indicative of other factors – for example a change in leadership that has caused employees to simply stop reporting bad news.

Operational risk financial performance measures are not treated in a balanced way in the industry. At times, firms try to measure the embeddedness and success of their operational risk management using only numbers (such as actual losses and capital position), thus underestimating the less tangible benefits of the framework, as discussed later in the chapter. At the other extreme, financial performance is sometimes excluded altogether, resulting in operational risk not being taken seriously and not treated on a par with other risk disciplines. For this reason, financial performance metrics should constitute an important *pillar* of the risk management framework, but must also be supplemented by other tools, namely the *use test* and *risk culture*.

Use test

The importance of impact on the bottom line cannot be underestimated, but financial measures on their own cannot paint a complete picture. This is particularly true for smaller-sized firms that may have neither a large dataset of past losses nor multiple opportunities for savings. In this case the trend analysis can be less meaningful than for larger firms. The so-called *use test* – frequently referred to by the Basel Committee and regulators in various jurisdictions – goes to the heart of actively using risk tools to enhance live decision making. The *use test* is a broad concept that encompasses many different aspects, from the risk framework and tools to responsibilities and value-add; collectively, all components covered in this book. It includes, for example:

- sophistication and fitness of the risk framework and toolset;

- clarity, usefulness and actionability of operational risk reporting;

- maturity and effectiveness of the operational risk appetite;

- responsibilities, brand and reputation of risk teams;

- roles and attitudes of functions outside the Risk department, including first line champions, subject matter experts, and risk and control owners, as well as the board, senior management, and other employees in the organization;

- the value proposition that emanates from risk management – it is impossible to truly embed risk management just by wielding a regulatory stick.

Some of the possible use test measures have been introduced in previous chapters. They may include:

KRI6: Number of material gaps emanating from gap analysis against Basel Committee Principles and other relevant requirements, as discussed in Chapter 2 (reflects the sophistication of risk framework and toolset).

KRI9: Gaps in accountability: percentage of 'orphan' RCSAs, or risks/ KRIs with no owner assigned (measures whether business units have embraced their roles and responsibilities for the management of operational risk).

KRI10: Number of departments/areas without an established first line operational risk champion (similarly, presents a view on the accountability – or the lack of it).

KRI7: Number and/or monetary value of investments in control improvements resulting from the use of operational risk tools (for example, emanating from RCSAs, OREs, SAs or KRIs; which demonstrate that significant risks are taken seriously, and that budget is allocated to enhancements where needed; indicative of the risk value proposition).

KRI8: Number or percentage of internal and external audit findings which were already known and self-identified via the use of operational risk tools (for example, RCSAs, SAs, KRIs, etc; again indicative of value proposition).

Risk culture

The topic of risk culture was discussed at length in the previous chapter. Undeniably, the effectiveness of operational risk management is closely linked to and largely dependent on the firm's culture, which can either support or hinder it. Additional measures of success in this area, which supplement *financial performance* and *use test* metrics, are as follows:

KRI11: Trend in employees' views on risk culture of the organization and/ or their perception of the Risk department (obtained via employee engagement surveys, focus groups or other means).

KRI12: Number and trend of issues raised through established risk channels (eg risk mailbox).

KRI13: Number or percentage of material risks, ineffective controls or significant gaps with no actions or where actions are overdue (reflective of the overall strength of response or the absence of it).

KRI4: Number or percentage of risk acceptances vs actions related to risk reduction (a healthy score indicates a mature and balanced approach to risk management, including considerations of the cost-effectiveness of mitigation).

KRI15: Number of times the Operational Risk department is asked to participate in initiatives in an advisory capacity (this suggests a department that is well thought of, and seen as a reputable advisor).

The outcome-based measures proposed above can be displayed in a balanced scorecard, as described in Figure 13.4. Collectively, they evaluate the embeddedness of risk management by reflecting on *financial*, *use test* and *risk culture* aspects. These measures partially overlap and fall into more than one category, as shown here in Figure 13.4.

FIGURE 13.4   Operational risk balanced scorecard

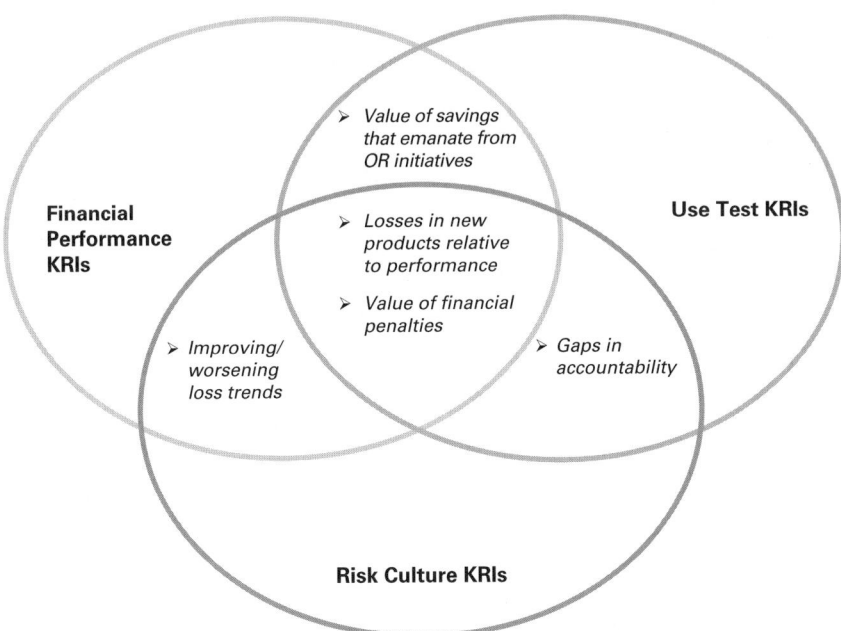

Business units' self-assessment of embeddedness

As an alternative to metrics and measures, a powerful mechanism for evaluating embeddedness is via business units' own self-assessment of how well they believe they are doing. This can be accomplished using a guided approach, where the second line operational risk function creates a questionnaire for the business with a choice of possible answers. The units then select the state they believe they are in, corroborating their responses with facts and evidence. The second line operational risk team reviews and constructively challenges the outputs.

An example extract from such a questionnaire for one component, RCSA, is presented in Table 13.1.

Self-assessment helps first line business units and support functions to understand what 'good' looks like, as well as to reflect on their own performance.

TABLE 13.1 Example questionnaire: self-assessment of embeddedness

RCSA aspects	Development phase: Early Stages	Development phase: Managed	Development phase: Embedded
Scope	Unclear justification of scope and/or boundaries of RCSA.	Clearly defined boundaries of what is within and outside RCSA scope.	Scope is clearly defined, interdependencies with other RCSAs are understood.
Risk assessment	No proactive risk identification. Risk profile is not in sync with actual OREs and KRIs. Risk owner(s) not explicitly defined.	Risk identification and assessment is facilitated by first line operational risk champion, in coordination with risk owners.	Named risk owners proactively and regularly consider changes in risk environment, including emerging risks. There are minimal surprises from Internal Audit – risks are already known.
Control assessment	Control owner(s) not explicitly defined. Control rating is not corroborated by evidence.	Control identification and assessment is facilitated by first line operational risk champion, in coordination with control owners.	Named control owners rate control design and effectiveness, with periodic testing of most important controls to support the assessment.
Actionability	No actions emanate from the exercise.	Tactical actions are in place, with clear owners and target dates.	RCSAs are considered in tactical and strategic decisions. Consideration is given to risk reduction and risk acceptance, demonstrating a balanced approach.
RCSA refresh	RCSA is updated annually, and not used in between updates.	RCSAs are referred to and reviewed during periodic risk and control meetings.	Trigger-based refresh is in place, with triggers including material ORE, change initiatives and/or KRIs.
Completion and sign-off	RCSA is filled in by the risk champion without the involvement of subject matter experts (SMEs) and unit head. There is no evidence of sign-off.	RCSA is completed by the risk champion with active participation of SMEs. RCSA is signed off by the risk champion of the business unit.	RCSA is facilitated by the risk champion in collaboration with SMEs and unit head. There is evidence that the head of the unit signed off, confirming that RCSA is a true and fair reflection of the unit's risk and control profile.

Importance of retaining evidence

We now digress slightly from the subject of embedded risk management to the ancillary topic of retaining evidence. 'Absence of evidence is *not* evidence of absence' is a quote attributed to Professor Martin Rees, the English astronomer and astrophysicist. Alas, auditors and financial services regulators would disagree; even if a firm is mature and constructive in its approach, if it is not able to produce *convincing evidence* of its operational risk management activities, this simply equates to the firm not managing operational risk at all.

In 2019, I led a study on this topic with the Best Practice Operational Risk Forum. In a live poll, practitioners opined on the strength of evidencing of operational risk management within their firms, the results of which are presented in Table 13.2.

TABLE 13.2 Industry study: evidence of operational
risk management

Strength of evidence	% Respondents
Insufficient	0
Partial	19
Adequate	81
Robust	0

Good evidencing involves both a disciplined approach to record retention (including the required duration and storage media) and, most importantly, agreed policies and standards on the actual content of the records themselves.

What is retained as proof

Effective operational risk management can be demonstrated via the following mechanisms:

- Business-as-usual operational risk tools, such as RCSAs, OREs and KRIs. The evidence may be stored in either an official system or other sources such as Excel spreadsheets, with a record of the results alongside actions and decisions taken.

- New product sign-off packs, which commonly include operational risk assessment.

- Risk consideration in change initiatives, either in the form of completed assessment(s) or the minutes of relevant committee meetings.
- Strategy documents and business plans. This area of record keeping was perceived by the forum as needing improvement from an operational risk perspective, which does not appear to be always explicitly considered in these documents.
- Risk assessments of technology changes.

Demonstrating challenge

When it comes to the role of the second line operational risk team, it is often difficult to effectively evidence all the good work the department does; in particular the *oversight and challenge* part, which will often take the form of discussion at a meeting or workshop, a phone or video call, email correspondence or all of the above.

Second line challenge can be evidenced via:

- Detailed minutes of operational risk committees or other relevant governance meetings, documenting what was discussed and agreed. It is also good practice to note options or risks that were considered and discounted (and on what basis).
- A separate second line opinion appended to first line business unit reports, thus providing a record of views from both sides.
- A presentation of common themes based on an overall analysis of OREs, RCSAs and other tools; identifying areas of weakness followed by the results of second line thematic reviews or deep dives. This documentation approach not only demonstrates a robust thought process but also generates real value-add to the firm.

Consequently, when it comes to evidence, it is better to follow Charles Dickens than astronomers such as Professor Rees, perhaps using the quote, 'Take nothing on its looks; take everything on evidence. There's no better rule.'

Common challenges and good practices

Common challenges

The following challenges may face organizations during their journey to embedding operational risk management practices.

LACK OF CULTURAL FIT

At times, leaders join a firm from a different organization and immediately launch into building the blocks which proved successful in their previous place, without spending sufficient time analysing what might work in their new environment. This can lead to failure, as the maturity journey is unique to each individual firm, including its pace and sequencing, and ways of working effectively together.

LINK TO STRATEGY NOT CONSIDERED

As discussed in Chapter 1, at times operational risk domain tends to go its own way, proceeding with framework implementation in a manner and pace that are not in sync with the firm's strategy and business goals. Keeping the vital link to what matters the most – the firm's business goals – and being cognizant of the bigger picture is crucial. The guidance on embedding operational risk framework issued by the Institute of Operational Risk also emphasizes the role of risk function is in supporting 'strategic planning and objective setting'.[3]

LACK OF EVIDENCE

Undoubtedly, the importance of retaining evidence has been increasing over the years. Firms with poor record retention practices are truly challenged during internal audit and external supervisory inspections. Evidence is also vital to the firm itself, in case it needs to look back and revisit prior decisions; for example, a particular new product that was approved, together with risks that have been accepted. Operational risk teams must be conscious of keeping the appropriate proof, and educating first line business units and support functions on good practices.

Good practices

MEASURING EMBEDDEDNESS AND COMPLETING MATURITY ASSESSMENT

Over the years, I have discussed the topic of maturity assessment with multiple regulators. They considered that the firms which did not complete such an assessment struggled to articulate to their supervisors a coherent picture of their current state, together with planned areas for development. By contrast, organizations that applied healthy practices of self-reflection and evaluation came across as cognizant of their strengths and weaknesses, transparent and prepared. These practices bring benefits to the firm itself, as well as external parties such as regulators. A globally accepted standard for risk management – ISO 31000:2009 – from the International Organization for Standardization also advises firms to develop strategies to advance their risk management maturity.[4]

PROGRESSING ELEMENTS IN TANDEM

There is no clear demarcation between the stages of operational risk maturity. The firm may be slightly more advanced in most aspects but stuck on one or two features, thus impeding its overall progress. For example, it may be progressing on target with a framework implementation project, but is not moving forward with embedding correct roles and responsibilities. In reality this often happens when a firm has to expedite the pace of deployment following regulatory criticism, perhaps having received a remediation requirement. In this case, additional efforts need to be refocussed on agreeing the responsibilities with senior management and developing a system of rewards (and sometimes punishment) to progress advancement in the accountability element, alongside any enhancements being considered to the framework itself. To achieve embeddedness, different components need to progress in tandem, at a sensible pace.

UNDERSTANDING ASPIRATIONS

Some firms have no aspiration to be best-in-class in their operational risk framework and tools; they do not need a Rolls-Royce and will be satisfied with a simpler model. So it is important to define the appropriate *point of arrival* for the overall journey. Requirements need to be proportionate to the size and nature of the organization. This may mean that, for some firms, not all elements of the framework will need to be fully developed. A useful tool to accomplish this proportionate outcome is presented in Figure 13.5.

In this figure, 10 desired outcomes have been articulated by the organization. The current position of each statement is outlined with crosses, while the desired state is marked with triangles. (Note: the *embedded* state remains an aspiration for many of the statements, but not all; in some cases, a lower *managed* position would be deemed acceptable.)

FIGURE 13.5 Defining point of arrival

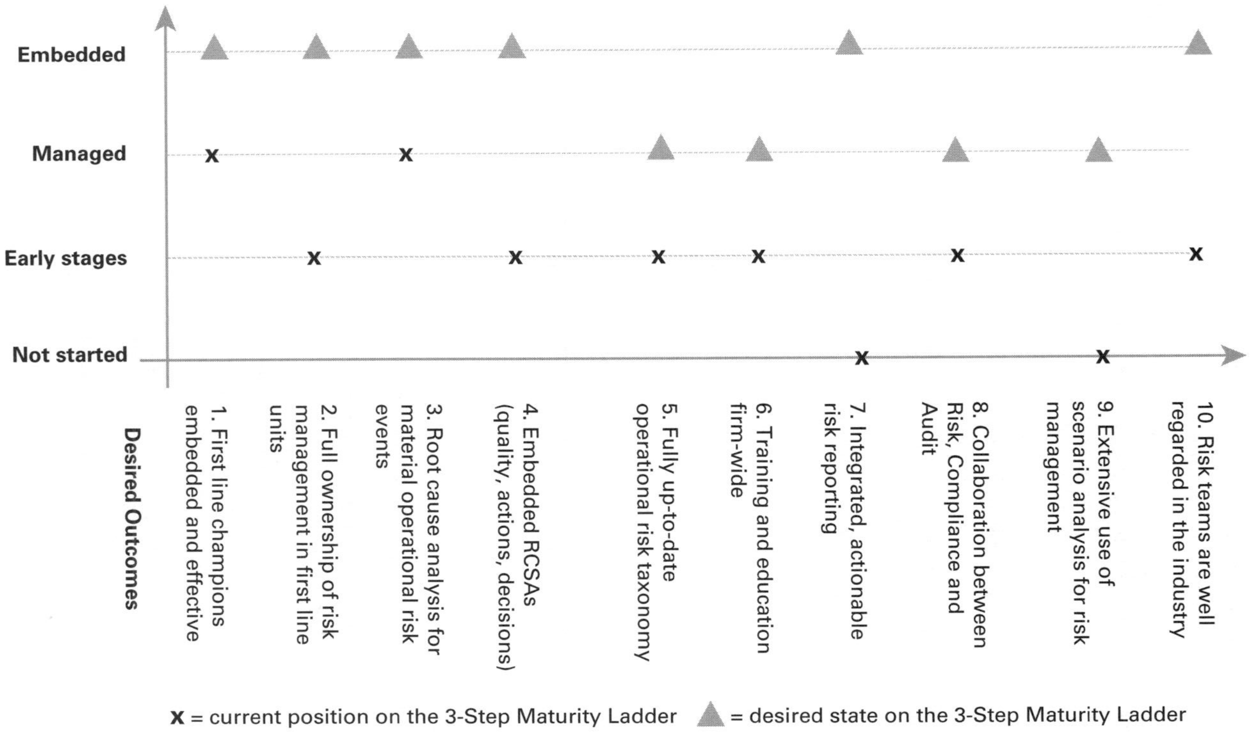

10. Risk teams are well regarded in the industry

9. Extensive use of scenario analysis for risk management

8. Collaboration between Risk, Compliance and Audit

7. Integrated, actionable risk reporting

6. Training and education firm-wide

5. Fully up-to-date operational risk taxonomy

4. Embedded RCSAs (quality, actions, decisions)

3. Root cause analysis for material operational risk events

2. Full ownership of risk management in first line units

1. First line champions embedded and effective

Desired Outcomes

Embedded

Managed

Early stages

Not started

▲ = desired state on the 3-Step Maturity Ladder

X = current position on the 3-Step Maturity Ladder

Industry benchmark, 2020

The Best Practice Operational Risk Forum discussed common practices related to the evaluation of embeddedness of operational risk management. As described in Figure 13.6, only half (54 per cent) of respondents said they conduct an assessment of maturity in a structured manner. Many organizations were still developing the practice; however, this appeared to clash with other key priorities on their agenda.

FIGURE 13.6   Industry poll: operational risk maturity assessment

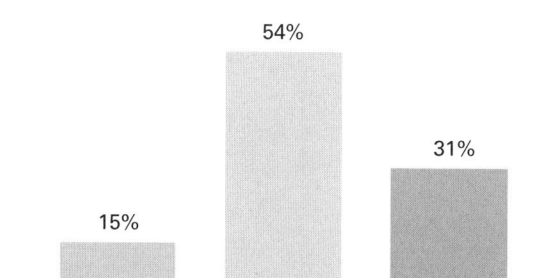

Do you periodically conduct Operational risk maturity assessment?

Best Practice Operational Risk Forum, 2020

FIGURE 13.7   Industry poll: three-step maturity ladder

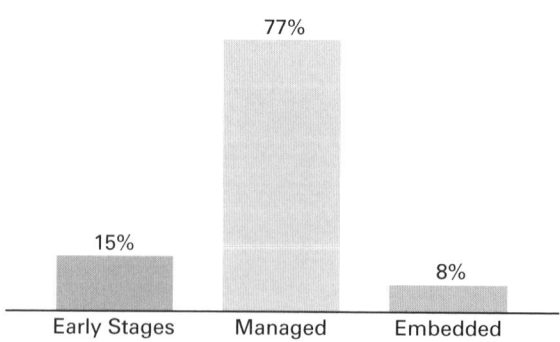

How would you rate your firm on a three-step Maturity Ladder?

Best Practice Operational Risk Forum, 2020

Considering how organizations perceived themselves on a three-step maturity ladder, 15 per cent believed they were operating somewhat as novices, while 77 per cent felt they were in a more mature intermediate phase, at least managing risk effectively. Only a minority (8 per cent) placed themselves in the *embedded* category (Figure 13.7). Those few organizations were in the habit of both measuring success via metrics and other robust processes, including requiring business units and support functions to conduct self-evaluations.

Practical workplace exercise

Consider how your organization evaluates its advancement along the stages of operational risk maturity:

1 Is there a maturity model or other mechanism in place to facilitate assessment of how well embedded your operational risk practices really are?

2 Is embeddedness defined, alongside its measures of success?

3 Is there any awareness of where the organization is on its journey and what its plans or next steps are?

4 What works well? Make a note of the strong features of the current maturity evaluation process, if they exist.

5 What can be improved? Note down how the evaluation of the operational risk implementation journey could potentially be enhanced.

6 In summary, this penultimate chapter discussed the importance of evaluating the progress of implementation of operational risk management, and proposed a number of ways of measuring success.

MAKE **A D**IFFERENCE (MAD) **A**CTION

Please note down one action that you will take after reading this chapter that will meaningfully enhance an evaluation of the maturity of your firm's operational risk journey.

In summary, this penultimate chapter discussed the importance of evaluating the progress of implementation of operational risk management, and proposed a number of ways of measuring success.

Moving on, the final chapter will discuss the topic of operational resilience and its link with the operational risk framework.

Notes

1 Antonucci, D (2016) *Risk Maturity Models: How to assess risk management effectiveness*, Kogan Page, London

2 Basel Committee for Banking Supervision (2011) *Operational Risk: Supervisory guidelines for the advanced measurement approaches*, www.bis.org/publ/bcbs196.pdf (archived at https://perma.cc/T5QN-5SC9)

3 Institute of Operational Risk (2020) *Embedding an Operational Risk Management Framework: Operational risk sound practice guidance*, www.ior-institute.org/sound-practice-guidance (archived at https://perma.cc/8L6M-DQ2R)

4 International Organization for Standardization, ISO 31000:2009, www.iso.org/obp/ui/#iso:std:iso:31000:ed-1:v1:en (archived at https://perma.cc/35EB-GTAD)

14

Operational resilience

What this chapter covers: The chapter introduces the topic of Operational Resilience, a subject which has close links with the operational risk discipline. It presents a call for action for operational risk teams to reach out and get involved in an area that has achieved an extraordinary degree of focus from firms and regulators in recent years, particularly in the light of the Covid-19 pandemic. Active collaboration between risk and resilience experts will help ensure a joined-up approach which is much needed in this space. The chapter includes an industry benchmark and the results of live polls which support the call for action.

FURTHER READING

• Basel Committee on Banking Supervision (2020) Consultative document, *Principles for Operational Resilience*
  Why recommended: Latest Basel Committee topic on operational resilience that needs to be read by operational risk practitioners.

Operational resilience: a step up from its predecessor

Business continuity, a predecessor of operational resilience, has always been a part of the agenda of financial services firms. And in a similar way to operational risk, it has always faced the challenge of being perceived as a rather administrative domain. Traditional operational resilience activities, by way of illustration, included completing a periodic business impact analysis, refreshing and testing the arrangements on an annual basis, and requesting employees to print and duly store a copy of the plan at home.

With increasing digitalization and reliance on technology, over the years the increased risk of serious disruption has led to business continuity gaining more focus and upping its game.

Firms started by augmenting the depth of their recovery capabilities and increasing the frequency of their testing. Then, following a series of significant system failures, operational resilience came clearly into the spotlight in 2018, when a joint discussion document by the UK regulatory authorities introduced the concept of *impact tolerances*, which prompted firms to start thinking hard about the types of failures that would be intolerable for both their customers and wider financial services markets.[1] This initiative generated significant worldwide debate, and response papers were subsequently issued by various industry bodies.

Needless to say, the emphasis of both firms and regulators during the Covid-19 pandemic in 2020 was almost entirely on the subject of resilience. The fact is that Covid-19 refocussed discussion in an area which had previously been largely technology-related. As noted by the Bank for International Settlements, operational resilience planning before the pandemic had been driven mainly by 'vulnerabilities brought about by technological change and an increasingly hostile cyber environment'.[2] Covid-19, on the other hand, created quite a different experience, with firms having to deal with a widespread long-lasting disruption which significantly impacted their most important asset: their people.

This chapter represents a Call For Action for operational risk teams to proactively reach out and join the efforts of their resilience colleagues. At a time of rapidly developing frameworks and approaches, this is a good moment to seize the opportunity and work towards maximum integration of the two disciplines, avoiding silos and reducing fragmentation.

OPERATIONAL RESILIENCE DEFINITION

Operational resilience can be defined as a firm's ability to 'prevent, adapt, respond to, recover and learn from operational disruptions'.[3]

It can be argued that operational risk management supports the operational as well as financial resilience of an institution. The *prevent* aspect of the above definition, in particular, is based on prudent and proactive risk management: identifying, understanding and mitigating threats and vulnerabilities. Assuming that disruptions are inevitable and will occur, post-event detective and corrective controls help firms to respond, recover and learn from incidents. Therefore, operational resilience is a continuous process, and certainly a step forward from business continuity:

Operational Resilience ≠ Business Continuity

And, as noted by the Basel Committee in its 2020 consultation document on operational resilience:[4]

Operational Resilience ❯ Outcome of
Operational Risk Management

Given the interconnectedness of the topics, it is important to explore these links further, and to examine a few areas where a united approach may prove to be mutually beneficial.

Integrating operational risk and resilience

The operational resilience life cycle can be described in Figure 14.1. Let's review some of these sub-components in more detail.

Business services and their dependencies (Steps 1 and 2)

To be operationally resilient, an organization needs to achieve a shift in mindset, developing a view of the firm from 'outside in', ie as a customer would see it. From the client's perspective, when an expected service is not delivered or a commitment not met, whether the process broke down within operations, technology or some other area is neither visible nor important. It is only the final product – the fact of the failure – that matters. In this light, it is becoming increasingly important for firms to understand the interconnectedness of different processes and harness an *end-to-end business service mentality*; one in which employees look out beyond their own narrow silos at the impact on the end-client. This is presented in Figure 14.2.

Against this background, potential areas for collaboration between risk and resilience functions include the following.

FIGURE 14.1   Operational resilience life cycle

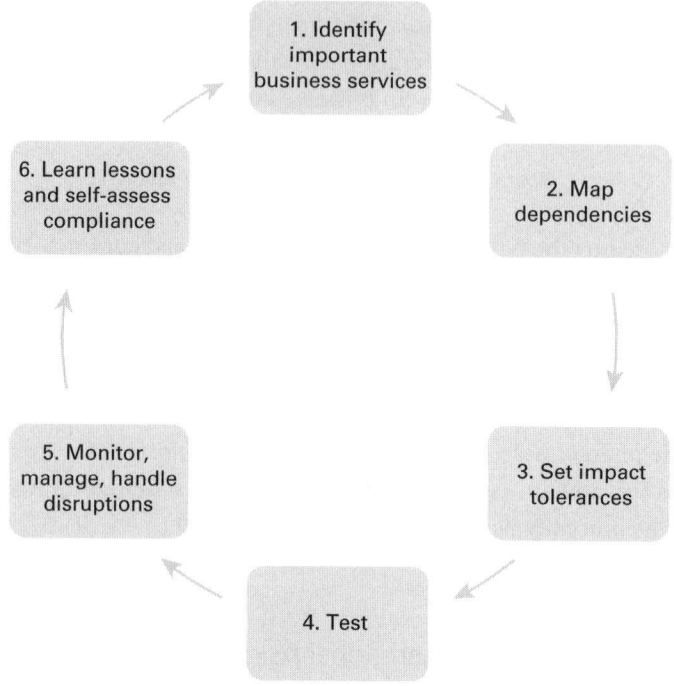

FIGURE 14.2   Business process dependencies

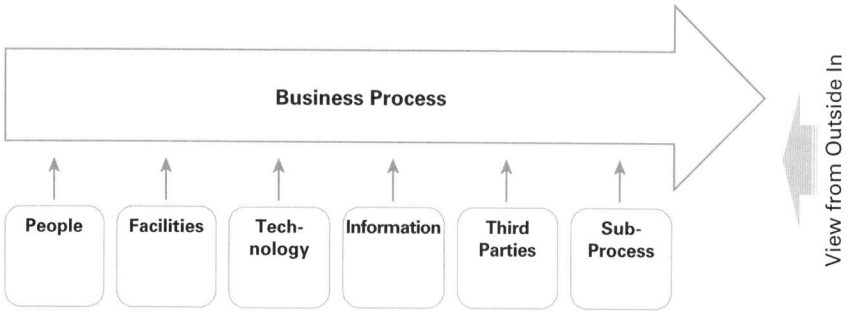

IDENTIFYING IMPORTANT BUSINESS SERVICES

The laborious and time-consuming task of mapping business processes may have already been accomplished as part of the operational risk framework. This is especially so if, as discussed in Chapter 5, PRSAs have been applied across the enterprise. If not, it may be resilience colleagues who initiate the journey of documenting and inventorying the resources that deliver and support their important business services. Indeed many organizations made good progress in this area as part of enhancing their financial resilience and complying with regulatory requirements around recovery and resolution planning. If this has occurred, it is crucial that operational risk teams also benefit from these outcomes, to ensure that future risk assessments are conducted on an integrated basis, taking into account the dependencies identified in the business mapping process. Additionally, as noted in Chapter 5, cross-functional process mapping exercises can help to optimize effectiveness and increase process efficiency.

DEVELOPING A BUSINESS SERVICES MENTALITY

Most firms have formal frameworks, policies and process maps which document their services and list dependencies. But there is an equally (if not more) important *softer side* to this process, whereby employees on the ground improve their understanding of how what they do impacts the whole business supply chain and external customers. When staff can visualize such interconnectedness, that enables more thoughtful and robust preventative action, and speedier, more coherent responses. Do employees have this customer-centric mentality? And if not, what training and education is provided by risk and resilience colleagues to enhance it? Operational risk teams are already in the habit of delivering staff training and education; which provides an excellent opportunity to incorporate some resilience components, rather than creating two separate training programmes.

CALL FOR ACTION

Collaborate with operational resilience colleagues to:

- review existing RCSAs and consider how to extract meaningful information by *business service*;
- agree a joint approach to process mapping and the identification of business services;
- jointly develop a 'business service mentality' among employees.

Impact tolerances and testing (Steps 3 and 4)

Another opportunity for teamwork presents itself when developing scenarios for setting impact tolerances and testing resilience capabilities. Impact tolerances articulate the maximum tolerable level of disruption to an important business service, including the duration of the disruption. Setting these tolerances requires firms to think through their worst case scenarios. As outlined in Figure 14.3, this creates a meaningful overlap between the operational risk and resilience universes.

Storylines in the operational risk space may well touch on themes such as fraud, regulatory non-compliance or employment lawsuits. While these are important topics to explore, they do not necessarily impact a firm's resilience capabilities.

In turn, major breakdowns of external infrastructure might be considered in order to proactively develop contingency measures, and review potential alternative means of operating. These kinds of scenarios may not be required for operational risk purposes, as a firm can hardly be expected to hold capital against the risk of external failures such as unavailability of the power supply or the national payments network.

Consequently, the area of overlap consists of topics of mutual interest. These might include:

- outsourcing and supplier failures;

- people unavailability;

- technology downtime;

- data corruption; or

- destruction to premises.

FIGURE 14.3   Operational risk and resilience scenarios

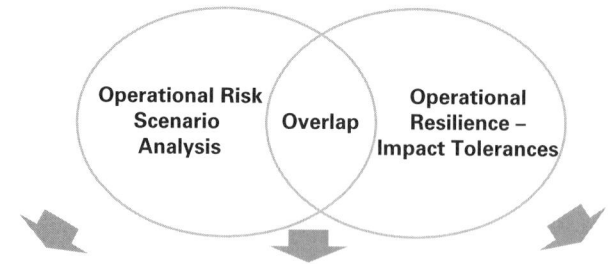

Operational risk
- Internal or external fraud
- Payment errors
- Regulatory non-compliance
- Employment lawsuits

Overlap
- Third-party (Outsourcing) failures
- Employee unavailability
- Technology and data issues

Operational resilience
- Failure of external infrastructure
- Failure of correspondent

These themes are relevant for both domains. By working together, scenario story lines can be aligned, enriching the whole experience on both sides.

In Chapter 8, the importance of using scenarios for *risk management* purposes was discussed, including taking actions to improve the control environment. This approach and philosophy are even more crucial for resilience purposes, where firms – in particular, boards and senior management – should be prioritizing their investment decisions on the basis of identified weaknesses that can threaten their ability to provide important business services. Hence the call for collaboration.

CALL FOR ACTION

Collaborate with operational resilience colleagues to:

- compare scenarios, align where possible and understand the differences;
- use operational risk structure, techniques and expert facilitation in running scenario workshops;
- jointly advance both scenario analysis and resilience testing frameworks;
- jointly work with relevant stakeholders to minimize duplication;
- jointly ensure actionability to address identified weaknesses.

Monitor environment, manage disruptions and learn lessons (Steps 5 and 6)

In order to remain within impact tolerances on an ongoing basis, it is critical to be able to avoid and recover from disruptions within set time frames and parameters, and to proactively identify and manage threats and vulnerabilities. As discussed in Chapter 1, each firm must decide how operational resilience fits into its taxonomy, enabling transparent and meaningful information flows across the organization. An example of a resilience dashboard, which displays essential risk and control indicators by business service, is presented in Figure 14.4.

Back on the topic of shifting mentality, organizations need to apply a business service lens to these kinds of reports, displaying the kind of information which enables a business service view. This is a challenging task, because in reality departments tend to both operate and report in silos.

FIGURE 14.4 Operational resilience reporting dashboard

Important Business Service: X						
People				**Facilities**		
Metric 1	**AMBER**	Remedial action:		Metric 1	**GREEN**	
Metric 2	**GREEN**			Metric 2	**GREEN**	
Technology & Information				**Third Parties**		
Metric 1	**AMBER**	Remedial action:		Metric 1	**RED**	Remedial action:
Metric 2	**AMBER**	Remedial action:		Metric 2	**AMBER**	Remedial action:

Another area for potential interaction between resilience and risk was described in Chapter 4, Operational Risk Events. Organizations can look to implement a *single notification route* for material disruptive events, whether IT-related or not. The channel used for reporting of operational risk *material* events can clearly be followed for swift escalation, enabling firms to respond more quickly to an event as well as communicate promptly with customers, employees and regulators.

And last but not least: *lessons learned* that are useful for operational resilience purposes may already exist in the operational risk space, for example, from OREs. The structure, format and rigour of the risk event management process can be replicated for resilience purposes, and in fact, implemented on an enterprise-wide basis.

CALL FOR ACTION

Collaborate with operational resilience colleagues to:

- agree on how operational resilience fits into the operational risk taxonomy;
- develop meaningful reporting capabilities, and agree governance, roles and responsibilities for effective monitoring and management of threats and vulnerabilities;
- jointly develop response protocols and channels for the escalation of threats;
- jointly institute a structured lessons learned process for operational resilience.

Finally, a few observations on future disruptions. Covid-19 has proved that firms could quickly adapt and transfer their entire business operation to a home-working environment. This was an extraordinary achievement which should not be undersold. Indeed the European Banking Authority has recognized publicly that 'banks proved their resiliency', and accordingly has assessed operational resilience in the second quarter of 2020 as merely a medium-level risk, with a stable trend.[5]

But despite the undoubted accomplishment, is it too early to claim victory? Covid-19 was characterized by three particular features. It was:

- relatively slow moving, allowing transition to home-working arrangements over a period of weeks rather than overnight;
- prolonged, enabling firms to learn, adapt and enhance their processes; and
- symmetric, affecting organizations across the globe in a similar way.

In the future, disruptions that are more sudden and firm-specific than Covid-19 will inevitably occur. In these circumstances, organizations that have invested in building sound resilience capabilities – with risk and resilience practitioners working hand-in-hand – will emerge stronger than any peers who succumbed to the temptation to celebrate their Covid-19 successes too early.

Industry benchmark, 2020

Results from the live poll conducted by the Best Practice Operational Risk Forum highlighted a positive trend: operational risk and resilience are moving towards integration. As demonstrated in Figure 14.5, 38 per cent of respondents are selecting a joined-up approach rather than a siloed operational resilience framework.

Firms that aim for integration have ensured that:

- operational resilience is not treated as a separate taxonomy category, but as an outcome of operational risks materializing;
- operational risk scenario story lines are compared and reviewed against resilience scenarios;
- RCSA outputs are also considered under operational resilience, and where possible, process-based RCSAs are used;
- there are some preliminary moves towards the convergence of risk event escalation with other types of incident (for example, technology-related); however this is considered an area where further joint work is needed with IT colleagues.

FIGURE 14.5   Industry poll: operational resilience framework development

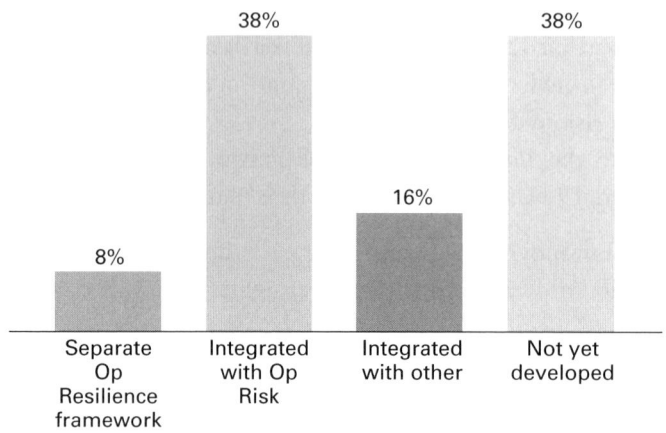

Op Resilience Framework

Best Practice Operational Risk Forum, 2020

FIGURE 14.6   Industry poll: operational resilience focus

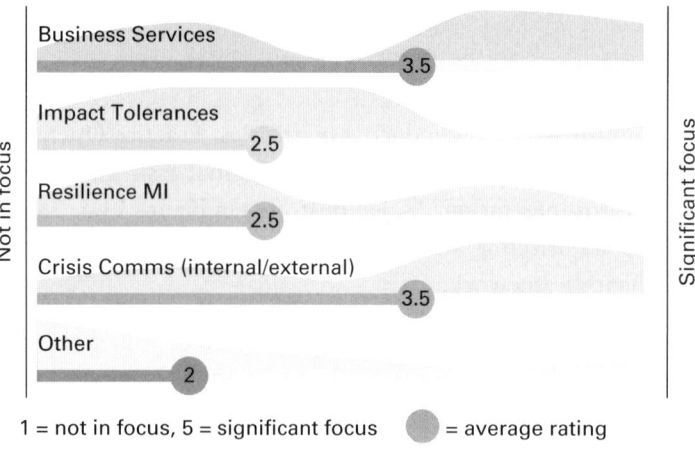

Op Resilience focus is on

Best Practice Operational Risk Forum, 2020

While firms are making progress with all components of their operational resilience framework, two areas have advanced further than others, as demonstrated in Figure 14.6.

These areas are:

- **Business services framework**: in some way, Covid-19 has expedited firms' study of important business services, as in practice organizations had to take decisions to suspend some services while continuing to offer others. This prioritization process has underlined the concept that some services are more important than others, and that during disruptions, firms should be concentrating on the resilience of those prioritized activities.

- **Enhancing crisis communication**: protocols for internal and external communication have been significantly enhanced, ensuring that prompt and accurate information is relayed to customers, and helping firms to work out ways to reach their entire client base quickly and effectively.

Great momentum has been achieved during the Covid-19 pandemic, with risk and resilience working in close collaboration. Carrying this momentum and energy forward will undoubtedly be beneficial for organizations in future years.

MAKE A DIFFERENCE (MAD) ACTION

Please note down one action that you will take after reading this chapter that will meaningfully enhance the integration of risk and resilience practices in your organization.

In summary, this final chapter discussed the importance of operational risk practitioners getting involved in firms' operational resilience activities, searching for synergies and implementing joint solutions.

Notes

1   Bank of England, Prudential Regulation Authority, Financial Conduct Authority (2018) *Building the UK Financial Sector's Operational Resilience*, www. bankofengland.co.uk/-/media/boe/files/prudential-regulation/discussion-paper/2018/dp118.pdf (archived at https://perma.cc/U58L-LK4U)

2   Bank for International Settlements (2020) FSI Briefs, *Covid-19 and Operational Resilience: Addressing financial institutions' operational challenges in a pandemic*, www.bis.org/fsi/fsibriefs2.pdf (archived at https://perma.cc/H3WC-4EB5)

3   Bank of England, Prudential Regulation Authority, Financial Conduct Authority (2018) *Building the UK Financial Sector's Operational Resilience*, www. bankofengland.co.uk/-/media/boe/files/prudential-regulation/discussion-paper/2018/dp118.pdf (archived at https://perma.cc/U58L-LK4U)

4   Basel Committee on Banking Supervision (2020) Consultative document, *Principles for Operational Resilience*, www.bis.org/bcbs/publ/d509.pdf (archived at https://perma.cc/DH3C-WASH)

5   European Banking Authority (2020) Risk dashboard data as of Q2 2020, www.eba.europa.eu/sites/default/documents/files/document_library/Risk%20 Analysis%20and%20Data/Risk%20dashboard/Q2%202020/933053/EBA%20 Dashboard%20-%20Q2%202020.pdf (archived at https://perma.cc/VL9T-7STP)

APPENDIX 1

Operational Risk Champion: role description

- Risk management is the responsibility of **each and every employee**.
- The **Head of each Business Unit** is ultimately accountable for ensuring that robust risk management practices are embedded within the respective Business Unit.
- The role of **Risk Champion** is to assist the Head of the Business Unit in ensuring that risks are identified, assessed, managed and reported.

The position

The Risk Champion is the Subject Matter Expert and the main liaison point between the second Line of Defence Risk Function and the Business Unit, facilitating the implementation and embedding of the use of risk management tools and techniques within the Unit, supporting the Head in continuous development and enhancement of the business unit's risk management practices.

Responsibilities

The Risk Champion's responsibilities include:

- ensuring all staff in the department are familiar with the operational risk event (ORE) identification and reporting process; and that there is clear understanding of what constitutes an event and what course of action should be followed;
- ensuring OREs are reported when they occur; with root causes analysed and actions taken to prevent reoccurrence;
- ensuring the unit's RCSAs are conducted; acting as a central liaison between second line risk department and the business unit in planning and organizing the RCSA workshops;

- ensuring the RCSA is fit for purpose and a is true reflection of the business unit's risk profile;

- raising the awareness of the unit's risk profile, ensuring all employees are familiar with and able to articulate the unit's top risks and mitigating actions;

- assisting the business unit head in the development of key risk indicators and the establishment of appropriate thresholds;

- identifying the business unit's risk training needs, and flagging new employees to the second line risk department for the provision of training;

- maintaining contact with other Risk Champions, to share information about relevant OREs, RCSA risks and lessons learned;

- developing risk procedures/desk instructions relevant for the business unit as necessary;

- coordinating with second line risk department to implement any new risk-related initiatives, processes and/or tools;

- participating in other risk initiatives as appropriate.

APPENDIX 2

Example operational risk event reporting template

Reporting business/function
Date of discovery
Date of occurrence (if known)
High-level description *Enter a clear and succinct description of the transaction/event that allows those who are not familiar with it to quickly understand the problem.*
How was ORE discovered? *Provide an explanation as to how the ORE was discovered and the area that identified it.*
Root cause (if known) – why did it occur? *Provide an explanation about the primary root cause of the event and any control breaks that contributed to the ORE occurring.*
Actual or estimated cost *Consider any direct out-of-pocket costs of the event and any additional costs to resolve the issue (eg legal fees, consultancy costs to investigate/solve the problem); if a near miss, a rough estimate of potential exposure client/reputational/regulatory impact.* *If the value is unknown, say so, detailing steps being taken to determine the exposure.*
Resolution target date
Remedial action *Highlight action steps already taken and any further plans to close the issue and prevent reoccurrence, including the person responsible for completion and target resolution date.*

(continued)

(Continued)

Event category *Select the most appropriate taxonomy category from the menu.*
Suspicious activity report filed (Y/N) *Refer to Compliance Manual.*
Status of loss: Pending / Incurred (paid) / Reserved / Recovered *If needed, discuss with finance, establishing a reserve or writing the amount off.*
Cost centre/Reference accounting entries
Conduct (Y/N) *Highlight whether or not the event has a conduct element.*
Department head sign-off

APPENDIX 3

ORA template

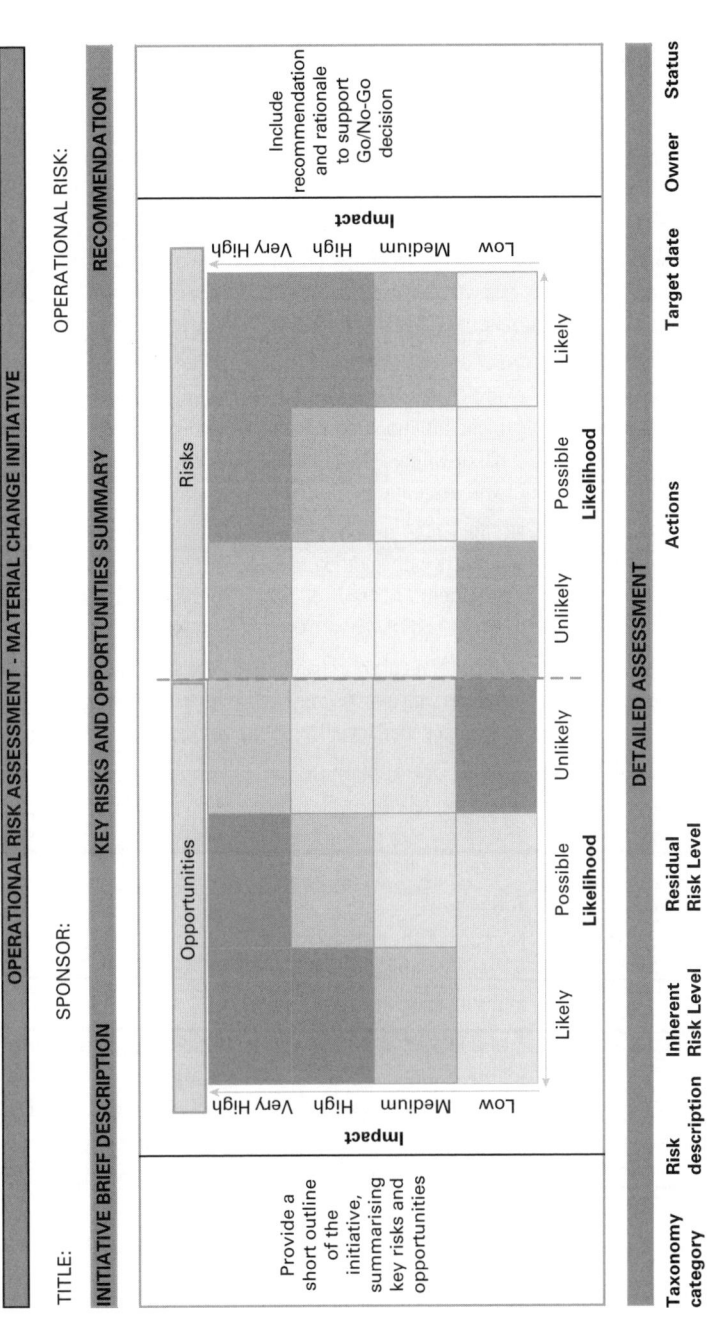

Table of 50 key risk indicators

No.	Risk or Theme	KRI Description	Why Useful?
1	Change Management	% of overdue and at-risk projects within active project portfolio	Presents overall health of change portfolio – overdue and 'at risk' projects vs on-track ones
2	Change Management	Number of change activities where post-implementation reviews (PIRs) highlighted material issues	Post-implementation reviews measure the success of project discipline; metrics tracks unsuccessful/poorly implemented projects
3	Change Management	Number of projects without project initiation document (PID) or where PID created late or with exceptions	Identifies projects with sub-optimal documentation and/or exceptions in approvals
4	Change Management	Number of change activities in scope without a completed risk assessment	Monitors compliance with the set process to ensure change projects undergo a risk assessment
5	Change Management	Number of regulatory change initiatives with at-risk status for a prolonged period (over x months)	Highlights a number of high-profile regulatory change programmes that require focus
6	Conduct and Culture	Number of exceptions to the New Product Approval (NPA) process, where product went live prior to formal governance approval	Monitors new products traded/sold to the client by-passing new product governance
7	Conduct and Culture	Number of conflicts/personal account dealings not reported and subsequently identified	Identifies potential insider trading
8	Conduct and Culture	% of operational risk losses not reported within timeline required by the policy	Helps identify poor risk management/risk culture issues in terms of not being open and transparent in reporting events quickly

(continued)

(Continued)

No.	Risk or Theme	KRI Description	Why Useful?
9	Conduct and Culture	% of staff background checks with 'high-risk' observations/ high-risk social media profiles	Where periodic screening of existing employees is performed, including social media screening, flags 'high-risk' observations
10	Conduct and Culture	Number of new accounts proposed by relationship managers and not approved	Monitors instances of potential account opening outside of the appetite, where subsequent approval was not granted
11	Conduct and Culture	Number/% of complaints related to client mis-treatment/ account mis-management	Provides a view on complaints, can be narrowed down, eg % to volume of payments, % that were 'material', % not resolved within policy
12	Conduct and Culture	Number of exceptions in product sales quality identified by quality assurance (QA) process	Monitors inappropriate sales identified via a spot-check quality assurance review
13	Cyber	Number of critical systems with vulnerabilities	Monitors most important (critical) systems' vulnerability and potential exposure to hacking
14	Cyber	Number of successful phishing attempts	Identifies repeat offenders within staff, who continue to click on internally created educational phishing emails
15	Cyber	Number/% of patches not updated on time	Predictive KRI; measures system health via timely installation of patches
16	Cyber	Number/% increase in malware alerts	Continuous monitoring of the volume of alerts, identifying spikes
17	Cyber	Number of table-top exercises to test response to a cyber incident conducted against plan	Monitors preparedness by ensuring periodic tests are conducted as planned; additional KRI can measure number of open actions emanating from the tests
18	Data Breach	% completion of mandatory information security training	Monitors adherence to mandatory employee training process

(continued)

(Continued)

No.	Risk or Theme	KRI Description	Why Useful?
19	Data Breach	Volume of attempts: staff sending emails/files to personal email addresses	Monitors email traffic focussing on attachments, identifying potential policy breaches
20	Financial Crime	% of new accounts opened with exceptions	Identifies non-standard accounts requiring additional approvals and sign-offs
21	Financial Crime	Open activity monitoring alerts not properly actioned	Control indicator; monitors how promptly the alerts are investigated and resolved
22	Financial Crime	Suspicious activity reports (SARs) – increase/decrease in cases reported	Monitors changes in volume and highlights spikes
23	Internal Fraud	Number of systems that permit staff to process payments or transactions single-handedly	Highlights exceptions where segregation of duties is not enforced, presenting a higher risk of error and/or internal fraud
24	Internal Fraud	Critical systems with user access not re-certified on time	Control indicator of system re-certification process; focusses on user access to ensure joiners/transfers/leavers are acted upon in a timely manner, preventing unauthorized access
25	Internal Fraud	% of movers or leavers with privileged access where access is removed outside of timescales	Identifies exceptions where leavers' access was not removed in a timely way
26	Internal Fraud	Whistleblowing – % increase/decrease in cases reported	Monitors unusual spikes and falls in the use of whistleblowing process
27	Internal Fraud	Premises access – unusual working patterns	Highlights unusual access to facilities, for example after hours or on weekends
28	Internal fraud	Number/% of staff that did not take mandatory leave	Monitors compliance with mandatory leave policy; applied to identified staff in scope, which can include trading, payments and others

(continued)

(Continued)

No.	Risk or Theme	KRI Description	Why Useful?
29	Internal Fraud	Trading policy breaches – trades in breach of trader's mandate	For trading business, monitors trades that have been erroneously or deliberately entered in breach of the prescribed mandate
30	Legal & Regulatory	Horizon scanning: number of new regulatory initiatives/consultations with potential significant impact in the next six months	Monitors regulatory developments and potential volume of change expected in the near future
31	Legal & Regulatory	Litigation: value at risk of active legal claims	Provides insight into potential value of settlement for legal claims
32	Outsourcing / Third-Party Risk	% non-adherence to service level agreements (SLA)	Monitors supplier performance against SLA, can be narrowed down to track most significant ('critical') suppliers
33	Outsourcing / Third-Party Risk	Number/% of overdue supplier due diligence reviews	Monitors timeliness of reviews as mandated by policy, dependent on the criticality of the supplier
34	Outsourcing / Third-Party Risk	Number/% of material exceptions to standard contract clauses	Identifies a proportion of providers with non-standard legal contracts that require additional attention
35	Outsourcing / Third-Party Risk	Number/% of critical providers without defined succession plan/not easily substitutable	Assesses reliance on a critical supplier which cannot be substituted in case of failure
36	People	Number/% of non-permanent staff in service over 12 months	Monitors long-term contract staff, indicating difficulties in filling open positions or a need to raise a permanent vacancy
37	People	Number/% of offers for preferred candidates rejected	Provides a view on the firm's attractiveness as an employer, and the risk of inability to recruit key staff
38	People	Maximum overlapping senior manager absences	Monitors instances where multiple senior managers are out of the office at the same time due to holiday, business trip, illness, resignation, potentially impacting business operation

(continued)

(Continued)

No.	Risk or Theme	KRI Description	Why Useful?
39	People	Senior managers' responsibility map: gaps or missing sign-offs in agreed accountabilities	Ensures that responsibility and accountability is clearly agreed between senior management, without gaps or duplication; especially relevant under the senior managers' regime
40	System Failure	End-of-Life hardware [software] as a % of overall hardware [software]	Predictive KRI; monitors reliance on software/hardware that is approaching the end of the service contract and needs to be replaced
41	System Failure	Average time to mitigate the highest impact technology incidents impacting service level agreements (SLA)	Provides a view to the firm's ability to recover quickly without significant internal or external impact
42	System Failure	System capacity	Predictive KRI; action needed when approaching/at capacity to prevent failure
43	System Failure	% change requests not signed off or signed off with exceptions	Monitors technology change management process, ensuring robust governance is applied
44	System Failure	Number of critical systems that failed periodic disaster recovery test	Raises awareness of systems that failed to recover within stipulated recovery time objective (RTO)
45	Transaction Processing	% staff with 2+ years' experience vs total staff	'Experience' indicator, valuable for complex processing units [eg derivatives, corporate actions]
46	Transaction Processing	Processing volume vs operations staff capacity	Monitors capacity and potential for over-stretching leading to risk of error
47	Transaction Processing	Number of cash/stock breaks outstanding > 30 days at month end	Monitors effectiveness of reconciliation and investigation process via number of 'aged' discrepancies
48	Transaction Processing	Manual processing: number of spreadsheets/end-user computing applications used in critical processes	Evaluates exposure to manual processing and risk of error, in processes identified as 'critical', eg payments

(continued)

(Continued)

No.	Risk or Theme	KRI Description	Why Useful?
49	Transaction Processing	% straight-through processing rate	Assesses rate of transactions without manual intervention
50	Transaction Processing	Number/% of bespoke non-standard client solutions	Monitors number of unique propositions/terms/work-arounds that require additional attention and are prone to error

INDEX